THE ANTIHEROINE'S VOICE

EDWARD H. FRIEDMAN

(THE ANTIHEROINE'S VOICE)

Narrative Discourse and Transformations of the Picaresque

University of Missouri Press
Columbia, 1987

Library of Congress Cataloging-in-Publication Data

Friedman, Edward H.

    The antiheroine's voice.

    1. Picaresque literature—History and criticism.
2. Women in literature. 3. First person narrative.
I. Title.
PN3428.F7   1987   809.3'87   86–30870
ISBN 0–8262–0641–7 (alk. paper)

∞™ This paper meets the minimum requirements of
the American National Standard for Permanence of Paper
for Printed Library Materials, Z39.48, 1984.

Jacket and frontispiece art by William Hogarth, engravings
from *A Harlot's Progress.*

TO SUSAN

Preface

Narrative thrives on the fact that all voices are not equal. This book describes the circumstances of narration and the production of messages in fictions of female characters. The focal point is the picaresque tradition: the early Spanish archetypes and feminine versions that vary and transform the discursive model. The progression is from male to female, from the condemnation to the exaltation of nonconformity, and from imposed silence to forms of eloquence. The agent of mediation is the implied author, who unites story and discourse. The works are self-consciously literary objects, and the goal of the study is a grouping and a (re)reading that will underscore the antiheroine's position in the text and beyond.

The section on *Lazarillo de Tormes* in Chapter 2 is a revised and expanded version of "Chaos Restored: Authorial Control and Ambiguity in *Lazarillo de Tormes*," which appeared in *Crítica Hispánica* 3 (1981): 59–73. The major portion of Chapter 5 is from "'Folly and a Woman': Galdós' Rhetoric of Irony in *Tristana*," published in *Theory and Practice of Feminist Literary Criticism*, edited by Gabriela Mora and Karen S. Van Hooft (Ypsilanti, Michigan: Bilingual Press/Editorial Bilingüe, 1982), pp. 201–28. I would like to thank the editors of these publications for permission to use materials contained in the earlier essays. Translations from the *Libro de Buen Amor* are from the edition with English paraphrase by Raymond S. Willis (Princeton: Princeton University Press, 1972), and those from *Tereza Batista* are by Barbara Shelby in Jorge Amado, *Tereza Batista, Home from the Wars* (New York: Avon Books, 1977). All other translations are my own.

My thanks in this project, as in all my work, must go to Elias L. Rivers and Harry Sieber for their classes in Spanish Golden Age literature at Johns Hopkins University. I am grateful for their guidance and for their example. I acknowledge with gratitude a summer stipend from the National Endowment for the Humanities, a faculty grant-in-aid from Arizona State University, and research support from the Arizona Center for Medieval and Renaissance Studies, all of which helped to make this study possible. I would also like to thank Marian L. Smolen for her dedicated assistance and the Data/Text Conversion staff at Arizona State University for aid in the preparation of the manuscript.

To the critics cited in this study, whose voices inform my own, I offer my respect and admiration. To my colleagues and students at Arizona State University, my appreciation for their friendship and for their dialogue. To Susan Krug Friedman, for bearing with me, my most profound and loving thanks.

E. H. F.

March, 1987

Contents

By the kind of silence he maintains, by the manner in which he leaves his characters to work out their own destinies or to tell their own stories, the author can achieve effects that would be difficult or impossible if he allowed himself or a reliable spokesman to speak directly and authoritatively to us.

    Wayne C. Booth, *The Rhetoric of Fiction*

A carnival participant is both actor and spectator; he loses his sense of individuality, passes through a zero point of carnivalesque activity and splits into a subject of the spectacle and an object of the game. Within the carnival, the subject is reduced to nothingness, while the structure of *the author* emerges as anonymity that creates and sees itself created as self and other, as man and mask.

    Julia Kristeva, *Desire in Language*

In thinking about women, writers have tended either to enlarge the differences between the sexes or to diminish them. Plato did the latter and Aristotle the former. . . . A woman declaring herself not significantly different from men tends to make a special plea for her own rationality and ability to speak. A woman accepting the designated polarities is more likely to turn toward emotion as a rule of response, and to stress the difficulties of utterance, the higher bliss of speechlessness.

    Lynn Sukenick, "On Women and Fiction"

How can a cultural model of women's writing help us to read a woman's text? One implication of this model is that women's fiction can be read as a double-voiced discourse, containing a "dominant" and a "muted" story.

    Elaine Showalter, "Feminist Criticism in the Wilderness"

Any attempt to codify context can always be grafted onto the context it sought to describe, yielding a new context which escapes the previous formulation.

    Jonathan Culler, *On Deconstruction*

Pleasure/Bliss: terminologically, there is always a vacillation—I stumble, I err. In any case, there will always be a margin of indecision; the distinction will not be the source of absolute classifications, the paradigm will falter, the meaning will be precarious, revocable, reversible, the discourse incomplete.

    Roland Barthes, *The Pleasure of the Text*

Introduction

This book examines a process of enunciation in narrative fiction. The point of departure is the Spanish picaresque novel, which builds on literary tradition and the cult of the norm as it explores the bases of communication and of alienation. The secular and satirical confession challenges blind faith in the stability of the universe and in the signifying powers of the word. In an age of disillusionment, reliability is the exception rather than the rule. Language obfuscates meaning, and narrative premises are made to be broken. The discursive aims of the narrator/protagonist are as deceptive and unrealistic as his quest for upward mobility, and as relegated to a preestablished hierarchy. Through the ironies of discourse, the author complies with the status quo as his character opposes it. Each text puts forth a "reading" of society and of preceding texts.

The feminine variations of the picaresque extend the illusion of control. Lowering the status of the speaker heightens the irony and increases the distance between desire and fulfillment. The antiheroine fuels the myth of male superiority while contributing to its destruction, or deconstruction. She occupies a privileged place in the text that documents her strength and ingenuity, albeit misplaced, along with her downfall. The silenced voice bears a message of repression and a sign of hope. Marginal existence finds validity in the rhetoric of self-defeat. Every act of defiance is double-edged, for crime and punishment keep the antiheroine's identity alive. Losing the battle may be the first step toward winning the war.

The picaresque novel develops, in part, as an alternative viewpoint, a vision of the world from below by a narrator unlike the reader. Works such as the anonymous *Lazarillo de Tormes* (1554), Mateo Alemán's *Guzmán de Alfarache* (1599, 1604), and Francisco de Quevedo's *El Buscón* (1626) grant a momentary release from a restrictive atmosphere and from literary prescriptions. The protagonists err, but their creators protect themselves by providing social justice for the offender and moral justification for the censor. The feminine variations take parody, delinquency, and a sense of the other one step further. Although sexuality is the antiheroine's major weapon against society, her schemes depend on wit as well. Social custom and an authorial presence hinder her success yet cannot deny her potential. The male authors may use women for all the wrong reasons—as objects of ridicule in a carnivalesque inversion of protocol—but the texts put women in center stage to air their grievances and to overshadow their masters, even those who would deprive them of the word.

Francisco Delicado's dialogic portrait, *La lozana andaluza* (*The Lusty Andalusian Woman*, 1528), anticipates *Lazarillo de Tormes* and gives the antiheroine and the author roles in the low comedy. The fictionalized Delicado becomes a harbinger of picaresque writers who intrude on their characters' verbal space. An example of this intrusive power is Francisco López de Ubeda, who shows up at the beginning and end of each chapter of *La pícara Justina* (1605) and who mediates the discourse of the middle. Alonso Jeró-nimo de Salas Barbadillo kills off the protagonist of *La hija de Celestina* (*The Daughter of Celestina*, 1612) before discourse begins, and Alonso de Castillo Solórzano employs essentially the same voice in *Teresa de Manzanares* (1632) and *La garduña de Sevilla* (1642), despite a shift from first- to third-person narration. The silencing of the antiheroine responds not only to the sub-jugation of women by men but also to a generic consciousness that subordi-nates discourse to story. The female voice could be the mirror to the psyche, but the authors do not choose this option. The interior self is not a part of the story, as in male archetypes. Nonetheless, the fiction of the antiheroine survives in the search for a happy ending and in the dialectics of discourse.

Spanish picaresque narrative offers a key example of what Russian Formalism calls "laying bare the devices" of a literary work.[1] The pretext of *Lazarillo de Tormes* is a contract between Lázaro and Vuestra Merced—narrator and narratee—and the (doubly) apologetic response calls attention to the act of composition: as explanation, defense, confession, autobiogra-phy, reworking of the intertext, and ultimately as a rhetoric of irony. Lázaro's document acknowledges, above all, the instability of the sign and the capacity of the word to function in numerous and often contradictory systems. Here, the creation of the text becomes synonymous with the creation of a "life." As Lázaro puts himself into the story, he selects events and verbal structures aimed to flatter or to excuse; in short, he seeks the best possible light for his self-portrait. The resulting text draws meaning from and at the same time adds meaning to the life. It shows the writer at work, to reveal (well before deconstruction reinvents rhetoric) the strategies of art and of the artist.[2]

St. Augustine's *Confessions*, operating in the modes of autobiography and confession, serves as a type of paradigm for the picaresque. The *Confes-sions* foregrounds a life, a metamorphosis, a thesis (or pretext), and a subjec-tive voice, and it sets forth a prescription for reading. The text self-con-sciously addresses the issue of reader response. As Eugene Vance notes, "Rhetorician that he was, Augustine was aware that in the limited and imperfect sphere of human speech, there are multiple alternatives in the choice of reality that one wishes to understand, and multiple alternatives in the mode of expressing a reality."[3] Augustine recognizes, as well, the high-er purpose of his confessions. When the (scriptural) word is potentially ambiguous, the narrator must direct the narratee to a theologically sound interpretation. Writing and reading must validate preexistent meaning. The right path, or strategy for reading, is that which leads to a previously determined message. When language is insufficient, the narrator steps in to restore a message that supersedes its medium. Imaginative fiction bears little of this doctrinaire burden. When "converted" and "freed" from its spiritual base, the confessional formula can move from the realm of the ideal to the unabashedly real. No longer subjected to a master text nor articulated by a narrator whose faith and reliability can hardly be impugned, the variable sign finds meaning in mutability itself.

The prologue to *Lazarillo de Tormes* presents a narrative "I" who lays claim to a reading public and to a public of one (Vuestra Merced). This divided "I" seeks authority through opposing measures, by promoting the book as an object in the marketplace and by acquiescing to the request of a social superior. The first story hopes to overcome the forces of oblivion, while the second resists direct disclosure. One foregrounds art, the other craft(iness). The fragmentation of the teller is a marker of what Wayne Booth and subsequent narratologists term the *implied author* to denote the "presence" of the author in the discourse of the narrator. The creation of the narrator's voice is a convention that permits the intrusion of a voice-over, a counterpoint to the story being told. The narrative engenders its own alternate reading, with an equally ironic censure (and censorship) of the nominal purveyor of messages. The author aligns himself with the social institutions of his day to put the narrator/protagonist in his place: in the margins of society and text.

In the case of the feminine variations, the complexity of the sign and the dubious authority of the picaresque narrator turn the union of author and society against the individual into an uneven battle of the sexes. The women who would challenge the status quo are figuratively and then literally silenced. The men who write these texts underscore the doubling of discourse and the double standard. The text is an analogue of social reality, which is, conversely, encoded in the text. The articulation of the anti-heroine's voice reveals a male-oriented semiotics whose subtext bespeaks suppression. The feminine picaresque is perhaps less a metanarrative than a dialectic between free speech and its demystified underside. If the discourse of *Lazarillo de Tormes*, *Guzmán de Alfarache*, and *El Buscón* shows the traces of an increasingly apparent authorial figure, the variations confirm this presence by failing to match voice with a discernible interior self. The feminine picaresque becomes the story of an absence, a gender-inflected sign of the duplicity of discourse, and a testament to the unliberated wor(l)d.

The interplay between narrator and implied author, as manifested in the picaresque, allows the text to display both antisocial and conservative positions. The narrator/protagonist's "misreading" of social options is matched by discursive strategies that backfire, that incriminate rather than defend the speaker. The implied reader, as recipient of the message systems (counterstrategies) of the implied author, may correct the misreading by viewing the verbal structure and its social referents ironically. The superseding voice of the implied author brings a restoration of order to the chaotic, or unconventional, measures proposed—through word and deed—by the déclassé character. This determinism on the level of discourse negates the authority of the outsider who attempts to achieve in the text a success denied by the social hierarchy. When the marginated figure is a woman whose voice is rendered (or left unrendered) by a man, the discursive model comes into clearer focus. The male author preserves institutionalized thought; he stands with the collectivity while diverting them with his fiction. Woman is object and object lesson, de-centered in the story (and in the discourse) of her life.

As society changes, however, so texts may change, through time and through exposure to new perspectives. The Spanish picaresque, which depends heavily on intertextuality, now forms part of the intertext. The patterns of discourse—the dynamics of (implied) author, narrator, and society—reflect the shifting status of the outsider. In the continuing conflict between individual and society, the implied author casts what could be considered the deciding viewpoint. The picaresque favors the rules of society over the civil disobedience of the individual. In this system of crime and punishment, overstepping one's place in the social order is an unpardonable sin. Enlightenment society seeks to rehabilitate its errant members, adding pardon to the cycle of crime and punishment. Romanticism and its aftermath give new stature, if not always success, to the outsider. The economic and political consequences of the industrial revolution rewrite the social record, and literature captures the transition by reflecting the seeds of change and the powers of resistance. Women in and out of fiction need to find their place in the new order. While their marginal status is an unfortunate constant of history, the implied author may reorient their story. When a postromantic, antisocial sensibility favors nonconformity over conformity, narrative discourse may invert the paradigm to unite implied author and narrator against the establishment. The texts studied here represent stages in the ongoing confrontation between society and the individual, as mediated by an author in control of narrative voices.

In the prologue to Daniel Defoe's *Moll Flanders* (1722), the authorial figure speaks of his role as editor of Moll Flanders's original manuscript. The hero of the revised text is society as redeemer of lost souls, and this organizing principle affects the antiheroine's discourse and her story. Society reforms her and editing alters her expression, all for her own good. Her feminine identity, like her voice and her message, lies between the lines. If Defoe finds spiritual comfort in reintegration and earthly penitence, Benito Pérez Galdós's *Tristana* (1892) returns to the impossible synthesis of the Spanish Baroque. A deterministic story leads to the defeat of the antiheroine, while the rhetorical subtleties of an ironic narrator advocate a reevaluation of the role of women. Man and nature conspire against Tristana, whose only sin is her desire for freedom. The paradoxically overdetermined text stands as an indictment against intolerance and as a defense of humanity. The Galdosian narrator aids the cause of feminism by failing to practice what he preaches.

The picaresque narrators are forced to espouse a philosophy that mocks their position in the community. While society accommodates the contrite sinner in *Moll Flanders*, the emended text imposes a conversional direction on the (unseen) original. The author as editor directs the narrator toward a strategy of conformity, claiming personal success as society's achievement. In *Hasta no verte Jesús mío* (*Until I See You, Sweet Jesus*, 1969), the Mexican novelist Elena Poniatowska sustains an ironic discourse, but antithetically so. She rewrites the commentary of an informant to indict society for its

abuse of women and the poor. Robbed of an identity in life, the narra-
tor/protagonist attains selfhood, status, and voice in the text. Jesusa Palancares is unaware of her verbal skills and emotional strength, which, real as
they may be, are now inseparable from the supplementary agenda of the
implied author.

The Spanish feminine picaresque texts—interludes in a male domain—
gradually remove the antiheroine from the discourse. Her conduct is entertaining, audacious, and ultimately unthreatening, backed by a pretext of
negative exemplarity. The Brazilian novel *Tereza Batista cansada de guerra*
(*Tereza Batista, Tired from Battle*, 1972) similarly excludes the protagonist
from the act of narration. The author, Jorge Amado, creates a fictional alter
ego who seeks and then structures information concerning Tereza Batista.
In this case, the ordering of events exalts the social rebel while condemning
a corrupt society. The antiheroine is a woman of action, aided by the words
of a narrator who supports her and who converts her life into legend, into
the stuff of romance. The strategy is no less manipulative than in the earlier
works, but there is a radical shift of allegiance on the part of the authorial
figure.

Jesusa Palancares of *Hasta no verte Jesús mío* has negligible impact on her
society. Poniatowska's text compensates for the omission by articulating
her courage, her kindness, and her intelligence. In the idealistic vision of
Tereza Batista, women may effect social change, but the antiheroine has no
voice of her own. Erica Jong's *Fanny, Being the True History of the Adventures
of Fanny Hackabout-Jones* (1980) portrays a character who is mistress of her
destiny and of her discourse. Fanny herself rewrites social and cultural
history to live in freedom and at peace with herself. To manage the synthesis, Jong goes back in time but forward in spirit. Fanny's diction belongs
to the eighteenth century and her conscience to contemporary feminism.
Superior to those around her, Fanny settles for isolation as opposed to
coexistence. Her utopian community excludes the traditional patriarchal
figure, and man becomes a commodity, an object. Liberation here is a
beautifully rationalized form of reverse discrimination.

The outsider's text responds to an intertextual past and to a historical
present. Picaresque narrative owes its development to literary idealism,
social stability, and the humanist vision of individual worth, all of which it
treats in terms of denial. The antihero never poses a serious threat, and his
failure enables the dominant groups to confirm their authority. Within the
text, an implied author controls story and discourse, but the unequal struggle has an ironic effect on message production. The markers that indicate
the rhetorical posture of the narrator implicate the voice-over as well. This
is especially apparent in the feminine variations of the picaresque, which
make little effort to sustain a feminine consciousness. The narrative reinforces the status quo while revealing a manipulation of discourse.

The contemporary narrative of the antiheroine manipulates discourse
in precisely the opposite way. The implied author takes the protagonist's
side against the prevailing social philosophy. *Moll Flanders* and *Tristana* are
transitional texts. Defoe finds—perhaps forces—compatibility between so-

ciety and the delinquent through revision and redemption. Galdós's plot seems to support society over the rebel, but the ironic discourse demonstrates a double standard of freedom. The twentieth-century examples present no ambivalence toward the subject nor reticence in decrying society. The various strategies, inversions of picaresque formulas, grant the antiheroine a dignity and an empathy that society does not accord her. The search for a voice mirrors the search for a positive identity.

The study is divided into three parts: The Model, Variations, Transformations. An episode of Juan Ruiz's *Libro de Buen Amor* (*Book of Good Love*, 1343) helps to define a crisis of signification that affects message production in later texts. As words lose their absolute value, language becomes more open and more easily manipulated. The relation between pretext and text and between narrator and implied author marks the signifying act as an object of inquiry, discourse as story. *Lazarillo de Tormes*, *Guzmán de Alfarache*, and *El Buscón* are "lives" and metalinguistic treatises. The picaresque narrators flout literary precedents, social practices, and semantic consistency, while an implied author exposes the rhetorical framework of their narration. The conservative position triumphs, but not without betraying its own rhetoric. In contemporary versions of the picaresque, including Camilo José Cela's *La familia de Pascual Duarte* (*The Family of Pascual Duarte*, 1942), ideologies vary while the discursive machinery stays true to its origins.

The narratives of the *pícaras* thrive on the distance between subject and object. These variations depend on the intertext and on a sense of difference. They are rereadings of literary models and satirical misreadings of social norms. Terms such as "variation," "male archetypes," and "antiheroine"— arguably sexist—convey the need to differentiate, to note the encoding of historical reality in the text and a space for alternative realities in the subtext. Feminist criticism cannot exist without acknowledgment of male dominion or a reigning myth of male superiority. This "homocentrism" or "metaphysics of male presence" (borrowing from Jacques Derrida)[4] invites a reexamination of the canon. The working hypotheses of Delicado, López de Ubeda, Salas Barbadillo, and Castillo Solórzano illustrate the strategical force of the implied author. What their protagonists achieve may be a function of the limits of aggression and a function, as well, of strategies of reading. Aesthetic response theory uses the term "negation" to refer to the invocation of familiar or determinate elements only to cancel them out.[5] The picaresque novel acts accordingly on idealistic fiction, autobiography, and confession; the feminine variations add the male world(view) to the field of negative determinacy.

The discursive model elaborated in the picaresque seems most obvious in the juxtaposition of a female voice and a male voice-over, as in the case of *La pícara Justina*. The authorial figure keeps rebellion in check. When antisocial behavior no longer separates means from end, the model adapts itself to shifting perspectives. The works labeled "transformations" respond to a complementary linking of protagonist and implied author. *Moll Flanders*, *Tristana*, *Hasta no verte Jesús mío*, *Tereza Batista*, and *Fanny* show a movement toward inversion of the paradigm. Still a question of oppositions, the discourse fashions an alliance of the individual and her creator against a male-dominated society.

The study does not pretend to exhaust the options nor to present a closed system; its goal is to define a model that will illuminate particular narrative strategies in a group of texts, considered individually and collectively. The approach is deconstructive, in the sense that it presupposes a rhetorical component at every stage of the creative process and in the social processes reflected through art. The author, conscious of his own rhetorical bent, hopes to serve in a modest way the (constructive) causes of poetics and poetic justice.

I
The Model

I THE WOR(L)D IN CRISIS
By Way of a Prologue

> The text is not an autonomous or unified object, but a set of relations
> with other texts. Its system of language, its grammar, its lexicon, drag
> along numerous bits and pieces—traces—of history so that the text
> resembles a Cultural Salvation Army Outlet with unaccountable
> collections of incompatible ideas, beliefs, and sources. The "genealogy" of
> the text is necessarily an incomplete network of conscious and unconscious
> borrowed fragments. Manifested, tradition is a mess. Every text is
> intertext.
>   Vincent B. Leitch, *Deconstructive Criticism*

Criticism of the picaresque novel—the Spanish texts of the sixteenth and
seventeenth centuries, notably the anonymous *Lazarillo de Tormes*, Mateo
Alemán's *Guzmán de Alfarache*, and Francisco de Quevedo's *Buscón*, and
their literary progeny—offers a generic analogue of the chicken/egg debate.
Much ink, if not blood, has been spilled in attempting to define the picaresque mode (genre, myth) and to determine those works worthy of inclu-
sion in lists of picaresque novels, lists that include as few as two works and
novels as disparate as Melville's *Confidence Man* and Gogol's *Dead Souls*. At
times, narratives generally acknowledged as picaresque serve as the basis for
definitions that end by excluding a part of the corpus from which they
derive.[1] Generic consciousness is alternately a function of author, narrator,
character, and critic. One article poses the question, "Does the Picaresque
Novel Exist?," and answers that the term has little use for literary analysis.[2]
Part of the problem may lie in an overemphasis on what the picaresque
novel *is* as opposed to what the picaresque novel *does*, in a privileging of
story over *discourse*.[3] The picaresque story is, of course, highly significant,
with its inversion of the patterns of idealistic fictions, its expansion of the
social panorama, and its foregrounding of the antihero. Even more significant, perhaps, is the form of expression, which encompasses and directs the
narrative.

No text exists in isolation. The concept of intertextuality, in its multiple forms, allows for synthesis between what a text owes to its literary and
cultural precedents, what an author creates by re-creating, and how contextualization affects the production of meaning. Intertextuality considers syn-
chronically what source studies view diachronically.[4] Every decision in the
process of composition implies a confrontation, if only intuitive, with other
texts and with the collectivity of texts. *Lazarillo de Tormes* borrows (and

3

secularizes) elements of the spiritual autobiography to challenge idealism and the social establishment. By changing the setting—the economic milieu and the narrative circumstance—the author reverses the premises and the perspective of the works he imitates. When the protagonist makes public a most modest lineage, when he nears death from hunger as opposed to love, and when he strays from the path of honor, he pays tribute to the texts that precede his own. The narrative homage takes the form of irony, in the flouting of conventions and confessions. Not only does the *Lazarillo* depend on books, but the act of writing becomes part of the story. Narrative events point beyond the text to society and to the world at large and within the text to personal and literary development; narrative events converge with linguistic events to complement and transform realities.

Lazarillo de Tormes presents man as a semiotic, signifying entity who must rely on words to authenticate his existence. Oral, written, and social codes govern his performance as narrator and protagonist, and he has a certain freedom to recode data according to rhetorical and self-serving strategies. The calculated manipulation of language is itself a sign of creative freedom, lending legitimacy to the enterprise of fiction. Discourse has an increasingly aesthetic function in texts that exhibit an awareness of their particular nature. Literature begins to deal openly with its powers and limits. The narrative act becomes a means of communication and an analogue of the events depicted, linking wordplay with worldview. As intermediary between author and reader, the narrator sets the points of reference and defines the discursive model. By virtue of his psychological complexity, his self-consciousness as a citizen and as a storyteller, and his affirmation of the dialectics of reliability, Lázaro initiates a moment of plenitude for narrative, a process that continues to the present. A masterpiece of medieval Spanish literature may help to determine an approach to the structures of discourse and to the voices that inhabit a text.

Building on a discursive system implicit in the fourteenth-century *Libro de Buen Amor* by Juan Ruiz, Archpriest of Hita, narrative indeterminacies in the picaresque reflect the chaotic aspects of human nature and of the universe in general. Through a multifaceted narrative persona, the *Libro de Buen Amor* demonstrates the conflict between saying one thing and showing, possibly meaning, another. Within the pseudo-autobiographical framework, Juan Ruiz concerns himself as much or more with bad love (*el amor loco*, carnal desire) as with good love (*el amor bueno*, devotion to God), supposedly to preach morality through negative exemplarity. The dual perspective on love and the shifting tone seem to reflect the archpriest's— and medieval man's—vacillation between God's law and natural law. Between man's impulses and his sense of the sacred stands society, as agitator rather than mediator of the tensions. Society simultaneously enacts rules to govern behavior and challenges man to break these rules, continually points to a higher order while offering earthly and immediate gratification of desires. The insistence on the priority of good love and the emphasis on bad love characterize man's wish to rationalize the divine and his need to satisfy the flesh. The compromised premise, the compromising conduct, and the exploration of language link the *Libro de Buen Amor* to *Lazarillo de Tormes* and its successors. Imitating social discourse, literary discourse leads, misleads, and finally validates its contradictions.

The *Libro de Buen Amor* depicts the tension caused by a primarily inflexible social code acting on man's flexible nature. Role models are well defined and acceptable in theory, but practice often contradicts the models. Man's union with God through the intercession of the priest (in communion) or through the Virgin (in supplicatory prayers) has an earthly and antithetical counterpart in man's attempted union with woman through the intermediary, or go-between. The correspondence between the elements of the triadic structure reaches its highest point when the man is a priest and the woman is a nun who allows herself to be courted. Both characters wish to function in two roles when society, as well as religious doctrine, demands clear recognition and fulfillment of one role. On the formal level, the lack of clarity in the narrator's voice calls further attention to the problem of identity. In the courtship of Doña Endrina (stanzas 576–891), the archpriest as narrator/protagonist yields his poetic space to Don Melón de la Huerta, who in turn disappears at the conclusion of the episode. The subjectivity of the first-person narration merges with the duplicity of the central character to produce a series of oppositions: the struggle between the spirit and the flesh that every Christian must endure, the confrontation between the narrator and his alter ego, and the battle between the purposeful didacticism of good love and the fictional multiperspectivism of bad love.[5] The episode of the courtship of the nun Doña Garoza (stanzas 1331–1507) serves as an analogue of the sustained tripartite framework and as an ironic point of contact between the incompatible realms of the spiritual and the carnal.

The episode responds linguistically to the tension between the two types of love. The account of the courtship of the thirteenth lady (the antepenultimate in a series of amorous misadventures) conveys the power of the word, and the use and abuse of language by the narrator, the go-between Trotaconventos, and Doña Garoza. Trotaconventos indicates a double function of discourse in the first stanza of the episode. The speaker (or writer) may develop conceits that supersede the literal level of reality—the archpriest becomes "don Polo," the north star of her amatory excursions[6]—and may give credence and a type of permanence to a lie through the spoken, and especially the written, word. Trotaconventos says to her master, "'Fé aquí buen amor.' Qual buena amiga buscólo" (1331d, pp. 360–61; "'Behold here good love.' Like a good friend she went to seek it"). This good love is, in fact, bad love, but the narrator, who has defined the categories, does not, for reasons that become apparent, refute the statement. The archpriest finally meets and falls in love with the nun, and he attempts to hide his sin by refusing to recognize it as a sin. It is, rather, a "limpio amor" ("unsullied love"), and "Dios fue mi guiador" (1503d, pp. 402–3; "God was my guide"). Through linguistic selectivity, the narrator glorifies sin by associating it with a platonic or spiritual relationship between two characters who pretend to serve God while they are serving each other. The ultimate literary paradox lies in the fact that the narrator proposes to give examples of bad love yet refers to the purity and the divine inspiration of this particularly negative case.

Deceptive language rather than a sense of righteousness controls the episode. Trotaconventos begins by painting a verbal picture of the convent as a storehouse of material objects, a veritable gastronomic paradise, whose inhabitants are the most beautiful and discreet of women: "'Todo plazer del mundo e todo buen doñear, / solaz de mucho sabor e el falaguero jugar, / todo es en las monjas más que en otro lugar'" (1342a–c, pp. 362–63; "'Every pleasure in the world and every nice love-word, most sweet enjoyment and affectionate fondling: all this is to be found in nuns, more than anywhere else'"). Later, on the other hand, she tells Doña Garoza that a suitor would provide sumptuous meals to replace the spartan diet of the convent: "'Comedes en convento sardinas e camarones, / berçuelas e lazeria e los duros caçones; / dexades del amigo perdizes e capones'" (1393a–c, pp. 376–77; "'In the convent you eat sardines and shrimp, cabbages and pittances and tough dogfish; you spurn partridges and capons from your suitor'"). Language here is rhetorical, functional, aimed at producing a particular effect from a specific object; it is everything but truthful. Through a sustained comic analogue of the conventions of courtly love and through the debate between Trotaconventos and Doña Garoza, the language of deception acquires an intertextual base. The two women present their arguments through exempla that support their points.[7] The debate demonstrates the strength of the literary recourse, in a match of ideology against ideology, creative ability against creative ability. And ironically, while language in effect determines the victor, it is not the one who tells the most effective stories who emerges victorious but rather the one who cannot believe her own stories who is defeated. Doña Garoza's exempla illustrate what she should say as a nun. She is acting well her part while feeling something else. Trotaconventos is arguing for bad love but calling it good love; Doña Garoza is arguing for good love but yearning for bad love.

The nun knows that theoretically she has an advantage over the go-between. God, so to speak, is on her side, and her statements reflect Christian dogma: "'Más valen en convento las sardinas saladas, / fazer a Dios servicio con las dueñas onradas, / que perder la mi alma con perdizes assadas, / e fincar escarnida como otras deserradas'" (1385, pp. 374–75; "'It is better to eat salted sardines in a convent, and do service to God with the venerated nuns than to destroy my soul with roast partridges and end up dishonored like other women who have gone astray'"); "'non deve ser el omne a mal fazer denodado, / dezir nin comedir lo que non le es dado; / lo que Dios e natura an vedado e negado / de lo fazer el cuerdo non deve ser osado'" (1407, pp. 378–79; "'a man should not have so much temerity as to do something wrongful, nor to say nor to think in his heart what is not given for him to do; what God and nature have forbidden and denied the wise man should not be so rash as to do'"). The exempla further magnify the dialectical space between righteousness and sin, between a Christian consciousness and a bad conscience, and between the holy image of God and the unholy image of man. The exemplum of the city mouse and the country mouse (1370–84), in which the Edenic urban setting proves illusory, may be considered a microcosm of the courtship episode. The presentation of the meal in the city—like the convent a paradise of forbidden fruit, with food as sweet as honey but bearing venom—mixes the pleasure of the moment with the fear of death and favors the tranquillity and security of the country.

Trotaconventos's advice, "'Amad al buen amigo e quered su buen amor'" (1452b, pp. 390–91; "Love your good suitor and accept his good love"), leads Doña Garoza to recognize the demonic nature of the go-between and serves as the point of departure for the exemplum of the thief who sells his soul to the devil, only to be deserted in the end. The thief says at one point, "'Ya yo só desposado/ con la forca'" (1455a-b, pp. 390–91; "I am already engaged to the gallows"), and one can note that the name *Garoza* means *desposada*, bride.[8] The devil remarks, "'Luego seré contigo, desque ponga un fraile / con una fraila suya'" (1466a-b, pp. 394–95; "I will be with you right away, as soon as I join a friar up with his nun"). The exemplum becomes a type of self-conscious memento mori: "'Quien al diablo cree, trával' su garavato; / él le da mala cima e grand mal en chico rato'" (1475c-d, pp. 396–97; "'Whoever trusts the Devil gets caught by his hook; the Devil brings him a bad end and great harm in a short time'"). Trotaconventos had earlier attempted to underplay the fear of death, and apparently she has failed to convince the nun. But only apparently, because after all is said and done, after the debate that Doña Garoza does not lose on the verbal level, after repeated expressions of spiritual faith and awareness of the consequences of sin, Doña Garoza asks for a physical description of the archpriest.

Like the archpriest, Doña Garoza lets herself be led astray by Trotaconventos's deceptive discourse, a discourse that links God and good love with amorous intrigue and sacrilege. Trotaconventos delivers a letter to the nun during mass, and the archpriest gets his first glimpse of Doña Garoza in church: "En el nombre de Dios fui a missa de mañana; / vi estar a la monja en oración, loçana" (1499a-b, pp. 402–3; "In the name of God I went to morning Mass; I saw the nun at prayer, full of life"). The inversion of terms offers a means of justifying the inverted value system that places God on the side of the lovers and evolves into a consummately ironic description of Doña Garoza's role: "Con mucha oración a Dios por mí rogava; / con la su abstinencia mucho me ayudava, / la su vida muy limpia en Dios se deleitava; / en locura del mundo nunca se trabajava" (1504, pp. 404–5; "With many a supplication she prayed to God for me; by her abstinence she aided me greatly; her immaculate life found delight in God; she never busied herself with the mad sensuality of this world"). The good woman, "la *buena* dama," the one who is being courted by a priest, is never distracted by earthly concerns, "las *locuras* del mundo," or so her admirer would have it. The semantic confusion reaches its uppermost limit. Using diversionary tactics to conceal, or attempt to conceal, his indiscretions, the narrator obscures the real issue in his conclusion: "Con el mucho quebranto fize aquesta endecha; / con pesar e tristeza non fue tan sotil fecha; / emiéndela todo omne quien el buen amor pecha, / que yerro e malfecho emienda non desecha" (1507, pp. 404–5; "In my great affliction I composed this dirge; because of grief and sorrow it was not done very skillfully; any man may emend it [if he is one of those] who pay a tribute to good love, for error and wrongdoing do not reject correction"). The nun dies, and the narrator laments the passing of a blessed figure who inspired his platonic love.

In an article entitled "Narrative Technique in Juan Ruiz' History of Doña Garoza," Robert Edwards notes what may be termed a union of story and discourse, in which "the narrative not only reports a love affair but, in the act of the story's coming into being, it also uncovers a poet working at his craft."[9] The particular structure elaborated by Edwards depends on shifts in discursive performance and on a metaliterary consciousness. For the critic, "the encounter between Garoza and Trotaconventos takes place outside the poet's awareness as a character in the story. To report the debate, an event he has not witnessed personally, the speaker must assume another voice. In a similar fashion, Garoza and Urraca [Trotaconventos] take on other roles as they move to different structural levels. Their roles as dramatic antagonists lead them to become narrators of their rhetorical exempla. So there develops a dual process of structural movement in the episode: the poet narrates a story and in the process becomes a dramatic character; and the women, dramatic characters in his narration, become narrators in their own right."[10] It follows, then, that the dialogue, traditionally an unmediated or mimetic form, is transformed into a series of mediated or diegetic forms.[11] The text, itself an exemplum, includes stories, such as that of Doña Garoza, that both serve as and contain exempla. The final semantic product, correspondingly, produces and reproduces itself in the story. The rhetorical focus shifts from the implied metaphor of the world as stage to synecdoche (the archpriest as a representative of humanity at large), to metonymy (the exempla as evocative of divine and earthly laws), and ultimately to irony (inversion and confusion of signifieds).[12] Doña Garoza, in essence, speaks in the manner of the archpriest; her words are polysemous, paradoxically direct, and ironic. The episode of Doña Garoza works discursively in the manner of the complete text. It commits itself, most emphatically, to established codes—theological, social, linguistic—only to reject them, equally emphatically, in the end.

The stated—somewhat overstated—intention presented in the introduction becomes part of a calculated indeterminacy that defines the *Libro de Buen Amor*. Anthony Zahareas, characterizing the irony of the courtship of Doña Garoza, speaks of "a device which for lack of a name we might call *deviating afterthought*: the afterthought (penance) modifies the preceding thought (sin). The deviating afterthought is Juan Ruiz's artistic manner of getting around the one-dimensional didactic form."[13] The exempla of the go-between and of the nun convey messages that apply to the narrative pretext and that, through irony, negate and reverse themselves. The speech events have both an immediate and a transcendent contextual field, and just as the archpriest becomes a character in the story, his early intervention renders him, as in the case of Cervantes in *Don Quijote*, a "segundo autor," or second author, one player more, functioning intratextually. Within the metaphorical literary universe, he is (in synecdochic terms) one of a number of narrators and the autobiographical, confessional "I," (in metonymic terms) the implied object of the narrated exempla, and (in terms of irony) the purveyor and pillager of discursive schemes.

Language describes actions, and language can distort actions. The narrator of the *Libro de Buen Amor*, whose name is the same as the author's, asks the reader to learn from his examples, when he himself has not learned from examples and when his own examples are, at best, ambiguous. He purports to give a didactic message while seeming to forget the need for clarity of expression in didactic works. The subordination of clarity to ambiguity symbolizes, to a degree, the triumph of fiction over dogma, of the literary imagination and its multiple resources over the limited vision of a sermon. The selective process works not only at the level of language but also in the matter of what to include and what to omit. The archpriest devotes the major part of the episode of Doña Garoza to the debate between the two women, a rather one-sided polemic. When the narrator reaches the culmination of the debate—the union of the nun and the priest—he has very little to say, and one can suppose the very worst. The archpriest's ego, or possibly his alter ego, reacts against synthesis of the extremes, and the *Libro de Buen Amor* reflects a reality principle that refuses to exclude the conflict of man's nature and allegiances, and, more importantly, that refuses to provide a resolution. The conflict is reflected in the conceptual and linguistic bases of the work. The literary language and silences of the unreliable narrator become elements of a contest between good love and bad love. This example of medieval art is capable of bringing the reader into the text to deal with contradictions and to relate semantics to selfhood. The *Libro de Buen Amor* is an anticonfessional work because words state and negate its message, and because the author will not sacrifice fictional creation to convert sinners. The moral frame strives to create order from chaos, but the text responds ambiguously to the professed intention.

While the archpriest says he is doing one thing, his book, in effect, does quite another. The narrator cunningly protects himself from precisely this charge by stating that there is nothing bad in the book, only that which is interpreted badly.[14] This position gives readers two unappealing alternatives: to deny the author's intention or to deny their own ability to read correctly. The answer, however, may lie in a text that proves chaotic, or that finds unity in chaos. The categories of good love and bad love, in any type of didactic framework, would have to remain mutually exclusive. Yet when Trotaconventos, the figure par excellence of bad love, dies, the archpriest laments the death of a saint and martyr to be compared with Christ, and curses death in a most un-Christian way, forgetting that the spiritual world is the source of good love and that only death can bring eternal life.[15] The (con)fusion of good love and bad love exemplifies both the conflict facing man and the ambiguous narrative that offers a discursive analogue of the conflict. The only way to reconcile the implicit ideological contradictions is to recognize that the contradictions form the ideological base of the work, that the only synthesis possible is a lack of synthesis. Interpretation is no longer an either/or situation, and the ironic narrator is the ideal candidate to present an ambiguous universe via an open, ambiguous text. The archpriest converts a go-between and a promiscuous nun into saints, without fully convincing the reader of his sincerity. Saying it is not enough, given what has been said before. The narrator, whose aim may not be to elucidate the situation, recounts (without witnessing) the dialogue between Trotaconventos and Doña Garoza, in which rhetoric displaces truth and emotion displaces codified speech. The unmediated discourse of the go-between and the nun is, in fact, mediated by defensive barriers erected in the linguistic foray and by the intrusive narrative presence.

For M. K. Read, the *Libro de Buen Amor* "gives expression to a deepening awareness in European culture of the problematic nature of language. A lingering vision of the mythical nature of the word is replaced by a playful exploration of the gap which separates the signifier from the signified. This exploration, leads, in turn, to a consideration of the profounder implications of man's alienation from language."[16] Linguistic structures produce "false myths" as the distance between signifier and signified "alienates" words from their original meanings. By creatively examining language, Juan Ruiz acknowledges the crisis between philosophical realism and nominalism and the growing opposition between philosophical and rhetorical ideals.[17] Apart from the intellectual superstructure, the *Libro de Buen Amor* allows metaliterary recourses to guide the text. The creative examination of language is not only a means to an analogical end but also an end in itself. The question of interpretation moves from the closure of directed reading and negative exemplarity to a counterpoint in multiple meanings, as illustrated in the debate between the Greeks and the Romans (stanzas 44–70), where gesture is at the same time symbolically abstract and defiantly literal. The account of the Greco-Roman contest redirects control from the narrator to the reader, from the one who employs or invents signs to the one who masters or reinvents them. As the text progresses, layers of words replace gestures to indicate innumerable interpretive possibilities. Old signs—from oral tradition, theology, fictional texts, allegorical conventions, regional and poetic variations—find new and changing significance in new and constantly expanding contexts. They become signifiers with modified signifieds, whose agent is appropriately a narrator/protagonist, with shifting functions in the text, and a literary double.

Language in the Doña Garoza episode, to cite one case, stems from women who represent the extremes of feminism: the bride of Christ and the devil's advocate. If Trotaconventos attains a certain spirituality in death, Doña Garoza becomes a sexual object in this life. Theologically prescribed behavior and allegorically inscribed fables form a linguistic repertory for the nun's pious role, while the latent significance (or modified signifieds) of her discourse bespeaks a latent sexuality. Consumed with feeling, she assumes both extremes of the feminine trajectory, longs for both types of love, and discovers a male counterpart in the errant archpriest. She disguises her emotions with moralizing stories that cannot conceal her immoral thoughts, and the barrage of fables yields to desire and to a rhetoric of form over substance. The narrator (as well as the reader) learns from Trotaconventos that the holy ladies have secular interests: "'Yo las serví un tiempo e moré aí bien diez años; / tienen a sus amigos viciosos e sin sossaños'" (1333a-b, pp. 360–61; "'I worked for nuns once and stayed there a good ten years; they keep their lovers in comfort and free from embarrassments'"). The nuns spoil men; their suitors are *viciosos*, spoiled, overindulged, corrupt(ed), and they themselves are corruptible. The archpriest's dialogue with Trotaconventos precedes the debate between the women, a debate interrupted by Doña Garoza's request for a verbal portrait of the pretender. The nun admonishes the go-between, "'Vieja, guárdeme Dios de tus mañas'" (1492a, pp. 400–401; "'Old woman, God preserve me from your wiles'"), and then arranges her first meeting with the archpriest, in church. In her figurative escape from God, Doña Garoza invokes the name of the Lord and encounters her suitor in the holy sanctuary. From that point on, she is silent, but the narrator speaks of the "good things" she did for him and of her "immaculate life," and ends by asking that "God forgive her soul and our sins" (p. 404).

Medieval theology grants a textuality to the world, where every object is a sign of something else. To triumph in the world or to win salvation results from successful and comprehensive semiotic activity, from correctly interpreting and deciphering the signs that present themselves in the course of existence. Marta Ana Diz shows the application of this thesis to a major prose work of the fourteenth century, the *Libro del Conde Lucanor* (*Book of Count Lucanor*) by Don Juan Manuel, a collection of fifty-one stories occasioned by a problem of the count and the solution, via exemplum, of his advisor Patronio.[18] The communicative event, ranging from the count's request to a moral in verse, distinguishes between a "real" situation and an invented or recalled analogue. The *Libro del Conde Lucanor* demonstrates a faith in the ability of the word to convey meaning and in a universal organizing principle to maintain consistency in meaning. Patronio has his master's best interests at heart; his discourse offers no hint of unreliability or ambiguity. Correspondingly, there is negligible tension between the circumstances of the problems and the content of the stories, and no subversion on the analogical level. The richness and variety of exempla attest to the comprehensive impact of the word and of the semiotic system it serves. Human beings and literary objects exist in the world and, by way of parallel, in the juxtaposition of the real and the literary in the text. The problem and its solution are to the reader what the exempla are to Count Lucanor. The stories are analogues within analogues and literary flourishes, sweet and useful, depicting a universe subject to reason. Don Juan Manuel and Patronio show faith in the signifying capacity of the word and, through the verbal medium, acceptance of a ruling harmony and logic. The *Libro de Buen Amor* casts the realm of the senses and binary opposition on the stability of this order, and the text reflects a spiritual crisis converted into a crisis of the word. The nun is an icon of the new order, both sinner and saint, bride and adulteress.

In the *Libro del Conde Lucanor*, the narrative pattern uses exempla, often fables, to deliver moral messages directed to receivers in the text (the count) and in society (the reader). Despite the multiple themes, subjects, sources, and settings, there is little sense of differentiation. Each story belongs to the general public, and each fits the narrative premise without forsaking an earlier significance. In the Doña Garoza episode of the *Libro de Buen Amor*, the fables continue to have meaning as fables, but their function extends to the specific context. They form part of the nun's and the go-between's textual identities and linguistic armor. They are not only the weapons of the debate but also a means of delineating character. The intertextual associations—for example, the allegorical connotations of the animals in the fables—heighten the tension of the debate and give it a sense of progression. While Patronio's fables relate directly to the case at hand, Doña Garoza's and Trotaconventos's fables stand as an ironic counterpoint to amorous feelings and ulterior motives. The archpriest takes an overcoded genre, whose clarity eliminates the need for an explicit moral, and reprograms the message to fit the intricate discursive schemes of the dialogue. The moral pieces ultimately serve the cause of immorality. Nothing—not the literary legacy, not even the convent—is sacred.

In the medieval vision, the vision of the *Conde Lucanor*, man serves a higher order and the social order that aspires to re-create the divine. Individual experience has exemplary value; the single person acts as representative of humanity, to instruct through shared concerns and responses. Within this system, texts tend to prioritize similarity over difference, lesson over event, and event over characterization. Morality reflects the collective will, and psychology takes the form of mass psychology. The *Libro de Buen Amor* represents a transitional stage in which the archpriest typifies the human struggle while he exerts himself as a distinguishable individual, a man who speaks and acts out of self-interest, who interacts with those around him, who has a personal history, changing attitudes, a physical side, a name. If the archpriest's proposal respects the past, its execution points to the future: antithetical categories merge, examples become ambiguous, words deceive. Men and women in the text find it difficult to pattern their lives on doctrines and saints when they find heaven on earth. The narrator recasts the literary object to conform to a modified view of the human condition. The work of art reifies epistemological questions, notably the problematical status of the signifier. When Doña Garoza rejects the force of her own discourse (stock fables that contradict her true sentiments) in favor of the description of her suitor and an immoral parody of her holy vows, she speaks on behalf of a growing alienation from the word and its bond with universal order. Literary tradition, as part of the earlier order, functions ironically in the new. No longer strictly subordinate to its message, fiction comes into its own.

From the secure consistency of Patronio, narrative moves to the indecisive, chaotic strategies of the archpriest. The fit of problem, exemplum, and moral in the stories of the *Conde Lucanor* proves the advisor's authority over the material and, to a certain extent, over the reading process. The archpriest, in contrast, sacrifices narrative control for the sake of perspectivism. The narrator—who shifts position and identity, who outlines the direction of the text but follows another course, and who detaches signifiers from long-standing signifieds—is not entirely unreliable. There is method in his inconsistency. Through the debate between the Greeks and Romans (and, more subtly, through the debate between Doña Garoza and Trotaconventos), he informs the reader that meanings vary according to the explicitness and setting of the message and according to the perception of the receiver. The text demonstrates that even set pieces, such as the fables, are defined by context as well as by content. As doubt and indeterminacy grow, so grows the role of the reader, who can no longer take discourse for granted.

The archpriest gives new significance and new fictional potential to old dichotomies. In mixing the sacred with the profane, the *Libro de Buen Amor* foregrounds the contradictory nature of man and of the world. It is noteworthy that identity and experiential conflicts include womankind. The loving and erring priest finds a true soulmate in Doña Garoza, torn by the demands of her given role and by emotions she cannot suppress. The same factors that dictate her behavior mediate her discourse. She is not free to say what she feels, so she resorts to the fictional analogue of moral doctrine, the fable. In reprimanding Trotaconventos, she employs commonplaces worthy of her position yet contrary to her desires. As soon as she submits to passion, she loses her textual voice and shortly thereafter her life. While the archpriest's attempt to promote her saintliness may be unconvincing, the gesture is nevertheless a narrative sign of her dilemma and an ambivalent concession to feminine sexuality. Trotaconventos and the women pursued by the archpriest face social, economic, and ethical pressures that discourage independent thought and action. To appease their instincts, they must deny a public and prescribed moral conscience. To garner respectability, they must deny their instincts. Like the narrator, they are caught in a double bind.

The *Libro de Buen Amor* places the author in a fictional world, and the fictionalized self offers a statement of intention, rendered enigmatic by self-conscious references to the act of interpretation (presented as variable) and by the text itself (incompatible with the stated purpose). The fragmented narrative persona devises a literary universe in which signs lose their certainty and characters face the loss with anguish and with creative impetus. Men and women must become more articulate, and perhaps more calculating, to compensate for the diminished capacity of the word. They must rely more on rhetoric as embellishment, in the double sense of the term. Linguistic diversity may lead to or derive from an incipient individualism, and fiction may put forth a subtext of conformity or nonconformity. In presenting a story, narrators avail themselves of discursive options to stress language for its own sake and to structure concepts. As the production of meaning in fiction becomes progressively complex—less explicit and more deceptive—discourse ceases to accommodate story and message as it had in the past. It evolves into a code to be analyzed, or broken, as part of the search for meanings. The Doña Garoza episode of the *Libro de Buen Amor* incorporates a narrative past into an ironic present. Although meaning has lost some of its force, the narrators share a faith in the power of the word to "remake" reality. Unlike Count Lucanor's problems, the problem of signification remains unresolved, and the text continually verifies the indeterminacy of discourse. The tentative status of language grants a higher status to the individual speaker, as well as to the individual reader. The nature of language becomes a central issue of writing and reading.

The author of *Lazarillo de Tormes* responds to the conventions of earlier works—and to the myths of society—to shed new light on genealogy, education, class, and honor. The text is a written statement of explanation that wavers between autobiographical and literary consciousness. A sense of remaking circumstance through verbal constructs permeates the narrative, which pairs maturity with linguistic competence and self-defense with variability of the linguistic sign. *Lazarillo de Tormes* works against the chivalric and sentimental idealism, spiritual renewal, and semiotic complacency that make its existence possible. The *Libro de Buen Amor* anticipates the skepticism toward the semiotics of an ordered world, a skepticism explored and exploited in the *Lazarillo*. The Archpriest of Hita confronts human nature against a backdrop of divinity. The distance between practice and preachment affects—reorients—art and the artist. The interplay of text and pretext, voice and character, heavenly and earthly messages tends to subvert prior concepts of signification. Despite their otherworldly armaments, literary works may be singularly unholy and certainly more inclined toward aesthetic response than toward moral instruction. Lázaro reduces the problem to the here and now of social survival and its textual correlative, the paradoxical case of unmediated discourse.

2 NARRATIVE ACTS, NARRATIVE ACTORS
Toward a Model of Picaresque Discourse

> Mimetic discourse mimetizes itself as world. It alienates itself
> and becomes its own object.
> Félix Martínez–Bonati, *Fictive Discourse and the*
> *Structures of Literature*

The sixteenth- and early seventeenth-century Spanish picaresque novels, together with *Don Quijote*, establish a set of conventions (and counterconventions) marked simultaneously by a consciousness of complex realities and a narrative self-consciousness. Process becomes as significant as product in an autobiographical framework in which a character moves from childhood to adulthood and at the same time from illiterate to man of letters. The reader is given a life story against the backdrop of the society of the time and amid the act of fictional creation. A model for the picaresque must take into consideration formal recourses and social implications, but perhaps the crucial factor in terms of continuity is the complex interplay between the participants in narrative discourse. The novelist explores language as a source of meaning and meaning as a source of multiperspectivism, and the picaresque may be not so much a myth as the structure that encompasses a myth. This structure projects itself in *Lazarillo de Tormes* and remains a part of the picaresque tradition in its multiple transformations. In the progression from discourse to story to meaning(s), the medium becomes the message. The character contends with the codes and conventions of the social system and the narrator with those of the literary system. The dialectical relation between the textual and the extratextual finds an analogue in the narration proper, which links the narrative voice with the agent who controls that voice.

Picaresque narrative originates, at least in part, as a reaction against the elevated style, diction, and circumstance of idealistic literature. Viewed from the lower depths, social phenomena such as lineage, rank, love, honor, and respectability lose their purity and elegance of expression. Because the intertextual identity signals a reversal of norms and expectations, as well as of linguistic pretensions, the effect is ironic, satirical. Narrative duties fall to a humble, uneducated outsider versed in deception, a social climber in a regimented and deterministic order. If this type of individual succeeds, according to the structured consciousness of the period, society is destined to fail. Since the social aspirations make their way into the discourse, language must somehow reflect the futility of the déclassé character's illusions of grandeur. The narrative situation suggests the need for a strategic denial of discursive proficiency to match the denial of ambition. The narrator's text calls for a "rewriting" from within.

Lazarillo de Tormes and its successors offer variations of what narratologists (following Wayne Booth) have termed the *implied author*, a presence in narrative fiction who affects the production of meaning, often subverting in some way the direction of textual discourse. Seymour Chatman calls this figure "'implied,' that is, reconstructed by the reader from the narrative. He is not the narrator, but rather the principle that invented the narrator, along with everything else in the narrative, that stacked the cards in this particular way, had these things happen to these characters, in these words or images. Unlike the narrator, the implied author can *tell* us nothing. He, or better, *it* has no voice, no direct means of communicating. It instructs us silently, through the design of the whole, with all the voices, by all the means it has chosen to let us learn."[1] The implied author is the reader's justification for analytical reading, for "reading into" the text those elements judged to be encoded by the real author. The real author exists outside the text, while the implied author leaves traces in the narrative. When the narrator is unreliable, whether consciously or unconsciously, these traces become more evident, as if intended to catch the attention of an *implied reader*.[2] In the early picaresque narratives, the principal markers of the implied author are discrepancies between the narrator's revelations and the protagonist's best interests.

At the end of *Lazarillo de Tormes*, for example, the narrator/protagonist informs the gentleman to whom he is addressing the account that he is living "in prosperity and at the height of all good fortune," yet his discourse belies this story. Lázaro's rhetorical strategy, as it were, works to transform dishonor into success, but the result is an ironically overdetermined text. His own words betray him, and the reader may doubt that they are his own words. When Lázaro's widowed mother moves to the city of Salamanca determined "to align herself with the good people," her situation goes from bad to worse. When Lázaro determines "to align himself with the good people" of Toledo in the final chapter, one may anticipate a reversal rather than a bonanza, despite commentary to the contrary. The repetition of the proverbial phrase, "Associate with good people and you will become one of them," unites the unpleasant social realities of the past with the present. More comprehensively, the narration stresses the importance of silence—the need to act hypocritically in a hypocritical society—while the narrative act breaks the silence and threatens to expose the real story behind the defensive rhetoric. Guzmán de Alfarache's narrative, replete with moral digressions, purports to trace a spiritual evolution, but once again the discourse allows for multiple, and antithetical, interpretive possibilities, including a rejection of the protagonist's conversion. Mateo Alemán creates a convert not only who looks to the past but also whose discursive present casts doubt on his repentance, his earnestness, and his reliability. Once the liar foregrounds his skills at deception, he becomes the victim of a discursive trap.

The implied author of *El Buscón* not only renders the discourse ironic but also creates a baroque metalanguage that hides its messages behind a compendium of verbal conceits. The linguistic complexity of the narrative suggests the imposition of an authorial figure, in this case one who controls events as well as language. Both discourse and story combat Pablos in his search for upward mobility; if Don Diego Coronel the character is his nemesis in life, Francisco de Quevedo as implied author is his nemesis within the text. The social hierarchy and the social status quo emerge victorious in a literary object in which the implied author, as defender of the established institutions, triumphs over the narrator in a hierarchical pattern of discourse.

Literature imitates life, in reflecting a growing cynicism toward absolute knowledge and a growing interest in the uniqueness of the individual. The ironic capacity of a text—its operation on distinct levels of significance—relates to the failure of language to be exact, which may be turned into the strength of linguistic variation and multiple meaning. The world must be perceived little by little; there is no such thing as completeness. The text unites numerous signs whose signifying potential is inexhaustible. Reading strives for completeness but is always incomplete, always in need of rereadings. (To this, the classic text and the art of criticism owe their survival.) The internal structure of a text situates the individuated discourse (or idiolect) of the narrator with events and other elements of plot. The union may take the form of correspondence or contradiction, or it may waver between the two. Within the miscellany of the *Libro de Buen Amor*, a first-person narrator who proposes to teach goodness through negative examples cannot, or perhaps does not wish to, separate the discourse of the good from the discourse of the bad. The archpriest of the text is not true to his holy role nor to his righteous premise. He, Trotaconventos, and other characters transfer the directness of dogma to the realm of rhetoric, where meanings depend on context and where contexts can change meaning. Words patterned to preserve the faith compromise doctrine and language while broadening the semiotic base of the text (and of future texts). The *Libro de Buen Amor* sets the stage for the discursive ironies of *Lazarillo de Tormes*.

LAZARILLO DE TORMES

The premise of *Lazarillo de Tormes* is based on the narrator's "reading" of his text, or the response he wishes to evoke from the addressee's reading. The narrative answers a petition that occupies the apparent center of discourse, but other elements combine to de-center the premise and the narrator's authority. Like Juan Ruiz's archpriest who calls his go-between a saint while pretending to instruct the public, Lázaro takes poetic license with traditional signifiers. The story of Lázaro de Tormes is the unmasking of an unreliable narrator who cannot keep the truth from coming out in his community or in his text. Because the markers of irony evolve within the text itself, they constitute a discursive mechanism of the comprehensive structure. This internal operation is the creation of the author (as is Lázaro's narration), but it needs to be differentiated from the external composition of the text. The subversion of discourse and story (the account) reveals the "real situation" that motivates the original request. By putting Lázaro in the writer's role and a gentleman associate in the role of the reader, the author focuses attention on the task of organizing events into narrative. The self-consciousness accentuates not only the finished product but also the demands placed on the narrator and the flaws in his method. Scrutiny of the narrative performance invites a different approach to the story. Whether it be called implied author or remain unnamed, the discursive device charged with altering textual presuppositions elaborates an ironic frame. The narrative situation, in its multiple facets, confirms the irony and the ironic presence.

Using speech-act theory as a model for point of view, Susan Sniader Lanser emphasizes three aspects of novelistic discourse: "the textual speaker's relationship to the literary act (status), the interactions between speakers and listeners (contact), and the attitudes of textual personae toward the represented world (stance)."[3] The category of status includes identity, credibility, sincerity, and other factors that comprise narrative authority, or lack thereof. Conventions and values—literary, linguistic, and cultural—function dialectically in the production and reception of narrative discourse. Contact centers on the narrator's role with respect to the addressee(s) of the verbal message. Stance refers to a speaker's disposition toward the material in question, to attitudes that derive from socialization, ideology, and individual psychology, "which precede the speech performance and which condition the speaker's response to the propositional content of the discourse."[4] By acknowledging its debt to the literary canon and to social practice, *Lazarillo de Tormes* illustrates the contextualization of perspective. The narrator's self-consciousness and his propensity for detail make him a particularly revealing subject.

Lazarillo de Tormes confronts the classical notion of decorum, substituting ignoble origins for lofty bloodlines, colloquial language and folk motifs for the erudition prized (and codified) in the Middle Ages, and a disreputable commoner and literary novice for the figure of authority. Lázaro's ironically symbolic birth on the river Tormes on the one hand gives him a humorous identity as compared with the chivalric heroes Amadís de Gaula (Gaul), Palmerín de Inglaterra (England), and their ilk, and on the other hand makes him a man without a country, without roots. The contradictory prose and the indeterminacies of the text, coupled with indications that Lázaro may be attempting to hide the truth, lend little credence to his status as narrator. The addressees, both the well-bred gentleman who requests the account and the reading public, presumably outrank the narrator. The social difference and possibly guilt lead to a patronizing, defensive posture. The internal premise of the account suggests a strategy on Lázaro's part to honor the request without defaming himself. The execution of the strategy, in contrast, points to another strategy (or stratagem) aimed at a denial of authority.

In the first part of the prologue to *Lazarillo de Tormes*, the speaker offers a conventional defense of his work, noting along with Pliny the Elder that no book is so bad that it has no redeeming features and with Cicero that honor fosters the arts. From the field of books and readers, the prologue shifts to the narrative premise: a gentleman recognized only as Vuestra Merced (Your Worship), a friend of Lázaro's patron, has requested a detailed explanation of what the speaker refers to as "the case" (*el caso*). Lázaro, willing to comply, proposes to start at the beginning in order to give a full account of himself. He observes that while fate smiles on those who inherit wealth, the less fortunate must forge their own direction in life. The text proper—the explanation—is divided into seven chapters, or *tratados* (literally, treatises), spanning pre-history to post-*caso*. The temporal and psychological distance between events and narration gives the narrator the opportunity to relate childhood experience (from the perspective of Lazarillo the boy) and to comment on that experience (from the perspective of the mature, self-conscious Lázaro).

Modest ancestry, an inauspicious birth on the river Tormes, and the indiscretions of both parents place the narrator/protagonist at a low point in the sacrosanct social hierarchy. Following the death of the father, Lázaro's mother entrusts the boy to a blind man, thus initiating the motif of service to a series of masters, a progression that reflects growth and education in the ways of the world. At first, Lázaro struggles for survival against masters who would starve him. Figuratively blind, the innocent child learns to outwit the avaricious blind man, only to encounter a priest who keeps food locked in a trunk and a squire who has no food at all. As hunger ceases to be a problem, Lázaro seeks respectability in a hostile and hypocritical society, with role models worthy of their milieu. For example, the fifth master, a pardoner, uses earthly wiles to feign divine intervention. From his mentor, the archpriest of San Salvador, Lázaro receives employment, a bride, and, so he claims, a sense of security.

The prologue to Lázaro's text introduces a reduplication of speakers and objects. An author, caught in the pages of his creation, contemplates the fortunes of his book in the public domain. An obvious goal here would be acceptance of a product by its consumers/critics. The defensive strategy calls on the reader to consider that there is some good in every book and to look for (redeeming) values rather than for flaws. Narrowing and internalizing the focus, a narrator puts forth his motive for writing the account, justifies the use of an autobiographical frame, and stresses his desire to fulfill Vuestra Merced's request. Classical allusions disappear, replaced by proverbial and anecdotal material, to signal the movement from the noble ideal to the crudely real. More importantly, a narratee or fictional receiver replaces the real reader within the narrative pretext.[5] In this part of the prologue, Lázaro approaches his undertaking with humility (calculated modesty, perhaps, directed to Vuestra Merced and to other readers) while seeking praise and sympathy for his rise in society without the advantages of heredity, positive examples, or property. A pattern of conflicting signs—an object in the marketplace versus a personal explanation, an epistle divided into chapters, pride in success alternating with rationalization of failure, offensive and defensive rhetorical strategies—establishes itself in the prologue and continues throughout the narrative. Similarly, two mysteries of the prologue, the identity of Vuestra Merced and the details of the case, remain elusive in a text supposedly built around clarification. The problem may ultimately be a key to the solution.

If traditional criticism of *Lazarillo de Tormes* describes the work as a loosely connected series of episodes united only by the presence of the protagonist and a formulaic master-servant relationship, criticism of the past half-century has dedicated itself to the elaboration of a complex structural unity earlier found lacking. Narrative events have not been chosen randomly, nor have they been recounted in an arbitrary fashion; a sophisticated unifying principle operates throughout the work.[6] Recognition of unity does not, however, produce uniformity of interpretation. Irony, linguistic variation, discrete resonances of the narrative voice, and a comprehensive ambiguity invade the facile linearity of the novel, and it becomes a paradox. The consistency of paradox lies precisely in its lack of consistency, a fact that one should bear in mind when analyzing the text. A significant, and perhaps overlooked, element is the chaos that frames the newly discovered order.

When in the prologue of his communication to Vuestra Merced Lázaro de Tormes rejects the in medias res convention of the ancient epic, both the narratee and the real readers may expect an unambiguous beginning and an unambiguous ending, as opposed to an assortment of surprises. The birth on the river may be a genealogical imperative turned genealogical burlesque, but it should be the undeniable starting point as well, just as the literary present should mark the logical stopping point. Neither of these assumptions proves true, a development that may substantiate the internal logic of the novel. The *Lazarillo* is a work built on the creation of ambiguities, and, within this system, the resolution of ambiguities would be a contradiction in terms.

While there is a clear distinction between Lázaro the narrator and Lazarillo, both subject and object of the text, there is perhaps a more significant distinction between Lázaro and the author. Lázaro's manipulation of narrative recourses is countered by an implied author's manipulation of the broader set of recourses that encompasses the metatext. The mature Lázaro is not telling a story but arguing a case, and his goal is to be judged innocent. Within this analogue, the author functions as a type of prosecutor working to undermine the validity of the argument. Through subtlety of expression, the narrator attempts to equate retelling with reexperiencing, in order to transform an impressionistic past into an objective present. The author's role is to subvert the verbal force of the metatext by exposing contradictory evidence. He accomplishes this by making the written response a form of self-betrayal, as Lázaro falls victim to his own words. The reader is the final arbiter, charged with recognizing the deceptive language of Lázaro and the ironic (counter)strategies of the author.[7]

Lázaro's apparent freedom of selection would seem to give him authority over the material. By purporting to include only those elements that relate to the case, he justifies the exclusion of irrelevant or, more properly, incriminating facts. Through his control of discourse and perspective, Lázaro seeks self-protection rather than absolute truth. The narrative force of his enterprise depends entirely on the transformational power of the written word: an exculpatory statement becomes a success story, dishonor becomes honor, and the victim becomes judge. The memories that shape the account are distorted by design; time is not the enemy of truth but rather the ally of metamorphosed truth. Lázaro subjects his life to a particular thesis, for which literary form represents a type of closure. The resulting document can only be undone by flaws in structure.

The narrative pretext of the *Lazarillo*, the explanation of a situation, mediates the selective process. While Lázaro is not anxious to speak of his state of affairs,[8] he is more than anxious to please Vuestra Merced. Up to this point, the self-imposed silence has served him well, but now he must find an elusive, seemingly contradictory, verbal correlative of the unspoken word. Lázaro's chief defensive maneuver is to convert an alibi into an indictment. He may choose episodes to his own advantage, put words into the mouths of others, and blame society for his errors. By focusing on his upward movement in the social hierarchy, he may also disregard the matter at hand. The positive statements that end both the prologue and the novel proper indicate the narrator's willingness to confuse a material progression with a moral retrogression and his conscious effort to move from autobiography to apology to ironic apotheosis.[9] Even before his account formally begins, Lázaro promises to address himself to one question yet in effect directs himself to another. Rather than be a report on a scandal, the text will be a justification of his involvement in the scandal, the product of an inverted theory of relativity in which rationalization is all. Lázaro hopes to negate his guilt by redefining traditional concepts of guilt and by establishing a pattern of collective guilt. The semantic proficiency of Lázaro's argument is surpassed, however, by defects in internal logic. As Lázaro's nemesis and the purveyor of textual discrepancies, the implied author offers a new text, essentially a cynical variation of the original.

In what proves to be a costly rhetorical miscalculation, Lázaro the writer openly indicates a predisposition toward poetic license. His verbal choices often invalidate the apparent messages, and complementary statements may turn into counterstatements through misuse of idiomatic and proverbial commonplaces. Lázaro's widowed mother goes to Salamanca to align herself with the good people, to become one of them; that is, she cooks for students and washes clothes for stableboys. Shortly afterward, she has an affair and an illegitimate son by Zaide, a stable attendant and thief. Whether the contextual incongruity is intentional or unintentional, the narrator fails to achieve the discursive expertise necessary to defend himself, even after exposure to various linguistic fields.[10] For if, on the one hand, he is trying to emphasize his mother's weaknesses—to show how far he has come—he is adhering to an ironic code, and the text must be read as a catalog of semantic inversions. If, on the other hand, he is trying to emphasize his mother's strength of character, he has failed miserably and the irony is equally overt. In either case, the tension between story and discourse is evident.

Lázaro suffers the consequences of his literary freedom in chapter 7. The negative depiction of the past (familial dishonor, subservience, near-starvation, events too demeaning to mention[11]) may accentuate the material comforts of the present, but it also forces Lázaro to criticize the same social sins that he now practices and to preserve in written form the correspondence between his parents' disgrace and his own. When Lázaro's little brother shudders in fright at his black father, Lázaro observes, "Yo, aunque bien mochacho, . . . dije entre mí: '¡Cuántos debe de haber en el mundo que huyen de otros porque no se veen a sí mesmos!'" (p. 11; Although I was but a young lad, I said to myself, "How many people there must be in the world who flee from others because they can't see themselves!"). The narrator commits himself early in the text (and early in his life) to a superior attitude over those who overlook the obvious, those victims of a figurative blindness who miss what others see. In the final chapter, Lázaro himself retreats into figurative blindness. As a result, either society assumes the superior position or Lázaro is misrepresenting his feelings. He can only respond to the lessons of his masters in a theoretical way; in practical terms, he has no desirable options, no release for his social perception, and no basis for the oblivious stance he wishes to project. The ultimate problem has not so much to do with vision as with speech. The situation calls for silence, but Lázaro, as a town crier and as an author, cannot keep silent.

The paradoxical relationship between speech (confession) and silence is discernible throughout the text[12] but most emphatically in the prologue. In the concluding section of the prologue, Lázaro announces both the unifying element (the explanation of the case) and the tactical focus (the poor man climbing the ladder of success) of his narrative. Although he offers a rationale of sorts—"confesando yo no ser más sancto que mis vecinos" (p. 6; I must confess that I'm no more holy than my neighbors)—he can arrive only at an awkward synthesis. Referring gloatingly to his relative prosperity, he must allude as well to scandalous events that would be best left unsaid. By pretending to ignore the contradiction here and in the seventh chapter, Lázaro sustains the deceptive linguistic scheme that treats polarities as interdependencies. The credibility of this position wanes as one considers that Lázaro's rites of passage into society include an initiation into the complexities of language. By informing readers of these stages in his development, he is simultaneously—and counterproductively—alerting them to the very verbal ploys that comprise the account.

Vuestra Merced asks Lázaro to relate the case in detail. It is Lázaro's decision to incorporate an autobiographical framework, in order to clarify his present status and to win sympathy for what may be described as complacent cuckoldry. For one who has come close to starvation and has prayed for his own death, has begged food for both himself and his master, and has been witness to deceitful and unmentionable acts, marriage and material stability are great steps forward. In a society committed to punishing the guilty (and the children of the guilty), Lázaro is motivated less by virtue than by survival instincts and the example of his masters. The final linguistic instruction comes from the archpriest of San Salvador, whose message presents a mutually beneficial fusion of innocence—actually complicity— with self-interest: "'Lázaro de Tormes, quien ha de mirar a dichos de malas lenguas nunca medrará; digo esto porque no me maravillaría alguno, viendo entrar en mi casa a tu mujer y salir de ella. Ella entra muy a tu honra y suya. Y esto te lo prometo. Por tanto, no mires lo que pueden decir, sino a lo que te toca, digo a tu provecho'" (p. 79; "Lázaro de Tormes, he who pays attention to what evil tongues say will never prosper. I mention this because it wouldn't surprise me if someone should comment on seeing your wife come and go from my house. She enters very much to your honor and her own. This I promise you. So don't worry about what they may say but about what concerns you, that is, what is to your advantage"). While in doctrinal terms the arrangement with the archpriest may resemble a pact with the devil, contextually it allows Lázaro to align himself with the good to produce yet another ironic alliance.[13] By directly quoting the archpriest, Lázaro proves that he is as innocent as his neighbors, or equally guilty.

The inconsistencies in Lázaro's story nullify the power that he ascribes to the literary object. The "true" language of the *Lazarillo* is that of the author, the creator of textual irony in the deceptive language of the narrator, also his creation. The exposition of an ironic structure, one that discloses the fallacious base of Lázaro's discourse, may in the end be an affirmation rather than a negation of verbal potentiality. While planting clues for the discovery of Lázaro's strategy, the implied author orients the reader toward a "truthful" reading. This reaffirmation of the word is made possible by a hermeneutic contract between the author and the reader: the author relies on the reader's recognition of the incriminatory nature of Lázaro's text, and the reader in turn seeks a consistent system of motifs and linguistic signs. The episodic elements of the narrative conform, then, to a major premise (the explanation of the case), a point of mediation (the revelation of an unreliable narrator), and a reversal of the initial premise (the acceptance of ironic levels of meaning). Within this perspective, the autobiographical device is a frame-up, similar to Quevedo's deterministic ordering of events in *El Buscón*. If Pablos's literary course is a blind alley, Lázaro's is a trap set from the beginning by the author. Lázaro is condemned to expose himself while trying to delude the reader. He is the victimizer turned victim, the victim of authorial irony. And yet this is only the penultimate irony of the *Lazarillo*.

Lázaro's narrative presupposes a multiple plan of action. He will conceal his social transgressions by controlling language and point of view, satirize the honor code to underplay his own loss of honor, and implicate all of society (in a panoramic vision that extends from his parents and the blind man to the archpriest) in his worldly education, or guilt. The attempt to defend himself against all possible accusations indicates desperation as well as comprehensiveness. Lázaro does not seem to realize the difference between asserting his innocence and rationalizing his guilt, and his emphasis on upward mobility and self-improvement calls into question his role as society's—or fortune's—pawn. The narrator cannot achieve a single effect by stressing both his impressive rise in a hostile society and the moral compromises implicit in his ascent. Vuestra Merced requests nothing but the truth, but Lázaro's art, like his life, is jeopardized by the truth. He takes refuge in a series of oblique visions and evasions, shielding himself from the clarity that would acknowledge the unconscionable. In Toledo, Lázaro endures his domestic circumstances by looking the other way and by forcing silence on others. In his account, he finds a literary correlative of evasion in an indirect approach to discourse.

Like the blind man's fatherly concern, the priest's religiosity, the squire's honorability, the pardoner's zealous devotion, and the archpriest's selflessness—as revealed and at least tacitly denied by Lázaro—the narrator's avowed truthfulness is a shallow and unconvincing pose. Men cannot be judged by their appearance or by their words, life has taught Lázaro, who inadvertently offers precedents for his own judgment by the reader. Giving Lazarillo a piece of bread he believes to have been gnawed on by mice, the priest says, "'Cómete eso, que el ratón cosa limpia es'" (p. 35; "Go ahead and eat this, for the mouse is a clean animal"). The message, of course, is that the man is a hypocrite in cleric's garb. Years later, when the archpriest tells Lázaro that his wife is "clean," the intended message may differ, but the real message is the same. Here, however, Lázaro is an accomplice in the hypocrisy, willing to certify that he has reached the height of all good fortune; yet the imposed silence on the marital issue is as articulate and as denunciatory as the key transformed into a serpent's "voice" in chapter 2. The predetermined cyclical pattern leads to Lázaro's downfall as writer and as protagonist, despite his highly developed verbal and experiential skills. In the first two chapters, Lazarillo seems destined to die of hunger whether he serves a master or not. The hypothetical remedy, a position with a master who will feed him sufficiently, is reversed in the third chapter when the apparently ideal master gives the boy an additional mouth to feed. At the end of the narrative, Lázaro finds himself in an analogous situation, threatened by the precariousness of his social status and called on to protect the archpriest's honor as well as his own.

The stages of the narration of *Lazarillo de Tormes* mark the process toward a unified perspective. According to the mature Lázaro, the selected narrative events work together to present the case and thus to comply with Vuestra Merced's written request. While respecting the petition of his social superior, Lázaro aims to turn the explanation into the vehicle of his redemption by contending that he is the moral equal of his neighbors. In this democratic system, all are innocent or all are guilty. Lázaro's testimony contains, as well, the elements of an ironic unity. The so-called vertical movement through society, associated in the text with the verb *medrar*, includes a variety of confrontations in which the social order and the individuals who guard that order humiliate Lázaro at every step. Through both linguistic and thematic repetition, the text produces an inverted progression that accentuates Lázaro's vulnerability rather than his success. The narrator emphasizes his mistreatment at the hands of his masters, but he also indicates his reactions to what he sees and hears. Even as a child, Lázaro proves himself capable of identifying character flaws, and these assessments allow the reader to consider Lázaro's behavior within the same judgmental base. As a result, Lázaro is caught imitating the example of the various masters. The pejorative narrative stance manifests itself only theoretically, since, practically speaking, the lessons have demonstrable effects on Lázaro's subsequent actions and his struggle to vindicate himself. In chapter 3, for example, Lázaro mocks the squire's exaggerated sense of honor and dependence on appearance, but as soon as he becomes self-sufficient, he emulates his former master's dress (chapter 6) and uses outward signs to point to social respectability (chapter 7). And like the squire's tale of honor (punctuated by the critical interjections of Lazarillo), Lázaro's text is meant to glorify his position but instead articulates the absurdity of his social role.

Seemingly unaware that he cannot redeem himself by denouncing those who have determined the direction of his life—the "neighbors" he berates and then emulates—Lázaro becomes entangled in his own linguistic and conceptual scheme. His intention is to show advancement; the ironic consequence is a backward and cyclical movement. The subversion of the narrative begins with the textual proposition, a duplicitous statement that seeks to deal with a negative experience in positive terms. Lázaro hopes to create a verbal standard of truth by representing (re-presenting) the facts, by treating the mutually exclusive premises as if they were complementary. While this is understandable, given Lázaro's dubious security, the narrative confusion causes a logical imbalance maintained throughout the text. The exemplary materials and rhetorical conventions employed by Lázaro to suggest his innocence more effectively corroborate his guilt. Paradoxically, the ironic reading of Lázaro's defensive memoir produces an explanation of the case as called for by Vuestra Merced. The narrator hints at the truth in spite of himself—in spite of his wish to do otherwise—and because the self-condemnation is so solidly carried out, one cannot help but suspect that Lázaro has another master, one who puts words rather than food into Lázaro's mouth.

In chapter 7, Lázaro reaches the pinnacle of his earthly accomplishments. He obtains an official post, gains the friendship of the archpriest, and marries the archpriest's servant girl, with his patron's favors as dowry. Very few words separate this section from the closing paean to prosperity, but the intervening paragraphs dismantle the self-congratulatory tone. The evil tongues that threaten to destroy Lázaro's matrimonial and communal bliss are not only evil but also truthful: "Mas malas lenguas, que nunca faltaron ni faltarán, no nos dejan vivir, diciendo no sé qué y sí sé qué de que veen a mi mujer irle a hacer la cama y guisalle de comer. Y mejor les ayude Dios que ellos dicen la verdad" (p. 78; But evil tongues, which have never been in short supply nor will they ever be, don't let us go about our lives, saying I don't know what and yes I do know about seeing my wife making his bed and cooking for him. And may God help them, for they're telling the truth). Lázaro does not so much doubt these assertions as wish to quell them. On a number of occasions, his friends have proved (*certificado*, the legal term) that his wife bore children before their marriage. Neither Lázaro nor the archpriest challenges public opinion. Silence must be maintained, not to protect the innocent but to shelter the guilty and to keep peace in Lázaro's house. By silencing himself and his friends, Lázaro expresses faith in the appearance of truth as the dominant social truth. Nevertheless, the central portion of this chapter conveys the real situation by outlining the dissimulation. Explaining the silence, the narrator eradicates the silence at the most crucial moment in the text, thus rendering ironic the concluding statement of triumph.

To comply with Vuestra Merced's request, Lázaro needs to introduce the hearsay linked to the case, but by no means is he compelled to verify the dishonorable aspects of the arrangement. For some reason, he seems determined to say more than he has to, and the deterministic pattern may be attributed to the implied author. At the end of the prologue, Lázaro informs Vuestra Merced that he will allude to events in his life which relate to the case. In addition to the linguistic lessons of the early chapters, the young Lázaro learns the importance of silence from the pardoner (chapter 5), and the mature Lázaro refrains from supplying compromising information in the episodes of the friar (chapter 4) and the painter (chapter 6). In the opening paragraph of chapter 7, Lázaro mentions briefly his misadventures with the constable. The encounter brings to light, if not Lázaro's cowardice, his strong interest in self-preservation. Leaving the service of the constable, he assumes a new and definitive role. He trades an "oficio peligroso" for an "oficio real," an uncomfortable position on the side of justice for a comfortable position on the side of obliviousness. To remain secure, he must block speech (in the form of gossip). Up to this point, he has demonstrated his willingness—though not always his ability—to do so, but in the final part of chapter 7, Lázaro blatantly contrasts his version of the story with the actual facts. Committed to guarding silence, he removes the ambiguities of both silence and indirect discourse.

Lázaro the writer attempts to dissemble dichotomies, by presenting the negative in a positive light and by speaking of matters that he would prefer to leave unmentioned. Precisely by gearing himself toward a synthesis of these former dichotomies—that is, by creating a literary form that would recast negative elements and convert silence into unrevealing discourse—the narrator realizes a certain consistency within the contradictory structure. Because a full synthesis is impossible and because from time to time Lázaro's "true" feelings intrude on his stylized recapitulation, there is a constant threat of self-exposure. Lázaro's overarticulation in the last chapter puts him on the side of truth at a point at which his defense, like the cuckolded husband who wishes to integrate himself into society, can permit only silence. He is no longer unwittingly giving clues from which the reader may guess the truth but rather confirming facts that belie his position. While Lázaro's credibility (as well as his formal consistency) is reduced by this narrative choice, the closing passages seem to verify the antithetical bases of the text.

Viewed from the perspective of an author in search of form for critical statements concerning society, the individual, and the literary work, the *Lazarillo* acquires a new consistency. The center of this analytical reading would be a polygraphic scrutiny of the narrator's voice and the result an increasingly complex paradigm of irony. When his mother offers him as a guide to the blind man in chapter 1, Lázaro writes, "Ella me encomendó a él, diciéndole cómo era hijo de un buen hombre, el cual, por ensalzar la fe, había muerto en la de los Gelves, y que ella confiaba en Dios no saldría peor hombre que mi padre" (pp. 12–13; She entrusted me to him, telling him how I was the son of a good man who had died for his faith in the battle of Gelves, and that she trusted in God that I wouldn't turn out a worse man than my father). As a convicted criminal, Lázaro's father has the option of fighting in the Holy Wars or completing a prison term. His service to the faith stems from this choice. By directly quoting his mother, Lázaro makes her the manipulator of less-than-literal language, yet he is the butt of the irony in a passage that does nothing to aid his own cause and that will eventually become more ironic. In the second chapter, reader sympathy derives from Lazarillo's mistreatment by the avaricious priest, but the narrator himself leads the reader toward a more detached reaction by devising an ironic biblical symbolism in which the boy is a serpent in this "breadly paradise."[14] In chapter 3, Lázaro undermines his acts of kindness to the squire by voicing disparaging remarks in the form of asides. Once again, this technique serves no useful function, and it signals the distinction between what Lázaro says and what he honestly feels. This time, moreover, he quotes himself, preserving in irrefutable form his incipient hypocrisy. In this instance, the reader becomes distanced from Lazarillo and more sympathetic toward the squire, the intended object of ridicule. After his "disappearance" from the text in the next two chapters, Lázaro—in his first act of independence—purchases a wardrobe to match that of the squire. The event is hardly the deviation from social norms that one would expect from a man who gives himself only one more opportunity (in chapter 7) to take a stand against false appearances.

Lázaro's weakness becomes the implied author's strength. What the narrator shows often conflicts with what he tells, and what he tells often goes beyond its primary intention to reveal a character flaw. The implied author's systematic betrayal of his narrator is especially effective because it takes the form of self-betrayal. When considered as part of an authorial strategy, the elements of Lázaro's rhetoric assume a more consistent pattern. While Lázaro may not succeed in convincing Vuestra Merced of his prosperous state or of his indifference to social codes, he does succeed in approaching the intricacies of language and the relationship between language and the reality it purports to represent. His aggressive and exhaustive experiments with language reflect both its powers and its limitations. The negation of Lázaro's narrative force may seem to accentuate the shortcomings of discourse, but the author's ability to control narrator and narrative is an affirmation (a negation of a negation) of verbal possibilities. The author interprets a facet of reality via a narrator whose words must be reinterpreted by a reader on the basis of critical and metacritical signs; an inconsistent text may produce a more consistent metatext.

Lázaro says that he will explain the case, and, despite an attempted cover-up, he does describe his exploits in society and the triangular relationship which seems to be the prime cause of this case. In chapter 5, the pardoner "proves" that the constable is a liar, when in fact he is telling the truth. Conversely, an ironic reading of the *Lazarillo* demonstrates the veracity of Lázaro's narration by signaling its deceptive qualities. The result, of course, is neither a transparent nor an unambiguous text. This is due, to a great extent, to irreconcilable contradictions on the part of Lázaro the writer and an implied author who imposes a mysterious superstructure on the work. Ironically, the one who offers means to clarify problems in Lázaro's account cannot seem to define his own position. The case, the point of departure for unity in the narrative, also becomes the source of its disjunction.

In *La novela picaresca y el punto de vista*, Francisco Rico contends that the case is not only the pretext of *Lazarillo de Tormes* but also the unifying element of the novel. The text—the letter—bases its organization around the convergence of diverse episodes in "el caso" of the final chapter.[15] For Rico and other notable critics, the case removes the *Lazarillo* from the realm of pure autobiography (and from subjection to the requisites of biographical unity). The formation of a structural plan oriented around the case helps to justify temporal and spatial shifts in the narrative, but there are several important questions that remain unanswered. What exactly is the case? If it is the scandal triggered by the "service" of Lázaro's wife to the archpriest, one can suppose that Vuestra Merced—friend of the archpriest and benefactor of Lázaro—would not be especially enlightened by Lázaro's response. He asks for an explanation and receives vague allusions. And why does Vuestra Merced request the explanation? Lázaro states at the end of chapter 7, "Hasta el día de hoy nunca nadie nos oyó sobre el caso" (p. 79; Up to now no one has heard us speak of the case). If he has been able to maintain silence for a certain amount of time,[16] thus shielding himself from the reality that would bring him dishonor, why would Vuestra Merced wish to reopen the case? What has happened during the intervening period, left unmentioned in the explanation of the case, to break the silence? Neither Lázaro nor his text provides answers.

One could perhaps argue that the lack of clarity in the *Lazarillo* affects not the narratee but the reader and that the selective process directs itself toward Vuestra Merced's foreknowledge of the case. The issue is debatable and, to a certain degree, irrelevant. The author creates and sustains the narrative voice of his protagonist throughout the text proper and in the second half of the prologue. He is manipulative but consistent in the presentation of the narrator's semantic resources. In the first half of the prologue, however, Lázaro—initiating his prefatory remarks with the narrative "I"—speaks not for himself but for the other author. The literary convention that establishes a framework for the novel and a marker for the implied reader is not only absent but also incompatible with the explicit message here. The first part of the prologue concerns itself with public reaction to an exercise in self-defense. Virtually every element of this section contradicts Lázaro's strategy for reporting the case.

The narrator, who will later stress the importance of silence in his life, opens with the hope that his work will be read (or heard) by many: " . . . que cosas tan señaladas, y por ventura nunca oídas ni vistas, vengan a noticia de muchos y no se entierren en la sepultura del olvido" (p. 5; that such notable things, by chance never before heard nor seen, may come to the attention of many people and not be buried in the sepulcher of oblivion). The ideas should be freely communicated to allow for differences in reader (or listener) reaction. Not only is there an emphasis on speech rather than on silence, but there is also an emphasis on multiple participants in the interpretative process, "porque, si así no fuese, muy pocos escribirían para uno solo" (p. 6; for if that were not so, very few would write for one person alone). The author is ideologically, if not physiologically, separating himself from Lázaro the writer, who is addressing himself to a single person and attempting to convey a particular message. The point of transition between the two divisions of the prologue is the Ciceronian adage that honor fosters the arts, followed by anecdotal references to man's desire for praise. The search for praise, linked in the examples with hypocrisy,[17] leads into the self-glorifying double plan of Lázaro's defense. The "yo" becomes the textual Lázaro in the last two paragraphs of the prologue, in which the case becomes the focal point. But after all is said and done, what is one to make of the quotation from Cicero? Even if one were to accept Lázaro's complacent attitude in chapter 7, it would be difficult to accept that either life or his book qua explanation of the case will bring him honor. As a final paradox and the irony of ironies, that honor is left to the anonymous author exalted in absentia.

Examination of the case gives a sense of order to an apparently chaotic text. Lázaro's narrative choices follow an outline presented in the prologue, while his linguistic choices prove more enigmatic. Considered from the perspective of authorial control, Lázaro's discourse seems to form part of an ironic system of self-betrayal. His unconscious associations and revelations confirm a conscious selection by the author. This second order complements the first but is by no means complete. As signs of the precarious relationships between appearance and reality and between word and meaning, the ambiguities of *Lazarillo de Tormes* negate any type of absolute concordance. In both text and metatext, the anonymous author explores partial truths, the nature of language, and the act of literary creation. His codes are, at times, indecipherable, and his spokesman is less than trustworthy. Yet for all this—because of all this—the true beauty of the vision lies in its openness.

Lazarillo de Tormes presents language in flux. Lázaro's discourse breaks a silence but desperately seeks a form of speech (or writing) that would function as silence. The drastic measure is an exaggerated example of the space between signifier and signified, of the search for identity in a system marked by differentiation. If the problematic order of the case suggests a return to chaos (and an implied order in disorder, to complete the paradox), the book-turned-explanation returns as a literary object directed toward a readership charged with identifying misrepresentation and irony. If every reading is a misreading,[18] it is appropriate that every act of writing be miswriting. The concept of mimesis may succeed as an approach, an approximation, but lack of mediation is an illusion. No discourse is pure; the diegetic intrudes on the mimetic to reflect design, artifice, appropriation. The gaps—logical, semantic, and presuppositional—cement the interdependence of story and discourse. The author of the *Lazarillo* seems to recognize that communication, be it social or literary discourse, calls for the imposition of structure. The narrative shows a text being made and unmade, or remade, by an implied author and an implied reader. The revision of idealistic fiction and spiritual autobiography inverts the high-spiritedness (or sanctity) of the story and the authority of the discourse. The self-conscious parody of earlier forms carries with it the strength and burden of transformation. The question of interpretation inspires and informs *Lazarillo de Tormes*, which speaks for the limits and the limitless potential of words.

Just as *Lazarillo de Tormes* undermines the literary precedents that condition its recourses, Lázaro the narrator shows the consequences of unwarranted faith in the expressive capacity of the verbal sign, whose meanings may be tempered by ironic opposition. The implied author of the *Lazarillo* exposes the strategies of the narrator but manifests his own reliance on rhetoric in the process. Lázaro, as no better or no worse than his neighbors, speaks synecdochically to Vuestra Merced, while the implied author "speaks" ironically to the implied reader, who may cast the discourse in still another mode. The openness of the text depends on the interplay between "facts," logical deduction or presuppositions, and indeterminacies, between those problems that seem to have a solution and those that do not. Because the implied reader receives markers or clues rather than unambiguous signs, no "truth" is indisputable, no statement is fully reliable. The force of irony upon irony determines and deflects meaning. The progression relates, precociously, to current philosophical and linguistic skepticism.

Jonathan Culler classifies Jacques Derrida's work in deconstruction as the attempt to "describe a general process through which texts undo the philosophical system to which they adhere by revealing its rhetorical nature."[19] Derrida refutes logocentrism, the assumption (underlying Western thought) that concept precedes and exists independently of expression, as a naive belief in the accuracy of signification. Meaning is not direct, as this "metaphysics of presence" would imply, but deferred, supplementary, a function of absence.[20] According to Vincent B. Leitch, "deconstruction practices two interpretations of interpretation. It aims to decipher the stable truths of a work, employing conventional 'passive' tactics of reading; and it seeks to question and subvert such truths in an active production of enigmatic undecidables."[21] Culler notes the (ironic) consequences of Derridean deconstruction: "Deconstructive readings identify this paradoxical situation in which, on the one hand, logocentric positions contain their own undoing and, on the other hand, the denial of logocentrism is carried out in logocentric terms."[22] Leitch, relying on a positive focus (that is, strategy) for his metacommentary, argues that the contradiction validates the system: "The production itself of deconstruction is necessarily a text. And each such work of critical writing contains its own blind spot. *Aporia* [impasse] is an accepted aspect of the deconstructive enterprise. Every deconstruction opens itself to further deconstruction."[23] In this sense, *Lazarillo de Tormes* develops as a deconstructive text, geared to subvert the noble elegance and piety of literary models through a mocking imitation of story and discourse. Lázaro, in turn, falls victim to an implied author, who mocks the narrator/protagonist by substituting incriminating speech and transparent (or negatively symbolic) actions for the saving grace of silence and freedom from irony. While uncovering Lázaro's defensive rhetoric, the implied author discloses his own rhetorical scheme, to be deconstructed by readers.

Lazarillo de Tormes is hardly without meaning, but it does not have a concrete meaning. Its signifying systems defer meanings to the rhetorical postures of both narrator and implied author, as analogues of the shortcomings of verbal expression. Lázaro's explanation is incomplete because it would not be to his advantage to tell the whole story. The ironic "text" of the implied author is incomplete because no single informant, for or against the subject, can relay the whole story. Silence and untold facts project significance by way of conspicuous absence. Layered meanings are matched by layers of indeterminacies, as well as by a critical corpus. The relationship between old and new is dialectical, part homage and part burlesque, repetitive and modifiable through context. The transformational power, which deconstruction calls iterability, allows discourse to grow and change. It is not Lázaro's method of presenting his genealogy but the insignificance of his peasant stock (as opposed to the pedigree of the chivalric heroes) that affects message production in the opening of the narrative. The literary norm and the social norm act on Lázaro's final occupation—*pregonero*, town-crier—at the level of discourse. The most resounding narrative misjudgment is the reference to the imposition of silence (chapter 7), which emphatically breaks that silence and puts the reliability of the closing statement in doubt. Since all discourse exists at some remove from absolute truth, calculated discourse intensifies the space between signifier and signified. In *Lazarillo de Tormes*, both voice and voice-over blatantly bespeak ulterior motives, yet the execution of discourse—the narrative performance and its ironic reenactment—only expands, for better or worse, the signifying potential of the text.

Critical controversy stems not so much from Lázaro's status as from his attitude toward his compromised respectability and the events he narrates. If he cares about honor, he is doomed in his own eyes and before society. If he substitutes material comforts for honor, he may reject all external criteria for honorability. In one case, his discourse deconstructs a strategy of indifference; in the other, his indifference would deconstruct a social myth.[24] In either case, the judgment depends on discourse. The authorial figure of the prologue relates writing to honor. In chapter 1, Lázaro presents his father's death as a sacrifice for Spain, a social and spiritual redemption. While he criticizes the squire's obsession with honor in chapter 3, he emulates the dress (and hypocrisy) of the third master. The description of his new wardrobe (chapter 6) denotes an obstacle overcome, a farewell to the threat of starvation, a first step toward integration into society. The purchase of clothes like those of the squire and the listing of the items in the text produce a message that operates on a subconscious level for Lázaro and on an ironic level for the implied author. The seventh chapter, despite its reference to social and domestic well-being, deals almost exclusively with the question of honor. Lázaro seems concerned with society's opinion of him and agrees to "explain himself" to Vuestra Merced. He approaches the addressee obsequiously, asks his friends to maintain silence, and often verges on circumlocution. Neither his stance, his strategies, nor his words create the impression of a defiant disregard for institutionalized behavior. He becomes, rather, an ironically eloquent spokesman for a society obsessed with the apparent. His entry into this society, however marginal, subjects him to its rules. Lázaro's actions and his discourse—especially his attempt to manipulate reality through language—proclaim him a product of his environment. Like his society, his own text forces him into a struggle for control.

Certain types of writing seek clear and straightforward exposition of ideas. Other types make the search for messages a major factor in the reading process, ultimately comprised of acts of decoding. The author of *Lazarillo de Tormes* organizes the text around other texts, placing established conventions in new contexts. The move is a descent from grace and a vulgarization of standards. The parody of spiritual autobiography and idealistic fiction appears within the text but comes from without. That is, there is no reason to believe that Lázaro would make his explanation of the case a literary satire, nor can the reader presuppose that the narrator is a reader of these texts. The explanation has a counterdirection, marked by intertextual signs and by elements that discredit Lázaro rather than strengthen his defense. Finally, there is no explanation of the case. Lázaro's story is a function of his discourse, a discourse that tells several stories. The irony of the text emanates from a narrator unaware of his debasement of literary tradition and equally unaware of his failure to comply with the narrative premise or with his strategy of self-advancement. He loses control of the discourse, which nonetheless produces specific patterns of messages. The author in the prologue and the agent of irony in the text proper guide the reader to the message behind the message, to the undoing of Lázaro's text.

As in the *Libro de Buen Amor* and *El conde Lucanor*, a conceptual structure defines itself in the structure of discourse. Society compels Lázaro to conform while keeping him at a distance. His way of life shows signs of stability from without as it crumbles from within. His text likewise exhibits the outward markings of a success story and the inner turmoil of an alienated soul. The prologue sets a discursive goal yet introduces at the outset a double purpose and a "second voice." An implied author catches Lázaro in rhetorical ploys and transmits an ironic version of the narrative to an implied reader. The "revised" text is no less rhetorical but more conformist, more conscious of its deviance from the norms of society and art, and thus more easily sanctioned by social and artistic conscience. The text achieves a compound meaning, subject to expansion in the reading process. The world and the intertextual base provide constant mediation of the signifying units and clusters. The protagonist must find his way in society and in the text, as both conspire to marginate him. The author of *Lazarillo de Tormes* connects writing with survival and respectability, so that Lázaro is not merely writing his life but writing for his life. The picaresque begins as a series of contests: between old forms and new, society and the individual, the narrator and the implied author, the signifier and resistant meaning. In the picaresque variations and transformations, the presence of an implied author who reacts to the narrator's vision of society and of the text remains a constant. Aware of the act of composition, narrators cannot conceal their rhetorical strategies, exposed by implied authors through strategies of their own. Both groups aim to win over a reader, who arbitrates the discourse.

Lazarillo de Tormes and the works that build on it demonstrate a structure of self-consciousness, an inescapable dependence on context in the widest sense of the term. In his study of deconstruction, Culler observes, "Any given context is open to further description. There is no limit in principle to what might be included in a given context, to what might be shown to be relevant to the performance of a particular speech act. This structural openness of context is essential to all disciplines: the scientist discovers that factors previously disregarded are relevant to the behavior of certain objects; the historian brings new or reinterpreted data to bear on a particular event; the critic relates a passage or a text to a context that makes it appear in a new light."[25] The study of other narratives against the structure of the *Lazarillo* yields a reciprocal sequence of discursive options, which develops as new texts appear to follow and to illuminate the old. The story of the outsider in a struggle against mainstream social ideology engages a double line of discourse to represent each side. In *Lazarillo de Tormes*, the implied author holds the narrator up to ridicule while showing an ironic integration into the hypocrisy of the social order. Succeeding texts offer variations on the theme of the marginated character and of the nuanced voice(s). In Spain, Mateo Alemán and Francisco de Quevedo enter narrative roads mapped but not taken by the author of the *Lazarillo*. The narrator of *Guzmán de Alfarache* divides the discourse into mutually exclusive packages of sin and penitence, which the implied author challenges by highlighting inconsistencies in Guzmán's rhetoric of conversion. *El Buscón* defends society in an uneven battle between the narrator/protagonist and an implied author who surpasses him in discursive intensity and control. In Quevedo's text, the antisocial becomes immoral.

The narrator of *Lazarillo de Tormes*, in face of the discursive trap set for him, manages to separate youthful perspective from commentary in the present. Notably in the first three chapters, he conveys the moment of experience as distinguishable from the detached perspective of the mature Lázaro. While the technique ultimately aids the implied author's strategy of betrayal, it does create the illusion of control, temporal as well as spatial, for the narrator. In *Guzmán de Alfarache*, the description of childhood experiences bears the signs of the present. Guzmán's evocation of the past cannot free itself of attitudes nurtured by an unfavorable destiny in a hostile world. In analyzing the discourse of the *Lazarillo*, one may ask what the case is that the narrator/protagonist is trying to explain and how effectively he explains it. As a corollary, one may attempt to determine whether Lázaro is as content with his current status as his closing statement would suggest. One answer, proposed here, is that through the subversive strategies of an implied author, the text disregards the restrictions of its pretext to accentuate linguistic and situational irony, a questionable union of showing and telling, and a condemnatory "breaking of silence." Lázaro's valiant efforts to shield the truth form the basis of a new text marked by its own rhetorical framework and ironic in its own right. Both the self-consciousness of the narrator and the incompleteness of the "rewritten" text justify a view of the narrative as an investigation into the changing status of the signifier in the text and beyond. In the case of *Guzmán de Alfarache*, the exploration of the signifier poses new questions for discourse analysis.

GUZMÁN DE ALFARACHE

Alemán's novel rests on the premise that the sinner of the past is the convert to righteousness of the present.[26] It is useful, then, to consider how narrative discourse reflects the spiritual conversion and to note signs that would cast doubt on the sincerity of the conversion. Does the narrator express his "true" feelings in the text, or does he assume a sanctimonious posture? Is there a proper balance between episode and digression? Lázaro ends his narrative "at the height of all good fortune," while Guzmán concludes with the commitment to moral conduct. If the good fortune seems to contradict the motive of the explanation in *Lazarillo de Tormes*, the post-conversional discourse seems to contradict the transformation around which *Guzmán de Alfarache* operates. Like Lázaro, Guzmán says more than he should; he reveals an inner being more tormented by the past than comforted in the present. Guzmán recognizes the correct course of action and strays from it. He similarly determines a discursive course and deviates from it, as feeling overcomes reason. Through word and deed, he intimates that it is hard to be good in a world that repeatedly treats him badly. Guzmán's self-image— and the central motif of his narrative—is that of victim. Fortune, circumstance, and grandiose designs subject the protagonist to constant humiliation, punctuated by a series of scatological scenes that recur to remind him of his fate. On a more comprehensive level, the theme of victimization relates to the authorial voice that opens the text and to the treatment of a spurious continuation that dominates the second part of the *Guzmán*. The consequence of suffering is a desire for revenge rather than for contrition. The implied author marks inconsistencies in Guzmán's discourse with regard to penitence but maintains consistency in presenting the *pícaro* and his creator as victims. As in the *Lazarillo*, one explanation supersedes another, to the detriment of the narrative premise.

Alemán dedicates part one of *Guzmán de Alfarache* to his superior in the ministry of finance, Don Francisco de Rojas. The author, in his own name, laces the apologia with abundant gratitude for his protector and unconcealed fear of his detractors. He points out that nothing can inspire greater terror in men than an evil intention, especially when it is deeply rooted in those cursed by tainted blood, humble birth, and base thoughts.[27] The predominant image is the hunt. Enemies lie in ambush, awaiting the occasion to pounce on him. To resist their attack, he has sought the favor of Don Francisco, in whom the three elements of true nobility—virtue, pure blood, and power—are manifest. With his master's support, the lowly tale of a *pícaro* will gain in stature; by dint of association, it will seem a work of grandness and majesty, and its protagonist will seem a courtly gentleman. In the dedication, Alemán demonstrates the hyperbolic force of discourse. The critics are venomous, the patron is princely. They are ignoble, he a model of nobility, capable of converting a minor work of art into an object of value. The author, not unlike his fictional character, is a victim in search of justice in an atmosphere of injustice, an unfavored member of a hierarchical society, a man dependent on the good will of others. Ironically, the blood, birth, and thoughts that characterize Alemán's enemies apply as well to Guzmán, perhaps emphasizing guilt (rather than redemption) through association. The supposition that illustrious patronage will transform the text is a rhetorical flourish devoid of logic. The problematic conversion sets the stage for the crucial conversion of the narrator/protagonist.

The following section, "To the Vulgar Public," features a battalion of rhetorical questions and commentaries to show the author's disdain for the tastes and tactics of the masses. He condemns a public that overlooks the didacticism of a work in order to focus exclusively on its entertainment value, the same public that will then berate the author for the misreadings. Then he addresses the "Discreet Reader," who is wise enough to know that (according to the lesson of Pliny and the author of *Lazarillo de Tormes*) no book is so bad that it does not contain something of value. One who reads discreetly will not forsake lessons for laughter, nor avoid reflection: "En el discurso podrás moralizar según se te ofreciere: larga margen te queda" (p. 94; On the discourse you can moralize as the opportunity presents itself; great leeway is left you). Thus, the perceptive reader will put morality first, while the vulgar reader will give priority to the picaresque adventures. Through the rhetoric of proper reading, the victim takes the defensive. Any parts of the narrative that may not be serious or well constructed owe their flaws to the roguish subject matter, but these are few and far between, according to the author.[28] The "Declaration for the Understanding of this Book" is not a statement on how to read the text but a defense of the narrator's fitness for the role. Guzmán's intellect, aided by study and by the knowledge of experience, turns punishment into a time for contemplation. He is educated and skillful, and he is repentant. He is prepared to include doctrine in the narrative without offending the laws of decorum and verisimilitude, as the discreet reader will concede.

The dedication and the notes to readers place the lofty patron against inimical critics and the vulgar reader against the discreet. Calumny is to misreading what nobility is to inspired reading. The underdog finds a power base in laudatory prose (a verbal connection with the nobleman) and in the oppositions of the reading process (in which goodness and badness have moral overtones). The enemies are not after his book but after him; nonetheless, the picaresque topic leaves him open to attack. To guard himself, the author relies on the acceptance of his work by Don Francisco de Rojas and by those readers inclined to follow a moral direction. He advises the discreet reader to savor the amusing episodes, but not at the expense of instruction. The "declaration," in turn, justifies Guzmán de Alfarache's suitability as the agent of morality. The introductory materials put forth a method of interpretation and the seeds of deconstruction. A rhetoric of irony may offer the final word.

In the opening chapter of *Guzmán de Alfarache*, the narrator speaks to the "curious" reader of his desire to recount his life. The carefully contrived narrative pretext of *Lazarillo de Tormes* is missing, and the narratee is a reader often addressed in the familiar singular *tú*. The autobiographical urge replaces the demand for an explanation, yet the implied case here is Guzmán's expression of remorse and subsequent conversion. The description of his less-than-exemplary parents puts into play a tension between the agony of his birthright and the humor of ostracism. Guzmán remarks, "Por no ser contra mi padre, quisiera callar lo que siento; aunque si he de seguir al Filósofo, mi amigo es Platón y mucho más la verdad, conformándome con ella" (p. 115; So as not to speak out against my father, I would like to keep my feelings to myself, but if I must follow the teachings of the philosopher, my friend is Plato and above all the truth, which I must preserve above all things). The father is a Genoese moneylender of Jewish origin (an unfavorable link to those who control Spain's economy), weak-willed and unmanly, who wears false curls and makeup. The narrator marginates himself from the (burlesque) discourse by pretending to answer the accusations of the narratee: "Si es verdad, como dices, que se valía de untos y artificios de sebillos, que los dientes y manos, que tanto le loaban, era a poder de polvillos . . . y otras porquerías, confesaréte cuanto dél dijeres y seré su capital enemigo y de todos los que de cosa semejante tratan; pues demás que son actos de afeminados maricas, dan ocasión para que dellos murmuren y se sospeche toda vileza" (p. 122; If it's true, as you say, that he used greases and creams, that his teeth and hands—which won him so much praise—were at the mercy of powders and other such rubbish, I must own up to everything and become the greatest enemy of him and of those who do the same thing; for in addition to being the acts of effeminate sissies, they give people the opportunity to gossip about them and to suspect them of every kind of depravity).

By "repeating" the words of another, Guzmán bows to truth without compromising himself, or so he may think, but he is dealing with a society obsessed with heredity. The negative judgment of his father fails as an attempt at self-elevation, despite the moral fervor and overdetermination ("afeminados maricas") of the passage. Disassociation has ironic consequences. Even Guzmán seems unconvinced by his discourse, as borne out by his decision to travel to Italy to make the acquaintance of his "noble relatives" following the death of his father. Point of view becomes confusing, at best. Can even the twelve-year-old Guzmán have believed that his lineage was illustrious? Can the reader, aware of the father's history and character, help but notice the absurdity of Guzmán's plan and the narrator's disregard for his previous commentary? The detachment, which earlier seemed forced, is now broken, as Guzmán sets out to reap the rewards of his lineage. It is as if the narrator/protagonist were conspiring his own doom.

Guzmán describes his mother at the time she met his father as, among other things, serious, discreet, and quite circumspect. She is, in fact, a prostitute, the mistress of an elderly gentleman whom she deceives with her husband-to-be, and a woman "criada en buena escuela, cursada entre los dos coros y naves de la Antigua" (p. 136; educated in a good school, enrolled with male classmates between the two choirs and naves of the Antigua chapel in Sevilla). She divides her time between the two men until the old gallant dies, and she informs her son that he has two fathers (since she has sued each for paternity). The ironic humor is again counterproductive. By making his mother ludicrously undesirable, or overly desirable, Guzmán establishes a difficult point of mediation between his aspirations and social reality. He chooses ridicule, ultimately self-ridicule, over silence. Guzmán disappoints his mother because he cannot ply her trade, as she has her mother's. Left to his own resources, he departs from home: "Salí a ver mundo, peregrinando por él, encomendándome a Dios y buenas gentes, en quien hice confianza" (p. 145; I set out to see the world, traveling through it and entrusting myself to God and good people, in whom I placed my faith). The road is long and hard, and the faith is misplaced.

Young Guzmán must fight for survival. Fatigued and hungry from his travels, he is served eggs about to hatch and mule meat when he orders veal. He is mistreated, robbed, duped by a muleteer, apprehended as a thief and beaten by officers of the law. New acquaintances lie to him, hold him up to ridicule, tell him stories, preach to him. The world he sees is one of deception, wickedness, and perversity, a world over which he has no control. He laments his fate, and no holy exemplum can keep him from wishing for revenge. Persecution and determinism mark his path: "¿Qué conjuración se hizo contra mí? ¿Cuál estrella infelice me sacó de mi casa?" (p. 184; What conspiracy has been planned against me? What unfortunate star dragged me from home?). The case of mistaken identity illustrates that justice and its agents are blind, that the trusting youth is an innocent victim, punished as a criminal though he has committed no crime. Guzmán's narrative strategy presents him as on a journey into solitude and despair, as one defenseless before the world at large. The implied author, in ironic compliance, makes him a victim of his discourse as well.

In the first book of part 1, Guzmán expresses mixed emotions through mixed messages. On the matter of his progenitors, he blends parody with unfounded pride. The father is by birth, religion, nationality, profession, and character a pariah. The mother is loose, unscrupulous, and unloving.

Guzmán barely laments his father's death, and he considers himself a burden to his widowed mother, who views her son in terms of opportunity cost. There is no anguished scene of separation reminiscent of Lázaro's farewell to his mother in Salamanca. Guzmán feels alone and neglected before his departure from Sevilla, yet he foresees a future worthy of his rank: "Yo fui desgraciado, como habéis oído: quedé solo, sin árbol que me hiciese sombra, los trabajos a cuestas, la carga pesada, las fuerzas flacas, la obligación mucha, la facultad poca. Ved si un mozo como yo, que ya galleaba, fuera justo con tan honradas partes estimarse en algo" (p. 145; I was in a wretched state, as you have heard: I stood alone, with no tree to offer me shade, troubles mounted on me and bearing a heavy load, my strength depleted, my responsibility great, and my possibilities meager. Consider whether a boy such as I, who had already begun to show what he was made of, should, with such honorable qualities as I possessed, rightly expect to amount to something). As he goes in search of a noble ideal that he expects to reach fruition in Genoa, he drops his father's last name to avoid recognition on the road, this despite the fact that "on my father's side, not even El Cid had an advantage over me." Illusions of grandeur vie with a sense of abandonment and shame, overconfidence with ingenuousness, and an illustrious journey with escape.

Guzmán is a humble boy posing as a nobleman, a comic player with tragic pretensions. His age and appearance betray inexperience and allow others to abuse him. He is at this point more sinned against than sinning, but each attack addresses his presumption; they are crimes against the stomach, against modest bearing and guilty mien. One cannot be taken for a thief unless one looks like a thief, and aristocrats do not look like thieves (or so a class-conscious subtext and the implied author would suggest). As narrator, Guzmán adds the bitterness and resentment of maturity to the youthful perspective without including signs of the conversion. Others speak of forgiveness, Guzmán speaks of revenge. He misses the doctrinaire value of the tales, digressions, and sermons of his own text. His trials are not exempla that lead to and then instruct the benefits of conversion, but rather they are stages in a process of disillusionment. By shifting positions on familial status, by structuring his dreams of social acceptability into patterns of irony, and by failing to incorporate his conversion into the commentary, Guzmán the victim loses reader sympathy. Guzmán the narrator does not practice what he preaches.

A similar strategy guides the discourse of book 2. Guzmán speaks of abject poverty and need and of the impact of recent reversals on his life and on his thought. He notes, in the past, "Vi claramente cómo la contraria fortuna hace a los hombres prudentes. En aquel punto me pareció haber sentido una nueva luz, que como en claro espejo me representó lo pasado, presente y venidero" (p. 248; I saw clearly how adverse fortune makes men wise. At that moment I seem to have felt a new light, which like a clear mirror held up past, present, and future to me). The statement suggests a turning point, a heightened realization of life's struggles, a coming to terms with earthly obstacles. Guzmán observes examples of selflessness in a world of avarice and interest, notably in the case of a humble friar who feeds him when those he has served abandon him without payment. The response indicates an awareness of God's benevolence and of an innate goodness in man: "¡Bondad inmensa de Dios, eterna sabiduría, Providencia divina, misericordia infinita, que en las entrañas de la dura piedra sustentas un gusano, y cómo con tu largueza celestial todo lo socorres! Los que podían y tenían, con su avaricia no me lo dieron; y hallélo en un mendigo y pobre frailecito" (p. 253; Immense goodness of God, eternal wisdom, divine Providence, infinite mercy, for deep within the hard stone You sustain the lowly worm and willingly come to the aid of all mankind with celestial munificence! Those that had and could have given refused me out of greed, while a poor and indigent little friar provided me). The statement, rhetorically an overstatement, promises a correlation of thought and action that Guzmán and his narrative do not deliver.

In the adventures that follow, Guzmán aids an innkeeper ("a worse master than a blind man") at deceiving guests, begs for alms in God's name, then makes his way to Madrid, where he takes up the profession of rogue. The fraternity of thieves teaches him its business, at which he is impressively adept. He is equally quick to surrender his scruples: "Te confieso que a los principios anduve algo tibio, de mala gana y sobre todo temeroso; que, como cosa nunca usada de mí, se me asentaba mal y le entraba peor, porque son dificultosos todos los principios. Mas después que me fui saboreando con el almíbar picaresco, de hilo me iba por ello a cierraojos" (pp. 260–61; I confess to you that at first my attitude was lukewarm, reluctant, and above all fearful, for, it being something I had never tried before, I was uneasy about the whole thing and got off to a bad start, since all beginnings are difficult. But as soon as I got a taste of picaresque delights, I got so good that I could have done the job blindfolded). The discourse moves from man's innate goodness to his propensity toward evil. Put to the test, Guzmán opts for hypocrisy and sin. He lectures on the vanities of honor while he steals from the public and from the employer of his new master, a cook, as he blames the kitchen staff for setting a bad example. The cook involves Guzmán in a theft that leads to dismissal. Here, as in succeeding episodes, Guzmán's humiliation finds an objective correlative in excrement. A move to Toledo, the purchase of a new wardrobe, and an active pursuit of women do little to alter his conduct or his fortune. In the town of Almagro, Guzmán passes himself off as a nobleman to join a company of soldiers bound for Italy. Before the departure, his money runs out and his companions desert him. He begins to serve the impoverished captain, whom he supports by stealing. Although he condones and profits from Guzmán's crimes, the captain fears that he may suffer from future villainies. When they arrive in Genoa, he informs Guzmán that he will no longer require his services, and the young rogue takes his leave to seek his noble kinsmen.

In the second book, Guzmán remains a victim of fate and of his fellow man (and woman). He changes his locale, clothes, master, name, strategy, everything but custom. He sermonizes, curses his behavior, cites the appropriate proverb, contemplates, demonstrates, remonstrates; he does everything but reform. The captain judges him a hardened criminal, unlikely to alter his course; once a delinquent, always a delinquent. The judgment calls to mind Prince Segismundo's decision to imprison the rebel soldier responsible for his escape from prison in Calderón's *La vida es sueño* (*Life Is a Dream*, 1635). After proving untrustworthy, the soldier becomes an outcast in the new society he has helped to create. Analogously, Guzmán the narrator stands before the reader as arbiter, showing a lack of agreement between discourse that represents past and present and conduct that offers a negative consistency. At the opening of book 3, he bemoans his poverty and his destiny as if free will were nonexistent. Perhaps more strikingly, he projects the same faith in his paternal legacy as when he set out from home: "Quise hacerme de los godos, emparentando con la nobleza de aquella ciudad, publicándome por quien era" (p. 356; I wanted to show off my Gothic blood, marrying into the aristocracy of that city, making it known who I was). Not only does the narrative present disregard the experience on the road, but the narrator disregards his knowledge of the outcome by imagining victory, thereby damaging his precarious credibility and accentuating— to his detriment—the ironic confrontation with his family.

The Genoese treat Guzmán badly and receive a verbal lashing from him. He discovers an uncle, who subjects him to a pre-dawn toss in a blanket, leaving him wallowing in the by-products of fear. He flees in such haste that "if Lot's wife had done what I did, she wouldn't have turned to stone, for I never looked back." Settling in Rome, Guzmán joins an order of false mendicants. His commentaries on poverty and charity seem to miss the point that his service to the "order" is hypocritical, even sacrilegious. His powers of observation span a broad spectrum, namely, the strengths and shortcomings of his neighbors, yet overlook his own role in the scheme of things. Moralizing and anecdotal, his discourse is conspicuously unself-reflective, which works to further emphasize the hypocrisy of his stance. Taken in by a cardinal and treated by two doctors who will not sacrifice their payment to expose the pretended beggar's imaginary illness, Guzmán begins a new career as a page. The kindly churchman has a trunk full of delicacies that Guzmán cannot resist. Caught *in delicto*, he must endure a dozen lashes as punishment. The episode is an ironic re-creation of Lazarillo de Tormes's misadventure with the cleric's trunk in chapter 2, ironic in the sense that while Lázaro steals from an avaricious master to stay alive, Guzmán robs a generous master to gorge himself on sweets. If Guzmán's cleric outshines Lázaro's, Guzmán himself fares poorly in the intertextual contest. His misbehavior has no reasonable explanation, no contextual qualification. The self-professed plaything of fortune acts up when fortune is on his side. When he turns to gambling, the cardinal discharges him and he becomes a buffoon (*gracioso*) in the home of the French ambassador.

Part 2 of *Guzmán de Alfarache*, anticipating part 2 of *Don Quijote*, finds itself inextricably bound to the earlier text and to a spurious sequel published in 1602. The title page bears a subtitle, "Atalaya de la vida humana" ("Watchtower of Human Life"), and the author's name is followed by "su verdadero autor," "the real author." In his dedication to Don Juan de Mendoza, Alemán refers to the challenge issued by the author of the false continuation, but—like Cervantes—he will take up arms in the text proper. In a note to the reader, he presents himself as an Esau who let the birthright slip away. He (over)praises the erudition and style of his opponent, only to turn the admiration into a critique of the second author's comprehension of part 1: "No escriban sin que lean, si quieren ir llegados a el asumpto, sin desencuadernar el propósito" (p. 466; Such people should not write until they learn how to read properly, if they want to get to the heart of the matter, without undoing the intention). By making Guzmán a poor student when he was actually very bright, this author ignores the goal of presenting, "as a watchtower," a flawless man overcome by vice and misery who reaches his lowest point in the galleys. Alemán berates his competitor for turning Guzmán into a master thief when his crimes were petty, for incorporating real people into the narrative, and for failing to carry through the revenge motif. Alemán, for his part, does not neglect revenge for a moment.

The sequel greatly affects the composition and content of part 2. Alemán sees as his task the removal of his rival's specter, as well as the continuation of Guzmán's autobiography. His strategy involves exposing the pseudonymous author of the sequel, pointing to the superiority of the authentic version, and bringing a false Guzmán into the text to kill him off. In terms of discourse, this strategy makes the authorial presence even more prominent in the text, for the battle for supremacy between Mateo Alemán and Juan Martí intrudes on the contest between narrator and implied author. The superstructure of vengeance becomes inseparable from the narrative progression, to the extent of echoing its indeterminacies. Alemán criticizes Martí's "reading" of part 1, but how accurate is his own reading? The narrator stands at a far remove from the perfect ("perfeto") man envisioned by the author; neither discourse nor story shows the effects of the conversion. Guzmán polarizes himself from the morality of the digressions, which seem more like appendages than tales from the heart. Guzmán up to now is neither so good a student nor so petty a thief as to warrant the invective. The author's design suffices as intention, according to Alemán, while Martí tacitly defends his own artistic freedom and, more importantly, his right to place the novel's discourse above its author's purpose. Whatever the reading, self-consciousness now operates on two levels.

In the oration that opens book 1 of the second part, Guzmán addresses the question of intention, examining his role as moralizer and the aims of his text. The perspective again recalls the middle ground between the youthful sins and the conversion: "A mí me parece que son todos los hombres como yo, flacos, fáciles, con pasiones naturales y aun estrañas. Que con mal sería, si todos los costales fuesen tales. Mas como soy malo, nada juzgo por bueno: tal es mi desventura y de semejantes" (p. 481; I imagine that all men are like me, weak, of loose virtue, with natural and even strange passions. It would be bad if all of us were alike, but since I'm bad, I judge nothing as good. Such is my misfortune and the misfortune of those of the same mind). Guzmán's suitability stems precisely from his errant life—who better to preach against sinners than the sinner?—and from his suffering. His purpose is to guide the reader through a system of negative exemplarity, but the reader has the obligation to follow the lead. No writer can please all the public, but Guzmán vows to seek the truth, no small undertaking given that his enemies are out to do him ill: "Seráme necesario, demás de hacer para cada uno su diferente libro, haber vivido tantas vidas y cuantos hay diferentes pareceres. Una sola he vivido y la que me achacan es testimonio que me levantan" (p. 488; It would be necessary for me to write a different book for each person, to have lived as many lives as there are different opinions. I've only lived one life, and the other one they're attributing to me is a testimony to the false witness they bear against me). The statement inscribes Alemán's complaint into his narrator's discourse and gives Guzmán a narrative pretext to encode into his own.

Guzmán's duties as go-between for the ambassador bring him into contact with illustrious citizens of Rome, where he gains notoriety for himself despite his alleged distaste for the office. When he "graduates" from this service, he discovers that the public is little disposed to pardon his folly. Guzmán, who leaves the sanctity of the cardinal's house to serve as go-between for the Frenchman, wants the reader to see him as a perpetual victim, acted on by a cruel fate and by an unforgiving humanity. He offers the wages of sin tempered with self-pity. The motif of deception continues, taking the form of a sermon with exempla and action featuring Guzmán as the instigator of tricks and later as the butt of a series of plots. Renewed solitude and public humiliation push Guzmán into the path of a young man calling himself Sayavedra and claiming to be a nobleman from Sevilla. If not heaven-sent, Sayavedra is nonetheless the answer to Alemán's prayers for revenge.

Juan Martí, author of the sequel, uses the pseudonym Mateo Luján de Sayavedra and changes his birthplace from Valencia to Sevilla. With the appearance of the character Sayavedra, Alemán initiates within the fiction an exposure and exorcism, which by its very success immortalizes the impostor in a classic text. Sayavedra saves Guzmán from a gang of ruffians as a means of endearing himself to the protagonist. Dismayed by his persecution in Rome, Guzmán plans a tour of Italy accompanied by Sayavedra. With the aid of his accomplice Alejandro Bentivoglio, Sayavedra robs Guzmán of his luggage, an obvious allusion to the "theft" of the literary usurper.[29] The narrator ends book 1 with a noble, paradoxically self-righteous peroration, which builds on experience, anecdote, and classical letters to condemn larceny in all its forms. The tone is bitter, personal, and vengeful, hinting that more than a rogue's possessions is at stake. In book 2, Guzmán meets up with Sayavedra, who prostrates himself before the wronged Guzmán, begs forgiveness, and swears to be his slave for life. Guzmán at this moment is a man torn by conflicting emotions, conscious of good and inclined toward evil. He remembers his determination on leaving Rome to strive for perfection, whether life may treat him favorably or unfavorably, and understands that to be honorable he must unite resolution with action ("Y no se sabe de alguno que con intención sin obra se haya salvado; ambas cosas han de concurrir, intención y obra," p. 600). His next action is a suit against Alejandro Bentivoglio for his role in the deception. Through his influence, Bentivoglio's father secures not only an innocent verdict for his son but also a prison term for Guzmán on charges of slander. The protagonist's only consolation lies in the certainty of divine judgment for those who have tampered with justice in this life. For his part, the case is another example of victimization, of the force that can turn a judicial process into a triumph for injustice.

Recognizing how earthly justice operates, Guzmán reaps the rewards of deception through gambling and acts of fraud, abetted by Sayavedra. On the road to Milan following one of their conquests, Guzmán asks Sayavedra to explain the motives of the robbery of the luggage, and Sayavedra responds with an account of his life. He claims a wealthy Valencian background and speaks of the hardships that have befallen him and his elder brother (Juan Martí, who changes his name to Mateo Luján). Alemán thus gives himself as well as his creation a double. Within the text of the "real" second part, both Sayavedra and Martí have biographical validity which, brilliantly, does not correspond to the apocryphal Guzmán or to the historical Martí. Sayavedra's discourse deviates from the spurious continuation to lessen the impact of his accomplishments and to complement the equally false biography of Martí.[30] Guzmán himself notes flaws in Sayavedra's exposition. If the effect is a revelation of the identity of Mateo Luján de Sayavedra and an unflattering comparison of the character Sayavedra to Guzmán, the narrative strategy evokes new forms of irony, as well. As Alemán intervenes to regain his literary honor, he removes Guzmán from his privileged discursive position to concentrate on Martí and Sayavedra. The "lowering" of Sayavedra as a delinquent raises him in moral terms, just as the "raising" of Guzmán contradicts the evolutionary spirit that the text pretends to portray. When Guzmán concludes that "Sayavedra era desventurada sardina y yo en su respeto ballena" (p. 646; Sayavedra was a miserable sardine and I a mighty whale by comparison), he takes a step backward on the road to perfection. The master thefts that follow grant him a dubious superiority, and his contention that the true science is robbery that allows one to prosper without risk ("Amigo Sayavedra, ésta es la verdadera ciencia, hurtar sin peligrar y bien medrar," p. 667) may make the reader lose faith in the powers of redemption. Amid the combined revenge motives of Alemán and Guzmán, the moral digressions have the narrative force of cries in the wilderness.

Alemán's direction of Guzmán's discourse is nowhere more evident than in the call to arms for revenge: "Si tú, Sayavedra, como te precias fueras, ya hubieras antes llegado a Génova y vengado mi agravio; mas forzoso me será hacerlo yo, supliendo tu descuido y faltas" (p. 669; If you were the man you say you are, Sayavedra, you would already have gone to Genoa and avenged the offense committed against me, but I'll have to take care of it myself to make up for your oversight and faults). Guzmán proposes that they change clothes and names "as you and your brother did." Sayavedra becomes Guzmán de Alfarache and Guzmán the Sevillian aristocrat Juan de Guzmán as they make their way to Genoa. After a lengthy harangue against stealing, Guzmán prepares for revenge on his uncle and others who mistreated him seven years earlier. His clothes, carriage, and noble pretensions make him a new man in their eyes. The uncle disassociates him from the youth who visited before, "a roguish kid who seemed like a thief or his assistant." Guzmán can hardly enjoy the festivities in his honor, so strong is his urge for vengeance. He invents an ingeniously elaborate plan to rob his relatives, which he carries out without the aid of Sayavedra and which follows a lengthy sermon on the evils of revenge. Morality notwithstanding, the text rushes headlong to complete the (extra)textual vendetta. Guzmán and Sayavedra set sail for Spain, and the rough sea and fever cause Sayavedra to hallucinate and speak nonsense. He calls himself the spirit of Guzmán de Alfarache and jumps overboard to his death. Guzmán's reaction is revealing: "Otro día, cuando amaneció, levantéme luego por la mañana, y todo él casi se me pasó recibiendo pésames, cual si fuera mi hermano, pariente o deudo que me hiciera mucha falta, o como si, cuando a la mar se arrojó, se hubiera llevado consigo los baúles. 'Aquesos guarde Dios,' decía yo entre mí, 'que los más trabajos fáciles me serán de llevar'" (p. 711; When the new day dawned, I got up bright and early and spent just about the whole day receiving condolences as if he were my brother, a close relative, or some kinsman dear to me, or as if when he threw himself to the sea he had taken along our trunks with him. "Let God watch over them," I said to myself, "and I'll handle the rest").

The ship lands in Barcelona, and from there Guzmán journeys to Zaragoza. Enjoying the fruits of deception, he remarks that if poverty made him overly bold, prosperity makes him over-confident. He falls in love with a beautiful widow who cannot remarry without forfeiting her wealth. Lowering his ambitions, he pursues ladies of the evening but remains unfulfilled and (again) befouled. Much of the first section of book 3 centers on the "Arancel de necedades," or tariff of follies, a list of faux pas under which offenders—such as Guzmán, who looks into his handkerchief after blowing his nose—must suffer the gibes of an innkeeper and his cohorts. Repeated humiliation puts him on the road to Madrid, where he becomes involved with a young woman who subsequently sues him for robbing her of her innocence. Discovering that this is the third suit for the same offense, Guzmán declaims on the abuse of men by women and their co-conspirators, the judicial system. In spite of the setback, Guzmán's fortune grows from his career as a "supremely elegant swindler." He marries the daughter of a colleague, and the honeymoon is quickly over. The bride is a spendthrift who eventually leads Guzmán to debtors' prison, and her death six years later leaves him penniless. He comments, "En sólo hacer mal y hurtar fui dichoso" (p. 796; I was only lucky in doing bad and stealing), but he vows to turn over a new leaf, to be good. The choice is extreme, the result less so.

The delinquent takes the path of greatest resistance. Holding in high regard his knowledge of the humanities, he hopes to parlay his gifts in the study of theology at the University of Alcalá de Henares: "No hallé otro mejor que acogerme a sagrado y . . . con esto me graduaré. Que podría ser tener talento para un púlpito, y, siendo de misa y buen predicador, tendré cierta la comida y, a todo faltar, meteréme fraile, donde la hallaré cierta" (p. 798; I couldn't think of a better option than to take shelter in holiness and so take a degree in theology. I might even find that I have talent for the pulpit, and, saying mass and being a good preacher, I can be sure to have food on the table, and should all else fail, I'll become a friar, where I'll have it for certain). The reader must take Guzmán's word for his early success in Alcalá. Since his decision to undertake religious studies is, by his own admission, humanly inspired, the validity of the discourse is in question. Guzmán praises his scholarly progress, but his description of activities in Alcalá focuses on the lighter side of education, on extracurricular rather than exalted matters. He goes so far as to call student life a "sister in arms" to the life he has always lead. In keeping with the motif of victimization, he says that he was first in his class but demoted in favor of an illustrious gentleman. In his last year of studies, he falls in love with an innkeeper's daughter named Gracia and marries her. A sermon on the harmful effects of love ("a prison of madness, . . . an excess of bestial lust") leads to the story of the ill-fated second marriage. Matrimony begins well, yet happiness does not last. Guzmán is waited on hand and foot, but "it was a dance of blind men, and I who was leading them was the blindest of all." When Gracia's father dies and the family must endure hard times, Guzmán returns to the university to study medicine and pretends to ignore—to be blind to—his wife's means of subsistence.

Guzmán's discourse reflects a lingering persecution complex, self-pity, and a groping for honorability, without regard for Gracia's position: "Mi reputación se anegaba, nuestra honra se abrasaba, la casa se ardía y todo por el comer se sufría. Callaba mi suegra, solicitaba mi cuñada, y, tres al mohíno, jugaban al más certero. Yo no podía hablar, porque di puerta y fui ocasión y sin esto pereciéramos de hambre. Corrí con ello, dándome siempre por desentendido, hasta que más no pude" (p. 831; My reputation was shot, our honor in flames, the house in burning ruins, and all this suffered for want of food. My mother-in-law kept her mouth shut, my sister-in-law solicited business, and, three against one, their game was more certain. I had no room to talk, because I had opened up the door and provided the opportunity, and without this we would have died of hunger. I accepted things as they were, playing dumb, until I could pretend no longer). Guzmán serves as his wife's procurer and moves her to Madrid, where the prospects are greater. Honor ceases to be an issue, as the two collaborate to fleece their customers. They ultimately fall into the hands of justice and leave Madrid for Sevilla. The judge, who knows Guzmán's family, informs him that his mother is still living, and Guzmán tracks her down. He, Gracia, and the mother (who has changed little) live in disharmony despite their common interest in the art of solicitation. Gracia steals their accumulated wealth and runs away with a captain. The broken ("roto") Guzmán embarks on a new series of swindles, which bring him a sentence of six years on the galleys. The similarity between the wife and the mother expands, as Guzmán's mother robs him of the money earned in thefts. Victimization comes full circle.

When Guzmán tries to escape from prison in women's dress, he is apprehended and condemned to the galleys for life. From despair he moves to contemplation: "Y por la mayor parte los que vienen a semejante miseria son rufianes y salteadores, gente bruta, y por maravilla cae o por desdicha grande un hombre como yo. Y cuando sucede acaso es que le ciega Dios el entendimiento, para por aquel camino traerlo en conocimiento de su pecado y a tiempo que con clara vista lo conozca, le sirva y se salve" (p. 874; For the most part, those who come to similar ends are ruffians and highwaymen, brutish types, and seldom or by great misfortune does a man such as I fall. And when that happens perchance it is because God blinds his understanding, so that through that road he may be brought to have full knowledge of his sin and time enough to examine it clearly, so that it may serve him and he may be saved). Guzmán accepts his earthly punishment as a sign from above. He bears mistreatment with thoughts of Christ's suffering. He prays to God and asks for guidance, "confessing often, reforming my life, cleansing my conscience, which took a number of days." Being of flesh and blood, he stumbles and sometimes falls, but he sees himself as a better man. Others have their doubts, interpreting his good deeds as hypocrisy. As Guzmán grows spiritually, his persecution by fellow prisoners increases, and his mortal enemy plots to incriminate him for a robbery he did not commit. His response is stoic: "No sé qué decirte o cómo encarecerte lo que con aquello sentí, hallándome inocente y con carga legítima cargado. Palabra no repliqué ni la tuve, porque, aunque la dijera del Evangelio, pronunciada por mi boca no le habían de dar más crédito que a Mahoma. Callé, que palabras, que no han de ser de provecho a los hombres, mejor es enmudecer la lengua y que se las diga el corazón a Dios" (pp. 899–900; I don't know how to tell you or express strongly enough how I felt at that moment, finding myself innocent yet with a legitimate charge placed against me. I didn't say a word nor did any occur to me, for even if I had spoken the Gospel, coming from my mouth, they would have given it no more credence than to Mohammed. So I remained silent, for if words are not to be of profit to me, it is better to make the tongue mute and let the heart speak the words to God).

Guzmán's silence is short-lived. His enemies plan a mutiny, and he betrays them to the captain. The rebels are cruelly punished, while Guzmán is free to roam the galley as the captain petitions a pardon from the king. Justice is done, virtue rewarded, the account of his evil days completed. Book 3, chapter 7, the final chapter, presents Guzmán at his lowest point to foreground his rise; the rich and contented fear falling from grace, the narrator remarks, while he himself has faith in rising, since he can fall no lower. His Christ-like suffering, in silence and when innocent, makes his freedom from bondage seem an act of God. The conversion on which his narrative rests demands credibility, and the closing episode stands as "proof" of Guzmán's truthfulness. If Guzmán has reformed, the ending is not only a case of poetic justice but also a moral base for all the textual discourse. After his conviction, Guzmán determines—as he has determined before, unsuccessfully—to be good. He bears the burden of a crime plotted against him, in part because he has no viable defense. Self-interest and vengeance may motivate his allegiance to the captain. The third part of the story announced in the last sentence, a work one could imagine to include the deeds of the converted Guzmán, never materializes. Without that story, the story of the conversion lies in the discourse of parts 1 and 2.

The negative exemplarity of *Guzmán de Alfarache* depends on the relation between a tainted past and a repentant present, between picaresque events and predicatory digressions. The promise of a sequel may be a common literary convention, and whether or not there is another story to tell, Guzmán's narrative "life" ends not at the moment of conversion but at the end of the composition of the text. The "new" Guzmán writes his autobiography following his transformation, in a "future" that does not make its way into the action of the work. The reader stands in judgment of the sincerity and the persuasive—that is, rhetorical—powers of Guzmán's discourse. The incidents themselves illustrate the progression toward criminality, while the interpolations are designed to instruct and to promote the image of the convert. Discounting the novelistic and anecdotal insertions, there is a varied pattern to Guzmán's moralizing. The digressions do not always pertain to the topic of the episodes. In the last chapter, for example, the narrator expounds on marital problems. In other cases, the teaching comes before the exemplum and thus loses some of its force. Certain speeches, notably Guzmán's lectures to Sayavedra, confuse the temporal scheme by placing morality in the delinquent past. Conversely, a vengeful, pessimistic tone invades the penitential discourse.

And there is the question of the narrator's self-acknowledged expertise at lying. The juxtapositions are often striking. In part 2, book 1, chapter 7, for example, Guzmán contemplates the amorous passion of his master, the French ambassador. It surprises him that the nobleman endangers his honor at the hands of a servant and that he should value the opinion of one "from whose mouth never came a truthful word." Guzmán analyzes the consequences of fabrication in general and in his current employment. He observes, in passing, that one must make amends for indiscretions gradually and in good faith: "Yo también he ido tras de mi pensamiento, sin pensar parar en el mundo. Mas, como el fin que llevo es fabricar un hombre perfeto, siempre que hallo piedras para el edificio, las voy amontonando" (p. 557; I have also acted on whim, without guiding my actions in a positive direction. But since I'm trying to build myself into the perfect man, wherever I find stones for this edifice, I rush to gather them up). The passage puts into Guzmán's discourse the "intention" of the narrative that Alemán accuses the author of the spurious sequel of having missed. It serves as an ironic interlude in the discussion, which resumes: "Vuelvo, pues, y digo que todo yo era mentira, como siempre" (Getting back to the subject at hand, then, I must point out that everything I said was a lie, as always). Since there are no narrative events beyond the conversion, with the exception of the secret message to the captain, the reader must rely on the honesty of the transformed Guzmán, who constantly reiterates his propensity for lying. As in *Lazarillo de Tormes*, message in *Guzmán de Alfarache* becomes a

question of credibility, but in Guzmán's narrative the implied author is at
the same time more evident and less predictable.

Part 1 of *Guzmán de Alfarache* conveys a sense of calculation through
adornment; the narrative strategies begin with the creation of an authorial
persona and voice. The dedication aspires to respectability through association with a high-ranking nobleman, while the text proper unfolds the picaresque autobiography in a setting of repentance and moral instruction. Guzmán's narrative expands the literary parody of *Lazarillo de Tormes* (in the
detailed sections on the parents' backgrounds, for example) and gives more
space to incidents and to expressions of thought. Ironic discourse affects the
production of meaning, a fact Alemán seems to anticipate, and perhaps
relish, in introductory commentary to two types of readers. Guzmán's low
social standing and Jewish blood deny him status, and his penitential stance
is somewhat diminished by undisguised resentment of his circumstances.
Good spirit is missing from the product of a so-called spiritual evolution.
Part 2, in response to the false continuation, modifies the "intention" to include a more self-righteous attitude toward the morality of part 1 (the process of becoming a "perfect man") and an attack on the sequel and its author
(a reorientation of story and a more bitter discourse). The successful exorcism of Martí's book and protagonist, as well as an exposure in print of the
pseudonymous author, ironically redirects the progression of the narrative.
Guzmán's "superiority" over Sayavedra lies in roguery and possibly in
intellect, but not in morality. In avenging Sayavedra and Martí, Guzmán
and Alemán ignore the effects of the conversion on the wayward protagonist; they forget that the narrating voice needs to speak for comprehension
and forgiveness. If revenge is an explicit theme in part 1, it is the controlling
theme in part 2. As a result, Martí lives in the pages of his enemy, and
Guzmán's conversion seems more doubtful. Throughout the narrative,
Alemán exerts more effort to defend the narrator/protagonist's erudition
and to relay his escapades than to convince the reader of his transformation.

The text portrays Guzmán as a helpless innocent and as a presumptuous social climber. The abuse he suffers may be a curse of destiny or of his
marginated status or a punishment for his presumption. After the ago-
nizingly descriptive presentation of the parents, the reader will probably
note the irony of Guzmán's decision to seek out his "noble relatives" in
Italy. The frustrations on the road, despite their consistency and their social
implications, fail to deter the noble quest. As in the rendering of the family
background, the mature narrator seems to insist, at his own expense, on an
ironic reading. Guzmán the moralizer could exploit the case of foolhardy
pride but chooses not to do so. He challenges the lineage of Sayavedra in
terms that the reader may apply to his glorified vision. The obsession with
rank joins with the parade of humiliations to suggest that Guzmán does not
learn from experience, that his goals are unrealistic, and that he has as little
control over words as over fate. His actions exhibit negligible movement
toward the ideal of perfection that he claims must be achieved little by little,
and his moral digressions resist logical connections and proof of the change

from evil to good. The problem relates not so much to form as to substance, to the specific nature of authorial intrusion.

In *Lazarillo de Tormes*, the implied author stands between the narrator
and an unknowable "truth" mediated by the space of fiction and by the
irony and duplicity of discourse. He uncovers Lázaro's rhetorical strategy
and in the process lays open his own. The result is a conclusive inconclusiveness, a literary paradox to mirror ideological questions treated in the
text. The specter of Mateo Alemán is obvious in *Guzmán de Alfarache*,
notably in the second part and its debasement of the sequel, but also in the
underlying tensions of the narrative. Alemán stands by social ethics in
ridiculing the pretensions of the *pícaro* whose tenuous position in society
resembles his own. Vengefulness stays with Guzmán after the conversion
because the conversion is a fiction and bitterness is a fact of life for creator as
well as creation. An implied author foregrounds the irony of Guzmán's
rhetorical blunders, while only the introductory materials determine the
moral direction of part 1. In part 2, the point of mediation shifts to the
spurious sequel and the need to "rewrite" the text. Superiority replaces
morality as the narrative pretext, and Alemán precedes Cervantes in exploring literature as macrocosm. Nonetheless, the beginning and ending, if not
all points in between, depend on a faith in change, on seeing the light, on
penitence, and on the act of transformation. The reader must pass judgment
on the plausibility of the conversion. If the argument is convincing, the
narrative complies with its pretext. If not, one may see the text as an
exercise in the intricacies of discourse, as a statement on the contradictory
aspects of human nature, or perhaps as the condemnation of a society that
worships man-made codes with spiritual fervor.[31]

The *pícaro*'s origin in satirical counterconvention reaches beyond satire
in *Lazarillo de Tormes*, and, in *Guzmán de Alfarache*, the individual—as
speaker, as character, as a unique creation—has a broader forum for expression and for development. The spiritual autobiography of a rogue provides
a synthesis of entertainment (the picaresque events) and instruction (the
conversion and the digressions), but as in the *Lazarillo* pretexts and categories do not remain stable. The temporal plan of *Guzmán de Alfarache* calls for
a distinction between the actions of the past and the voice of the present, yet
the resentment that should have been suppressed by repentance appears in
the "now" of discourse. In the first part of the narrative, morality becomes
conventionalized to serve the cause of literary composition; negative exemplarity satisfies the holy and amuses the unholy or the indifferent. Recalling
the *Libro de Buen Amor*, the markers of evil do not always keep their distance
from the markers of good, especially in the case of the "current" attitude of
the penitent Guzmán. It would be difficult to affirm or to deny the conversion, but it would be reasonable to contend that the "new man"—"el
hombre perfeto"—is not an obvious presence in the discourse. The pretext
of part 1 does not count on the intervention of Martí, and Alemán must deal
with two crucial issues, morality and rivalry. As a reader of part 1, Martí
has missed or chosen to ignore the moral base. Alemán dismisses this as

poor reading, not poor writing. The authentic second part must lead to Guzmán's conversion and contextualize the literary feud. Since conversion implies forgiveness, the aims of the second part are somewhat incompatible. The vengeance of the author calls attention to Guzmán's vengeful tone, while in contrast there is no heightened moral quality in the narrative voice. The role of the implied author in *Guzmán de Alfarache* is as enigmatic as the ultimate message of the work. This is not so in *El Buscón*.

EL BUSCÓN

Quevedo's *Buscón* (*buscón*, meaning robber, petty thief, rogue) combines the circularity of *Lazarillo de Tormes* with the revenge motif of *Guzmán de Alfarache*, adding revealing layers of language and of irony. The protagonist/narrator Pablos, mindful of, but undeterred by, his humble origins, determines to move upward in society. When society responds negatively to his pretensions, he turns to delinquency to reciprocate and to deception to disguise his true lineage. Event after event in the hierarchical and uncompromising milieu nurtures a sense of shame evident in early childhood. His best-laid plans nearly succeed but are visited upon by an inescapable past. Out to deconstruct the myth of determinism, Pablos only verifies the importance (or curse) of heredity. His childhood friend, Don Diego Coronel, serves as a sign of social stability—as a sign of the past—to thwart Pablos's audacious violation of the operative codes. Yet Don Diego plays a relatively minor role in the entrapment. Pablos's discourse indicates a conflict between desire and reality, an irreconcilability that neither word nor incident can camouflage. It is significant that *El Buscón* contains no lofty premise. *Lazarillo de Tormes* wants to be a success story, and *Guzmán de Alfarache* wants to be a success story on the divine level. The *Buscón*, in contrast, relates a failure accepted as such by the narrator, who seems more than willing to document his folly and to use language against his own best interests. The result is a magnificent verbal display and an ironic paean to institutionalized thought.

Pablos's separation from social prominence and from social possibilities alienates him without destroying his wish to assimilate and conquer. The elevated goals cannot conceal the misdirected zeal; antisocial behavior will not lead to social acceptability. More importantly, the hierarchical order greatly resists change by aligning itself with a sacrosanct divine order, so that the rebel defies heaven and earth. The text preserves the status quo by blocking Pablos's triumph, by creating internal agents of fate, and by deferring narrative discourse. In certain forms of Spanish baroque literature, recodification becomes the prime mover of the act of writing. A purposely obscure metalanguage replaces conventional signs, thus making decodification the primary task of the act of reading. The poetry of Luis de Góngora (1561–1627) and his contemporaries presupposes an elite public, disposed to decipher texts that approach the indecipherable. This *culteranismo* or *gongorismo*, as it is called, has a semantic counterpart in *conceptismo*, a form of conceptual multiperspectivism in which surprisingly few words, stratified and fragmented, offer numerous interpretive variations.[32] Conceptism is wordplay to the *n*th degree, a paradoxical union of signifier and signified, amplification through reduction. When applied to the picaresque model, the baroque style defines a discursive analogue of the protagonist's social margination. The implied author of the *Buscón* is a consummate artist and a defender of collective morality, whose conceptist diction spews forth from Pablos's mouth and whose anti-individualistic social stance determines Pablos's destiny. Text and context conspire against the *pícaro*, subjugating the narrator into a (syn)tactically indefensible position. Pablos's shame and solitude, his controlled anger and uncontrolled rhetoric, and his dogged persistence amid defeat attest to the dialectical relation between competing voices.

In the spirit of deconstruction, the implied author avenges Pablos's nonconformity by undermining his discourse and by crushing his designs, only to lay open the rhetorical bases of his own intervention in the text. The narrator's words try to mask the obvious, and his actions show little knowledge gained from experience. When he does not cause his own downfall, fate (here, literary determinism) lies in ambush to oppose him. The process of victimization within the narrative may inadvertently point to a form of oppression in society. Pablos's voice, drowned out by verbal conceits, and his frustrated efforts signal a correspondingly untenable role in the world at large. The lack of options becomes a saving grace, in that powerlessness may bring about reader sympathy and an examination of authoritarianism. Pablos's defeat is not absolute, for his figurative silence bears a message that may force a reevaluation of other messages in the narrative.[33] The implied author of the *Buscón*, through a blatantly offensive strategy, plots an eloquent and ironic defense for the narrator/protagonist.

The dedication to the reader ("or listener, since blind people cannot read") immediately establishes a humorous, though hardly benevolent, tone. The speaker promises every type of roguish entertainment and exhorts the reader to profit from the sermons; the text proper complies with a variety of diversions while falling short in the area of admonitory prose. Pablos's narratee, addressed as *señor*, is unspecified, and the *pícaro* expresses no other motive for the literary enterprise than sharing his autobiography. What he ultimately shares is a hunger for nobility, a social crime of the highest order, as well as the catalyst for his humiliation and delinquency. The linguistic veneer elicits a tension between the ingenuity and comic richness of the discourse and the self-deprecatory nature of its message. As narrator and as protagonist, Pablos plays a game of exposing and hiding his feelings, which replicates love, hate, and guilt in a system of contradictory signs. Like the author of the prologue to *Lazarillo de Tormes*, he may wish to gain through his writing the honor denied his social station, but even if the work wins him artistic praise, the combination of wit and immorality seems a dubious means by which to acquire honor. One could argue that self-critical laughter is a retreat from despair, yet a narrative built around ignoble blood and debasement of the individual seems an unlikely cure for self-contempt or ostracism. When all else fails, Pablos the character turns to delinquency to validate his selfhood, and his text may reflect a similar projection. To be ridiculed by society and by the reading public is to achieve notoriety, to possess an identity. Nevertheless, the markers of authority suggest that Pablos wages an unsuccessful battle for control of his "life."

The first chapter of *El Buscón* takes the parodic lineage convention to new lengths by intensifying both language and pseudohistory. Everything Pablos says about his family is demeaning (that is, truthful), but the discourse "dresses up" the flaws in euphemism, circumlocution, and misplaced elegance. The result is not so much a cover-up as an overdetermined text, which impresses in terms of linguistic skill, depresses in terms of heritage, and betrays its lowly subject despite the gloss. Pablos begins by identifying himself as a native of Segovia, at that time a colony of Jewish and Moslem converts. His father is a barber, a thief, a drunkard, and a cuckold. Pablos describes him as "tundidor de mejillas y sastre de barbas" (a shearer of cheeks and tailor of beards), adding, "Dicen que era de muy buena cepa, y según él bebía, es cosa para creer" (They say he was born of vintage stock, and considering the amount of wine he consumed, one could surely believe it).[34] The mother is a prostitute, go-between, and witch, "so charming that she bewitched all who crossed her path." She was so celebrated in her time that "casi todos los copleros de España hacían cosas sobre ella" (p. 44; almost every poet in Spain exercised his art on her). Pablos's younger brother, a "little angel," follows the paternal example by "stealing the heart of everyone who saw him." The father is imprisoned for his transgressions (making a "holy" exit with two hundred *cardenales*, cardinals of the church and bruises), and the mother comes close to being tarred and feathered. The parents fight over whose profession Pablos will follow. He separates them, and each resumes business as usual—she to make a rosary of dead men's teeth, he to scrape off a beard or a pocketbook ("Mi madre tornó a ocuparse en ensartar las muelas, y mi padre fue a rapar a uno—así lo dijo él—no sé si la barba o la bolsa," p. 48)—leaving their son to thank God for parents so mindful of his welfare.

The narrator overlooks an essential fact of autobiography, that what he says about his family reflects on him. He uses language to distance himself from events and attachments, but he cannot avoid contact. He is the butt of every joke about his parents' background and propensities. The exaggerated discourse forces the reader to look beyond the words for "true" meanings and feelings. A narrator who would dare to assert that he gave thanks to God for such parents is self-consciously unreliable. If this were a strategy to vent his rage while pleasing the public and detaching himself from the past, there would be no room in the narrative for absurd pretensions, delinquency, or repetition of the crimes of his parents. Since precisely the opposite is the case, the structure seems to bear the imprint of an implied author, who imposes irony on Pablos's ironic account. Beginning with the second chapter, an antithetical force pursues Pablos in his quest for upward mobility and for freedom from the binds of heredity. The young boy, already intent on attaining nobility, overcompensates for his rank by groveling before his colleagues and his teachers. When a schoolmate calls him the son of a whore and sorceress, his mother refuses to deny the charges. The moment is a turning point for Pablos: "Yo con esto, quedé como muerto, determinado de coger lo que pudiese en breves días, y salirme de casa de mi padre: tanto pudo conmigo la vergüenza" (p. 51; The shock almost killed me, and I made up my mind to gather up what I could and get away from home in the shortest possible time, that's how ashamed I was). Before the departure, fate subjects him to further humiliations, which, like Guzmán's misadventures, feature scatological elements. In his tenure as boy-king, for example, Pablos falls from his horse into an open latrine to effect an ironic variation of the symbolic fall.

Pablos finds employment as the servant and companion of Don Diego Coronel in the boarding school of the parsimonious Licenciado Cabra. Chapter 2 represents the culmination of the hunger motif in picaresque fiction, employing bountiful description to depict a scarcity, nay, absence, of food. The situation is as rich in conceits as it is poor in nutrition, and Pablos's path toward respectability commences with omens of disaster and images of death, grotesquely juxtaposed with the excesses of wit. Rescued and recovered, Pablos and Don Diego journey to Alcalá de Henares for higher education. On the road, they fall victim to the pranks, scatologically punctuated, of ruffians and impostors. Both boys feel a deep sense of shame and defenselessness, but when they arrive in Alcalá, Don Diego is in his element and Pablos is on his own. The semblance of equality is over, and while Don Diego is looked after by friends of his father, Pablos is spit on, showered with mucus, beaten, attacked, and covered with excrement. He observes that one day in Alcalá has brought greater suffering than the entire period with the wicked schoolmaster. Don Diego entreats him to be on guard, and Pablos vows to adapt himself to his surroundings, to begin a "new life," to be a prince among rascals.

Disillusionment directs the movement of the *Buscón*. The stability of traditional family life, friendship, and education decomposes within the text. Genealogy is a curse, not a blessing, for Pablos, who fancies himself a gentleman. His zeal for approval leads to disaster. Decked in feathers and filthy from the latrine, he blurts out to those who would stone him, "I'm not my mother," a witch ripe for tarring and feathering. The response is involuntary, a rupture of dissembling, not unlike the discourse itself. The first stage in the plan for prosperity is education, but the experience with the Licenciado Cabra is a step backward, intertextually speaking, to his picaresque roots. In Alcalá, Don Diego shatters the illusion of solidarity, plunging Pablos into a solitude from which he never escapes. The students who taunt him refer to him as a Lazarus (Lázaro) in need of resurrection, and the realization of his plight echoes Lazarillo de Tormes's ordeal with the blind man and the loss of innocence. When a Moslem convert seems set to spit on him, Pablos shouts, "I'm not *Ecce Homo*," the type of unfavorable remark that belittles the speaker as the victim of his heredity and of his words. In chapter 6, Pablos puts into practice his determination to begin anew. In the inverted value system of the *pícaro*, he meets with great success; by society's standards, he fails miserably. Pablos himself—or his discursive alter ego—

accentuates the gap between the norm and deviation from the norm, in a comparison of master and servant: "Era de notar ver a mi amo tan quieto y religioso, y a mí tan travieso, que el uno exageraba al otro o la virtud o el vicio" (pp. 91–92; It was worthy of note to behold my master so quiet and devout and myself so mischievous, for the virtue of one exaggerated the vice of the other, and vice versa). Through notoriety, he achieves the identity, albeit antisocial, that eludes him through conventional channels. He turns disillusionment into a rhetoric of pragmatism.

Pablos "confesses" the inordinate pleasure he derives from his life as a student/delinquent. At the height of his youthful escapades, he receives a letter from his uncle, a hangman, reporting that his father has died in a most dignified manner on the gallows and that his mother, held prisoner by the Inquisition, is near death. He treats the tidings as a blessing in disguise: "No puedo negar que sentí mucho la nueva afrenta, pero holguéme en parte: tanto pueden los vicios en los padres, que consuelan de sus desgracias, por grandes que sean, a los hijos" (p. 106; I can't deny that I was greatly distressed by the latest disgrace, but I was also somewhat relieved: parents' vices may be so great that their demise, however deeply felt, may serve to console their offspring). Meanwhile, Don Diego's father, having heard of Pablos's exploits, orders his son to dismiss the servant. Pablos admits his regret to the reader, but when Don Diego offers to find him a similar position, he answers, "Señor, ya soy otro, y otros mis pensamientos; más alto pico, y más autoridad me importa tener. Porque, si hasta ahora tenía como cada cual mi piedra en el rollo, ahora tengo mi padre" (p. 106; Sir, I'm a different person now, and my goals have changed; I'm shooting for something higher, something that will give me more authority. Because if up to now my lot has been like everyone else's, now I have my father behind me). Pablos sets out for Segovia to collect his inheritance and to get to know his relatives, so that he may steer clear of them.

The confessional aspect of Pablos's narrative proves both revealing and ironic. He informs the reader of his thoughts, while adopting a pose for Don Diego. The uncle's letter is euphemistic and grandiloquent in its treatment of the basest subjects—as is Pablos's discourse in the opening chapters—and the nephew as reader of the letter pretends to be convinced by the florid prose. He tells his master that he will strive to live up to his father's reputation as he plots to take the money and run. The apparent message is that for Pablos, the linguistic artifice may help to shield the truth when that is advisable (as a motive for his false bravado before Don Diego, for example), but in no way does the careful reader ignore the meaning behind the artifice. In Pablos's account, the subtext shows concealed emotions, a despised heritage, obsequiousness toward social superiors, and a reckless abandon for the sake of self-preservation. Attuned to ironies around him, the narrator misses his own. His flight from the past can only be a journey home.

Pablos regretfully leaves "the best life I ever had." In his solitude, he reflects on the hardships of the virtuous life: "Iba yo entre mí pensando en las muchas dificultades que tenía para profesar honra y virtud, pues había menester tapar primero la poca de mis padres, y luego tener tanta, que me desconociesen por ella. Y parecíanme a mí tan bien estos pensamientos honrados, que yo me los agradecía a mí mismo. Decía a solas: —'Más se me ha de agradecer a mí, que no he tenido de quien aprender virtud, ni a quien parecer en ella, que al que la hereda de sus agüelos'" (p. 119; I was going along thinking about the great difficulties involved in the practice of honor and virtue, since first I would have to hide how little of each my parents had, and then I would have to act so honorably and virtuously that no one would suspect my background. And these honorable thoughts impressed me, and I congratulated myself for thinking them. I said to myself, "I deserve a great deal of credit, for I haven't had anyone to teach me virtue nor to serve as an example, like those who inherit it from their ancestors"). The self-congratulatory thought places the narrator in a logical bind. He lives in a society that exalts acting well one's part in the great theater of the world, accepting rather than rejecting the role allotted by destiny. Dissimulation is practical but not necessarily honorable, and virtue is rarely a function of hiding one's lineage. According to Pablos, he has had a model of exemplary behavior in Don Diego Coronel, who could have taught him virtue had he been willing to learn. The illusions of grandeur and the contradictions remain.

On the road, Pablos meets a variety of social types, all fair game for (an implied author's) satire. They include a priest who fancies himself a poet, a hermit who dupes the protagonist at cards, and a Genoese businessman, "one of those anti-Christs who usurp Spain's wealth." Together, they provide a panorama of hypocrisy, which the narrator notes but does not relate to his own conduct or to the object of his mission. Pablos reaches Segovia, "greeted" by his father, or by the remains of his father, quartered by the uncle and scattered at the entrance to the city.[35] He puts on airs in seeking out his uncle and "could have died of shame" when the uncouth hangman rushes to embrace him. He redeems the legacy of his parents, taking French leave after penning a telling letter: "Tras haberme Dios hecho tan señaladas mercedes como quitarme de delante a mi buen padre y tener a mi madre en Toledo, donde, por lo menos, sé que hará humo, no me faltaba sino ver hacer en v.m. lo que en otros hace. Yo pretendo ser uno de mi linaje, que dos es imposible, si no vengo a sus manos, y trinchándome, como hace a otros. No pregunte por mí, ni me nombre, porque me importa negar la sangre que tenemos" (pp. 148–49; Since God has shown me great mercy in taking my good father from me and in detaining my mother in Toledo, where I'm certain she'll go up in smoke, all I need now is to see your worship gain the reward you so eagerly give others. I want to be a singular member of my line, for it would be impossible for me to be double unless I were to run into you, who could carve me up like the others. Don't inquire about me, don't even mention my name, as it's of the utmost importance to me to deny the blood we have in common). In this thought made public, Pablos hopes to sever his ties with his origins, to deny his blood. In Madrid, he finds a new "family" and old problems.

Pablos's rites of passage to Madrid come from a fellow traveler, Don Toribio, a would-be gentleman who makes illusion his reality. If the schoolmaster Cabra takes hunger to the limit, Don Toribio outdoes the squire of *Lazarillo de Tormes* in insubstantial elegance. He and his companions, Pablos's adoptive family, exploit the complexities of appearance. They manipulate material objects, events, and people to convey prosperity, poverty in disguise. Pablos is quite comfortable in this milieu. After a brief training period, he puts theory into practice, taking advantage of acquaintances, inviting himself to meals, affecting wealth and rank, changing his name to fit the occasion. One fateful day, however, the entire school of rogues ends up in jail.

Don Toribio's kingdom of the ersatz is a most appropriate home for Pablos in his flight from the realities of heredity and environment. Until he can be a gentleman, he settles for the appearance of a gentleman. Until he can integrate himself into society, he is content to beat society at its own game. Within this perspective, nobility becomes as intangible and illusory as the property of the gentleman rogues. Pablos tends to confuse the noble with the good, but that hardly matters, for he is unsuited for the first and disinclined toward the second. The "gentlemen" in Madrid are mature versions of the delinquents in Alcalá, replacements for the parents he rejects. The text moves from the world of immateriality to the surreal world of the prison and its inmates, another variation of the family situation. The jail episode offers a view of hardened criminals and criminality in the penal system. The freshman pranks of university days bow to the threatening presence of the inmates, and excrement once again reminds the *pícaro* of his lowliness. To escape danger, Pablos bribes a jailer to let him stay in his quarters. He ingratiates himself with the jailer's wife ("a whale") and two daughters ("prostitutes in spite of their faces") by claiming to be their cousin. Since these ladies seem to have Jewish blood, Pablos moves—in hierarchical terms—from the fry-pan into the fire. With this familial support and additional bribes, Pablos gets out on probation while his cohorts suffer public shame and exile. There is a lesson here for Pablos, one that he chooses not to obey.

Released from jail, "alone and friendless," Pablos determines to win respect and to influence people by changing his name and pretending to have money. Fortune seems to smile on him when a young lady at his boarding house sets her sights on his (nonexistent) income and arranges a nocturnal tryst. In another ironically symbolic fall, this time off a ledge, Pablos shatters his hopes and a good part of his body. "Shamed and offended," he plots to leave the lodgings without paying. He loses face but not ambition; he invents a new name and begins to serve an aristocratic lady. As the courtship progresses, he organizes a luncheon in the park, and a false sense of security consumes his thoughts: "Yo confieso que no pude dormir en toda la noche, con el cuidado de lo que había de hacer con el dote. Y lo que más me tenía en duda era el hacer dél una casa o darlo a censo, que no sabía yo cuál sería mejor y de más provecho" (p. 210; I confess that I couldn't sleep all night, worrying about what I was going to do with the dowry. What really troubled me was whether I should buy a house with it or invest it in an annuity, since I couldn't figure out which would be better and more profitable). While fate prepares for a radical turn of events, the implied author, master of Pablos's fate, maximizes the irony of the discourse. By having Pablos count his chickens before the reading public, the voice-over calls attention to a consistency of attitude, a youthful presumption undeterred by successive failures, and a continued dream to eradicate the past. The *pícaro* is in for a nightmarish awakening, for one of the guests at the luncheon is none other than Don Diego Coronel, the cousin of Pablos's intended. The events that follow re-create and exaggerate those that have preceded. The victim of the design—the symmetry of plot and the conspiracy of discourse—is the narrator/protagonist.

Recognizing his childhood companion, Don Diego cries out, "No creerá v.m.: su madre era hechicera, su padre ladrón y su tío verdugo, y él el más ruin hombre y más mal inclinado que Dios tiene en el mundo" (p. 214; Your worship won't believe this, but the man you resemble had a witch as a mother, a thief as a father, and a hangman as an uncle, and he himself was the most despicable and evil-minded person that God ever put on the earth). Pablos follows a familiar pattern of dissembling as he burns with shame and rage from within. He borrows a horse to parade in front of the lady, and the animal dumps him in a puddle while the owner berates Pablos, with Don Diego and his cousin as witnesses. The narrator confides that even a public flogging carries less shame. The incident increases Don Diego's suspicions, and soon he is able to verify Pablos's identity. Pablos discovers that two of his "good friends" have absconded with his inheritance and his winnings from gambling, then he encounters men hired by Don Diego to beat him up. He is truly at the height of all bad fortune: "Acostáronme, y quedé aquella noche confuso, viendo mi cara de dos pedazos, y tan lisiadas las piernas de los palos, que no me podía tener en ellas ni las sentía, robado, y de manera que ni podía seguir a los amigos, ni tratar del casamiento, ni estar en la Corte, ni ir fuera" (pp. 223–24; I was put to bed and remained in a daze all night long, finding my face slashed in half and my legs so maimed from the blows that they couldn't support me and felt numb, and having been robbed as well, I could neither pursue my friends nor work on getting married, neither afford to stay in the capital nor get away). At this point, the narrative becomes the journal of a descent, broken only by a dramatic interlude in which Pablos finds an outlet for his protean nature.

Nursed by a landlady vaguely reminiscent of his mother, Pablos turns to begging and to kidnaping children, so as to claim a reward on their return. He heads for Toledo, where he initiates a career as an actor and playwright. As he prospers on and behind stage, his discourse takes on a satirical cast. The writing samples he includes are humorous for their poor quality and ironic for their ethical content. When the company manager is imprisoned, Pablos abandons the troupe, an action which he views as a move away from the bad life. The spiritual ascent, valid in an ironic sense, is Pablos's courtship of a nun. If the Archpriest of Hita presents his relationship with Doña Garoza under the guise of pure love, Pablos deconstructs his literary precedent by robbing his holy lover. He gives the episode an open ending: "Lo que la monja hizo de sentimiento, más por lo que la llevaba que por mí, considérelo el pío lector" (p. 247; As far as the nun's feelings about the loss—of her property more than of me—that is something the pious reader must determine). In Sevilla, Pablos becomes a full-fledged member of a company of thieves, a professional criminal pursued by the law. He makes up his mind to flee to the New World with a female companion and waxes philosophical as he concludes the narrative: "Determiné, consultándolo primero con la Grajal, de pasarme a Indias con ella, a ver si, mudando mundo y tierra, mejoraría mi suerte. Y fueme peor, como v.m. verá en la segunda parte, pues nunca mejora su estado quien muda solamente de lugar, y no de vida y costumbres" (p. 254; I decided, after talking it over with La Grajal, to go to America with her, to see if by changing from the Old World to the New and by settling in a new country, I could improve my luck. But things got worse, as your grace will see in the second part, since one can never improve his lot by changing his location and not his way of life). The unwritten continuation would have the same message as its predecessor. There is no room for change.[36]

While Lázaro de Tormes argues for his prosperity and Guzmán de Alfarache for his conversion, Pablos makes no unsubstantiated claims. Negative exemplarity marks the course of the narrative, with no crosscurrent of success or spirituality. In *El Buscón*, the dialectical play does not stem from the failure of the text to conform to its presuppositions, as in the earlier works, but—ironically—from the antisocial narrator's willingness to voice the establishment position at his own expense. In terms of the social mentality of his time, Pablos's pursuit of noble standing is reprehensible, ludicrous, and ironic. The text—supposedly formed of the protagonist's words—makes this position clear, perhaps too clear. Pablos the narrator sins of overstatement. The portrait of his family, the presentation of his delinquency, and the praise of his social superiors are hyperbolic, unnecessarily self-deprecatory, and calculatedly ironic. The implied author announces his presence through conceptist eloquence and through a building intensity of failure, a prediction and patterning of doom held to be the organizing principle of the narrator. The Pablos who hides his feelings in society exposes them in the text, to reveal the plight of the marginated individual with no control over his place in the accepted order. By foregrounding his own role in the text, the implied author creates a narrative analogue of social determinism. Whereas Lázaro's breaking of silence incriminates him, Pablos's discourse paradoxically does the opposite. Pablos articulates his dissimulation, thereby separating the internal from the external self. His parents, his environment, and his social status fill him with shame, and he can do little to change society's perception of him. Despite his admission to the contrary, he is Don Diego's equal in the boarding school and on the road. The difference stems from the association of human worth with bloodlines, which begins in Segovia and culminates in Alcalá. Pablos's ideal is incongruous, but society shares responsibility for his delinquency.

As narrator, Pablos attempts to ingratiate himself with the reader by ridiculing his heredity and environment. He expects the reader to elevate him from his source, but the narrative strategy links him to that source. The complex discourse ensures an educated, but not necessarily sympathetic, public. By resorting to mockery of his background and abuse of traditional signifiers (in elaborate wordplay and substitutions such as "angel" for "thief" in the case of the brother), the narrator prioritizes effect over cause and appearance over reality. His pretensions and his narration make the *Buscón* a type of fool's journey in which the speaker seals his own fate. Pablos wants to be a nobleman, not do noble deeds. He rejects his family to join equally undesirable "families." Like Don Toribio and his companions, he concentrates on the outer trappings of gentility. And, significantly, he thrives on criminal behavior; he is, as Don Diego points out, inclined toward evil. The dishonest, insincere, and contradictory aspects of the discourse unite the narrative persona to the character. Pablos thanks God for his concerned parents, says that he has always respected Don Diego for the great affection his master showed him, calls his time in Alcalá the best life he ever had, describes his encounter with mock-gentlemen after forsaking his heritage in a search for new blood, courts a nun after leaving what he characterizes as the wicked life of the theater, and so on. Story and discourse lend themselves so easily to ironic interpretation that the excessive conceits and conceit, the ordering of events around repeated humiliation, and the self-defeating nature of the text become the markers of semantic and social determinism. The implied author falls victim to his own rhetoric of irony.

El Buscón, probably unconsciously, opens to debate issues its society considers closed. The question of narrative control is crucial because control of one's fate underlies every facet of Pablos's autobiography. The narrator maintains to the end that he has chosen badness over goodness, but the course of events indicates that social prejudice pushes him toward delinquency. The hierarchical system frowns on upward mobility and ostracizes those at Pablos's level. The *pícaro* can neither ascend nor defend his inherited position without incurring the wrath of his superiors, the people who establish and sustain the norm. There are several turning points in the protagonist's life. The first is his mother's confession of her bewitching ways. The second, and arguably the most significant, is the initiation in Alcalá. On the road, Pablos and Don Diego are equal, anonymous, defenseless. When they reach the university, they do not change, yet the academic community recognizes a distinction in rank. Colleagues flank the privileged son to protect him and torture his unfavored companion. Pablos's move to delinquency relates to self-survival both as a response to persecution and as a plea for salvation from those forces that would deny him an identity. Pablos praises Don Diego for his piety but envies his nobility, a birthright that guarantees him clear passage. Delinquency is a defense against and an acknowledgment of social determinism. The defense may ultimately be unconvincing as a moral option, but it succeeds, documenting Pablos's failure, as a sign of the lack of options facing the outsider. Authorial intervention strengthens the coercive hold on Pablos while accentuating his helplessness, compromising but not completely silencing him.

While Pablos's status is never in doubt, the tone of his narrative shifts radically. Pablos mocks himself, his family, and other undesirables as he begs for pity and even empathy. His solitude, frustration, and shame break through the burlesque frame to focus on the alienated individual in a class-conscious society. Society wins, with the narrator's compliance, but the text registers the emotions of an outcast, a concession in itself. Pablos's enigmatic relish in deriving humor from mortification bespeaks discursive opposition in the form of an implied author. This imposing presence stands above the material to deride both subject and audience. His role within the text is directly antithetical to that of Pablos as an embodiment of pre-romantic sensibility. The narrative explores the two extremes and the space between them. *El Buscón* provides an excuse for ingenuity, a generic inside joke, a parody of a parody, a picaresque novel for the intelligentsia, yet the variation is not lifeless. Pablos records events from his childhood to maturity, alternating narration with commentary and the feelings he hides from society. True to conceptist doctrine, Quevedo offers layers of meaning superimposed on the picaresque model. The discourse of *El Buscón* is a doublespeak of wit and desperation, determination and determinism, meditation and mediation. The implied author forces Pablos into a web of contradictions that reflects on both of them. Armed with a classical flaw (overbearing pride) and impeded by an unkind fate (an implied author working at cross purposes), Pablos becomes a tragic hero in the mode of irony and a standard bearer of baroque disillusionment, articulate in his speech and in his silence.

Conceptism is the property of an elite public trained in the intricacies of language and thought. The artistic flourish functions in multiple associative fields, and the image deciphered is the witticism ripe for further exploration. A sociology of conceptism would probably rule out a person of Pablos's educational and experiential background from the reception and almost certainly from the creation of this highly stylized and complex form of art. The disparity between the first-person narration and the conceptist artifice separates the literary illusion from the realities of literary convention. Quevedo enters the narrative scheme to determine the course of action and language. Pablos is a displaced person in society and, fittingly enough, in the verbal object that reflects the social structure. The artist is conspicuous by his presence, the subject equally conspicuous by his *controlled* wit. The subversion of authority in the picaresque is a logical consequence of the subordination of the individual in the hierarchy of the age. The underprivileged individual gains titular force as narrator and protagonist of his story only to be ridiculed and rebutted by what may erroneously be called his own words. Determinism, which carries theological if not epistemological weight, operates on the internal structure of the *Buscón* in much the same way that it operates in the world order of Quevedo's time. The marginated figure is many times removed from the base of power, and even the professed power of the pen cannot withstand the strokes of irony. The ironizing spirit is the source of control and the intersection of storytelling and story.

The anonymous author of *Lazarillo de Tormes* lowers his sights from idealistic fiction and spiritual autobiography to focus on the marginal self, the end point of individual worth inspired by Renaissance humanism. The change in station of the narrative persona brings a modification of authority. Truth becomes more problematical and unreliability a strong possibility, but there comes a new beauty in the subjective vision of the world and in contemplation of the act of writing. Self-consciousness foregrounds expression as inseparable from meaning and involves the reader in evaluation of narrator and narrative. The social context and the literary text become interdependent; the indeterminacies of one become part of the structure of the other. The narrator/protagonist's position in the text mirrors his position in society. He is at the mercy of an ironic structure that allows his defense to work against him. A second, inimical voice exposes the strategies of the narrator while revealing its own rhetorical force and its own ambiguities. The prologue to *Lazarillo de Tormes* accommodates both a narratee and an implied reader, as well as a pattern of indeterminacies. The text proper builds on this base, and the picaresque model includes a dialectical struggle between the narrator and the other voice, that of an implied author.

The professed complacency of Lázaro de Tormes turns to spirituality in the case of Guzmán de Alfarache. The autobiographical narrator digresses to bring the morality of his new life into the story of his old. Intended to convince the reader of a conversion, the digressions may indicate more resentment than reform. Within the interplay of belief and suspicion, Alemán internalizes his rage at the author of the spurious sequel to avenge the invasion of his textual territory. The retaliation adds another dimension to the narrative voice(s), but the cost of revenge is dear, as the desire to show Guzmán's superiority over Sayavedra (and Alemán's over Martí) tends to subsume the original pretext. The implied author of *Guzmán de Alfarache* mediates the narrator's discourse and the author's response to the continuation. Part 1 points back to the *Lazarillo*, and part 2 adds a Cervantine cast to the delicate imbalance of signifier and signified. Quevedo's *Buscón* intensifies language and picaresque motifs in Pablos's account of his delinquent past. The unreformed sinner defends the establishment position against his criminality and against his plans for social advancement. The baroque energy in discourse and story, which defines a structure for the rebel's tract against rebellion, may serve to explain the ironic situation. Pablos's failure in society has a discursive analogue in the self-defeating articulation of his career. The diction, the ridicule, and the conservative ideology of the text suggest the presence of an implied author, who teasingly makes the *pícaro* the agent and object of satire. In the course of subverting Pablos's strategies, however, the implied author reveals his own, and he is not entirely successful at drowning out the narrator's voice. Pablos records the plight of the alienated soul confronted by a hostile society. The hostility of the implied author only confirms the untenable position.

LA FAMILIA DE PASCUAL DUARTE

In *Lazarillo de Tormes* and in the novels that emulate and modify its structure, rhetoric measures itself against an individual and collective conscience.

Established doctrine and literary tradition regulate discourse, event, and dénouement. The narrative voice is deceptively singular, able to capture social and antisocial perspectives. The status of the speaker forces a hierarchical system onto the text, with ironic results. Author, narrator, and reader engage in dialectical play in which the fate of the outsider and the fate of the word are at stake. Picaresque narrative grants the lowborn figure a new prominence, often reluctantly, but status, like society, is subject to upheaval. As points of reference and institutions change, discourse reflects changes in attitude toward the marginated character, but irony and a lack of synthesis remain constant. The de-centering of social (and literary) reality and the self-consciousness of the enterprise promote an opposition between detachment and subjectivity, a questioning of motives within and beyond the text. *Don Quijote* explores the issue of universal truth and the myth of difference between history and fiction from the perspective of a protagonist who chooses his course of action. Idleness, literature, and madness notwithstanding, it is he who rejects society and not the opposite. Lázaro, Guzmán, and Pablos face ostracism from birth, and free will is the myth their discourse respects and their stories deny. Social inferiority and conflicting authority in the text mark the picaresque models, their variations, and transformations. Intertextuality and (mis)reading project an ironic history of the outsider in narrative and in society, as the form survives, prospers, and exalts its origins by defying them.

The *pícaro* offers a voice for every age but becomes an especially striking sign of modern disillusionment. An example of the classic form in a contemporary context is Camilo José Cela's *La familia de Pascual Duarte*, published almost four centuries after *Lazarillo de Tormes*.[37] Cela's narrative repeats the pattern of unresolved tensions, stressing the conflict between man's control over his actions and his inability to affect the forces that direct his life, between man as a responsible being and as a plaything of destiny and circumstance. The author separates himself from the material only to accentuate his presence, just as the narrator/protagonist devises a strategy of separation that heightens rather than diminishes his involvement in the episodes recounted. Each adopts a rhetorical posture that becomes part of the message of the text, a commentary on complicity disguised as disengagement. Narrative discourse has the dual function of exposing the irony of the speaker's stance and of demonstrating the validity of the ironic mode of presentation, ultimately the most humanitarian recourse in a time of destruction.

In a transcriber's note, the fictionalized author tells of finding Pascual Duarte's manuscript and negates his own role in the composition: "No he corregido ni añadido ni una tilde, porque he querido respetar el relato hasta en su estilo. He preferido, en algunos pasajes demasiado crudos de la obra, usar de la tijera y cortar por lo sano; el procedimiento priva, evidentemente, al lector de conocer algunos pequeños detalles—que nada pierde con ignorar—; pero presenta, en cambio, la ventaja de evitar el que recaiga la vista en intimidades incluso repugnantes, sobre las que—repito—me pareció más conveniente la poda que el pulido" (I haven't corrected or added even a tilde, because I wanted to respect even the style of the original. I preferred, in the case of some particularly crude passages of the work, to make use of the scissors and excise the offending parts. The process obviously deprives the reader of knowing some minor details—which are no loss at all—but it offers, in contrast, the advantage of avoiding a confrontation with intimate and even repugnant items that, I repeat, I considered more convenient to prune than to polish).[38] The transcriber then points to a reading that follows the convention of negative exemplarity: "Es un modelo de conductas; un modelo no para imitarlo, sino para huirlo; un modelo ante el cual toda actitud de duda sobra; un modelo ante el que no cabe sino decir: —¿Ves lo que hace? Pues hace lo contrario de lo que debiera" (p. 5; It is a model of conduct, not a model to imitate but to flee from, a model before which all question of doubt is superfluous, a model before which the only thing one can say is, "You see what he's doing? Well, he's doing just the opposite of what he should be doing"). In the narrative proper, Pascual confuses apology with self-justification. Cela the transcriber initiates this confusion by identifying his subject in terms of the "other" (the family) and by explaining the revisions of the "untouched" manuscript, by prescribing a reading, and by setting a tone of levity for the violent proceedings.

In the letter that accompanies the manuscript written from his jail cell, Pascual Duarte calls his work a public confession. He warns the narratee, Don Joaquín Barrera López, that the text is silent where memory has failed him and on matters too painful to treat. Pascual expresses hope for divine forgiveness, since human forgiveness has eluded him. Given the evil that has followed him in life and his tendency to succumb to instinct, he accepts the prospect of death, fearing that freedom would only force him to revert once more to violence. The opening statement of the memoir itself—"Yo, señor, no soy malo, aunque no me faltarían motivos para serlo" (p. 11; I, sir, am not bad, although I would have good reason to be so)—initiates Pascual's narrative strategy, in essence a rationalization of his past behavior. Pascual sees himself as the victim of a predetermined fate and of a hereditary and environmental curse. Every positive sign in his life portends disaster, and every decision reflects his social conditioning. The emphasis on intuitive responses that guides the letter leads into a defensive text, relegated to determinism yet never quite freeing its subject from complicity. Like the *Lazarillo*, the text is ironic because the narrator both strives for more than he can achieve and reveals more than he intends. The conflict on the intentional level finds discursive support in the grotesquely comic language and narrative distance employed to convey tragic and intimate events. Cela, the so-called transcriber, makes Pascual's retrospective vision and self-judgment an exercise in duplicity.

Pascual begins his narrative by distinguishing between those who are born to proceed along a road bedecked with flowers and those impeded in their course by thistles and cacti. The representative of the first group is Don Jesús González de la Riva, owner—significantly—of a flower garden tended by Pascual. In the Duarte household, the only flowers are those painted on a plate, and, symbolically, one unable to come into full bloom:

Pascual himself, characterized by the village priest as a rose in a dungheap. From birth, Pascual is imprisoned, according to his own description, in a sterile house in a "lost" village on a road as dull and long as the days of a convict condemned to death. The son of parents lacking virtue and unwilling to submit to God's commandments, he is quick to acknowledge an inheritance of unrestrained impulses and violence. Throughout the narration, Pascual points to the inevitability of his self-destruction, as clearly predictable as the perdition of his sister Rosario, a prostitute and a thief, and the hellish existence and premature death of his retarded brother Mario. By alluding to his role as victim, he exonerates himself from culpability, a recourse that he extends rhetorically through narrative detachment from the crimes he has committed. The strategy reaches a culminating stage when Pascual the narrator remarks that Pascual the protagonist seems like a complete unknown to him.

Pascual, like his predecessor Lázaro, provides evidence to undermine his plea of innocence. The shooting of his hunting dog Chispa, described with no thematic or chronological motivation in chapter 1, serves only to indicate the gratuitous violence that typifies Pascual's conduct. Seeing himself reflected in the dog's eyes, eyes that remind him of a father confessor's, he allows his displaced anger and remorse to cause an unprovoked death. Once this precedent has been established, the rationale that supposedly will justify Pascual's acts (including the climactic killing of his mother) loses its full impact. While attempting to portray himself as a passive entity, the narrator demonstrates his direct involvement in the events. Seeking to analyze the external forces that have brought about his downfall, he ends by elaborating the very choices he holds to be lacking.

The intervention of the implied author is apparent in the circumstantial irony and in Pascual's "unconsciously" ironic language, intensely poetic and intensely revealing. The revelations are not necessarily flattering. Pascual says of his enemy El Estirao, "No me parecía hombre valiente más que con las mujeres" (p. 28; He didn't impress me as especially brave, except with women), immediately before presenting an encounter in which he himself avoids the anticipated confrontation. He begs the reader's pardon for using words such as *guarro* (hog) and *trasero* (buttock), while registering no such delicacy in the grotesque survey of Mario's misfortunes or the graphic descriptions of the killings. Violence becomes so ingrained that it produces no self-consciousness on Pascual's part. The displacement and rationalization that attend this violence work at cross purposes with the defensive tactics of the narrative. Similarly, the details that Pascual provides often incriminate him rather than free him from incrimination. The lengthy sequence that leads to his first wife Lola's miscarriage, for example, underscores Pascual's irresponsibility and ultimately his guilt. While he views himself as physically and morally removed from the tragedy, incident and imagery show otherwise. The matricide, in a sense the most justifiable of Pascual's crimes, turns into a symbolic (and ironic) suicide. The yearning for escape definitively destroys his chance for freedom from his impulses and from his destiny. The final breath of relief is illusory, marking a change from one type of imprisonment to another. In the closed world of the penitentiary, Pascual is distanced from the family yet bound to it by memory and by the writing of the text.

When asked if he has completed the story of his life, Ginés de Pasamonte, galley slave and autobiographer in *Don Quijote* (part 1, chapter 22), responds that the narrative cannot have ended while he is still living. Pascual Duarte addresses himself to this question in the letter to Don Joaquín: condemned to die, he assures the narratee that little of consequence awaits him. Even more emphatically, Cela discovers a way to close the narrative, by appending a second transcriber's note and two letters from witnesses to Pascual's execution. Ironically, something has happened in the interval, but the transcriber has been able to ascertain only a few facts. From the epigraph preceding chapter 1, the reader knows that Pascual has killed Don Jesús, and the transcriber relates this event to a rebellion in the village in 1935 or 1936, at least thirteen years after the death of Pascual's mother. This may be the matter too painful to discuss—the source of the literary silence alluded to in the letter[39]—though one can hardly imagine a more horrifying recollection than the death match between Pascual and his mother. Cela clouds the issue further by stating in the second transcriber's note that Pascual wrote the letter between the composition of chapters 12 and 13 (a judgment based on ink color) and by including a number of narrative inconsistencies and misinformation. A case in point is the early reference to the sleeping arrangements in the Duarte house, in which Pascual has himself and his wife sleeping in a room next to that of his parents and has his children scurrying to the kitchen, when in fact his father dies before the marriage and his only son dies at eleven months.[40]

If the manuscript is contradictory and historically incomplete, its end point captures perfectly the intensity of Pascual's rage against his fate and against those around him. The chaotic text preserves the linguistic indeterminacy (or polysemy) and the ambiguity of the archetypal picaresque novels, as it reflects the violent and self-destructive force of the larger social scenario, the Spanish Civil War and its aftermath. The narrative superstructure captures Pascual's textual strategy and his unconscious mind, standing as a mirror to the world and possibly to a collective unconscious. The mother symbolizes a motherland about to be devoured by her children; the assassin seems more concerned with decorum of expression than with the implications of the matricide. In *La familia de Pascual Duarte*, as in the earlier narratives, misplaced values and lack of focus alternate as medium and message. An implied author eternizes the narrator's design and his own, creating and challenging a myth of solitude.

La familia de Pascual Duarte sustains the confessional form and penitential premises of the picaresque novels. For whatever reason, the narrator, following precedent, deals in partial truths and an incomplete story. Like Lázaro, he confuses defense and rationalization, and the full implication of his words escapes him. Like Guzmán, he takes responsibility for his guilt without incorporating a metamorphosed self into the discourse. What for Guzmán may be an insincere repentance is for Pascual a conditioned insensitivity to humanity and a lack of awareness of his own character. Circumstance has robbed him of positive examples, and the revelations in his account are often closed to him. The elegance of Pascual's prose suggests the baroque opulence of the *Buscón* as a sign of the implied author. While Quevedo practices conceptist art and preaches society's lesson, Cela achieves a meaningful incongruity between discursive form and message. The transcriber as editor and censor shields the reader from the spontaneity of creation, blurring object and objective. The intrusive scribe and the inexplicably poetic language signal an ironic counternarrative. Cela captures the isolation of his protagonist by placing the narrator among the other voices of the text. This is the paradox and the paradigm of the picaresque.[41]

Lazarillo de Tormes examines the social and literary hierarchies from below. Authority in the text reflects control in society. The narrator is not created equal; his mastery of discourse is an illusion. The narrative resists its guiding premise and redirects messages. The first-person point of view places the speaker in the ironic position of refuting his own pretensions. The self-betrayal comes complete with patterns of imagery and speech to celebrate the irony. Overdetermination incriminates the narrator and suggests the presence of a third party, who stands between the author and Lázaro. The implied author distances himself—in status and pretext—from the outsider. He seeks a reader capable of penetrating the structure of signifiers to perceive the "real" story. The effort is so effective that the narrator displays and thereby undermines his rhetorical strategy. In deconstructing the discourse, however, the implied author manifests his own rhetorical stance. Competing and contradictory signifieds show that the word, for all its power, is at the mercy of shifting contexts, embedded irony, and an interpreting subject. *Lazarillo de Tormes* self-consciously confronts the intertext and lays itself open to rewriting, in every sense of the term. The model of 1554 holds firm to the present, and its application to the female voice in fiction may add a new page to her story.

II
Variations

3 THE VOICELESS NARRATOR

The Spanish Feminine Picaresque and Unliberated Discourse

> Men, in determining the "acceptable" values and assumptions (which include the inferior status of women), subject women to experiences that men are not subjected to; but men's language structure does not include the ready means for women to express the thoughts and behavior that result from their subjugation.
>
> Cheris Kramarae, *Women and Men Speaking*

A salient feature of narrative is its paradoxical resistance to historicist principles. As narrative forms proceed historically through time, they both expand the recourses of earlier texts and validate the presence of the new—the novel—in their predecessors. *Don Quijote* stands as a monument to the synchronic backdrop of intertextuality and to the defiant chronology of narrative development. The absurd and counterhistoric temporal scope of Cervantes's novel underscores, perhaps precognitively, the interplay between history and fiction and the powers and limitations of the verbal sign. *Don Quijote* erects barriers between the real and the imaginary; it establishes categories of experience and writing before theories of history and literature legitimize such distinctions. *Don Quijote* reacts to nineteenth-century narrative realism over two centuries before European literary realism takes hold, and it challenges narrative presuppositions from the perspective of author, narrator, character, and reader. Practice encompasses theory, and theory raises rather than answers questions. The problem of truth and the amplification of perspective foreground the self-conscious literary object as a microcosm turned macrocosm, a system of devices that uses artifice to seek essence. By placing himself in the work—by fictionalizing himself—Cervantes acknowledges the comprehensive nature and the inverted hierarchy of his narrative performance. The irony of his vision points forward to twentieth-century skepticism and backward to the discursive strategies of picaresque narrative, in which an implied authorial presence directs language and event. The feminine variations of the picaresque offer new patterns of discourse while forming the basis for further transformations of the model. Quite fittingly, they also anticipate the dialectical discourse and rhetorical effects of the picaresque archetypes.

Borrowing from the tension between stated intention and uncompliant text (and between the author and his alter ego) in the *Libro de Buen Amor*, the early writers of picaresque fiction project ambiguity on various levels of narration. The doubling of the author and narrator in the prologue of *Lazarillo de Tormes* initiates the relationship between implied author and narrator/protagonist that regulates the irony of the text proper. The prologue speaks, without transition, of a book to be judged by a reading public and an explanatory manuscript with a readership of one. Lázaro himself is both man and boy, writer and character, participant and observer. From the standpoint of discourse, he is unreliable and reliable, because the authorial figure encodes the text with fixed patterns of irony and revelations of truth that betray Lázaro's defensive rhetoric. *Guzmán de Alfarache* heightens rhetoric and defense by moving the explanation to a spiritual plane. Guzmán's text is a confession in the double sense, the story of a professed conversion presented through the discourse of a repressed individual. The separation of episode and moral digression establishes the opposing sides of a narrative competition in which the reader may accept or reject the penitential stance. To read *Guzmán de Alfarache* is to determine priorities, to validate the narrator's redemption or to expose the unredeemed self. Authorial control becomes more prominent in *El Buscón*. The intensification of language, the identifying sign of a baroque stylist rather than of a narrative novice, finds an analogue in the incriminating discourse and fatalistic events of the text. Quevedo announces his presence verbally, in technical and rhetorical terms; neither the words nor their message belong entirely to Pablos. The idiolect, the negative determinism, and the implicit denial of upward mobility mark the intrusion of the creator in his creation, to oppose and ultimately to silence the narrator.

Just as *Don Quijote* makes the process of composition a part of the narrative product, the archetypal picaresque novels allow particular strategies of storytelling to guide message production. The markers of discursive play set opposing systems into motion. The dual direction of the prologue in *Lazarillo de Tormes*, the division between narrative and commentary in *Guzmán de Alfarache*, and linguistic self-consciousness in *El Buscón* suggest a dialectical chain of connections that unite discourse, story, and signification. The premise of each work—Lázaro's explanation of the case, Guzmán's indictment of sin following his conversion, and Pablos's record of his entry into the world of crime—leads to a possible counterargument that would redefine the focus of the work. Lázaro's ascent in society may, in fact, be a descent into complacent depravity, Guzmán may be a hypocrite instead of a convert, and Pablos may adopt a bold tone to camouflage his shame. The narrators as pawns of the authors, real and implied, function as analogues of the individual at the mercy of a regimented society, but the literary space grants the narrator a forum that society does not provide and that an author cannot completely dominate. The discursive structure ironically features variations on the theme of silence, specifically attempts on the part of the narrator to conceal the truth and on the part of the (implied) author to discredit or render problematic the words of the speaker. The ironic consequence is a duplication of narrative voice, which adds a richness of ambiguity and a subtext for speech and social acts.

The earliest of the male picaresque forms secularize the spiritual confession to delineate a character who confronts society and the blank page. Lázaro breaks a protective silence to publicize his disgrace, as the speaker in the first part of the prologue alludes to honor attained in the pursuit of the arts. While boasting of his newly acquired prosperity, Lázaro stresses the importance of silence (and figurative blindness) in the honor-obsessed Spain of his time. Rather than remove him from the preoccupations of his countrymen, his words seem to concede his faith in the power of illusion. The narrative continually reiterates the contradictory force of its existence. Unity comes not so much from the execution of the narrative premises as from the ironic correspondences and "unconscious" revelations of the text. Guzmán links the sacred and the profane in an attempt to negate a sinful past through contrast with a calculatedly exemplary present. To give credence to the earnestness of Guzmán's conversion, the reader must take him at his word and ignore to some extent the comprehensive impact of his words. The discourse of *Guzmán de Alfarache* subtly belies the stated intention and the avowed repentance. Between the adventures of the *pícaro* and the moral lessons of the reformed sinner lie the thoughts (made public) of one made bitter by his rejection by God and his fellow man. This psychic middle ground disrupts the balance created by the textual division to favor the sinner over the would-be saint and a rhetoric of discord and resentment over a language of inner peace. In *El Buscón*, the extended verbal conceits announce the presence of an extranarrative mediator who makes his way into the story by controlling causality as well as discourse. Pablos publicizes his dishonor through words not fully his own, and a fate guided by the implied author conspires to deny him escape from the past. The connecting threads of the narrative relate to the superstructure of linguistic and situational determinism.

The doubling effect, characterized by irony of discourse and circumstance, brings into question the concept of an objective reality or of absolute values. The narrative mirrors the dilemma of man before nature, society, and fate, only partially in control of the events that beset him. While the literary vehicle privileges him, the authorial figure compromises his autonomy at every turn. Message systems interact and at times contradict each other, finding an order of sorts in the evasive syntheses and ironic patterns of narration. When a female protagonist replaces the male, the distance between empathy and contrivance increases. Women do not necessarily sound like women, nor do authors always give them a voice in the narrative. The precariousness and inequality of their social roles are reflected in literary works that often reduce feminism to the status of motif. Male authors bring women into the domain of the picaresque without giving them freedom of speech and without liberating them from the constraints of their social inferiority. The female rogues achieve a degree of success by plotting against men, but society at large, if not the individual, avenges their deviation from behavioral norms. The *pícaras* face despair, unhappy marriages, and even death for their tricks and for their rebellion. The texts that portray their lives marginate them from discourse. Their stories are immoral yet entertaining interludes in the male-oriented scheme of things, and their creators undermine their words as society undermines their actions. Like their male counterparts, the female protagonists achieve an identity in spite of the factors that work against them, and some manage to escape the silence that threatens their discursive authority.

A beauty and an enigma of the picaresque trajectory is the generic consciousness of writers, narrators, readers, and critics, ranging from mythic to socio-historical, from moral and conceptual to purely formal considerations. The feminine picaresque, with its inherent need for modification of the model, lends itself to the study of the "readings" (and anticipation) of the picaresque archetypes by those authors who choose to present antiheroines. The *pícara* is an orphan, an outsider, a trickster, whose story relies on an episodic structure and a system of poetic justice based on the social status quo. The incipient psychological realism of the *Lazarillo*, the *Guzmán*, and the *Buscón* counts less in these readings than the re-creation of antisocial events to conform to the female characters. Discursive mediation becomes more evident in the presentation of women's lives. The external self—the male view of the opposite sex—dominates the narratives, which nonetheless bespeak woman's place in society and in the text. The discourse contains a number of voices, one of which belongs to the protagonist. Her confrontation with competing voices offers a key to the production of meaning, as well as a social statement.

The dialogic format of Francisco Delicado's *La lozana andaluza* links the work to the tradition of Fernando de Rojas's *La Celestina* (1499, 1502), with its emphasis on verbal portraiture and social panorama. Significantly, however, *La lozana andaluza* points forward to the picaresque mode through an ambiguous prologue, rich in moral intention and challenged by the text proper, and through a doubling of the author, who becomes a character and commentator in Lozana's story. As the object of story and discourse, the protagonist acts and interacts with those around her. As a participant in the dialogue, she develops a voice to complement (and perhaps to rectify) the descriptive and narrative components of the text. In *La pícara Justina*, Francisco López de Ubeda foreshadows the linguistic intricacies of Quevedo's *Buscón* with a voice-over that puts morality at the service of the written word. The baroque idiolect subordinates self-revelation to diversion, accentuating the role of the implied author over the delineation of Justina's inner being. The intertextual motive for the artistic display—and the target of López de Ubeda's moral indolence—is Alemán's *Guzmán de Alfarache*. In Alonso Jerónimo de Salas Barbadillo's *La hija de Celestina*, the authorial figure once again becomes the agent of morality. The narrative commentary, the chronology, and the intervention of fate adhere to a moral order that occupies more narrative space than weight of conviction. Death looms in the background (and in the foreground of narration) for Elena the sinner, the victim of an ignoble heredity, a corrupt environment, and a third-person narrator who gives her little opportunity to speak for herself.

The movement from *La lozana andaluza* to *La hija de Celestina* gives priority to entertainment, instruction, and feminism, generally in that order. The carnivalesque world of inversion and wish-fulfillment informs the feminine picaresque, despite its antifeminist subtext of social hierarchies and male superiority. Alonso de Castillo Solórzano draws on the picaresque models for plot and form, while avoiding a certain ambivalence of discourse. The archetypes are models rather than myths, and discourse is no longer an end in itself. The evidence is a first-person perspective in *Teresa de Manzanares* that changes only slightly in the shift to the third person in *La garduña de Sevilla*. As a unit, the antiheroines' narratives cover the discursive range of their brother works. They become counterfictions when the differentiated voices of the texts convey a sense of variation and sexual consciousness, when the female presence begins to affect the production of meaning. The semiotic (and economic) system associated with these women is the body, a visual and sexual commodity. Their tricks and their words depend on desirability, and the transition from object to subject illustrates the tenuous interiority of the female character. To a degree the texts define identity in negative terms or in terms of what is left unsaid. Discourse becomes a literary response to a social question.

LA LOZANA ANDALUZA

> *Lozana*: Mirá, dolorido, que de aquí adelante que "sé cómo se baten las calderas," no quiero de noche que ninguno duerma comigo sino vos, y de día, comer de todo, y d'esta manera engordaré, y vos procurá de arcarme la lana si queréis que teja cintas de cuero. Andá, entrá, y empleá vuestra garrocha. Entrá en coso, que yo's veo que venís "como estudiante que durmió en duro, que contaba las estrellas."

> Look here, heartsick boy, as of now "I know how to stir the cauldron," and I don't want anybody to sleep with me at night but you, and in the daytime, I want to eat some of everything, and in this way I'll fatten myself up, and you'd better check out the territory if you want me to get some hides under my belt. Come on, enter, and employ your spear. Enter the ring, for I can see that you're approaching "like the student who slept on a hard bed, the one who was reaching for the stars."

The Spanish feminine picaresque both addresses itself to the male archetypes and prefigures the dialectical narrative of the models. *La lozana andaluza*, published twenty-six years before *Lazarillo de Tormes*, strives to reproduce reality through the devices of fiction, in a portrait that brings the artist into his work. Expanding the role of the *auctor* from sentimental romances such as Juan Rodríguez del Padrón's *Siervo libre de amor* (*Free Slave of Love*, mid-fifteenth century) and Diego de San Pedro's *Cárcel de Amor* (*Prison of Love*, 1492),[1] Delicado populates his literary creation with characters from an identifiable real world and places them in authentic settings, notably in the holy and corrupt city of Rome. He escapes the fantasy realm of idealistic fiction by concentrating on the lower elements of society and the baser instincts of humanity. The author fictionalizes himself to add credence to the portrait and in doing so gains control of the text from both sides of the figurative canvas. He is a writer, an observer, and an actor who influences events and calls attention to the task of composition. He is not only author as character but also character as author. The literary product becomes the macrocosm, subjecting the elements of reality to the conventions of art. The author manipulates the material from within and beyond the text, while Lozana derives her power as the focal point of the discourse and as a speaker. The progression of the text is panoramic rather than emotional, but Delicado does include a final moment of disillusionment for his protagonist and with it the possibility of redemption. The individual and morality lie within the portrait, which places extension over depth. As in every portrait, the center carries a privileged status, and at the center of *La lozana andaluza* stands a woman with a well-defined past and an ingenious talent for reaping rewards in the present. She is an unabashedly sensual product of her time and milieu, artistically enriched by the complementary facets of the portrait, one of which is a voice of her own.

In his dedication to an illustrious personage, Delicado stresses the pleasure derived from things related to love, "que deleitan a todo hombre" (which delight every man),[2] especially in the case of so expert a practitioner as the subject of the portrait. Alluding to Juvenal's skill at observation, he purports to reveal only what he has heard and seen. A faithful rendering of events in a less than exemplary moral climate necessitates a degree of poetic license for the sake of reader satisfaction: "Mi intención fue mezclar natura con bemol" (p. 34; My purpose was to mix nature with sweetness), to soften the truth in order to heighten the enjoyment. Delicado modifies the Horatian dichotomy of the sweet and useful, aiming for authenticity over instruction, or perhaps for instruction through an accurate portrayal of life. Morality and didacticism are at the service of art, an art that establishes an order for quotidian reality.[3] For those who would question his motives, Delicado comments, "Si, por tiempo, alguno se maravillare que me puse a escribir semejante materia, respondo por entonces que *epistola enim non erubescit*, y asimismo que es pasado el tiempo que estimaban los que trabajaban en cosas meritorias" (pp. 33–34; If, in time, someone were to wonder that I would bring myself to write such things, I would reply then that a letter does not blush, and likewise that the time is past when they respected those who busied themselves in worthy matters). The ambiguity of this passage, with its debt to Cicero, sets the tone of the work. In unpraiseworthy times, literary scruples cede to verisimilitude, as art reflects life in a double sense. If the *Libro de Buen Amor* rationalizes its carnal obsession under the rubric of negative exemplarity, *La lozana andaluza* relates its scurrilous episodes and vulgarities of language to fidelity in the artistic representation of nature.

Following the dedication, the author offers a brief description of the materials contained in the text. He once again emphasizes the completeness of the portrait and its faithfulness to nature, while using classical sources to justify the need for an artistic arrangement of events and a "dressing up" of the material for the cause of creativity.[4] Thus, in the story Lozana will come to be much wiser than her real-life model ("verná en fábula muncho más sabia la Lozana que no mostraba," p. 36), remade to enter the literary tableau. The analogy to painting expresses the tension between natural phenomena and their transference to another medium, between absolute truth and truth in art. Artistic creation involves re-creation according to the principles of the chosen mode. Delicado acknowledges this distinction, despite repeated references to his accurate rendering of the life around him, by foregrounding his own role in the creative process and later by entering the fictional world. In the preliminary sections of this precursor of *Lazarillo de Tormes* and *Don Quijote*, the author notes, whether consciously or unconsciously, the ongoing dialectic of fiction. Unmediated reality provides multiple options. The writer designs a model, selects some elements at the expense of others, and asks the real to comply with the norms of the imaginary. The contradictions inherent in a verbal approach to reality—standard features of the picaresque and a motivating force of *Don Quijote*—direct the self-consciousness of *La lozana andaluza*. The more the author and his alter ego ponder the act of writing, the more obvious their imposition on reality becomes. By transforming himself, Delicado punctuates the transformation of reality. By defending the veracity of his portrait, he illustrates the pervasive influence of literary artifice.

  La lozana andaluza reflects the trope of synecdoche, which centers on the representative part to symbolize the whole. The sinful existence of a courtesan corresponds to the decaying morality of the Roman populace, avenged by Spanish and German soldiers in the 1527 sack of Rome. The portrait is not art for art's sake but art with a foreboding of doom. The historical moment is as significant a part of the structure as setting, character, and speech. The sack of Rome is determined by political, social, and (for Delicado) ethical factors and predetermined by history. As exposition and warning, the text exists in an ironic present and in a parabolic atemporality. Lozana's story evokes a precognitive or precocious determinism, a combination of her *converso* background, her sex, and her exposure to poverty, crime, and sin. Delicado presents the stages of her decline in a systematic fashion. He begins with her birth and ignoble lineage, follows her along the path of destruction, and ends with a spiritual solution to discontentment. The vision of the lower depths, so to speak, offers an early form of naturalism that takes into account the desires, instincts, and motives of the characters. The realistic view of society seen from below builds on the exploration of multiple social levels in *La Celestina* and precedes the anti-idealistic tenor and focus on the individual in *Lazarillo de Tormes*. *La lozana andaluza* works from the isolated subject to a segment of society to society and humanity at large. Lozana's destiny relates to circumstances beyond her control, as well as to her conscious choices. The author supplies a family portrait to complement the panorama of Rome, allowing descriptive voices to take the place of the introspection that will mark subsequent narrative discourse. As the mediating presence within the unmediated form of dialogue, the author in his dual role sets the terms and the boundaries of Lozana's story.[5]

  La lozana andaluza is divided into three parts containing sixty-six *mamotretos*, or memoranda, and several closing pieces. The first *mamotreto* gives a brief biographical introduction, while the second initiates the dialogue form sustained throughout the text, interrupted only by infrequent commentary by the author (outside his role as actor). Perhaps unwittingly, given his zeal for realistic depiction, Delicado questions the narrative devices he employs. The author who in the dedication attests to having seen and heard the events portrayed in the text cannot have seen and heard everything, nor could his recounting of the dialogue be exact. Like Cide Hamete Benengeli in the *Quijote*, he claims to be a witness to events he could not possibly have observed. Note, for example, the author's remark in *mamotreto* 14 concerning Lozana and her servant/procurer Rampín, with whom she has just spent the night: "Quisiera saber escribir un par de ronquidos, a los cuales despertó él y, queriéndola besar, despertó ella" (p. 76; I wish I knew how to write down a couple of snores, which woke him up, and when he tried to kiss her, she woke up). The statements supporting the validity of the text underscore their implausibility. The author at work within his fiction—a fiction that applauds its historicity—embraces and opposes a reality perceived by the senses and modified by words. Realism's loss is literature's gain. Delicado exposes what Cervantes exploits: the writing process itself, the creative distance between signifier and signified, the inversion of microcosm and macrocosm. The figure of the author in *La lozana andaluza* makes problematic the elements that he attempts to clarify. Objective reality becomes subjective, absolute truth yields to poetic license, and the poet reveals the tools (and the tricks) of his creative trade.[6]

The author provides a moralizing voice in the text, to the point of confronting Lozana herself on the issue of God's omnipresence and omnipotence (*mamotreto* 42), a passage that places the creator in a superior position to his creation. The moral stance of the author as character approximates narrative perspective, setting up a type of analogy between the historical veracity and moral validity of the text and the credibility of Lozana's penitent attitude at the end of her story. The discrepancy between a moral position and a profane text and between a historical position and an artistic text may predispose a somewhat skeptical reaction to the change of heart, overshadowed by a volume of sinful acts. The quantitative imbalance resembles that of the *Libro de Buen Amor*, in which the rhetoric of bad love proves a formidable combatant to the doctrine of good love. An important difference, however, is the presentation in *La lozana andaluza* of family origins and the origins of antisocial behavior, leading to sin and eventually to despair. Just as Don Quijote and the authorial figure(s) share the spotlight in Cervantes's novel, Lozana and her author(s) command attention in Delicado's work. The author establishes the terms of the socio-biographical account, placing himself within the narrative to report, comment, and interact. Lozana performs mimetically to substantiate his case and to offer her own.

Born in Córdoba to New Christians, Aldonza (later renamed Lozana for her feminine ripeness) travels throughout southern Spain with her widowed mother. The author hints of early sexual encounters and a free-spiritedness that increases on her mother's death. In Sevilla, Lozana's aunt introduces her to a successful merchant, Diomedes, whose mistress she becomes. She journeys toward Italy with Diomedes and barely escapes death at the hands of his irate father, who imprisons Diomedes and arranges to kill Lozana. The protagonist makes her way to Rome, where she settles in the section known as Pozo Blanco, largely populated by Spanish *conversos*. She finds a kindred spirit in the women of Pozo Blanco, many of whom specialize in the cosmetic arts. Through them she meets a Neapolitan woman whose son Rampín becomes a guide, companion, and sexual partner. Trigo, a wealthy member of the Jewish community, sets Lozana up in a house, where she uses her sexual and economic expertise to profit from her clients. She also practices her skills in the treatment of venereal diseases. At the end of part 1, she comes to the aid of a canon and his pregnant mistress, and at the beginning of part 2, the author discovers that Lozana herself will bear a child by the canon.

The events of what may be termed Lozana's pre-history greatly affect her story, as do the circumstances of her early years. Her impurity of blood, her unstable family life, her status as an orphan, her emerging sexuality, and her mistreatment at the hands of men rob her of youth, innocence, and dignity. Fate brings her to Rome and to Pozo Blanco, where she finds the comfort of group identity and a continuity of ostracism. She becomes the queen of whores in a society that denies her respectability, and the text does not reveal that she would wish it otherwise. The dialogue form gives Lozana an active role in the literary structure, and she has reached a discursive maturity before she begins to speak in the text. She is hardened, cynical, and adept at linguistic as well as sexual expression. The Renaissance predilection for physical beauty customarily manifests itself in paeans to the female form, in works such as Juan del Encina's *Egloga de Plácida y Vitoriano* (*Eclogue of Plácida and Vitoriano*). When Lozana sees Diomedes for the first time, she reacts excitedly to his physical charms, shattering the model (and decorum) to acknowledge feminine sexual urges. In Rome, she recalls her successes: "Fui festejada de cuantos hijos de caballeros hubo en Córdoba, que de aquello me holgaba yo. Y esto puedo jurar, que desde chiquita me comía lo mío, y en ver hombre se me desperezaba, y me quisiera ir con alguno, sin que no me lo daba la edad" (p. 49; I was courted by as many gentlemen's sons as there were in Córdoba, which gave me great satisfaction. And I swear that from the time I was a young girl I could feel the cravings of my sex, and just seeing a man stirred me up, and I would have liked to go off with one of them, but age got in my way). Whether to satisfy her desires or to repay men for their abuse, Lozana—whose name suggests her maturity—thrives as a prostitute, swindling her patrons as she gratifies their desires.

Lozana is the antithesis of the ethereal, virginal, elusive beauty, and she is far removed from the aesthetically erotic love objects of idealistic fiction. She shows little concern for the children she has borne Diomedes, she sleeps with Rampín on their first night together, and she combines prostitution with theft. Like Pablos of *El Buscón*, she is a retrogressive over-achiever, the most flagrant of courtesans, as he is the most flagrant of delinquents. While she deals in cosmetology and legerdemain—arts of illusion—her language reflects the directness of her approach to lovemaking. Her tastes are natural, her needs immediate, her actions shameless, and her discourse is graphic, colloquial, and to the point. When a headwaiter who requires her services approaches her, Lozana says, "'Señor, dijo el ciego que deseaba ver'" (p. 96; "Sir, the blind man said that he wanted to see," that is, "Put your money on the table"). She refers openly to sins past and present, to syphilis and other consequences of these sins, and to sexual topics in general, lying only when the deception of the moment demands it. The following passage, in which Lozana addresses a group of Spanish women living in Rome, illustrates her lack of discursive restraint: "¡Ay, señoras! Contaros he maravillas. Dejáme ir a verter aguas que, como eché aquellas putas viejas alcoholadas por las escaleras abajo, no me paré a mis necesidades, y estaba allí una beata de Lara, el coño puto y el ojo ladrón, que creo hizo pasto a cuantos brunetes van por el mar Océano" (p. 50; Oh, ladies, do I have things to tell you! Just let me make water, since because I had to push through all those old painted whores downstairs, I couldn't stop to answer my needs, and among them was a pious hypocrite from Lara, with her smelly cunt and thieving eyes, who I think has rolled in the hay with every sailor who sails the high seas). Lozana's goal of independence extends to her lexicon. Her language, like her lifestyle, is consciously rebellious, unladylike, and worthy of the basest profligate, male or female.[7]

Delicado's depiction of Lozana is an analogue within an analogue. The antiheroine becomes a symbol of the depravity that is Rome, as Rome itself is a symbol of the triumph of evil. Language, event, and attitude mark a type of semiotic consistency, as all signs lead to sin. Vulgarity is intrinsic to the portrait and to its message, even though the seriousness of the message remains a subtext in a text that seems to take its scandalousness quite seriously. The author forges (or forces) his way into this world, sharing its language and partaking of its temptations yet aware of retributive justice. In *mamotreto* 4, he describes Lozana as "muy contenta, viendo en su caro amador Diomedes todos los géneros y partes de gentilhombre, y de hermosura en todos sus miembros" (p. 43; very happy, discovering in her dear lover Diomedes all the goods and parts of a gentleman, and with beauty in all his members). Later, in *mamotreto* 17, he discusses the wayward life with Rampín as one who knows from where he speaks but who knows, as well, the wages of sin. Lozana, for her part, concentrates on the here and now of a commercial venture that unites sexual passion with financial security.

The author as character takes a more active role in part 2, separating himself to a certain degree from both the extratextual author and the intratextual biographer and commentator. A companion provides the exposition of Lozana's affairs, of her victories over men and their pocketbooks, after which the author speaks directly to the protagonist. He is now a lovesick gentleman, she a consultant in matters of the heart. Lozana advises the author to eat sage with his mistress, but prescribes another remedy—monetary in nature—for the companion, who is in love with her. The first *mamotreto* (24) of part 2 presents Lozana in action among three men, including the author, who praise her beauty and ingenuity, avail themselves of her multiple talents, and finally judge her licentiousness as symptomatic of the ills that beset Rome. In the sections that follow, Lozana pursues all manner of meretricious business, giving counsel and giving of herself. In *mamotreto* 31, she tells of a dream in which Rampín falls into the river, and she fears for his safety. Immediately afterward, the chief constable apprehends the servant for robbing a grocer. On his release, Rampín ironically validates the dream by falling into a latrine. The dream vision and its actualization relate to the impending disaster and to the importance of Lozana's dream in *mamotreto* 66, the last memorandum, a dream that may lead to her salvation. In part 2, however, the emphasis is on destruction, personal and communal. Lozana advances as a deceiver of men, and Rome moves toward defeat. In *mamotreto* 34, a squire echoes Silvio's earlier warning of the danger facing Rome, while Lozana disregards the warning and the future to seize the day.

Part 3, which promises to be more entertaining than the preceding parts,[8] gives greater space to the individual and brings the author into the dramatic events and Lozana into the commentary. The protagonist has periodically evaluated her course of action, and she continues to do so, finally realizing that slight modifications cannot benefit her, that the change must be radical. The text devotes little attention to the crisis of conscience and none to the penitence itself. The diversion comes from further variations of Lozana's craft and craftiness. In a lengthy soliloquy at the beginning of part 3, Lozana expresses a desire to separate herself from the prostitute population in order to have greater control over her destiny: "Ya no quiero andar tras el rabo de putas. Hasta agora no he perdido nada; de aquí adelante quiero que ellas me busquen. No quiero que de mí se diga 'puta de todo trance, alcatara a la fin.' Yo quiero de aquí adelante mirar por mi honra, que, como dicen: 'a los audaces la fortuna les ayuda'" (p. 172; I don't want to follow behind whores' tails any more. Up to now I haven't lost anything; from here on I want them to come after me. I don't want it said of me, "a whore all along, a beggar in the end." From here on I want to watch out for my honor, for, as they say, "fortune comes to the aid of the bold"). Even allowing for honor among thieves, there is a certain boldness in Lozana's words. More than honor, what she apparently wants is status within the demimonde. She is the ultimate pragmatist, willing to do anything to stay one step ahead of her neighbor. The road to redemption is thus far the road not taken.

Mamotreto 42 features a debate between Lozana and the author on the legitimacy of her strategies for survival. Lozana elaborates the various branches of her practice, which include paramedical and pseudoreligious rites and the interpretation of dreams. The author chides her for profiteering from the fears and the superstitions of her customers, cautioning her against playing God. Lozana counters that she performs a service by satisfying the needs of the people and that her prognostication is based on fact and common sense. Having observed those around her, she predicts great carnage in Rome. The author recants, ending the polemic by restating his adversary's case: "Y digo que es verdad un dicho que munchas veces leí, que, *quidquid agunt homines, intentio salvat omnes.* Donde se ve claro que vuestra intención es buscar la vida en diversas maneras, de tal modo que otro cría las gallinas y vos coméis los pollos sin perjudicio ni sin fatiga. Felice Lozana, que no habría putas si no hubiese rufianas que las injiriesen a las buenas con las malas" (p. 178; And I maintain as true a saying I read many times, that "whatever men do, their intention saves them." Whence it seems clear that your intention is searching for life in diverse ways, such that another raises hens and you eat chickens, without prejudice and without causing trouble. Fortunate Lozana, there would be no whores if there were no bawds to mix the good with the bad). The dialogue puts the protagonist's activities into moral and practical contexts. Along with the author, the reader discovers the range of Lozana's enterprises and a logical—as well as rhetorical—force that rivals that of Celestina. In spite of his argument to the contrary, the author accepts the instinctive, self-serving rationale of his forensic opponent. Both recognize, nonetheless, that men and women must answer to a higher authority for their conduct. The author looks to the hereafter and Lozana to an imminent hell on earth.

The debate between the fictionalized creator and his creation attests to the persuasive and multiperspectivist capabilities of the literary work and to an emerging self-consciousness on the part of the artist. Just as the character Miguel de Unamuno allows Augusto Pérez to present a superior argument centuries later in the climactic confrontation of *Niebla*,[9] Delicado gives his protagonist the final word in the debate, using his foreknowledge of the sack of Rome to justify her prophetic claims. Rhetoric triumphs over absolute values, self-preservation over virtue. *La lozana andaluza* offers no psychological progression, but the author's position in the debate conveys an understanding of the protagonist's social predicament. Lozana builds from weakness, using her marginated identity to survive in a hostile world. She becomes mistress of the illegitimate, specialist in the unholy, advisor/confessor in cases of love. Alienated from social acceptability, she inverts the hierarchies of society to control fragmented (and errant) souls. The author places himself in the role of the reader, and his reaction to Lozana's speech guides the reader of the text to a more sympathetic response to her antisocial behavior. Because of his involvement in Lozana's story—he is, in fact, one of the errant souls—the author achieves a dual credibility, as director and participant. By allowing Lozana to "outvoice" him, he gives a victory of sorts to the female outsider and to the evolution of narrative discourse.

The foregrounding of Lozana in the debate serves the transition to her withdrawal from the world, an escape that the text presents as her own decision. *Mamotreto* 44 sustains the ambivalent portrait of Lozana and of the prostitute in general by addressing the issue of security. As an active member of the community within a community, Lozana lives "better than the Pope," yet her unceremonious language suggests a concern for and kinship with the older prostitutes whose days of glory have come to an end. She dares to recommend that society provide for the former ladies of pleasure in order to ensure continuity among the ranks. She defends this stance with a traditional argument in favor of prostitution: "Cuando a las perdidas o lisiadas y pobres y en senetud constitutas, no les dan el premio o mérito que merecen, serán causa que no vengan munchas que vinieran a relevar a las naturales las fatigas y cansancios y combates, . . . y de aquí redundará que los galanes requieran a las casadas y a las vírgenes d'esta tierra" (p. 184; When the lost and crippled and poor and elderly don't receive the recompense or recognition they deserve, it will turn out that many who would have come to relieve the regulars from their weariness and toil and conflicts won't come, . . . and from this it will follow that gentlemen will court the married women and virgins of this land). Human interest competes with sin, and scruples with logic, in a speech that has greater impact because it follows Lozana's case (with the author's endorsement) for resourcefulness and survival at any cost. The presentation of the problem by Lozana herself stresses the importance of perspective on message production. The prostitutes are agents of sin and guardians of purity; by corrupting themselves, they save others from corruption.

In the debate, the author offers a compassionate and socially advanced affirmation of Lozana's views. Here and in the following memoranda, he gives the antiheroine a voice to identify and elicit sympathy for her sisters in sin. As a character, he yields the floor to Lozana's rhetoric of self-defense. As manipulator of the text, he fosters the cause of the underdog while vacillating slightly in the area of feminine discourse. It is implicit in the statements concerning sexual roles that women fall into one of two categories. They are either good (chaste or married) or bad (prostitutes). Men, in contrast, can have it both ways. Their sexual activities do not affect their honor or their social status. When Delicado has a prostitute rationalize the benefits of her profession for society as a whole, he bestows a somewhat suspicious magnanimity on the figure of the scapegoat. Although he may be accused of putting words into the speaker's mouth, one must note that the double standard has endured far beyond the early sixteenth century and that Lozana's voice, however contrived, has a significant function in the text.

In the concluding sections, Lozana labors as a sexual and medical counselor and cosmetics specialist, mixing with all types from pimps to jurists. She is aggressive, cynical, ready to compete for business. More mature and more pensive than in the preceding parts of the text, she continues to seek notoriety in the margins of society. *Mamotreto* 51 represents a turning point in the protagonist's life, as the deceiver of men becomes the trickster tricked, duped into giving her affection for nothing. She takes this as a personal affront, and her speech to that effect contains numerous linguistic signs of her rage. The episode forms part of a progression toward her total disenchantment with the things of this world and toward the decision to isolate herself from the past. While Delicado's structure has a beginning, a middle, and an end, the order of events does not reflect a calculated building of momentum. After the deception, it is business as usual for Lozana until she registers dissatisfaction with her earthly existence in the final memorandum. *La lozana andaluza* is an outline rather than a manifestation of psychological realism. The text provides a compendium of scenes, a portrait of

Lozana's enterprises and of her environment, and a re-creation of her speech. The transformation, be it spiritual or self-serving, is a fitting culmination to the material presented in the text. The rigors of her profession, which have a cumulative force in the work, take their toll on Lozana, and she determines to pursue the road to eternity.

Delicado returns to the motif of the dream to inspire Lozana's reformed outlook. Lozana's dream in *mamotreto* 66 draws images from mythology, legend, and astrology to conclude that "'el hombre apercibido medio combatido'" (p. 244; "forewarned is forearmed"). From the tree of human destiny, she will reach for the fruit that will lead her to paradise. The vision allows her to put her present existence into perspective: "Ya estoy harta de meter barboquejos a putas y poner jáquimas de mi casa, y pues he visto mi ventura y desgracia, y he tenido modo y manera y conversación para saber vivir, y veo que mi trato y plática ya me dejan, que [no] corren como solían, haré como hace la Paz, que huye a las islas, y como no la buscan, duerme quieta y sin fastidio" (p. 245; I'm tired of putting chin straps on whores and applying home-made depilatories, and since I've seen my fortune and misfortune, and I've had the ways and means and conversation to know how to live, and I see that style and repartee now leave me, for those things don't flow forth the way they used to, I will do as Peace does, which is to flee to the islands, and since they don't seek it out, it sleeps tranquilly and with no burdens). Lozana will retire to the island of Lipari, leaving behind the vanities of her life in Rome, in the hope that a new setting may calm her troubled soul. The author closes with the wish that his portrait may lead its readers to peace, as he has led the protagonist to righteousness. If the resolution is abrupt, the motive is worthy. Lozana laments her age and fading beauty, neither of which has an earthly remedy, and the dream gives her an extramundane alternative that begins with atonement. The reader may applaud the intention and hope for the best or consider Pablos's closing words in *El Buscón*, published a century later, to the effect that a change of locale does not bring a change of habits.

La lozana andaluza ends with several short compositions, including an apology, an explanation, an epilogue, two letters (one an epistle written by Lozana), and a digression. In the apology, the author answers possible objections to his work. He refers to the moral intention evoked in the dedication to remind the reader what the text proposes. He cites modesty and verisimilitude to justify its imperfections, its crudeness of episode and language. The apology advances the story by stating that Lozana did, in fact, go to live on the island, where she changed her name to signify her change in attitude. The author mentions that he composed the work—which he calls "estas vanidades," this nonsense—to pass the time while recuperating from a grave and lengthy illness. He closes with an admonition to the reader to place the spirit above the body, as those of the portrait do not, to win God's approval and salvation. The explanation defines *mamotreto* as a book that contains diverse arguments, in this case secular, thus emphasizing the idea of multiple items of interest and multiple perspectives. Delicado gives the background of Lipari, traditionally a home of condemned criminals, and notes that Lozana's three names (Aldonza, Lozana, and Vellida) all derive from words meaning exuberance and beauty. He adds, "Por tanto, digo que para gozar d'este retrato y para murmurar del autor, que primero lo deben bien leer y entender, *sed non legatur in escolis*" (pp. 250–51; Therefore, I say that in order to enjoy this portrait and to criticize the author, they first ought to read and comprehend it well, but "it should not be read in school"). The apology and the explanation, along with the introductory materials, offer a literary frame (and moral framework) for the portrait of Lozana.

In the "Letter of Excommunication against a Cruel Maiden in Good Health," the author presents the suffering of love from the viewpoint of a gentleman overcome by the fire of passion, a lover who laments his lost freedom and blames the ungrateful woman (described in courtly detail) responsible for his metaphorical demise. Significantly, the speaker here is Cupid, a figure whose effect on humanity informs *La lozana andaluza*. Sixteenth-century Rome rejects Christian doctrine to worship the pagan deity of love, and moral chaos and destruction follow. Lozana's epistle deals directly with the sack of Rome. Addressing her sisters in love, she points out that sin, the cause of the devastation, must now yield to reconstruction, for the prostitutes have only past glories to celebrate. Delicado's digression, written in Venice, places the sack of Rome in the context of divine retribution for mortal errors. On a more personal level, the author recounts the situation that brings him to have his manuscript (which he does not count among his "legitimate" writings) printed in Venice. In addition to the dual culmination—the sack of Rome and the publication of the text—the digression asserts the authority of Delicado's voice in the dialogue, bringing the "real" author into his work to validate his fictional counterpart. The result may be an inversion of this principle; the touted diversity of the memoranda may include the fragmentation of the author.

La lozana andaluza creates verbal portraits of an antiheroine and her milieu with a consciousness of history, causality, and the act of composition. The protagonist is an outcast among outcasts, poor, foreign, a New Christian, and a woman who works as a prostitute in a Jewish quarter of Rome. The precocious naturalism of the text relates to Delicado's conception of portraiture as a detailed rendering of reality and to his analogical vision of corruption as a prelude to disaster. The portrait "freezes" a moment to present its richness and its historical irony. Lozana is an agent of sin and a product of the society that ostracizes her. Her position in the portrait is genetically and socially determined, a testimony to the importance of bloodlines for social respectability and responsibility. Up to the final memorandum, Lozana is a character without a conscience and without a sense of the hereafter.[10] Disillusioned at last, she retires to Lipari as a form of penitence, thereby abetting the author in his claim of a moral intention. The same author seems to relish the freedom that Lozana's licentiousness gives him to convert her negative energy into a justifiably scatological text. The tension between the expressed purpose and the direction of the text typifies the interplay of author and narrator in the later picaresque models. The dialogue format of *La lozana andaluza* effects a unique strategy of authority that nonetheless points the way to succeeding fictions.

By projecting himself into the text, the author brings the real world into the realm of fiction while pretending to do precisely the opposite. He is artist and character. He interacts with Lozana and her associates and develops a portrait according to the conventions of literature. He respects truth but subjects his work to the criteria of poetic truth and artistic unity. He makes the writing process a part of the product. One can distinguish between the several faces (or voices) of the author as creator, participant, witness, and mediator. His presence heightens the verisimilitude of the events and at the same time puts narrative reliability into question. The direct discourse calls for exact reproduction, and the privacy of a number of scenes precludes the intrusion of a witness. The author must approximate, must create new realities from old, and must reinvent the world to conform to the demands and the limitations of fiction. The arguments for literary realism and the divided self indicate the distance between the world and the work of art. Literary reality is faithful to its source in an analogical, symbolic way, a fact lost neither on the picaresque authors nor on Cervantes. Self-consciousness turns restrictions into assets by expanding the horizons of literature, by incorporating the problematic relation between life and art into the text. Delicado seems to intuit both the delicate balance and the means of using it to his advantage through the author's multiple functions in *La lozana andaluza*. As in the later forms, realistic and counterrealistic tendencies coexist.

The fragmentation of the authorial figure and the use of dialogue make possible a variety of perspectives. Several characters describe the protagonist, and she completes the portrait by acting and speaking in the text. Through her, Delicado seeks a discursive correlative for immoral behavior in a richly indecent speech. *La lozana andaluza* is a display of colloquial and dialectal speech, proverbs, classical sententiae, lists, literary allusions, maledictions, and the sexual lexicon of its period. The antiheroine is the principal informant, a storehouse of linguistic data. Because she offers counsel on beauty and carnal matters, her discourse provides not only a vocabulary but also a state of the art, and perhaps an experiential statement about the author. Discourse reflects character, as the wayward Lozana freely expresses her emotions, with little or no concern for polite society. Language becomes a form of release, a means of decrying social inequity, a verbal analogue of promiscuity. The author's discourse mirrors the ambiguity of intention by uniting moral insertions with vulgar speech. His language alternately places him above the characters he depicts and makes him one of them. He pleads for piety in an age of sin but shows compassion for the sinner, fights for spiritual ideals but defends the tactics of survival in this life, shows the protagonist on the road to hell but leads her toward peace. Using a non-narrative form, he fashions a multiperspectivist object in which the author interacts with the antiheroine and discourse parallels story. Lozana's language, like her lifestyle, is unrestrained, yet she is free only in a relative sense. A higher authority regulates her conduct and her discourse.

Considered historically, *La lozana andaluza* points to the subtle inter-play between author and narrator/protagonist in the picaresque. As is often the case in the archetypal novels, the more the speaker (here, the author as character) says, the wider the distance between the expressed intention and the messages produced by the text itself. Discourse works ironically to shatter the foundations of a positive or moral purpose. Speech intervenes when only silence will protect secrets or serve didacticism. Lozana's dis-course hardly progresses toward the change of attitude reflected in the final memorandum. The linguistic consistency conveys a pattern of thought and behavior. Lozana is as much a product of heredity and environment at the end of the work as she is at the beginning. The text does not prepare the reader for a conversion, so that the shift from sin to repentance may carry a note of skepticism. The intervention of the author in the work, as both moralizer and womanizer, intensifies the system of mixed messages. The anonymous author of *Lazarillo de Tormes* announces his presence in the prologue and within the text as the manipulator of irony. Alemán extends the interpretive possibilities in *Guzmán de Alfarache* by allowing the al-legedly reformed sinner to describe his errors and provide moral commen-tary. When the inner thoughts conflict with the outward stance, Guzmán may reveal more than he intends. Like his author, he may accept morality as a necessary premise while responding more fully to the world of feeling and spontaneity. Quevedo's *Buscón* unites stylized discourse with a coercive story to acknowledge the intrusion of the author into his fiction. Published between *Guzmán de Alfarache* and *El Buscón*, *La pícara Justina* has a different historical (and intertextual) role than *La lozana andaluza*. Borrowing a gloss of morality from Alemán and offering a prelude to the linguistic achieve-ment of Quevedo, López de Ubeda forges a new direction for the pica-resque.[11]

LA PÍCARA JUSTINA

> No quiero, pluma mía, que vuestras manchas cubran las de mi vida, que (si es que mi historia ha de ser retrato verdadero, sin tener que retratar de lo men-tido), siendo pícara, es forzoso pintarme con manchas y mechas.

> I don't wish, my pen, to have your stains cover those of my life, for—if my story is to be a valid drawing, without having to withdraw from deceptive events—being a *pícara*, it's essential to paint myself with stains and threads showing.

La pícara Justina opens with a dedication, two prologues, and a general introduction. In the dedication to his patron Don Rodrigo Calderón, López de Ubeda puts forth certain facts "out of character." He emphasizes the diversity of the material and its great entertainment value, which will give respite from the grave issues of state that concern Don Rodrigo. In the prologue to the reader, written in a comically sycophantic tone, he recog-nizes that a totally playful book should not be published and that a totally solemn one would not be read, and so he opts for leisure reading with a message. To the frivolous adventures of a free woman he has appended moral messages in the style of the fabulists. The author claims to avoid the love plot of *La Celestina* by focusing on the greater evil of deception for financial purposes. He replaces a carnal structure with a commercial structure that incorporates all manner of sin. For every crime there is an implied punishment and for every punishment a lesson: "En este libro hallará la doncella el conocimiento de su perdición, los peligros en que se pone una libre mujer que no se rinde al consejo de otros; aprenderán las casadas los inconvenientes de los malos ejemplos y mala crianza de sus hijas; . . . y finalmente, todos los hombres, de cualquier calidad y estado, aprenderán los enredos de que se han de librar, los peligros que han de huir, los pecados que les pueden saltear las almas . . . pues no hay en él número ni capítulo que no se aplique a la reformación espiritual" (In this book, the maiden will find knowledge of her perdition, the danger into which a woman who will not heed the counsel of others places herself; married women will learn the consequences of bad examples and inadequate rearing of their daughters; and finally, all men, of every rank and status, will learn the snares from which they must free themselves, the dangers that they must flee, the sins that may rob them of their souls, since there is in it no item nor chapter that does not apply to spiritual reformation).[12] The second prologue uses the words of the protagonist, directed to her fiancé Guzmán de Alfarache, to summarize the major episodes of the text through epithets that collectively affirm her protean nature.

In the three parts of the general introduction, Justina Díez addresses herself to the act of writing. The point of departure is a reaction to a hair on her pen. In an apostrophe to the writing instrument, she wonders if the hair has appeared to cover her blemishes or rather to show that hair will never cover her blemishes, an allusion to the loss of hair from venereal disease. Submitting that artful treatment may make an ugly object valuable, she will present a truthful picture of herself and hope that, as in other creatures of nature, the spots will enhance her worth. She plays on the verb *confesar*, to confess, and her status as *confesa*, converted Jew, to synthesize the writing process with its social implications. In the second part of the introduction, Justina again works with variations of the word *mancha* (spot, blemish) as she complains of the ink stains she has received in removing the hair from her pen. Attempting to remove the stains, she gets ink on her skirt, a situation treated as emblematic. In the third part, the narrator reacts to the small snake that serves as watermark on her paper, at first fearing the symbol and then indicating its positive qualities. Similarly, negative incidents may have illuminating results, and her book will allow readers to see the light as it entertains them. Thus, with pen and paper in order, the composition may begin.

The writing process has, of course, already begun. The introduction defines the goals and the parameters of Justina's text and establishes the direction of the discourse. The author enters the text to frame the narrator's story with a verse resumé at the beginning of each section and moral commentary (*aprovechamiento*, application) at the end. The commentaries represent a concession to didacticism, with a special nod to the digressions of

Guzmán de Alfarache. Despite their prominent position in the text, the concluding passages register as truthful but uninventive adages competing
against the resourceful and sophisticated discourse of the antiheroine. *La
pícara Justina* is a static work from the perspective of psychological or ethical
development. The protagonist liberates herself from the dictates of society
to pursue monetary rewards. She knows that she is wrong to place wealth
and pleasure above all else, but she chooses to obey the mandates of pocketbook and heart over the admonitions of Christian dogma and conscience.
The text alternately celebrates this freedom and condemns it, placing entertainment in the context of final judgment and reminding the reader that
freedom abused is license. As an object unto itself, *La pícara Justina* prioritizes a lack of restraint in deed and discourse, while the *aprovechamientos* link
the text to the world and make the present moment part of an eternal
scheme. The narrator justifies her work as entertainment without fully
convincing the reader of its enlightened vision. As a self-consciously conventional gesture, the author coats the wanton account with studied virtue.

The introduction presents a framework for the text and a format for the
relation between author and narrator, and it foregrounds Justina's linguistic
skills. Here, as throughout the narrative, one discovers a mistress of the
word whose art becomes a type of structure of consciousness. If Guzmán de
Alfarache alternates story with moral digression, Justina does little but di-
gress at every phase of storytelling. The hair of the first section, for example, leads to word plays, symbolic interpretations, historical and mytholog-
ical allusions, fables, rhetorical analogies, refrains, and hieroglyphic or
emblematic representation.[13] Blowing on the hair, she stains herself and her
clothing and thereby progresses into a new set of verbal tricks. From there,
she finds additional digressive possibilities in the watermark. The obsession
with hair illustrates the inevitable suffering for sins of the past, as her
crowning glory falls prey to syphilis. The constant shifts aid the cause of
multiperspectivism, for Justina devotedly complements the bad with the
good, the bitter with the sweet, and the sweet with the useful. Within this
miscellany of free association, Justina speaks of the exemplary nature of her
manuscript, of her current social and physical status, and of the picaresque
life. There is method in her tangents. The salient features of her discourse
are its directness, its commitment to honesty at the expense of modesty, and
its virtuosity. Her willingness to push self-examination to the limit may
denote the presence of a male author who takes every opportunity to criticize and to satirize her actions or to make her the mouthpiece of such
criticism. Justina is quick, perhaps too quick, to make her impure blood,
her infirmities, and her calamitous existence the object of verbal abuse.
There are signs to indicate that the author does not withdraw from the text
between the opening verses and the closing admonition, and that he controls the irony of Justina's discourse.

Whatever subtextual strategies may be discerned from the discourse of
La pícara Justina, it is important to note that López de Ubeda creates a
protagonist who recounts her life from birth to her first marriage (with the
promise of a sequel) in a consistent style and with a literary sensibility.

While the author has the last word in each section, Justina has the major voice, even if it is not entirely her own. López de Úbeda makes the anti-heroine a specialist in proverbs, tales, historical and geographical data, and symbolic meanings. Justina ventures into the realm of the senses—debatably from the male perspective—to discuss general feminine psychology. The judgment of her own actions comes primarily from the author's commentaries as opposed to narrative introspection. More dedicated to details than to motives, Justina moves chronologically (and tangentially) from one episode to the next. In her role as narrator, she periodically considers the ramifications of her deceptions. As a character, she has little regard for the future and little regret for her errant ways. The four books of *La pícara Justina* share a common ground in Justina's greed and tricks to ensure economic security, in a figurative and literal return to her roots, and in the discursive plan. To comply with his moral aim, the author employs the narrator as speaker in the introduction to undermine the success and the self-determination of the young protagonist. In the text proper, he assumes the task of guardian of morality, while, at least quantitatively, Justina dominates the discourse. The interdependence of author and narrator marks an impressive collaboration that nonetheless precludes discursive freedom for Justina.

Book 1, "La pícara montañesa" (from the mountains, where most people have pure blood), begins with the narrator's comments on writing and with a defense of her endeavor. She has barely started to write when her first critic appears. Perlícaro ridicules the presumptuousness of her act. Is her story holy or significant? Is she a legitimate artist? Does posterity require the thoughts and deeds of a lowly, untrained, and undesirable woman? This case of devil's advocacy on the part of the author confronts the question of justification. Justina devotes far more space to answering Perlícaro's charge that she is old than to answering his condemnation of her literary enterprise, but the implied argument, based on fables and verbal emblems, is to let the book speak for itself and to judge it after the fact. The author comes into the text to censure Justina's vanity and humanity's inclination to use words for evil rather than for good. The antiheroine's discourse has detractors before her story commences.

The narrator maintains that the picaresque nature is hereditary, a premise supported by her family tree. The none-too-impressive ancestry leads to her parents, shrewd and unscrupulous innkeepers who give Justina a practical, if not pious, education. Justina's grief at the loss of her parents is short-lived. Of her lack of tears upon her mother's death, she notes, "Hay veces que, aunque un hombre se sangre de la vena cebollera, no quiere salir gota de agua por los ojos, que las lágrimas andan con los tiempos, y aquél debía de ser estío de lágrimas, y aun podré decir que unas lagrimitas que se me rezumaron salían a tragantones. ¿Qué mucho? Vía que ya yo me podía criar sin madre, y también que ella me dejó enseñada desde el mortuorio de mi padre a hacer entierros enjutos y de poca costa" (pp. 144–45; There are times when, although a man may even resort to peeling onions, not a drop of water will come from his eyes, for tears are at the mercy of the occasion, and this must have been the summer of tears, and I can even say that some little tears that did leak out came out in gulps. Indeed, I saw that I could get along without a mother, and she herself taught me on my father's death how to bring off a dry and cheap funeral). The passage shows an inherited insensitivity and an acquired self-sufficiency, as well as a comic and colloquial form of expression. The *pícara* is now an orphan who must fend for herself. She leaves her village to see the world and conquer.

Book 2, "La pícara romera," takes its title from the practice of making pilgrimages in memory of loved ones. Justina's adventures in the town of Arenillas are more secular than spiritual, as is logical of one whose goals are to dance and to travel. Justina has an extremely brief career as a religious devotee, then finds herself pursued by a zealous suitor, a bacon and pork dealer. Escaping him through deception, she participates in a celebration with acquaintances whose envy and ill treatment force her to move on. She meets up with a group of student-rogues dressed in religious habits and involved in mock-religious celebrations. The captain or "bishop" of the company, called Pero Grullo after a character in folklore, takes a liking to Justina and wants to add her to his flock. The rogues kidnap her and prepare for her seduction by their leader. Using reason, her feminine wiles, and a great deal of wine, Justina manages to outwit them and to hold them up to ridicule. To complete her revenge, she leads them to Mansilla, accuses them of robbery, and watches in delight as they flee. Home again, she enjoys the notoriety of her triumph. Having set out to complete a holy mission, she falls in with an unholy alliance. She prays only when Pero Grullo threatens to violate her, yet her salvation hardly makes her more devout. Her escape is not a moral victory but a demonstration of her ability to trick the trickster. The townspeople praise her as chaste, astute, and brave. The author denounces her as loose-living, lazy, and hypocritical.

Justina confesses that she has never felt any particular affection for the men of her village. Now that she has risen above the rustic life, she departs for León. Her journey marks the beginning of the second part of book 2. The author remarks, "Pondera, el lector, que los males crecen a palmos, pues esta mujer, la cual, la primera vez que salió de su casa, tomó achaque de que iba a romería, ahora, la segunda vez, sale sin otro fin ni ocasión más que gozar su libertad, ver y ser vista, sin reparar en el qué dirán" (p. 224; Ponder, if you will, reader, that evil grows by leaps and bounds, for if this woman, when she left home the first time, used the pretext that she was going on a pilgrimage, now, the second time, she goes without any other end or reason than to enjoy her freedom, to see and to be seen, without any regard for what people will say). In the midst of the holy activities of the cathedral city of León, Justina may observe the religious sites, but her mind is on money and men. An episode with a student-cardsharper shows Justina blinding her admirer with love only to defraud him of a gold crucifix, a symbol of the sacred ideals that she is rejecting. The (implied) author cleverly juxtaposes this episode with Justina's commentary on why hypocrites are abhorrent, based on an encounter with a thief dressed in hermit's garb. The protagonist is, of course, not beyond duping the hypocrite of his money.

Never quite devoted to her role as pilgrim, Justina covers herself with a cloak and places herself at a church door to beg for alms. Shortly after the account of her experience as a mendicant, she delivers a "sermon" on the glories of virtue, which ends, "No predico ni tal uso, como sabes, sólo repaso mi vida y digo que tengo esperanza de ser buena algún día y aun alguna noche, ca, pues me acerco a la sombra del árbol de la virtud, algún día comeré fruta, y si Dios me da salud, verás lo que pasa en el último tomo, en que diré mi conversión. Basta de seso, pues. Quédese aquí. Voy a mi cuento" (p. 303; It's not my custom to preach, as you know, for I'm only reviewing my life, and I tell you that I have hopes of being good someday and even some night, for I'm approaching the shade of the tree of virtue and someday I'll partake of its fruit, and if God gives me strength, you will see what happens in the last volume, where I'll tell of my conversion. Enough food for thought, now. Let's leave it here, and I'll get on with my story). She is still some distance away from the tree of virtue. She tricks a student, a widow, a barber who has helped her rob the widow, and others before a second triumphal return to Mansilla.

Book 2 of *La pícara Justina* sustains the format of book 1, differing only in the intensification of story and discourse. The tricks become more complex, with several cases of repeated crimes against the same victim. There is greater emphasis on role-playing and disguise and on the sacrilegious nature of Justina's behavior. She is an insincere pilgrim who uses León as her base of operations and nominal religious practice as a means to financial ends. Her contact with clerical figures is economically rather than divinely inspired, and she prays for the success of her sinful ventures. Just as Justina exploits those around her, the author forces his narrator to sermonize against the very transgressions that typify her behavior. Neither her promised conversion nor his promised sequel materializes, a fact that consciously or unconsciously adds to the irony. The successful homecoming is a return to the sins of the past and a prelude to those of the future. The motif of inheritance appropriately dominates the third book of the narrative. Throughout the text, Justina Díez acts according to a parental and ethnic legacy, a public notoriety, and an ironic code of self-betrayal inherited from her picaresque predecessors.

In book 3, "La pícara pleitista" (litigant), Justina quarrels with her siblings over the estate of their parents and is disinherited: "Para mí fue la justicia justicia, para mis hermanas misericordia" (p. 391; For me the court of justice was just, while for my sisters it was compassionate). To avenge the decision of the magistrate, she convinces a roguish admirer to rob the family coffers, and, with the newly acquired wealth, she departs for the town of Ríoseco. There she uses the stolen money to renew her claims. A "perverse" solicitor enters a suit but consumes her resources in the process. With finances depleted but spirit intact, she endears herself to three spinners—having changed her costume to fit the enterprise—whom she relieves of wool and profits. Justina meets her match in an elderly Moorish woman, a sorceress whom she calls "great-grandmother of Celestina." During the time that Justina resides with the old crone, she finds her ingenuity (formerly termed "grandiose," she informs the reader) of little avail. Fate intervenes, however. The old woman dies, and Justina claims to be her grand-daughter and only heir. Her acting achieves what her legitimate defense does not; a constable grants her the rights of inheritance. After resisting the "importunate" sacristan who handles the burial, Justina once more returns to Mansilla. Motivated by pride and encouraged by prosperity, she appeals the earlier judgment and obtains a favorable sentence. Now that she has resolved the problems of the past, she turns to domestic possibilities for the future.

Book 4, "La pícara novia" (bride), traces Justina's steps to the altar and, in the process, allows the narrator (and the implied author) to satirize some members of male society. The first of the suitors is Maximino de Umenos, a turner with illusions of grandeur. Ironically, or hypocritically, Justina rejects him for pretending to be more than he is. The next candidate is an equally presumptuous washerwoman's son who appears as a flagellant to woo Justina. In the third chapter of book 4, the narrator catalogs the aspirants to marriage, emphasizing vices that range from insincerity, egotism, ostentation, and rustic impropriety to excessive gravity. For Justina, the bottom line in courtship is the economic status of the suitor: "Gustamos las damas que haya pasajeros por nuestra puerta, que no es buen bodegón donde no cursan muchos. Pero no es ese el *finis terrae*, que ya la gallardía, gravedad, señorío—y aun el gusto y el amor—, por pragmática usual se ha reducido a sólo el dar. . . . El amor se declina por sólo dos casos, conviene a saber: dativo y genitivo. El primero por antes de casarse y el segundo por postre. ¡El diablo soy, que hasta los nominativos se me encajaron!" (p. 448; We women like to have travelers pass by our door, for a tavern can't be any good if few frequent it. But this isn't the be all and end all, since gallantry, seriousness, distinction—and even pleasure and love—as a general rule have been reduced to only giving. Love is declined in only two cases, to wit, the dative and the genitive. Devil that I am, even nominatives cramped my style!). Justina sacrifices some of her illusions to marry Lozano, a soldier given to gambling and defender of her estate in the suit against her brothers and sisters. She concludes the text with a description of the wedding ceremony and wedding night, then alludes briefly to her second marriage to a wealthy old man named Santolaja and a third and blissful marriage to none other than Guzmán de Alfarache.

In *La pícara Justina*, López de Ubeda creates a loquacious, irreverent, and intelligent narrator full of misdirected energy. Justina's verbosity is a family trait, her delinquency a product of heredity and environment, and her knowledge a synthesis of reading (a collection of works left in her parents' inn) and experience. The misdirected energy is the synthesis of a synthesis; the craving for financial security is the logical final stage of her upbringing and marginated position in society. Lineage and circumstances work against her, so she must fight on her own behalf. Unlike the defensive tenor of Lazarillo de Tormes or the confessional air of Guzmán de Alfarache, Justina's account carries no apologetic overtones. The narrator/protagonist follows the way of the world by differentiating theory from practice, by making action and diction functions of situation rather than of doctrine. She states boldly, "Ya ves que hago alarde de mis males, no a lo devoto, por no espantar la caza, sino a lo gracioso, por ver si puedo hacer buena pecadora" (p. 401; So you see I make a show of my wrongdoing, not in a devout manner, so as not to spoil my prospects, but in an amusing manner, to see if I can make a good sinner). Fully conscious of her picaresque tendencies—and given to dropping forms of the word *pícaro*—Justina relishes her nonconformist performance on the stage of life and on the pages of her manuscript as one who has nothing to lose. It is the author, not she, who professes to make a moral point.

The author superimposes himself on the structure of the narrative, poetically at the beginning of each section and morally at the end. In the poems, he strives for variety and a touch of humor. In the *aprovechamientos*, he appends instructive but commonplace adages to a blatantly antisocial text to remove *La pícara Justina* from the threat of inquisitorial stricture. The benefits are reciprocal in that the author enjoys moral superiority over his creation and the narrator enjoys a certain freedom of speech. From the opposing perspective, equally reciprocal, the author's presence in the text proper seems evident and Justina's liberated discourse may be an illusion. The depth of information, literary and otherwise, contained in the work suggests a background far more diverse than Justina's. The autobiographical thread belongs to the narrator, while the great quantity of non-narrative material—descriptions, judgments, anecdotes, customs, emblems—bears witness to the educational and experiential range of the author. The treatment of hypocrisy reflects an ironic strategy in which the narrator betrays herself by condemning others for a sin that she continually commits; this is the author's discursive version of tricking the trickster. In terms of plot, López de Ubeda builds unity around the themes of freedom, deception, and inheritance, with special emphasis on the latter. Justina is a product, perhaps victim, of biological and socio-historical factors that dominate her existence. She responds to and pursues the family legacy, fighting her closest blood relations and fighting the discrimination caused by her blood. Her means of survival in an inimical world is deception, just as the only power she can achieve is wealth. Criminality is freedom only in the most relative sense, and Justina is subject to control from without, both in society and in the text.

Following the lead of Delicado's Lozana, Justina flouts the rules of proper (feminine) speech, as well as the social proprieties. López de Ubeda makes a concerted effort to include what may be termed women's topics in *La pícara Justina*, but the series of observations bespeaks a male viewpoint. The manipulation of the female voice to evoke antifeminist (or pre-feminist) responses signals the inversion of perspective characteristic of the picaresque variations. In book 1, chapter 1, number 2, Justina discusses the basic generic roles: "El hombre fue hecho para enseñar y gobernar, en lo cual las mujeres ni damos ni tomamos. La mujer fue hecha principalmente para ayudarle (no a este oficio, sino a otros de a ratos, conviene a saber:) a la propagación del linaje humano y a cuidar de la familia" (p. 98; Man was made to instruct and govern, in which we women have no give or take.

Woman was made primarily to help him [not in this duty but in others from time to time, namely:] the propagation of the human race and looking after the family). In book 2, she provides male-oriented theories as to why women are restless, why women respond to rejection, why women favor possessions over the welfare of men (an inheritance from Eve) and why they are vain about their beauty.[14] Justina also credits her sex with the invention of false stories and stratagems: "La primera que oyó ficciones en el mundo fue la mujer. . . . La primera que buscó aparentes remedios para persuadirse que en un daño claro había remedio infalible, fue mujer. La primera que con dulces palabras hizo a un hombre, de padre amoroso, padrastro tirano, y de madre de vivos, abuela de todos los muertos, fue una mujer. En fin, la primera que falseó el bien y la naturaleza, fue mujer" (p. 345; The first in the world to hear falsehoods was woman. The first to seek outward cures to persuade herself that a clear injury had an infallible cure was woman. The first to use sweet words to turn a man from loving father to tyrannical stepfather and a mother of the living to grandmother of all the dead was a woman. In sum, the first to falsify goodness and nature was woman). Few readers, it seems, would deem this unqualified freedom of expression for the *pícara*.

In the throes of courtship and imminent marriage, the narrator further examines the nature of male-female relations in book 4. In chapter 4 ("On the Obligations of Love"), she declares that there are three reasons why a woman loves. The first is wealth, which she places above honor. The second is to preserve, albeit temporarily, the natural order and have man submissive to her as a slave of love. Justina notes that women react against dominion and subjection "although it is natural and for our own good" ("aunque sea natural y para nuestro bien," p. 455). The third reason stems from woman's nature to please ("dar gusto"). Wishing to make the best match possible and yet not disappoint anyone, women respond most strongly to the men who are most persistent. True to her sex, Justina yields to interest, presumption, and persistence in agreeing to marry Lozano. Idealized love and honor have no place in this pragmatic approach to holy matrimony. López de Ubeda transforms the sexual reprobate of *La lozana andaluza* into a virgin sinner. Justina's body is a selling point, but not for sale; she takes men's money and escapes before they can abuse her. On her wedding night, she laments her lack of education in the wifely duties and faces the nuptial couch with a certain degree of modesty. At the end of the narrative, Justina alludes to future volumes that will include accounts of her widowhood and a second and unfortunate marriage to Santolaja, which nonetheless leaves her with property she may share with Guzmán de Alfarache. She refers somewhat ambiguously to her current happiness ("el felice estado que ahora poseo," p. 465) while saying that she will be called the poor one ("la pobre," p. 466) in the fourth volume of her account. In any event, the interest from her second marriage presumably allows her to modify the criteria for selection of a third partner, a love match with the infamous Guzmán.

Early in the narrative, Justina mentions that she wrote the manuscript quite a while before ("Mil años ha que hice esta obrecilla," p. 79), so one must assume that the narrating voice is a composite of past and present. The text barely reflects the dual temporal scheme, however. There is no interplay between an unreflective past and a reflective present nor a dialectic of experience and contemplation, and there is only negligible difference between the Justina of the introduction and the Justina of book 4. For all her loquacity, insights, and data, the narrator resists self-examination, stressing detail and cross-reference over the implications of events. A dubious prosperity, reminiscent of *Lazarillo de Tormes*, marks an ending that shifts from the first wedding ceremony to the third marriage. A conversion that would link the work to *Guzmán de Alfarache* is conspicuous by its absence, with the exception of a fleeting remark. López de Ubeda responds parodically to Alemán's novel, retaining the moral lessons but separating them from the narrator/protagonist and greatly reducing their quantitative impact.[15] The *aprovechamientos* vindicate the author from negative reaction to story and discourse, while the associative thinking of the narrator justifies unlimited interpolations. Justina provides the reprehensible examples, the author provides a rhetoric of righteousness. Alemán and later Quevedo create protagonists who fight to deny their heritage, whereas López de Ubeda shows Justina's struggles to attain her birthright. With no facade of piety and no defensive maneuvers, she moves doggedly forward to reach her objective, as the author recasts her temerity in the framework of eternity, or of eternal damnation. The intricate use of language, exhaustive range of materials, and ironic exposure of hypocrisy proclaim an authorial presence who combines invention with subversion. *La pícara Justina* heralds the linguistic flourishes and discursive intrusions of *El Buscón* and the narrative syntheses of Salas Barbadillo and Castillo Solórzano.

LA HIJA DE CELESTINA

> Eran sus ojos negros, rasgados, valentones y delincuentes: tenían hechas cuatro o cinco muertes, y los heridos no podían reducirse a número; miraban apacibles a los primeros encuentros, prometiendo serenidad; pero en viendo al miserable amante engolfado en alta mar, acometían furiosos y—usando de aquella desesperada resolución "Ejecútese luego"—daban fin a su vida.

> Her eyes were black, almond-shaped, arrogant, and delinquent: they had caused four or five deaths, and the number of wounded was beyond calculation. They looked gentle on early encounters, promising serenity, but on seeing the unfortunate lover adrift on the high seas, they attacked furiously and—using that desperate decree "Execute at once"—put an end to his life.

In *La lozana andaluza*, the protagonist has a decisive voice in a dialogue that makes her its object. In *La pícara Justina*, the narrator/protagonist develops a voice despite the intrusive tactics of the author. The title character of *La hija de Celestina* is dead at the time of narration. Reviving her for the cause of literature, the third-person narrator gives her space in which to recount her family background and early years. She has an opportunity to demonstrate her ingenuity and rhetorical skills in the dialogue, while he provides the structural and moral frame. Salas Barbadillo makes self-consciousness a function of the detached narrator, presenting the protagonist Elena in action rather than in contemplation. The synthesis of story and discourse stems from a commitment to style, to humor, to the picaresque tradition, and perhaps only secondarily to instruction. Salas Barbadillo treats crimes as entertainment and punishment as compliance with a social and literary order. He brings morality into the picture after establishing a burlesque tone, after dealing with his sinful antiheroine in terms more jocular than doctrinaire. The concern with ethics becomes anticlimactic and somewhat inconsistent with the narrative discourse. Through a determinism rooted in socio-genetics and intertextuality, Elena repeats the errors of her mother, a woman who invites comparison with Celestina herself. The frequent intervention of fate in the narrative underscores Elena's destined retribution for the evil that she pursues—and that the writer and presumably the reader enjoy—but it also indicates a lack of free will. The protagonist falls victim to the flaws of genealogy, the whims of fate, and the ironies of discourse, none of which she is in a position to control. At the expense of motivation and a female voice, the narrator organizes the material to distance Elena from the spirit and the actualization of the text.

La hija de Celestina has no prologue; the "intention" is to be found in the text proper. The narrative begins with Elena's arrival in Toledo, where she initiates a scheme that becomes the major episode of the novel. The story opens in medias res, with a promise to save the details of the protagonist's birth and origins for a "more agreeable place." The narrator's description of Elena accentuates her beauty and her mendacity, as well as his interest in verbal wit: "mujer de buena cara y pocos años, que es la principal hermosura; tan subtil de ingenio, que era su corazón la recámara de la Mentira, donde hallaba siempre el vestido y traje más a su propósito conveniente. Persona era ella que se pasara diez años sin decir una verdad: y lo que más se le ha de estimar es que nunca la echaba menos, y vivía muy contenta y consolada sin sus visitas" (a woman fair of face and of few years, which is the foremost beauty; so subtle of intellect, that her heart was the dressing room of Falsehood, where she always found the clothing and costume most suitable to her purpose. She was a person who could go for ten years without saying a word of truth, and what is even more noteworthy, she never felt its absence, but lived happily and comfortably without its visits).[16] Elena can weave a web of lies that lasts a full year. So adept is she at "weaving" that one could scarcely find a more industrious or "homespun" type. Her black, bold, and "delinquent" eyes have killed a few and wounded countless others. Her every deed warrants a chronicle of its own. In sum, "¡Oh, qué mujer, señores míos!" (p. 134; Oh, what a woman, my good sirs!), cries the narrator to his reading public. In this introduction to the protagonist, one can note an enthusiasm on the narrator's part for his subject and for writing as a creative process. She is a femme fatale who breaks hearts and bends the truth. He is a humorist who can speak of the "noble spirit" that guides her actions and keep a straight face. At this point, neither seems particularly consumed by moral questions.

Following the introductory portrait, the narrator foregrounds Elena's modus operandi. He links her to the cunning society of *pícaros*, which he describes with tongue in cheek: "Mezclábanse al descuido entre la gente, y, como padres comunes de bolsas desamparadas, si hallaban alguna huérfana la recogían con tanta caridad que la hospedaban en su mismo pecho" (p. 137; They mingled nonchalantly among the people, and, like common fathers of helpless pocketbooks, if they found one orphaned they would take it in with so much charity that they gave it a home in their very breast). In Toledo, Elena meets and immediately enamors Antonio de Valladolid, a wealthy gentleman's page, who reveals that the old man is in the city to attend the wedding of his nephew and heir. The bridegroom, Don Sancho, is a profligate whose treatment of women has caused the uncle a considerable amount of grief and has cost him a considerable amount of money. Elena uses all her wiles to conquer Antonio. Satisfied that she has sufficient information to initiate her scheme, she locks Antonio in a room and absconds with a dagger belonging to Don Sancho. With the aid of her lover ("brother") Montúfar, she appears before Don Rodrigo de Villafañe claiming to be a woman dishonored by his nephew. She employs the feminine weapon of tears ("perhaps more powerful than speech") and delivers the dagger as proof of her forced seduction. Elena requests funds for entry into a convent, and Don Rodrigo complies. Having converted a true story into a lie, the antiheroine displays her powers of invention. Richer for their efforts, she and Montúfar escape toward Madrid.

In chapter 3, commenting on the flight of Elena and Montúfar from Toledo, the narrator strikes a moral chord. Those who live badly, he says, will never have a permanent home and will always be awaiting punishment through human and divine justice. Criminals often die young, or, if they survive, they face desertion once their skills falter. Who would choose the lowliness of a vice that may rob one of twenty years at the hands of an executioner over devotion to God and honor? As the criminal pair travel, they feel fear ("a very hard bed in which no one rests") and, in Montúfar's case, a certain regret. To distract him, Elena speaks of her early years and of her family. This distraction is a narrative pretext to present the origins of the protagonist. Elena was born in Madrid to a Galician footman named Alonso Rodríguez, a great friend of the vine, and to a Moorish slave named Zara, who entertained men when sent to wash clothes along the banks of the Manzanares. Zara's expertise in the bewitching arts, notably the restoration of virginity, wins her the title of "Celestina" after the queen of bawds. Her husband, meanwhile, is so faithful to his drinking habit that his "devotions" often last for days on end. Alonso dies after entering a bullring in a drunken stupor; the neighbors comment on the appropriateness of his form of death, a cuckold (*cornudo*) killed by horns (*cuernos*). The surviving wife and daughter force a few tears and go about their business. Before Elena reaches the age of fourteen, her mother decides to offer her to the public ("abrir tienda," to set up shop) and finds a number of takers. Zara sells Elena three times as a virgin, to a rich clergyman, to a titled lord, and to a Genoese who spends all his money on her and dies in debtors' prison. Fearing the law, Elena and her mother flee toward Sevilla. On the road, thieves kill Zara, and Elena returns to Madrid, where she meets Montúfar and gives her heart for the first time.

The narrator opens chapter 4 with a condemnation of impure love, which makes its victims abandon what is natural and good for the unacceptable: "Tan torpe es la condición de nuestro apetito, que aborreciendo el manjar limpio y saludable, jamás se ve harto del más dañoso y grosero" (p. 166; So vile is the nature of our appetite that, loathing the clean and healthful dish, it never has its fill of that which is most harmful and crude). Don Sancho, a prime example of the errant soul, awakens from his wedding night with thoughts of the beautiful woman he saw on the streets of Toledo, none other than Elena. When his uncle informs him of the deception, he sets out in a rage to catch up with the perpetrators. His servants detain Elena's coach, and he rebukes them for suspecting so angelical a figure. Elena invents an identity for the occasion, passing herself off as a married lady willing to arrange a tryst in Madrid at a later date. Beauty and ingenuity stand her in good stead for the moment. Free from danger but warned by fate, Elena and her accomplice make their way to Madrid.

Burning with passion, Don Sancho searches in vain for his beloved lady, while Elena, Montúfar, and an elderly female companion named Méndez dress as pilgrims and leave for the city of Burgos. So, coincidentally, does the jilted lover, to attend to his dying brother. At this time, Elena begins to have negative feelings toward Montúfar, whom she considers cowardly and shallow. Méndez shares the opinion. She reminds Elena that she is not getting any younger and advises her to parlay her wealth into a respectable marriage. When Montúfar becomes seriously ill, the two women spout hypocritical platitudes about accepting death gracefully and take their leave. Montúfar recovers, vowing to avenge their desertion. He finds them, binds them to a tree, parodies their sermons on death, and flees. Don Sancho, whose brother is convalescing nearby, discovers Elena and Méndez, who recognize him and believe that heaven has now caught up with them for the sins of the past ("le reconocieron y pensaron que el Cielo había señalado aquel día para que pagasen en él todos los pecados que habían hecho en muchos," p. 190) A peasants' quarrel distracts Don Sancho for a few moments, and when he returns, the women have vanished. Fate works in strange ways.

In chapter 7, the narrator responds to a hypothetical objection to plot developments, specifically the issue of verisimilitude in the disappearance of Elena and Méndez. "Calm down, pedant," he cries to the potential detractor as he cites the proverb, "Quien bien ata, bien desata" ("He who ties well, unties well"). It turns out that Montúfar quickly regrets his decision to rid himself of his source of income. He frees the women and, in the spirit of renewed friendship (and self-interest), the three colleagues in crime make their way to Sevilla. They spend several profitable years in the southern city, donning religious habits and prospering from donations collected in the name of the poor and unfortunate. When a former acquaintance threatens to expose the sinners, Montúfar practices deception through honesty, publishing his wicked ways for all to hear. The calculated repentance wins more converts to the unholy cause. People of all social classes seek their advice, request their prayers, and give them money. Lest one might think that the success endures, the narrator interpolates: "Enojóse el cielo y, no pudiendo sufrir que tanta maldad durase permaneciente, corrió la cortina de la hipocresía de golpe y viéronse desnudos sus vicios" (p. 205; Heaven was angered and, being unable to tolerate that so much evil would endure, all of a sudden unveiled the hypocrisy and exposed their corruption). Montúfar routinely beats his servant, who in retaliation denounces him before the law. Elena and Montúfar escape in time, while Méndez receives four hundred lashes for her complicity and dies shortly thereafter. The other servants receive a punishment of two hundred lashes and banishment from the kingdom. The narrator notes that all leave jail on the same day, she for the grave and they to begin their exile. Temporarily pardoned, Elena and Montúfar continue on the road to perdition, a road that comes to an end in the final chapter.

Rich and newly married, Elena and Montúfar make their way to Madrid after verifying that Don Sancho is in Toledo. The "honorable gentleman" arranges for his wife to have frequent paying visitors. All goes well until Elena admits the attentions of one Perico el Zurdo. Overcome with jealousy, Montúfar punishes his wife, who answers in kind, with poison in his dessert and a death blow from her lover. For their efforts, Perico is hanged and Elena garroted and her body thrown into the Manzanares. In her will, Elena stipulates restitution for Don Rodrigo de Villafañe (now deceased) and Don Sancho (now moved to reform). The third victim of the swindle, the page Antonio de Valladolid, mends his ways to enter the religious life. The narrative ends with a satirical epitaph for Elena, written by an "illustrious" poet of Toledo who draws on her ignoble birth, life, and death for his composition.

The narrator elects to close Elena's story with a comic variation of a serious form. The narrative frame of La hija de Celestina prioritizes humor and verbal show, inserting moral doctrine either after the fact or in conformance with the satirical tone. The protagonist's posthumous retribution allows for the type of updating found in later novels. The principals of the major episode, the libertine Don Sancho and the undisciplined Antonio, vow to mend their ways, yet there is no deep moral message here but rather a tying up of loose ends. Elena's final act may make her seem less reprehensible, but again this serves no moral purpose, given that she fully merits the verdict rendered her for killing Montúfar. Final judgment comes from the court and from above; the narrator offers little ethical commentary in the second half of the narrative. He calls Montúfar's beating by the crowd in Sevilla a "just reward" (chapter 7) and then allows honesty to perpetuate the deception. When Montúfar serves as Elena's pimp (chapter 8), the narrator refers to him as a "beloved husband" who tries to introduce his wife to men of substance, though "more in the pocketbook than in the mind."

The sins against the sacrament of marriage occupy a humorous rather than a moral space in the text. The final showdown between the jealous husband, the vengeful wife, and her lover would lend itself to a discussion of poetic or divine justice, but the narrator offers instead an epitaph that mockingly speaks of the departed protagonist's virtue and innocence. The poet of the epitaph recalls her uninspired origins, just as the end in the Manzanares brings the narrative full circle to the site of her parents' first encounter. Elena is trapped in a deterministic blind alley. In a regimented and intolerant society, she fulfills a destiny that gears her to repeat the errors of the past. In an equally predetermined text, she becomes the victim of the narrator's verbal and structural machinations, literary defenses against her identity and authority.

If Lozana strives for survival at all costs and Justina for financial security, Elena—who also seeks as much comfort and wealth as possible—seems devoid of any sense of remorse for her crimes. Corruption appears to be, for whatever reason, the only option available to her, and she makes a sport of her transgressions. Only in her will does she show a sign of generosity or a departure from self-interest. In life, she uses her beauty to entrap men and to rob them of their purses, taking recourse to the eternal only as a means of defrauding the righteous in the here and now. The alliance with Montúfar parodies the ideals of a Christian marriage and the goals of Christian charity. At one point, each leaves the other to die, and at another point, they fight to the death. When the narrator presents Elena's thoughts, they invariably relate to criminal or selfish concerns. When Elena herself becomes the narrator of her family history, her discourse echoes that of the other narrator, with the added irony of her role as agent and object of the humor.

Through the willingness of the antiheroine to reveal the flaws of her parents, as well as through the intertextual tie with Celestina, the implied author negates the value of her voice. She is not a woman speaking for herself but an extension of the narrator. The reference to her sexual initiation(s) bears no trace of resentment, introspection, or modesty; she provides facts but no feeling, no sympathy, not even self-pity. One must conclude that she is so hardened to her environment that she rejects or does not recognize other options, or that the lack of freedom in society finds an analogue in the restrictive text, a text in which the narrator quotes her in his own voice. Whether heredity, environment, fate, or literary determinism is responsible, Elena's story gives the protagonist no room for development, no comprehension of her status in society, and no conscience. The discourse of *La hija de Celestina* reflects this situation by making entertainment the primary message and by denying Elena an individuated voice in the text that bears her name. The death of the antiheroine is as much a subtextual statement as a punishment.

Salas Barbadillo acknowledges his debt to literary tradition in the epic convention of an opening in medias res.[17] Although Elena changes very little in the course of her story and her retrospective view of the past has no notable impact on what precedes or follows it, the narrator makes a case for the present as a function of the past. Zara's relation to Celestina gives Elena a fictional as well as a biological antecedent for waywardness. The self-consciousness of the writing process on the part of a narrator separate from the protagonist corresponds to the general structure of *La lozana andaluza*, in which the figure of the author carries the discursive burden. In *La hija de Celestina*, the self-conscious commentary seems to have several functions: to avert criticism of the narrative technique, to highlight literature over reality (and thereby differentiate between the two), and to accentuate the humor of the text. The jocular attitude of the narrator toward the material belies the alleged moral commitment and, metacritically speaking, a concept of the picaresque as a study of the interior self. The protagonist does not lament her wrongdoing, nor does she profess a last-minute conversion. She attempts to settle accounts on earth without looking toward a final judgment. She offers no defense of her actions and in fact does not speak in the last three chapters of the novel. Her silence puts her at the mercy of a narrator (and an implied author) more disposed to fit a dose of morality than a bit of soul-searching into the comic base. The discourse of *La hija de Celestina*, specifically the satirical tone and linguistic humor, directs the reader to the mode of comedy. If the events themselves suggest another—and tragic— story, that does not seem to be the story that interests Salas Barbadillo. The ready-made woman of (criminal) action follows her fateful course as the narrator converts her sins into a diversion with appended morality.

TERESA DE MANZANARES AND *LA GARDUÑA DE SEVILLA*

> A los nueve meses de casados ya Teresa de Manzanares había visto este mundo, saliendo a él con buen alumbramiento de mi madre. Fue grandísimo el gusto que tuvo el francés con mi nacimiento y, igual a él, el cuidado con que me crio hasta edad de siete años; salí con razonables alhajas de la madre naturaleza en cara y en voz; mi viveza y prontitud de donaires prometieron a mis padres que había de ser única en el orbe y conocida por tal.

> When they celebrated their ninth month of marriage, Teresa de Manzanares had already come into the world, making my way in a safe childbirth for my mother. My father the Frenchman reacted to my birth with the greatest of pleasure and, by the same token, treated me with great care during my first seven years. I turned out with reasonable gifts from Mother Nature in regard to face and voice. My liveliness and sharpness of wit showed my parents that I had the promise to be unique in the world and famous as such.

Like Salas Barbadillo, Castillo Solórzano uses the picaresque model more as a source of narrative unity than as an exploration of the self or of the individuated voice. Moving from Italianate forms to a sustained narrative in *Teresa de Manzanares*, *El bachiller Trapaza*, and *La garduña de Sevilla*,[18] he shifts from first-person to third-person narrative and from female to male protagonists with little change in technique or tone. Social codes marginate the central characters, who must rely on their wit to survive. They oppose the society that opposes them, taking recourse to role-playing and deception only to be exposed and punished in the end. Events proceed in rapid succession, relieved by verbal humor and literary variations. Introspection and morality rarely intrude, and then merely to comply with conventions observed by the author. Castillo Solórzano's narrative persona, be it Teresa de Manzanares or a third-person narrator, becomes the agent of a burlesque discourse that favors storytelling over social psychology and the status quo over social change. A subtle determinism marks the direction of Castillo Solórzano's texts. Bloodlines, class consciousness, society's view of justice, and (in the case of Teresa and Rufina of *La garduña de Sevilla*) gender limit the possibilities of success. The implied author underscores the liabilities by removing the protagonist from the discourse, first figuratively and then literally.

In the prologue of *Teresa de Manzanares*, the author asks that the tricks of the antiheroine dissuade the public from falling victim to those of her ilk. He insists that readers who would condemn the work as malicious miss the point of its negative examples; the "intention" is to warn against moral oversights and to teach a lesson while entertaining. In a brief introduction, he repeats the admonitory rationale in the hope that the life of the protagonist will shield the readers from the dangers of a loose ("libre") existence. At the beginning of the introduction, between the obligatory attempts at justification, he describes the work in terms that reflect the adventurous spirit of the protagonist, his own interest in verbal creation, and a synthesis of sorts between heredity and natural inclination: "Escribo la vida, inclinaciones, costumbres y máquinas de una traviesa moza, de una garduña racional; taller de embustes, almacén de embelecos y depósito de cautelas. Con sutil ingenio fue buscona de marca mayor, sanguijuela de las bolsas y polilla de las haciendas. Con lo vario de su condición fue malilla de todos estados, objeto de diversos empleos y, finalmente, desasosiego de la juventud e inquietud de la ancianidad. Parte de estas cosas heredó por sangre y mamó en la leche, y parte ejecutó con travieso natural y depravada inclinación" (I write the life, leanings, habits, and schemes of a roguish girl, of a rational thief: a factory of deception, storehouse of tricks, and depository of guile. With subtle inventiveness, she was a pilferer of the highest order, a sponger of purses, and a consumer of property. In her variable state, she was a trump card for all purposes, the object of diverse employment, and, finally, a cause for restlessness in the young and uneasiness in the old. Part of these things she inherited through blood and absorbed in her mother's milk, and part she carried out with dissolute temperament and depraved inclination).[19]

The account that follows shows Castillo Solórzano's willingness to make entertainment his top priority. By subordinating Teresa's voice and the professed moral intention to the profusion of events and the mocking tone of the narrative, he demonstrates a picaresque consciousness based on plot and pre-history. The author within the text of *La lozana andaluza*, the moral commentaries of *La pícara Justina*, and the third-person narrator and death of the antiheroine in *La hija de Celestina* supply forms of didacticism in the earlier feminine picaresque. Apart from the prefatory materials, Castillo Solórzano leaves it to the reader to determine exemplarity through induction. Delicado's portrait of Lozana is at once a portrait of Rome's demimonde, a view of self and circumstance that ends with a departure from the city, and a promise of conversion. López de Ubeda and Salas Barbadillo reduce the panoramic vision to focus on significant events in the life of the protagonist. In a synthesis of sorts, Castillo Solórzano keeps the antiheroine in the narrative center while projecting her into numerous situations that reveal her modus operandi and seal her fate. She moves through Spain and through forms of narrative, poetry, and drama to return to her source. Her protean nature facilitates changes of identity without discovering an interior self equipped to triumph in society. The author who controls her voice allows the rules of social discourse to frustrate her pretensions. He foregrounds the factors and motives of her evil deeds and ignores a compensatory human goodness. The text that provides a voice without interiority mirrors a world dependent on appearance. The text settles for humorous episodes and language, the world for a self-protective status quo. Among the victims of these systems are women subjected to silence. The silence is, of course, figurative. Teresa's speech occupies the nineteen chapters of the text, beginning with the courtship of her grandparents and ending with marriage to her fourth husband.

Teresa's grandmother conceives her mother out of wedlock, marries the man responsible, and dies with him from overeating. The orphaned Catalina, seduced and abandoned by a canon's servant, finds her way to Madrid. Washing clothes on the banks of the Manzanares, she has a steady stream of admirers, including a peddler from Gascony who capitalizes on the *locus amoenus* and then marries Catalina. Shortly after Teresa's birth, her father dies on a drunken spree. Her mother runs a lodging place, takes on a lover who dupes her out of her money, and dies of shame after being abandoned by him. This leaves the ten-year-old Teresa an orphan and a precocious skeptic concerning men. Teresa, already known as an adolescent trickster ("la niña de los embustes"), goes to live with the two widowed sisters who have taught her needlework, but her social and monetary appetites lead her to seek a husband, whom she finds in an elderly and wealthy widower. Marital bliss is short-lived, largely due to the old man's inordinate jealousy. Teresa's scheme to frighten her husband is so effective that it provokes his death. On the road to Córdoba, her party of travelers is assaulted and robbed, and Teresa escapes just as she is about to be raped by the band of thieves. She is given shelter by a hermit, who narrates the amorous cause of his reclusion. With the aid of the hermit, Teresa finally reaches Córdoba, where she establishes herself as a tradeswoman. One of her admirers is pursuing a woman who has given her attentions to a eunuch, and Teresa invents a plot to punish the eunuch. To escape vengeance, she takes refuge in Sevilla but returns to Córdoba in disguise to see the dramatic interlude (*entremés*) commissioned as a continuation of the scheme.

Recalling the hermit's tale, Teresa travels to Málaga and claims to be Feliciana, the long-lost daughter of Don Sancho de Mendoza and the hermit's former lover, Doña Leonor. She is treated regally until the real Feliciana, who has been ransomed, appears. Her plan thwarted, Teresa moves to Granada. She attends a play and discovers that her former lover Sarabia is playing the leading role. They marry shortly afterward, and Teresa gains fame as an actress and singer. Sarabia begins to gamble heavily, and his indifference encourages Teresa's love affair with a nobleman. When the theater manager—angered because of his unrequited love for Teresa—cuts her role, she feigns sickness and submits white wine for urinalysis. Sarabia composes an *entremés* to ridicule the doctors tricked by Teresa. They, in turn, hire assassins to kill Sarabia. The company has been in Sevilla at this time, and the widowed Teresa decides to remain there. She is courted by the wealthy Don Alvaro Osorio and pretends to be of noble birth. After their marriage, Don Alvaro keeps Teresa secluded, and her only companion is his sister, Doña Leonor. On one of their rare excursions, Teresa and Leonor meet two gentlemen who show interest in them. One day when the women have arranged a rendezvous, Don Alvaro surprises them, but he sees only Leonor and stabs her to restore his honor. He then retires to a monastery, where he dies of grief. Leonor, who has recovered, receives the major portion of the inheritance and marries her suitor. Teresa's noble aspirations are quelled when one of the members of the acting troupe identifies her and Leonor's husband forces her to leave his home. Teresa moves to Toledo, where she plots an elaborate trick, resulting in the robbery of her own money and jewels. Having returned to Madrid, she weds for the fourth time, claiming total discontentment with her new partner, a merchant from Alcalá who gives her three stepchildren. Teresa promises a sequel, to be entitled *La congregación de la miseria* (*The Congregation of Misery*), which will recount her life with the merchant and the four children she bears him.

In *Teresa de Manzanares*, Castillo Solórzano combines what he calls bad blood and evil inclinations to produce a compendium of tricks, justified in ethical terms by the allusions to negative exemplarity and by the continual defeat of the antiheroine. Diversions in themselves, the tricks become the unifying threads of Teresa's life. In a world of appearances, the highest reality is social acceptability, which must be inherited, not won. Those who challenge the hierarchical structure must fail if the system is to be preserved, and, as long as Teresa fails, the author can amuse his reader with her antisocial escapades. Through the irony of discourse, the narrator's voice works against her to reveal the illegitimacy of her pretensions. The narrator goes out of her way to ridicule her family and herself. Society makes her the butt of its prejudices, and an implied author makes her the butt of verbal humor and a self-betraying discourse. The text proceeds from one deception to the next with no attempt on Teresa's part to defend herself, to reconcile her actions, or to comprehend her behavior. The scope of the narrative and the arrangement of events present a demythified eternal return, a vacuous circularity that the author attributes to lineage and temperament and that the subtext attributes to a lack of options. The elusive social freedom finds a discursive analogue in the wordplay and mockery that alienate the narrator from her story. Teresa's insensitivity (to the eunuch, for example) matches an authorial insensitivity to her human dimensions. The implied author removes the character from her psychological context and underplays society's role in her conduct. Heredity and personal inclinations, not environment, mark Castillo Solórzano's determinism, yet Teresa's nature is fully the product of social conditioning. She follows the lead of her mother and her grandmother because that is her only course.

The early chapters of the novel illustrate the intervention of an implied author, who puts the narrator in the position of satirizing her family tree. She associates her grandfather with thieves and describes the premarital intimacy of her grandparents in a ludicrously antipastoral setting, a pasture where cattle are grazing. These are people who die not from service to God, country, or love but from gluttony, who embarrass rather than glorify their progeny. Saving herself for marriage, the orphaned Catalina capitulates when she becomes enamored of Tadeo, like Quevedo's Pablos a native of Segovia. She robs her aunt and Tadeo robs her, leaving her stranded and unable to return home. Making her way to Madrid, she repeats history by conceiving Teresa in a far from idealistic locale (the Manzanares, replete with washerwomen) and by marrying a man with immoderate tastes. The motif of the inn—where Catalina works for her aunt, where she gains her first employment in Madrid, and where she earns a living as a widow—accentuates the sense of repetition. More strikingly, the background information stresses man's abuse of woman. When Catalina's lover absconds with her money, she dies of shame, leaving Teresa to fend for herself. First replaced in her mother's attentions, then removed from their shared bedroom to the maids' quarters, and finally deprived of maternal guidance, she recognizes that men are not to be trusted. As a trickster, Teresa often directs her stratagems against men who have done her little harm, perhaps in retaliation for the crimes of the past.

Teresa's guardians give her a "long sermon" on virtue, the only dowry and recourse for an orphan in search of honor. While pretending to accept this advice, Teresa serves as a go-between for the daughter of one of the widows and engages in trysts of her own. She claims to be the natural daughter of a nobleman to win her elderly first husband and discovers that marriage intensifies her subjugation. After the old gentleman's death, she decides to go into business for herself, practicing the art of wigmaking she has learned in Madrid. She chooses Córdoba because several ladies tell her that the trade is unknown there. Narrowly escaping death on the road, she meets the hermit, who implores her to lean toward the good and the virtuous. Following a brief and troubled career as a wigmaker in Córdoba, Teresa makes her way to Málaga to enact a metadrama based on the hermit's fact. If wigmaking reifies the powers of deception, the conversion of the hermit's account into a plan for self-advancement has sacrilegious overtones. Caught in one lie, she invents another to escape the wrath of Don Sancho de Mendoza. She says that heaven has declared the truth, then proceeds to lie about her origins and tearfully places herself at the mercy of the old gentleman. When Don Sancho allows her to leave with dresses and jewelry, Teresa considers this an act of the Lord, "so that we may know His goodness," but she avoids goodness as adamantly as she avoids the truth. She rejects a trade that would make her self-sufficient (and that is appropriate to her social class) in favor of an upward mobility that society and the author deny her. In Granada, she resolves to a degree the dialectic of ambition and caste by transferring her desires to the stage.

When Teresa attends a play in Granada, she discovers a link with the past in Sarabia, whom she had known when he was a penniless student in Madrid. Previously, the two had invented plots to mock her first husband, who died as a result, and now they form a theatrical team specializing in fictional plots. Both their marriage and their acting triumphs go sour through mutual dissatisfaction and an inability to separate dramatic illusion from social reality. Sarabia mistreats Teresa, which leads to his death. Teresa resists the advances of the manager of the troupe, acting offstage the devoted wife and widow. In Sevilla, she must contend with the confinement of her third marriage (which closely resembles the first) and with the threat of exposure. Again, her deceptive strategies bring about the death of her husband, the revelation of her background, and dismissal from a respectable household. As in the case of Pablos in *El Buscón*, her nemesis is named Don Diego, one who brings the past to bear on the present and who repudiates the concept of social climbing. Assuming a new identity in Toledo, Teresa leaves the stage but not the performing arts. Her plan to defraud an unsuspecting suitor is intricate yet unsuccessful, and she flees to Madrid, "like waters that return to their source." She takes up residence in what she calls the "pleasure district" of the city, where she suffers for her tricks. Rebuked and betrayed, she calls on Teodora, the daughter of one of her guardians, to arrange the fourth marriage. From this union, she acquires a mate, two sons and a daughter ("as wretched as their father"), and negligible assets and status. It is as if destiny conspired to castigate Teresa for her lofty goals. The past, here symbolized by Teodora, is inseparable from the present. For the person who denies this, the punishment is servitude in a "congregation of misery."

This conspiracy, as it were, reproduces itself in the discourse. When Teresa describes Tadeo, who robs her mother of her virginity, she uses the phrase "natural de Segovia, de los refinos hijos que aquella cuidad cría" (p. 141; a native of Segovia, one of the refined sons that city raises). The irony of the passage has meaning for the author and for the reader but not for Teresa as narrator, who would have little purpose in joking about her mother's disgrace, even if she were planning to attribute her own failures to her upbringing. When Tadeo deserts Catalina, Teresa recounts her mother's plight, stating, "Aquí comenzaron los trabajos de la gallega Olimpia, viéndose dejada del segoviano Vireno" (p. 143; Here began the trials of the Galician Olimpia, finding herself abandoned by the Segovian Vireno), an allusion to Ariosto's *Orlando Furioso* that perhaps befits the author more than the narrator. If the Segovian recalls Pablos, Teresa's conception on the banks of the Manzanares relates intertextually to Elena of *La hija de Celestina* and to Lazarillo and the Tormes, as well as to ironic discourse. Following the death of her first husband, Teresa momentarily rejects her suitor in a resolve to be a model for women ("con propósito de ser espejo de mujeres," p. 189), becoming instead a model of improper conduct. Protected by the hermit after the mishap on the road to Córdoba, she listens to his words and is apparently moved by them, but only until she leaves the spiritual refuge for more worldly ventures. The episodes in Córdoba, including the public embarrassment and disfigurement of the eunuch, provide the strongest examples of gratuitous crime in the narrative. From Córdoba, Teresa goes to Málaga, where she turns the hermit's tragic history into a charade. Saved from punishment, she continues her schemes in Granada and Sevilla. Sarabia's death gives her another occasion to profess disinterest in the obligations and conventions of love ("deseando huir de empeños y más de amor," p. 266), a determination undermined by the ironies of the third and fourth marriages.

In a few instances, Teresa expresses her feelings about events that affect her. While unduly coy about her lineage, she does not conceal her despair when her widowed mother takes a lover: "Así se enlazó en ambos una firme amistad, que la obligó a hacer expulsión de mí, acomodándome a dormir en la cama de la criada, cosa que yo sentí en extremo, y aunque niña, bien se me traslució la causa por que se hacía aquella novedad conmigo, con lo cual tuve ojeriza al huésped, que no le podía ver delante de mis ojos, de suerte que su presencia me helaba en lo más sazonado de mi humor" (p. 154; So a firm friendship linked the two of them, which obliged her to throw me out, setting me up to sleep in the maid's bed, something that grieved me deeply, and, though just a child, I clearly recognized the motive for such a change and held such a grudge against the guest that I couldn't stand the sight of him, to the extent that his very presence hardened me to the core). The expulsion from her mother's bed is a turning point for Teresa, a sign (like Lazarillo's encounter with the stone bull in chapter 1) that she must look out for herself and a notice that she must view man as the enemy. Because it is unique in the text, the passage carries discursive weight as an intimate revelation. Conversely, the infrequency of such passages supports the idea of an authorial voice-over, who gives the narrator limited space in which to air her views.

From her loveless marriages, Teresa becomes an authority on marital conflict. Calling herself Doña Teresa de Manzanedo and claiming distinguished predecessors, she marries Saldaña—three times her age—at sixteen. She considers her lies more a virtue than a sin, since everyone must strive for greater social prominence, but she soon regrets her decision to wed a man who turns into the stereotypical jealous husband. She warns parents not to allow their daughters to fall into this trap, noting that self-interest is the cause of the unnatural alliances. Sarabia is the one man that Teresa marries for love, yet the affection lasts only a short time. He gambles, pawns her clothes, beats her, and, worst of all, offers to have her serve her suitors. Teresa addresses the issue: "Una de las cosas que más hacen perder el amor que tienen las mujeres a los hombres es el verse desestimadas de ellos, y en particular ser tratadas como mujeres comunes y de precio. Visto lo que Sarabia me había dicho, desde aquel punto se me borró el amor que le tenía, como si no fuera mi esposo y le hubiera amado tanto" (p. 252; One of the things that most make women lose the love they have for men is to see themselves belittled by them, and in particular to be treated like common women available for a price. After what Sarabia had said to me, from that point on the love I felt for him was wiped away, as if he weren't my husband and I hadn't loved him so much). Embittered by domesticity, Teresa surprises herself by marrying a third time: "Escapé de un celoso; di en un jugador, y en el tercer empleo hallé un indiano que, si no fue jugador, era la suma miseria y los mismos celos" (p. 270; I escaped from a jealous one and landed on a gambler, and on the third go-round I found a Spaniard returned from the New World who, if he wasn't a gambler, was the height of stinginess and jealousy incarnate). Even the trauma of this marriage cannot diminish her idealistic and ultimately ill-conceived vision of wedded bliss.

On her arrival in Madrid, Teresa notes, "Nací en la corte y volvíme a mi centro, con algún caudal granjeado, no puedo decir que con buenos modos, porque el lector sabe cómo han sido en el largo discurso de mi vida, de que podía temer su poca duración, pues lo mal ganado ni llega a colmo ni se conserva" (p. 301; I was born in the capital and I returned to my center, with something of a fortune in stolen goods—though I can't say with the best of intentions, since the reader knows what these have been in the long discourse of my life—of which I well might fear its short duration, for that which is ill-earned never reaches culmination or lasts). In effect, the victims of the swindle in Toledo make their way to Madrid to avenge the theft. Teresa's servants betray her, and facing poverty she truly comes full circle. Her idealism fades as her prospects grow dimmer, and she settles for the merchant from Alcalá, "the crudest and most wretched man that nature ever produced." As Teresa closes the narrative with the promise of a sequel, her discourse merges with that of the author: "Para la segunda parte remito contar las vidas de todos, con nombre de *La congregación de la miseria*, libro que será de su gusto, cuyo volumen promete el autor de éste dar a luz con la historia de *Los amantes andaluces* y *Fiestas del jardín*, siendo Dios servido" (p. 309; I will hold off for the second part an account of their lives, with the title of *The Congregation of Misery*, a book that will conform to the reader's taste and that the author of this volume promises to bring out with the story of *The Andalusian Lovers* and *Garden Parties*, God willing). Teresa's voice conveys no pretense of freedom from its creator; its resonances are humorous and ironic, not personal. In his succeeding picaresque works, *El bachiller Trapaza* and *La garduña de Sevilla*, Castillo Solórzano allows a third-person narrator to carry the full burden of perspective.

In Castillo Solórzano's static view of psychology, ancestry and temperament—as opposed to developmental processes—rule human actions. Teresa ends where she begins. Rather than forming part of a progression, characterization and discourse relegate themselves to a series of misadventures. Despite its picaresque conventions, *Teresa de Manzanares* operates chronologically and psychologically in the world of romance, where character is ready-made and discourse uniform. The idea of improving one's lot, a desideratum common to picaresque narrative and linked to the verb *medrar*, is generally employed in an ironic sense. In the social system propagated by *Teresa de Manzanares*, the antiheroine is as doomed to fail as society is entitled to succeed. Teresa's proposal to outwit the establishment by taking advantage of its dependence on appearance exacts a high degree of adaptability. She selects a profession aimed at deceiving the eye (wigmaking), invents noble backgrounds, and changes her name to meet the circumstance. She lives in a world in which people make theatrical performance (for example, the interludes) a part of life, and she achieves fame as an actress. Ultimately, she attains neither wealth nor respectability in her union with two jealous old men, an uncaring young one, and a none-too-prosperous nor aristocratic nor sensual merchant who makes her mistress of a miserable household. In one of the rare cases in which Teresa rationalizes her misdeeds, her discourse reflects the world-as-stage metaphor and the precarious double bind of poverty and station. Not surprisingly, context determines content, and a second party determines the ironic direction of the narrator's words.

Following the death of her third husband, Teresa comments on her aspirations in Sevilla, "Pues en lugar donde tan conocida fui con varios papeles que había representado en sus teatros, supe hacer también el papel de la honrada, que merecí por esposa un principal hidalgo de lo mejor de Navarra sin que nadie me conociese, que no fue el menor embuste mío publicar estimación donde no la había para pescar aquel novio. No soy la primera que de esta estratagema se ha valido, ni seré la postrera; pues se debe agradecer en cualquier persona el anhelar a ser más, como vituperar el que se abate a cosas inferiores a su calidad y nobleza" (p. 284; Since in a place where I was so well known for the various roles I had played in its theaters, I also knew how to play the role of upright citizen, which I earned as wife of one of the foremost noblemen of Navarra without anyone knowing my real roots, it was not one of my lesser tricks to publicize my worthiness where it didn't exist to hook that suitor. I'm not the first to profit from that stratagem, nor will I be the last; moreover, one has to appreciate in anyone the yearning to be more and likewise should condemn one who would lower himself to things inferior to his rank and nobility). Fate and the implied author respond negatively to Teresa's explanation, suggesting that the end does not justify the means and that nobility is a function of birth. Honor, while not absolute, favors the upper classes and their self-perpetuating morality. The noble figures of *Teresa de Manzanares* exceed their social inferiors not in moral stature but in status, yet society resists the distinction. Teresa's expertise in the (meta)dramatic arts is of no avail. She cannot hide from the past, nor can she arrange a marriage that would give her honorability. Her nuptial couches are procrustean beds that bespeak the presence of an author aligned with the social hierarchy. The text substantiates the strictures of society against the individual, of pure blood against the impure, and of fixity against change.

Just as the picaresque archetypes invert the terms and the participants of idealistic narrative, *Teresa de Manzanares* represents a downgrading of the novel of lofty adventures, the *novela cortesana*.[20] The emphasis on a profusion of events, each with negative impact, creates a panorama of wrongdoing to complement the noble tone of the courtly works. Teresa's failed marriages oppose the sacrament of holy matrimony and the conventional ending of romance, as every stage of her story brings her further from her goals of riches, rank, and love (probably in that order). Castillo Solórzano substitutes union with a miserly merchant for reunion with a long-lost lover, thus placing the protagonist on a picaresque course of retribution for crimes against society. Circularity and repetition mark Teresa's ties with a constraining (and intertextual) past. Only in the theater do her dreams materialize. In an atmosphere of metaphors within metaphors, illusions prosper while illusory reality crumbles. Role-playing works in drama but not in life. If Teresa's world is a stage, the performance is directed from without by an author who re-creates a deterministic universe. Free will and control of self and circumstance are the true illusions.

Teresa's limited discursive authority becomes more evident in a comparison of the text with Castillo Solórzano's subsequent picaresque narratives. In *El bachiller Trapaza* and *La garduña de Sevilla*, the author relies on the combination of blood and temperament, role-playing, pseudonyms, a succession of tricks, and the specter of the past as a factor in the present. He asks the reader to penetrate the texts to discover an ethical message. He subjects the protagonists to humiliation and subordinates the carnivalesque world of diversion and deception to a hierarchy that he sustains and presumably respects. And, significantly, he creates a narrative voice not unlike the voice of Teresa de Manzanares. The comic, mocking tone of the implied author of *Teresa de Manzanares* reappears in the third-person narrator of the later works. Since storytelling here depends more on humor and on variations of trickery than on a shared intimacy between narrator and reader, the shift is hardly noticeable. Teresa is little given to introspection, and there is no narrative pretext comparable to Lázaro's response to Vuestra Merced. Self-consciousness derives from a synthesis of narrative tradition rather than from a focus on the act of composition.

El bachiller Trapaza contains two interpolated novels, an interlude, five love poems, and three satirical poems.[21] The character of Don Tomé in chapters 11 and 12 shows obvious traces of the squire in the third chapter of *Lazarillo de Tormes*. Trapaza is condemned to the galleys, as is Guzmán de Alfarache, to return as Rufina's father in *La garduña de Sevilla*. Like Pablos of *El Buscón*, he aspires (and conspires) to marrying above him by passing himself off as a wealthy nobleman, only to be defeated by the revelation of his lowly origins. In Salamanca, for example, he courts a lady from the most eminent family until he is exposed by her former suitor. The mortified Trapaza changes his residence and spends a period in isolation. As a final blow, his servants quit because his rank is lower than theirs. Again following Pablos, he reacts to social restrictions through unrestricted delinquency, settling for notoriety over nonentity. His tricks are often pernicious and—as in the case of Teresa's crimes against men—more an expression of general resentment than an attack on the victim. Time and again, poetic justice makes him a trickster tricked. Trapaza finds a kindred spirit, colleague, lover, and eventually a betrayer in the maid Estefanía, who turns him over to the authorities and bears his daughter Rufina.

Castillo Solórzano continues to emphasize storytelling as literary display in *La garduña de Sevilla*. Using an antiheroine, third-person narration, intercalated materials, and manifestly fraudulent behavior, he offers a portrait of Rufina with generic and even genetic ties to *Teresa de Manzanares* and *El bachiller Trapaza*. In a prologue to the reader, the author warns his public to read with discretion ("con buena intención"), for, if not, one may be tempted to reap only gratuitous diversion. Although the dedication presents the manuscript as a cautionary and reform-minded tract, the reader may find it difficult to detect a moral base. Life is not easy for Rufina, but while Teresa and Trapaza are left suffering, Castillo Solórzano closes *La garduña de Sevilla* with the antiheroine free from persecution and as owner of a modest business. There is no authorial message in the concluding passages, only the promise of a second part to feature "more witty tricks and ingenious swindles" ("más sazonadas burlas y ingeniosas estafas").[22] *La garduña de Sevilla* provides neither a personality nor a narrative persona in formation. Without the benefit or burden of self-analysis, Rufina makes society at large the object of her hoaxes. She responds to her legacy—lineal and literary—as the proverbial fish to water. With blood lines granting little hope, she depends almost exclusively on instinct. Her instincts lead to no good.

Rufina is mistress thief of Sevilla and a hook for her neighbors' purses, "garduña de Sevilla y anzuelo de las bolsas," related in habit to the marten (*garduña*), a relative of the weasel known for nocturnal thefts. The initial description of the protagonist sets the stage for the narrative events and recalls Castillo Solórzano's brand of determinism in *Teresa de Manzanares*: "Fue moza libre y liviana, hija de padres que, cuando le faltaran a su crianza, eran de tales costumbres que no enmendaran las depravadas que su hija tenía. Salió muy conforme a sus progenitores, con inclinación traviesa, con libertad demasiada y con despejo atrevido. Corrió en su juventud con desenfrenada osadía, dada a tan proterva inclinación, que no había bolsa reclusa ni caudal guardado contra las ganzúas de sus cautelas y llaves maestras de sus astucias" (p. 523; She was a loose and licentious girl, the daughter of parents who, when they could manage to attend to raising her, had such customs of their own that they could hardly correct the depraved habits of their daughter. She turned out quite in harmony with her progenitors, with a roguish temperament, too much freedom, and daring resolve. In her youth, she ran with unbridled boldness, given to such evil temperament that there was no such thing as a purse out of reach or a fortune safe from the picklocks of her cunning and the master keys of her astuteness). Rufina's inheritance from her parents is documented in *El bachiller Trapaza* and in her conduct. The lifelike portrait ("pintura al vivo") is, according to the narrator, a composite of a common type drawn to make the errant take heed, the reckless refrain, and the unwary take warning. With this third admonition to the reader, the text itself refrains from self-justification to proceed with the antiheroics.

Estefanía arranges to have Trapaza released from the galleys, and they marry in the presence of their five-year-old daughter. Trapaza returns to his former ways, putting his wife in such a state of anguish that she has no time to instruct and correct Rufina. The narrator comments, "Culpa de muchas madres, que por tener omisión en esto, ven por sus casas muchas desdichas" (p. 12; A fault of many mothers, who, neglecting this, see much disgrace fall upon their homes). Estefanía dies of despair over her situation. Rufina is twelve years old, the apple of her father's eye, and his only hope for financial security. The object here is a prosperous son-in-law, and to that end he allows Rufina the freedom to look and to be seen and the free will to make her own decision in the matter. His sole criterion is that "Rufinica . . . fuera una red barredera de las bolsas de la juventud que la festejaba" (p. 13; his little Rufina be a dragnet for the purses of the youths who courted her). The early pages of the novel contain the narrator's precocious concession to environment as a factor in Rufina's development. The illegitimate birth, the imprisonment of the father, the tumultuous reunion of the parents, the mother's negligence, and the father's self-interested permissiveness produce the antithesis of an exemplary childhood. Rufina will live up to—or down to—the example of her parents.

The fruit of the implicit contract between father and daughter is Rufina's marriage to Don Lorenzo de Sarabia, a gentleman in his fifties who has made his fortune in the New World. Sarabia is a kind and honorable man, willing to bear the burden of his father-in-law to win the bride. Rufina goes out every morning, supposedly to pray but actually to meet her lover, the roguish Roberto. When Roberto deceives her, Rufina plots revenge within hearing distance of her father, who challenges the young man to a duel and dies defending the honor of his adulterous daughter. Rufina's new lover, Feliciano, avenges the crime in a duel that takes place near Sarabia's study. Overwhelmed by his wife's betrayal of the holy sacrament, Sarabia dies of shame. A nephew takes Rufina to court and wins the estate for himself, leaving her "a widow and, what is even worse, poor." Given the tragic consequences of the events in this section, the narrator employs a consistently comic tone. Note, for example, the treatment of Trapaza's death: "Trapaza fue llevado a casa de su yerno, donde fue recibido dél agridulcemente: agria, en haberle de poner en costa el enterrarle, y dulce, por quitarse aquel embarazo de su casa" (p. 532; Trapaza was carried to his son-in-law's house, where he was received bittersweetly: bitter, for incurring the costs of burying him, and sweet, for removing that obstruction from the house). At the same time, "Rufina lloró a su padre con entrambos ojos. Diráme algún crítico que cuándo se ha visto llorar con uno" (Rufina cried for her father out of both eyes. Will some critic please tell me when a person has been seen to cry out of just one). The dishonored Sarabia takes so long to compose a letter explaining Rufina's treason and his plan to kill her that his heart gives out as he is midway into the fourth draft. Rufina moves to another part of the city, recognizing that her beautiful face is the key to her survival.

Rufina, whom the narrator calls spirited and lusty ("briosa y lozana"), finds her next mark in Marquina, a wealthy and middle-aged veteran of New World exploration. Marquina is such a miser that he fasts in order to guard his savings, which he keeps hidden in trunks behind his bedroom. Aided by Garay, a galley companion of her late father, Rufina wins Marquina's confidence with a made-up story of tragic love, complemented by feigned tears. Equally importantly, she wins his love. The narrator celebrates the victory with commentary on first love that occurs late in life, a passion capable of converting a miser into a prince of magnanimity and a Midas into an Alexander, and ultimately a madness that will destroy its victim. The commentary includes metacommentary on Rufina's ability as a storyteller, noting certain inconsistencies that would have compromised her had not Marquina been blinded and made deaf by all-consuming love. If her authorial skills need polishing, Rufina is an expert practitioner of the art of deception. She escapes with Marquina's treasure (sharing the silver with Garay and hiding the gold for herself), while the discovery of his loss sends the enamored miser from figurative to literal madness. Book 2 adds still another version of the smitten lover, in this case a Genoese merchant who allows Rufina to recuperate in his home after she becomes ill on the road. Octavio Filuchi, "a bird ripe for plucking," cannot defend himself against Rufina in the role of a noble widow and Garay in the role of an alchemist. He entrusts his wealth to them, and they depart for Málaga.

While hiding in the woods to escape arrest, Rufina and Garay hear robbers speaking of their leader Crispín, who conceals his identity in the guise of a hermit. "He knows so well how to dissemble with studied hypocrisy that he can deceive anyone," says one of the thieves. Books 3 and 4 are largely devoted to Rufina tricking the trickster by relying once more on her physical assets and quick wit. With spontaneous hypocrisy, she has Garay tie her to a tree, where she "lies tears and feigns anguish" so that the false hermit may save her. During her stay at the unholy hermitage, she conspires to relieve Crispín of his stolen goods. In this battle of impostors, captured by the narrator in a rhetoric of deception, Rufina manipulates her opponent by blinding him with her charms. She serves Crispín a soporific drug, appropriates his riches, notifies the chief magistrate of his whereabouts, and makes her way to Toledo with Garay. The law punishes all the robbers but one: Crispín walks out of jail on the day he is to be hanged, dressed as a woman and bent on punishing the woman who has betrayed him. In Toledo, Rufina and Garay establish new identities, she as a young noblewoman and he as her father. Crispín tracks them down and hires a Valencian rogue named Jaime to assist in the vengeance. Jaime wins Rufina as she had won Crispín, but in the process he falls madly in love with her and joins her to incriminate the former hermit. Crispín goes to the gallows and Garay, caught flagrante delicto, to the galleys. Rufina and Jaime marry in Madrid, where he plays the role of a poet to rob a theater manager, and end up in Zaragoza as silk merchants.

In *Teresa de Manzanares* and *El bachiller Trapaza*, Castillo Solórzano entertains his public while punishing the protagonists for their antisocial behavior. Teresa and Trapaza follow a pattern of initial success countered by poetic justice; they are constantly tricked by a fate that has literary dimensions. Each wants a noble spouse and is willing to use ignoble means to deceive the intended, only to contend with phantoms from the past and determinism from within. Their final (textual) rewards are a miserable fourth marriage and a term in the galleys, respectively. Their varied misadventures amuse readers while providing unobtrusive instruction. *La garduña de Sevilla* operates under the same general premises. It is a book of entertainments, mixing picaresque misdeeds with acknowledgment of a number of literary forms and containing three interpolated novels, five love poems, a satirical poem, and a satire on the drama of the day. A major difference, however, stems from the narrative system of crime and punishment. Although the narrator of *La garduña de Sevilla* breaks away from the rigid determinism of the earlier novels to speak briefly of environmental factors, he passes over the doctrinaire premise by permitting Rufina to succeed as a thief and swindler. After losing Sarabia's inheritance to his nephew, Rufina triumphs over Marquina, Octavio Filuchi, and Crispín, among others. She finds her male counterpart in Jaime, marries for love, and evades the law. The moral imperative inaugurates the discourse, fades, and then disappears. The text calls for what may be termed a moral vacation, a reading that disregards the disastrous results of Rufina's swindles and the concept of poetic justice. The antiheroine is not content to rob Crispín but schemes to cause his death. Their first encounter goes a stage beyond metatheater, as does Jaime's masquerade with the theater manager. The union of Rufina and Jaime is the ideal marriage turned inside out, an incipient victory for carnivalesque inversion.

The three novels of Castillo Solórzano vary the ironic treatment of honor found in *Lazarillo de Tormes*. The *Lazarillo* presents a debasement (perhaps deconstruction) of the lofty principles of the honor code when presented in the context of the lower classes. Lázaro's concern over social respectability, his imitation of the squire, and his reaction to domestic troubles parody points of honor already parodied in the ignoble birth, the service to the impoverished squire, and the marriage arranged by the archpriest. Castillo Solórzano involves dishonorable characters in honor tableaux. The chivalric duels of *La garduña de Sevilla*, for example, evoke a certain sense of incongruity when one considers the participants (a former criminal and his adulterous daughter's lovers) and the object (a woman who lies about her birth to dupe an elderly suitor). The desired ascent in society fails to materialize. Teresa marries a merchant and inherits his brood of undesirables. Trapaza, betrayed by his mistress, leaves for the galleys. Rufina must work for a living. Nothing disrupts the hierarchical social structure, and the antisocial activities of the protagonists promise earthly and divine retribution. Even the ambiguous conclusion of *La garduña de Sevilla*, viewed in the light of its literary precedents and the self-righteous introduction, suggests a continuation of crime and eventual punishment for Rufina.

Castillo Solórzano makes the series of swindles a constant of his narrative plotting. To give the tricks a gloss of edification, he devises a conventional moral frame. The intercalated materials add further adornments to the literary product, as do the variations on idealistic fiction. Somewhat ironically, the shift from antiheroine to antihero and the shift from the first- to the third-person narrator effect minimal changes in narrative direction. Teresa and Trapaza depend on lies about their social and economic status to seek noble spouses; a pseudonym accompanies each attempt. Teresa's trump card is her beauty, Trapaza's is his willingness to sacrifice all for the cause of delinquency. She narrates her own story but with a voice never really her own. Lázaro's discourse is ironic because he unknowingly (and with the aid of an implied author) reveals more than he seems to intend. Teresa's burlesque account of her origins and her adventures has no narrative pretext. There are no distinctly feminine qualities to her discourse and little that would distinguish her from the male narrators of *El bachiller Trapaza* and *La garduña de Sevilla*. Irony derives from linguistic and situational humor rather than from tension between story and discourse. *Lazarillo de Tormes* complements character development with a foregrounding of the act of composition. Castillo Solórzano's protagonists develop to a great extent outside of the text and thus promote no analogy with narrative process. The interrelation between story and discourse lies on levels of discordance. The texts mock the antiheroic figures as these figures mock social convention, thereby sustaining the status quo while offering emotional release and amusement. Nonconformity never exceeds established (or establishment) limits.

The Spanish feminine picaresque begins with a dialogic format that places the antiheroine in two models of interdependence, as the central feature of a portrait and as the object of discourse. *La lozana andaluza* depicts the protagonist's actions and re-creates her voice within a specific milieu. In both cases, circumstance helps to define self. Lozana interacts with her society and with the fictionalized author. He, in turn, uses multiple voices (including a variation of his own) to characterize Lozana. Verisimilitude and linguistic authenticity are obvious concerns of Delicado, who foregrounds the antiheroine's voice in the discursive scheme of the work. The portrait examines Lozana by combining words with deeds and by emphasizing the panoramic vision, by extending the pictorial analogue to story and discourse. The controlling presence of the author sets the direction of the text and at the same time brings the nature of the literary object into question. An ambivalent morality and a problematical reality make their way into the portrait, setting up the conceptual issues explored in *Lazarillo de Tormes*. The author of the *Lazarillo* directs discourse from behind the scenes, creating a paradigm of implied authorial control for the picaresque. Delicado anticipates the technique by allowing the artist a role—or rather, multiple roles—within and beyond the text. The artist fosters a dialectic between subject and object, not always differentiated. *Lazarillo de Tormes* builds on this base to present author and narrator, narrator and protagonist, and individual and society in opposition.

In *La pícara Justina*, López de Ubeda creates an antiheroine who narrates her own story, in conjunction with an implied author whose picaresque consciousness hints of satire. It is not the carnal desire of *La Celestina* that preoccupies Justina, but survival and success in a hostile society. For those without rank, success translates into money. *La pícara Justina* continues the mocking reaction to literary lineage (a prominent element of *Lazarillo de Tormes*) in the treatment of the protagonist's heritage and inheritance. The relish with which Justina undertakes deception seems a natural phenomenon, and each major episode leads her home. The economic attachment to her family ironically reinforces her marginal role in the social order and the stability of that order. In *Guzmán de Alfarache*, Alemán maintains an equilibrium of sorts between the formation of the delinquent and the conversion of the sinner. Guzmán speaks for both sides of the human struggle, while Justina commits herself only to delinquency. A second, authorial voice appends moral commentary to Justina's story in a manner that exaggerates its conventionality and its subordination to antisocial and linguistic play. Nonetheless, the authorial voice dominates the discourse of *La pícara Justina* as it does that of Quevedo's *Buscón*. Erudition, verbal intensity, and a lack of introspection suggest a manipulation of discourse by an implied author, who ridicules the narrator as she ridicules society. Justina's strategy is to take the offensive against those who would ostracize her by distancing herself from the mainstream. If she cannot have society's respect, she will settle for its wealth. If she cannot marry a respectable gentleman, she will settle for one who protects her and joins her in flaunting convention (Lozano), one who gives her financial security (Santolaja), and finally one who embodies picaresque plenitude (Guzmán de Alfarache). The author's strategy, on the other hand, is alternately to hide behind the narrator/protagonist and subvert her power, to let her challenge the social system as he upholds it.

Delicado's "portrait" extends beyond the subject to her ambience, experiential and linguistic. López de Ubeda's "book of entertainment" draws more heavily on literary precedent, and Justina's ramblings include forays into myth, fable, legend, and symbology. Salas Barbadillo's *La hija de Celestina* uses a classic chronology (beginning in medias res) and traditional morality (ending in death for the sinner) to present the misadventures of Elena. The antiheroine's voice appears in dialogue and in her account of her ancestry. For obvious reasons, this voice is a re-creation by the narrator, who moves from effect to cause and back to effect in portraying Elena's demise. The question of priorities centers on the case as (im)moral example and as an exercise in roguery replete with linguistic humor. Although the narrator leads the protagonist to her death in accordance with systems of earthly and divine justice, the tone of the work is far from serious. Like the professed exemplarity, the retributive justice is a concession to social pressure and the cause of righteousness, but the crux of *La hija de Celestina* is the beauteous creature who enamors her victims only to defraud them, a woman who operates without conscience against an alienating society. As in the case of the authorial figure in *La pícara Justina*, the narrator defends law and order while Elena engages in extreme forms of social protest. Crime is the principal concern, but punishment legitimizes the proceedings. The anti-heroine is a casualty of social and literary determinism, unable to conquer genetic or discursive obstacles. In the first instance, her identity is pre-established and negated. In the second, she loses her voice—her narrative identity—to a narrator without sympathy or interest in the interior self.

Salas Barbadillo makes discourse a function of the narrator, who deprives the protagonist of even nominal authority. Discursive irony and tone serve the production of meaning, but the antiheroine is distanced from the narration proper. A similar pattern regulates meaning(s) in Castillo Solórzano's *Teresa de Manzanares*, despite a return to first-person narration. Teresa has no reason to tell her story, no specified narratee, and few verbal habits that would link narrator and protagonist. The novel rarely focuses on interiority, emphasizing instead variations on the theme of trickery. Blood and temperament predetermine Teresa's disposition toward sin, and the text displays cause and effect relationships on the level of deception, not on the level of personality. While humor outweighs morality, the narrative presents a modulated vision of failure. Wit, beauty, and ambition notwith-standing, Teresa goes from bad to worse, coming full circle in the city of her birth and in a disastrous fourth marriage. In *La garduña de Sevilla*, the narrator/protagonist disappears without noticeable discursive consequences. Since Teresa never really appropriates the narrative voice, Rufina has little to lose in this regard. The rapid succession of events and the burlesque tone of the narrator, as well as the space allotted to three interpolated novels, overshadow a moral plan outlined in the prologue and in the first pages of the text (and abandoned in the end). Somewhat inexplicably, poetic justice suffers at the hands of picaresque love. Rufina finds in Jaime a male version of herself, a means of destroying her nemesis, and a partner in matrimony and business. The text displaces the female voice and the moral premise to accentuate the schemes of the antiheroine amid other entertainments. With no narrative control, negative exemplarity, or mythical dimensions, the feminine rogue becomes a stock character in a fiction that ultimately dis-regards its working hypotheses.

The first work of the series, *La lozana andaluza*, anticipates the sus-tained narrative presence of the *pícara* in Lozana's participation in a dialogue that has her (and her social backdrop) as its object. Delicado strives for linguistic verisimilitude, so the created voice both fits and defines the anti-heroine. The other voices in the dialogue complement the portrait. The intervention of the author in his work points in two directions: first, to the relation between a narrator/protagonist and an implied author and, sec-ondly, to a confrontation between the artist and his creation over questions of validity in literature and life. (More succinctly, the distinction relates to the picaresque versus the quixotic.) *La pícara Justina*, reacting to male mod-els, highlights the voice of an implied author while parodying the notion of the picaresque as moral treatise. Authorial control is more subtle but just as strong as in *La lozana andaluza*. López de Ubeda synthesizes, probably as much intuitively as consciously, the voice-over, the interplay of entertainment and ethics, and the verbal intricacies of the picaresque mainstream. In addition, he makes the antiheroine the major character in a "book of entertainment," so that a part of the generic consciousness (and legacy) will rest on this association. Salas Barbadillo and Castillo Solórzano stress the entertainment values of deception as they routinely acknowledge the moral consequences of sin and as they turn away from the joint creation of narrator and protagonist. Elena, Teresa, and Rufina comply with a birthright of deconstructed idealism. Their repertoire of tricks represents a flouting of idealized love, social customs, and instructive literature. They release the reader from the conventional, as it relates to world and text.

The feminine picaresque narratives from *La pícara Justina* to *La garduña de Sevilla* offer "readings" of the picaresque archetypes and put generic consciousness into practice. The use of a female protagonist is a major variation. While the distance between male sinner and male saint may be great, it is more so in the case of women. The *pícaro* is a social reality; the *pícara* combines reality with saturnalian inversion, the poverty-stricken orphan with the seductive temptress. The early *Lozana andaluza* takes the humanist devotion to the individual to an extreme position by filling the literary canvas with a wayward woman and those around her. López de Ubeda's Justina wields her feminine charms to seek economic security. If heredity fails her, she will substitute a share of the inheritance. The men whom she deceives are the psychological equals of the brothers who plot to disinherit her. While fighting and defrauding, she manages to protect her virginity. Justina's wedding links ironic conventionality with her unconventional past and a less than ideal marital prize. In *La hija de Celestina*, Elena's criminality extends to the murder of her husband (who is also her go-between) with the aid of her lover. For Castillo Solórzano's Teresa de Manzanares, poetic justice takes a more humorous form. Her swindles bring her not the noble matrimony she desires but four unhappy marriages to jealous old men and uncaring young ones. Rufina of *La garduña de Sevilla* is a hardened criminal who leaves men dead in her path. Ironic discourse removes her story from the realm of the tragic by favoring her tricks over her motives. At the hands of writers who create female rogues, the picaresque moves from a tortured interior self to the free-spiritedness of carnival. The *pícara* is not free, however, to voice her predicament or to challenge, through discourse, the forces that subdue her in society. The text is as inhibiting as the world.[23]

Lazarillo de Tormes, *Guzmán de Alfarache*, and *El Buscón* make a dialectical struggle of first-person narration. The author concedes narrative responsibility to the protagonist while undermining his authority through circumstantial and, most notably, discursive irony. The self-incriminating and ambiguous discourse points to a controlling presence, an implied author who steals the final word—if not the final meaning(s)—from his creation. The protagonist as foil is most evident in the feminine variations, where sexual difference is a major factor in the opposition of the *pícara* and her discursive nemesis. The chronological frame records a type of retrogression. The dialogic form of *La lozana andaluza*, which predates the *Lazarillo*, offers multiperspectivism while showing the author exercising his craft and giving the protagonist a voice in the document that portrays her role in society. In *La pícara Justina*, which responds to the picaresque genre, López de Ubeda sustains the contrapuntal discourse of the male models to the point of opposing the loquacious antiheroine with an implied author bent on displaying his erudition and satirizing his subject. In *La hija de Celestina*, the protagonist loses her voice to a third-person narrator, to regain it—only nominally—in *Teresa de Manzanares* and lose it once more in *La garduña de Sevilla*. The feminine picaresque transformations represent, to a great extent, a search for the elusive narrative self.

III
Transformations

4 THE ENLIGHTENED NARRATOR
Moll Flanders and the Social Imperative

> IT will not be strange, if I now began to think, but alas! it was but with very little solid Reflection: I had a most unbounded Stock of Vanity and Pride, and but a very little Stock of Vertue; I did indeed cast sometimes with myself what my young Master aim'd at, but thought of nothing, but the fine Words, and the Gold; whether he intended to Marry me, or not to Marry me, seem's a Matter of no great Consequence to me; nor did my Thoughts so much as suggest to me the Necessity of making any Capitulation for myself, till he came to make a kind of formal Proposal to me, as you shall hear presently.
>
> THUS I gave up myself to a readiness of being ruined without the least concern, and am a fair *Memento* to all young Women, whose Vanity prevails over their Vertue.

In the archetypal picaresque novels, the protagonists face a hostile society and authorial figures resistant to upward mobility. Narrative discourse reflects a semiotics of change countered by a semiotics of irony that inverts the message of the speaker while revealing unlimited ironic (and thus interpretive) potential. Voice becomes voices, message becomes messages, and the limited point of view opens itself to the reader. Context, action, and consistency influence the powers and the deficiencies of the word and of the narrator. Within his world and often within his text, the *pícaro* is a solitary man in a futile search for prosperity and peace. Just as the world rejects his ambitions, an implied author may invalidate or question his narrative premises. The texts function analogically, as the narrators vie with their creators and the protagonists with the social establishment. A narrative conflict mirrors the conflict of the individual versus society. Manipulation of the narrator's voice exposes linguistic, logical, and existential flaws and at the same time unmasks the authorial presence. The self-consciousness on both levels characterizes the production of meanings in the picaresque.

In the early feminine variations of the picaresque theme, the antiheroines provide a new set of narrative and social conventions and an increased detachment between narrator and character, a detachment marked by a silencing of the female voice. The novels of Castillo Solórzano illustrate this point. The shift from a first-person perspective in *Teresa de Manzanares* to the third-person in *La garduña de Sevilla* effects only minimal changes in narrative discourse. Teresa's diction, style, and strategies of presentation are, in essence, those of the omniscient narrator of the later work. Her voice is the author's voice-over, and she is a long way from the liberated female character, one who would be free to oppose the social norm and free to articulate this opposition in her own terms. Daniel Defoe's *Moll Flanders* occupies a narrative middle ground between the dominated voice and the pronounced dialectical play of narrator and implied author. The discourse changes, to a large degree, because the story changes.

López de Ubeda's *La pícara Justina* offers formal ties and a kindred spirit to *Moll Flanders*. In the Spanish text, the narrative voice shares discourse with a moralizing authorial presence who acknowledges—though not necessarily seriously—the digressions of *Guzmán de Alfarache*. Justina's own voice, like that of Pablos in *El Buscón*, struggles for expressive control with the conceptist idiom of a baroque stylist. The narrator/protagonist competes with an author who addresses his remarks to a male readership ("varones"), who defines his method and his message, who edits and imposes himself on the text, and who obviously counts Justina's linguistic expertise and corpus of knowledge as his own. As Justina recounts her fight to maintain her inheritance and her virginity, the implied author mocks established views of heredity and purity at her expense. Despite the literary armament raised against her, she wins several important victories. As a victim of social determinism, she cannot alter her marginal status, but she can ridicule and defraud the bourgeois male, find an outlet for her intellect, and celebrate her marriage to the man (men) she chooses, thereby ending her "life" with a defiant nod to literature's symbol of reintegration into society. Defoe is far less conspicuous in his narrative than López de Ubeda in *La pícara Justina*, yet he does modify an original manuscript and register its significance. Moll Flanders's voice is not entirely her own, but the author's concern with realism gives the narrator a modicum of control. And significantly, society makes reintegration a reality.

Society as represented in *Moll Flanders* is no longer the enemy of the individual but the agent of redemption.[1] Sharing the enlightened worldview of her creator, Moll repents for her sins without introspectively analyzing their origin. As a narrator, she is more interested in effect than in cause, viewing her decline primarily as a function of her salvation. Within the text, however, one may detect an incomplete reconciliation between the reformed and morally conscious Moll Flanders and the Moll Flanders forced by circumstances into a life of crime, between one who speaks reasonably and one who acts intuitively. The ultimate success may be attributed to society, but that same society must share responsibility for the initial rebellion. The subtlest of voices indicates the discrepancies between the rights of rich and poor, men and women. In a manner ironically analogous to the narrative duplicity of *Lazarillo de Tormes*, *Moll Flanders* sets forth a story and a story-behind-the-story, the latter being not the events of her life but the subtext of her discourse. The striking structural relationship between *Moll Flanders* and *Roxana* accentuates the discursive priorities of the narrator and the authorial presence. Following the anonymous author of the *Lazarillo*, Alemán, and Quevedo, Defoe revises the picaresque story in accordance with social institutions.[2] The changing role of society coincides with a linguistic project (the creation of female narrators) and a generic project (the creation of private histories), each with new forms of irony and ambiguity.

The dynamics of picaresque discourse begin to operate in the prologue to *Lazarillo de Tormes*, which presents an author directing himself to a readership and a narrator directing himself to a narratee. The author treats the text as a marketable object with social implications, while the narrator adheres to an explanatory intratextual premise. The narrative is at once a book to be sold, read, and appreciated, perhaps even to bring honor to its creator, and the account of a "case" privately dedicated to a public of one. By making his presence known and distinguishable from the narrator/protagonist, the author gives himself a role in textual significance. His intervention justifies the ironic counterdirection of a work that purports to tell one story while telling others. If the text as object encompasses the explanation of a social situation, the implied author controls the discourse of his narrator, whose independence and authority may be illusions. In short, the comprehensive text predominates over the narrative pretext, as the act of narration becomes an integral part of the events described. The speaker avoids a direct response to Vuestra Merced's petition yet depicts the evolution of his own social position, indirectly and often unfavorably, as if forced to reveal more than he intends. The character in formation parallels a discourse in formation, a discourse that makes its way into the story. *Lazarillo de Tormes* and *Guzmán de Alfarache* sustain a dialectical struggle between narrator and implied author, and *El Buscón* gives the victory to an author who uses a baroque idiolect and literary determinism to suppress the social aspirations of the narrator/protagonist. With the possible exception of *La pícara Justina*, the feminine picaresque narratives of the same period appropriate the story (or myth) and discursive conventions without emphasizing the ironic dualism of storytelling as process. In the eighteenth century, Defoe synthesizes and modifies the discourse of the archetypal models and the story of the feminine variations to construct voices and visions of his age.

As in the case of the *Lazarillo*, *Moll Flanders* and *Roxana* project a tension between the prefatory material and the texts themselves. The implied author explicitly states his role as editor, censor, and unifier of the original manuscripts of Moll Flanders and Roxana. If social redemption is an Enlightenment issue and solution, the author here becomes a "redeemer" of the wayward text, making the voices purer, the content more consistent, and the end more morally edifying. The unity of the narratives centers on a consciousness of errors in judgment on the part of the repentant sinner, brought low by civil and spiritual crimes and raised by penitence and social salvation. Or so the author of the prefaces would have it. The didactic message of the narratives is not as obvious nor the penitence as sincere as the prefaces would suggest. The forces of mimesis lag behind those of diegesis; that is, the antiheroines' texts, even in their revised versions, do not fully illustrate the conversions claimed by the author. The problematical interaction between story and discourse offers a new treatment of a standard feature of the picaresque tradition. The author opposes the narrator/protagonist, in this case by rewriting the text according to a preestablished message. In *Lazarillo de Tormes*, the prologue serves as a marker of semantic duplicity. The author announces his presence, then disappears from the story but not from the discourse. Lázaro writes an account, and the implied author casts the record in the ironic mode. The author does figuratively what Defoe does literally. Mediation in *Moll Flanders* and *Roxana* takes place prior to the act of reading, so that the only basis for analysis is the transformed text. Rather than detect the implied author in the words of the narrator, the reader may seek the original voice of the narrator in the structure devised by the author. Irony in Defoe's novels derives from the distance between poetic justice, as advocated in the preface, and the individual will, as celebrated in the text. Didacticism operates within the confines of human nature.

Moll Flanders moves from the alienation of the self to reintegration into the social order. Society saves and forgives its lost souls in an earthly rendering of eternal salvation. The remorseful protagonist does penance in Newgate Prison and in the wilderness of Virginia, and returns at the conclusion of the narrative to England and presumably to the path of righteousness. Despite the claims of rehabilitation and restitution, one cannot be certain that the penitence fits the crimes. The narration, events, and decisions of Moll Flanders underscore this discrepancy by showing the antiheroine as much mistress of her destiny as plaything of fate, heredity, and environment. While *Moll Flanders* questions the validity of the preface, *Roxana* comes close to mocking the author's presuppositions. *Roxana* belies its self-professed morality through a more decisive narrative voice and a more transparent social foundation. The abruptness of the didactic message, reminiscent of the Spanish feminine picaresque, negatively affects the earnestness of the message and the ethical pretensions of the author. In this light, the preface and the ending become literary trappings unsupported by the major portion of the text. The immorality of Roxana and the structural similarities of the two narratives determine a reading of *Moll Flanders* based on the hypothetical existence of an original manuscript and the intervention of an author/editor. The reader may reconstruct the first by deconstructing the second. The oppositions between preface and narrative, author and narrator, and statement and documentation find a counterpart in society's redeeming qualities and economic practicalities.

The Fortunes and the Misfortunes of the Famous Moll Flanders, "Written from her own Memorandums," includes in its lengthy subtitle the passage "at last grew *Rich*, liv'd *Honest*, and died a *Penitent*." From the beginning, repentance and its rewards become keys to the authorial vision and unity of the text. In the preface, the author advocates a particular approach to narrative realism in this "private History," as differentiated from the novel and the romance. The first rupture, in terms of authenticity, comes with the alteration of the original language of Moll Flanders: "She is made to tell her own Tale in modester Words than she told it at first; the Copy which came first to Hand, having been written in Language, more like one still in *Newgate*, than one grown Penitent and Humble, as she afterwards pretends to be."[3] The discourse that marks the repentance simultaneously undermines its apparent intention. The penitential lexicon belongs to the editor, not to the subject who (ambiguously) pretends to have repented. The "new dressing up" of the story will avoid lewdness, indecency, and "some of the vicious part of her Life, which cou'd not be modestly told" (p. 2). The author signals a gap between the converted sinner and the sinful commentary, perhaps causing the reader to speculate that the modified discourse tells a modified story. The author, in fact, appeals to the reader to favor the moral over the fable, as if the text were dependent on the value system of the consumer rather than encoded with values of its own. In contrast, he stresses the editorial craft as it pertains to unity, a unity produced by adherence to the concept of poetic justice: "There is not a wicked Action in any Part of it, but is first or last rendered Unhappy and Unfortunate: There is not a superlative Villain brought upon the Stage, but either he is brought to an unhappy End, or brought to be a Penitent: There is not an ill thing mention'd, but it is condemn'd, even in the Relation, nor a vertuous just Thing, but it carries its Praise along with it" (p. 3). The implication is that the responsible reader will perceive the moral scope of the narrative and that the admonitory structure is self-evident, but the double protection may prove to be a double bind.

By writing his explanation, the narrator/protagonist of *Lazarillo de Tormes* breaks the silence that has guarded him from full exposure. His attempt to find a verbal correlative of silence is futile and leads to his undoing as a reliable narrator and as an upright citizen. In much the same way, the author's discussion of the transformed manuscript of Moll Flanders credits the moral position to him rather than to her. He not only makes deletions but also identifies the deletions. If the text is "garbl'd of all the Levity, and Looseness that was in it" (p. 3), the reader understands that Moll's diction is not entirely virtuous, but it is difficult to assess her role in the instructive areas of the text. The life story is Moll's, the discourse an edited and censored version of her manuscript, and the directions for reading a contribution of the author. The structured exhortations, directly following examples of negative behavior, testify to a controlling presence and to a calculated unity. Moll Flanders may view her private history as autobiography with lessons in sin and salvation, while the author seems to regard it (or professes to want the reader to regard it) as a moral treatise whose autobiographical trajectory is spiritual in nature. Every evil act has a recriminatory counterpoint, and the corpus of vices leads to a sentence of death, reprieve, repentance, redemption. The author points out that "all the Exploits of this Lady of Fame, in her Depredations upon Mankind, stand as so many warnings to honest People to beware of them, intimating to them by what Methods innocent People are drawn in, plunder'd, and robb'd, and by Consequence how to avoid them" (p. 4). The question is not, however, whether there is a moral in Moll Flanders's story but whether there is a moral in her discourse.

The author echoes Ginés de Pasamonte's dictum in *Don Quijote* that the first-person narrative can have no definitive ending, but Defoe's consciousness of the Spanish literary forms extends beyond allusions. The conversion motif acknowledges, at least intuitively, the interplay between spirituality and hypocrisy in Alemán's *Guzmán de Alfarache*. The reader chooses between a prescribed set of priorities and messages encoded in the text, essentially the option of narrative reliability versus unreliability. The construct of the implied author relates reading to the process of composition, in that the text contains markers to interpretation and analysis. Literary structuralism focuses attention not on specific meaning and intention but rather on the elements that produce meaning in a text. In this sense, one may search for patterns of consistency (or inconsistency) in Guzmán's discourse to determine the potential significance of his story and the appropriate mode(s) of critical inquiry. In *Moll Flanders*, Defoe intensifies the problem by denying the reader access to the narrator's "true" voice. The description of the edited manuscript provides the first marker for discourse analysis and possibly for a concealed story. According to his statements in the preface, the author adjusts the discourse of the narrator to comply with his own reading, a desired reworking of the manuscript. The reader needs to discover the voice—to differentiate between the discursive identity of Moll Flanders and the mediating authority of the editor—before making judgments concerning the narrative as a whole. Like the *Guzmán*, *Moll Flanders* alleges to portray a conversion. In one case, the reader must deal with mimetic and diegetic correspondences and contradictions to formulate an approach to narrative truth. In the other, the initial distinction lies in the competition between a suppressed and an imposed voice and in a separation between the textual premises and the text.

The prologue to *Lazarillo de Tormes* isolates the author from the narrator, the reading public from the narratee, and the message from the explanation of the case. The overcoded text functions on multiple semantic and ironic levels, drawing on what may be inadvertent verbosity and even silence to extend the production of meaning. The preface to *Moll Flanders* uses literary convention to merge author with narrator. Playing on the idea of an immodest discourse in the original version, the author allows himself the option of purifying the language, which in turn leads to authorial projection on the development of the story. The author, fictionalized within the preface, has access to Moll's story as well as to her discourse. His intervention in each realm of the dichotomy represents a deviation from the original. If he substitutes decent words for indecent words, it is possible that he substitutes moral thoughts for immoral or incriminatory thoughts. There is textual evidence to support the conjecture, first because the author makes his ploy a part of the text and secondly because Moll's revised narrative fails to convey the penitential spirit for which the author praises her and the work. The author of the preface defines a system of interpretation based on his reading (real and ideal), editing, and ordering of the material, yet this invasion of the narrator's domain enhances rather than eliminates ambiguity. In the memoirs, Moll Flanders distinguishes, as the author does not, between awareness of the consequences of sin and the virtuous suffering of repentance. The narrative collaboration shows an exemplary sinner but not necessarily an illustrious penitent.

Because the reading process involves conventions, illusions, and concessions, the individual reader may follow one of many paths. The preface to *Moll Flanders* could guide a reading of the text or be considered an appendage to a self-contained document. Just as realistic drama draws the public away from the trappings of theater, the private history (Defoe's version of realism) strives for a faithful portrait of the individual in society from the perspective of the subject, but not without setting boundaries and order for the literary reality. As the ultimate creator of the vision, the author places himself in the text to influence the reading experience. Poetic justice and repentance serve as points of reference in this directed interpretation of Moll Flanders's narrative. Within the context of the preexisting manuscript, the voice of the protagonist is a combination of voices reworked to express authorial priorities. The reader may accept the author's case for moral unity, test or challenge it, or disregard it in favor of the freedom of direct confrontation with the narrative proper. The reader may disregard, as well, the fact that Daniel Defoe invents story and discourse, original and revised, by entering the "historical" world of Moll Flanders via a suspension of disbelief. Whether the analysis evaluates the coordination of preface and narrative or the narrative alone in terms of the theme of repentance, the result is paradoxically similar. The text demonstrates neither the stages nor the mental process of contrition, and the particular circumstances of Moll Flanders's redemption demand few sacrifices on her part. Social justice models itself after divine justice, with relative rather than absolute consequences. Perhaps unconsciously, the text reflects a less than absolute transformation. Moll's triumph is undebatable, unlike those of Lázaro and Guzmán, but the victory may belong more to literature than to society, more to the narrative voice than to the still, small voice.

Born to a prisoner at Newgate, "left a poor desolate Girl without Friends, without Cloaths, without Help or Helper in the World, as was my Fate" (p. 8), Moll Flanders (who never gives her real name) finds herself at the age of three with a group of gypsies. Abandoned by them, or abandoning them, at Colchester, she receives aid from the town magistrates, who put her with a kindly guardian. This nurse teaches her to read and to work, serving as an example of piety, cleanliness, and courtesy. When the magistrates order the child to "go out to Service," Moll begs her guardian to intercede on her behalf; she wishes to be a gentlewoman, that is, an independent worker. Her pretensions to gentility attract the attention of the local society, including the mayoress. She more than earns her keep and even spends time at the home of an aristocratic family. The experience raises her class consciousness: "I was not so easie in my old Quarters as I us'd to be, and I thought it was fine to be a Gentlewoman indeed, for I had quite other Notions of a Gentlewoman now, than I had before" (p. 16). The nurse dies when Moll is fourteen years old, and her daughter, taking charge of the estate, casts Moll into the world. The solitude does not last for long, for her earlier benefactress takes her into her home and gives her the advantages of rank, including an education. Moll acknowledges that "I could not be better than where I was" (p. 18). The opening of Moll Flanders's narrative establishes a pattern for discourse sustained throughout the text, a contrast between professed isolation and the magnanimity of fate. The narrator/protagonist is rarely as alone as she would have it, nor does destiny frown on her as often as she would suggest. Through luck and fortitude, she rises above the status of victim to control her fortune, while poor judgment negates the benefits of freedom.

The narrator speaks at the beginning of her memoirs of being "expos'd to very great Distresses, even before I was capable, either of Understanding my Case, or how to Amend it, nor brought into a Course of Life, which was not only scandalous in itself, but which in its ordinary Course, tended to the swift Destruction both of Soul and Body" (p. 8). Heredity is clearly unkind to Moll Flanders, and the stigma of her ignoble birth lasts throughout her life. It is equally evident, however, that a solitary and destitute child could have had a worse plight. The magistrates take pity on her, the nurse teaches and protects her, the noble ladies cater to her, and, when she again faces alienation, a wealthy family treats her with love and generosity. Her movement from "gentlewoman" to gentlewoman marks an upward progression hindered only by the threat of poverty and abuse. The townspeople consistently act on her behalf, and none of the causes of fear materializes. Moll does not suffer, she does not go into service, she does not starve after her guardian's death. The death, in fact, opens the way for her rise in society. The nurse educates her in piety and practicality, while the new mistress offers her an education in the liberal arts and social graces. She is in this respect an equal of her "sister" gentlewomen. While lineage favors them, nature favors her: "First, I was apparently Handsomer than any of them. Secondly, I was better shap'd, and Thirdly, I Sung better, by which I mean, I had a better Voice; in all which you will I hope allow me to say, I do not speak my own Conceit of myself, but the Opinion of all that knew the Family" (pp. 18–19). It is conceit—or, more properly, vanity—that leads to her undoing, through circumstances attributable to free will rather than to determinism, to the ironies of the emotions rather than to a tragic fate. In direct contrast to her discourse, Moll's story bespeaks a benevolent fate.

Moll's beauty and intelligence mean little in the general code of social, or economic, determinism. Once again, fate would seem to conspire against Moll Flanders, but in fact she overcomes the obstacle of poverty to fall victim to the egalitarian principle of love. Even then, destiny shields her. Both sons of her mistress fall in love with Moll. With a promise of marriage, the older brother conquers her. Moll's description of the act may perhaps betray a man's rendering of a woman's voice: "I made no more Resistance to him, but let him do just what he pleas'd; and as often as he pleas'd; and thus I finish'd my own Destruction at once, for from this Day, being forsaken of my Vertue, and my Modesty, I had nothing of Value left to recommend me, either to God's Blessing, or Man's Assistance" (p. 29). The generic significance notwithstanding, Moll seemingly reduces her options by venting her passions, but the younger brother (unlike his insincere sibling) offers her social redemption through a marriage proposal. In doing so, he disproves the obstacle of class in the mating ritual. The poor, lowborn, and dishonored Moll has the opportunity to live in prosperity as the wife of an aristocrat. The scales of justice, social and poetic, weigh in her favor, yet she disrupts the positive turn of events by forsaking reputation for love. She vows to the older brother that she would rather be his whore than his brother's wife. After a lengthy illness caused by psychological conflict—and convinced by her rational, if unloyal, lover—Moll consents to marry the other brother: "Thus in a Word, I may say, he Reason'd me out of my Reason; he conquer'd all my Arguments, and I began to see a Danger that I was in, which I had not consider'd of before, and that was of being drop'd by both of them, and left alone in the World to shift for myself" (p. 57). Marriage to Robin, which could have been culmination of her aspirations to gentility, becomes the lesser evil, but at the same time a manifestation of her freedom of choice. If the outcome is not fortuitous, Moll must bear the burden of responsibility.

Almost despite herself, the abandoned girl seeking to become a gentlewoman gets her wish. The trajectory toward matrimony transcends the social obstacles while Moll Flanders, no longer a victim of fate, creates her own emotional barriers. Ironically, the would-be gentlewoman prefers whoredom to an honorable match. She implies in the opening passages of the narrative that she was "brought into" a scandalous course of life, when the events and their narration indicate a strong-willed character who determines her own fate. From her arrival in Colchester, God and the good people—to recall a phrase from *Guzmán de Alfarache*—work to aid Moll. She responds by rejecting virtue in favor of vice, goodness (personified in Robin) in favor of evil (personified in her lover). Although the older brother speaks of marriage, it is important to note that Moll gives up her virginity and conceivably her hope for future happiness to live in sin. The earnest and somewhat ingenuous Robin represents a continuation of Moll Flanders's blessings, a means by which she may transgress without suffering the consequences. She repays his faith as a dutiful wife during the five years of their marriage, but on his death she leaves her two children with their grandparents and sets out in search of greater economic prosperity. She admits that she never lost her feelings for her brother-in-law ("I committed Adultery and Incest with him every Day in my Desires") and is relieved to be rid of the children ("taken happily off of my Hands," p. 59). Her language demonstrates her priorities; she supplies the details of her financial status but not the names, ages, or sex of her children. The lack of maternal affection and appreciation for her family, offset by a preoccupation with wealth and an exaggerated awareness of her physical assets, characterizes a vain and unfeeling Moll Flanders but significantly not a woman trapped by social structures. She is by no means a defenseless innocent. She programs a future based on the acquisition of capital. When Robin dies, she relinquishes the past to pursue greener pastures.

Moll Flanders's case is a puzzle in causality, or in social determinism. One could argue for the impact of heredity to justify her sinful ways and the disowning of her children, yet Moll herself seems to attribute her flaws to a fate more logically related to environment. Given the receptive treatment by the nurse and the adoptive family, especially Robin's defense of love over social standing, the protagonist has the means to counter her inauspicious entry into society. Her successive guardians alter social practice to spare her the disadvantages of her birth and to accommodate her dream of gentility. In spite of its repetition in the text, Moll's fear of solitude remains an abstraction; people are eager to come to her assistance. Benign strokes of fortune and exposure to upright behavior fail to mold her into an exemplary citizen. Economic matters and sexuality replace idealism, motherhood, and the quest for virtue. Moll places the blame on vanity engendered by her youth and beauty, while the real cause may be a wayward nature, an inexplicable (and unexplained) change from gentlewoman to golddigger, and worse. The new dream of increased prosperity leads to a life of crime, a bout with death and with the past, and finally to happiness. At each stage, fate is on her side. As she sets out from Colchester, Moll Flanders ironically views her solitude as a sign of liberation.

There is irony, as well, in the contrast between what Moll leaves behind and what awaits her. She gives up respectability to desert her children and her husband's family, taking with her a "small fortune" that becomes smaller before it becomes greater. The desire for money makes her a schemer in a world of schemers, a woman who will judge her future matches in economic rather than in social terms. In a sense, she reverts to the male role in the domestic market by attempting to dominate the proceedings as opposed to being dominated. Moll is ultimately more successful at intrigue than at matrimony, partly because the men involved are as manipulating as she and partly because the past makes its way into the present. Awaiting a worthy candidate for her second husband, Moll Flanders lives honorably, motivated by interest more than by morality. The choice, a "Gentle-Tradesman" (a parody of the earlier emphasis on rank), proves unwise, as the new spouse is a spendthrift who threatens to deplete Moll's capital as well as his own. In debt, he flees England to escape prosecution, leaving Moll again as a widow on the lookout for a match. Fearing the company of men without nuptial possibilities, Moll once more laments her solitary existence. Her third marriage eliminates the fear of starvation while introducing new and more menacing fears and ironic variations on the motif of solitude.

After a digression on feminine psychology, in which the narrator advises women to resist abuse and to aggressively pursue a good marriage, Moll strives to "deceive the deceiver" by creating an inflated vision of her finances. She ends up in a double snare, marrying a man who uses the same ploy. Not only does history repeat itself, but irony forces a tragic confrontation with the sins of the past. Because of the mutual deception, for which neither Moll nor her third husband bears a grudge, the couple find themselves in economic straits. The solution is a move to the New World, where he has a plantation in Virginia. The marriage is a happy one until Moll deduces that her mother-in-law, a woman given to recounting adventures from her youth, is her mother. Moll recoils at the thought that she has unknowingly committed incest, bearing two children and pregnant with a third from her brother. The situation recalls Moll's sexual experiences with the two brothers at Colchester and reifies the stigma of her birth. Following a pattern of recurrence, one may see in the old lady a projection of her daughter's future: "In her younger Days she had been both WHORE and THIEF; but I verily believe she had lived to repent sincerely of both, and that she was then a very Pious sober and religious Woman" (p. 89). Moll's love for her husband turns to revulsion and then to pity. After having changed her name and station to suit the circumstance, she must now deal with the problem of her true identity. The solution, which cannot help but cause pain to her family, is a return to England after eight years in Virginia. Destiny reenacts the departure from Colchester, as Moll Flanders finds herself alone in London. While the interlude in the New World marks the direction—geographical and psychological—of the narrative events, economic security remains Moll Flanders's chief concern.

In the Bath at Bristol, Moll meets a "compleat Gentleman," a married man with a "distempered" wife. The platonic relationship is broken by one night of passion and a resulting offspring, and the amorous ties endure for four more years. Moll's bittersweet reminiscence of the time echoes the ambiguity of the closing passage of *Lazarillo de Tormes*: "And now I was indeed in the height of what I might call my Prosperity, and I wanted nothing but to be a Wife, which however could not be in this Case, there was no room for it; and therefore on all Occasions I study'd to save what I could, . . . knowing well enough that such things as these do not always continue, that Men that keep Mistresses often change them, grow weary of them, or Jealous of them, or something or other happens to make them withdraw their Bounty" (p. 118). Moll presents the story as a warning to readers against gratifying the senses at the expense of virtue, yet her emphasis, as always, is on survival rather than on ethics. She comments, "Tho' I was not without secret Reproaches of my own Conscience for the Life I led, and that even in the greatest height of the Satisfaction I ever took, yet I had the terrible prospect of Poverty and Starving which lay on me as a frightful Spectre" (p. 120). The aviso cannot disguise the nature of Moll Flanders's concerns. There is, at this point at least, no piety in her words, no consciousness of the wages of sin, no deferment to eternal principles. It is not hell at the end of a wicked lifetime but fear of poverty at the end of an affair that motivates her response. In the realm of the here and now, the specter of hunger is stronger than the specter of her mother. Ironically, the repentant party is the gentleman, whose recovery from a near-fatal illness promotes a crisis of conscience and an end to his relations with Moll. For her part, Moll relieves her penitent lover of a tidy sum of money and relieves herself of the onus of motherhood, entrusting her child to the care of another. As the narrator speaks of solitude and vulnerability, the protagonist recommences her search for a spouse, at the age of forty-two.

As in the previous cases, deception is the key element of Moll's fourth and fifth marriages, interconnected in the narrative. The first prospect is a clerk, cuckolded by his wife and hopeful of obtaining a decree against her, who asks Moll to wait for him. In the meantime, she meets the wealthy brother (who turns out to be neither) of a friend, an Irishman who the sister claims has a large estate in his homeland. Moll is not above intimating to the family that she will convert to Catholicism or allowing her friend to spread false reports of her wealth. When the Irishman proposes, Moll—admitting that she has lost the power to say no—assents. Pleased with the possibility of great wealth, she feels slightly guilty about her abandonment of a man all too familiar with feminine deceit. Here, however, the guilt is unfounded. Once more the victim of a double snare, Moll discovers that her new husband is penniless. Although he loves her, he is forced to flee after the two share a month of bliss in the countryside. Upset but undeterred, Moll manages to give birth to a son and to maintain the interest of the clerk, who by this time has been granted the decree. She gives up the child to return to her trusting suitor. She lives a modest existence with the fifth husband and mistakenly foresees a reversal of fortune: "Now I seem'd landed in a safe Harbour, after the Stormy Voyage of Life past was at an end; and I began to be thankful for my Deliverance; I sat many an Hour by my self, and wept over the Remembrance of past Follies, and the dreadful Extravagances of a wicked Life, and sometimes I flatter'd my self that I had sincerely repented" (p. 188). The repentance is an illusion, and the change is for the worse.

A recognizable structure emerges. Moll Flanders's fifth husband, like her first, dies after five years of marriage and two children. Moll broods over her misfortune, gives up her children, and begins a new way of life as a thief. She blames the devil for prompting her to steal and for forcing her to continue in this vice. Whatever the initial provocation, she becomes a consummate professional, "a compleat Thief, harden'd to a Pitch above all the Reflections of Conscience or Modesty" (p. 202). Need leads to crime, crime promotes avarice, and avarice subjugates conscience. Moll's lengthy treatment of her criminal adventures stresses her knowledge of wrongdoing, her increasing prosperity and lessening need to steal, and the obsessive nature of the affliction. Despite a number of close calls and the unmerciful punishment of her comrades in theft, she relies on continued good luck. She is audacious enough to have an affair with a man she has robbed, the details of which "are not so proper for a Woman to write" (p. 233). The variety and ingenuity of Moll's criminal art shine in her discourse, yet there looms in the background the shadow of Newgate. Shortly before her arrest, she returns to Colchester, finding only news of death. One day fate works against Moll Flanders, as she is apprehended and sent to Newgate: "My very Blood chills at the mention of its Name; the Place, where so many of my Comrades had been lock'd up, and from whence they went to the fatal Tree; the Place where my Mother suffered so deeply, where I was brought into the World, and from whence I expected no Redemption, but by an infamous Death" (p. 273). The imprisonment in Newgate, with its omens of death, opens the road to redemption.

The road is a difficult one. While Moll fails to emulate the exemplary conduct of her guardians during the early years in Colchester, she is quick to imitate her criminal colleagues: "I was become a meer *Newgate-Bird*, as Wicked and as Outragious as any of them; nay, I scarce retain'd the Habit and Custom of good Breeding, and Manners, which all along till now run thro' my Conversation; so thoro' a Degeneracy had possess'd me, that I was no more the same thing that I had been, than if I had never been otherwise than what I was now" (p. 279). At her trial, she is found guilty of felony and sentenced to die. The turn of events moves her good friend and accomplice to repent, and Moll follows suit: "It was now, that for the first time I felt any real signs of Repentance; I now began to look back upon my past Life with abhorrence, and having a kind of view into the other Side of time, the things of Life, as I believe they do with every Body at such a time, began to look with a different Aspect, and quite another Shape, than they did before" (p. 287). A sympathetic minister, sent by her friend, prepares the way for Moll's transformation. Moved emotionally and spiritually, she bears her soul to him: "He reviv'd my Heart, and brought me into such a Condition, that I never knew any thing of in my Life before: I was cover'd with Shame and Tears for things past, and yet had at the same time a secret surprizing Joy at the Prospect of being a true Penitent, and obtaining the Comfort of a Penitent, I mean the hope of being forgiven" (p. 289). Moll convinces the minister of the sincerity of her repentance, and he wins her a reprieve. She will be transported to the colonies. The past acquires new meaning for Moll, who relives the crime and punishment of her mother. She discovers that her fourth husband is also a prisoner at Newgate, awaiting trial but with the option of transportation. She pleads with him to come to America, through logical arguments and tears ("that known Womans Rhetorick," p. 302). Following numerous complications, they make their way to the coast of Virginia.

Moll Flanders's narrative of her years as a thief may be classified as a rogue's history with a conscience and with a consciousness of earthly justice. The sense of divine justice comes later, after the religious experience in Newgate. The successful career makes Moll forget her mortality, while the death sentence awakens her to the gift of existence. In the episode of her fourth marriage, she notes the element of hypocrisy in her attitude toward the Irish Catholics. In the Newgate section, on the other hand, she stresses the sincerity of her penitence, which coincides with the reunion with her fourth husband. Echoing the author of the preface, Moll concerns herself with the place of spirituality in her memoirs. She beseeches the reader to reflect on the significance of her conversion and to accept a didactic counterpoint to her exploits: "This may be thought inconsistent in itself, and wide from the Business of this Book; Particularly, I reflect that many of those who may be pleas'd and diverted with the Relation of the wild and wicked part of my Story, may not relish this, which is really the best part of my Life, the most Advantageous to myself, and the most instructive to others; such however will I hope allow me the liberty to make my Story compleat: It would be a severe Satyr on such, to say they do not relish the Repentance as much as they do the Crime; and that they had rather the History were a compleat Tragedy, as it was very likely to have been" (p. 291). Repentance is an internal matter, able to be tested only in terms of correspondence between the declaration of change and the manifestation of the transformed self. Facing death, Moll puts her faith in divine mercy. The reprieve answers her prayers, and the question of a lasting conversion, as it relates to the text, depends on the strength of her discourse in the final portion of the narrative.

Through an elaborate plan devised by Moll and her friend in England, the couple escape the years of slavery awarded to transported convicts. Stolen goods and money from Moll's days as a thief give them freedom and economic peace of mind in the New World. The protagonist discovers that her mother has died and that her former husband resides near where they have landed. Seeing the old man and her son, whom she cannot recognize at this point, grieves her: "Let any Mother of Children that reads this, consider it, and but think with what anguish of Mind I restrain'd myself; what yearnings of Soul I had in me to embrace him, and weep over him; and how I thought all my Entrails turn'd within me, that my very Bowels mov'd, and I knew not what to do; as I now know not how to express those Agonies" (p. 322). This is Moll's most pronounced display of maternal remorse. In a consideration of consistency, one could point to a discrepancy between her concern here and the ease with which she has previously abandoned all her children, or alternately view the sentiments as the expression of a converted sinner. Moll and her husband settle in southern Virginia, and she returns to confront her son with the truth, the father being too sick to receive her. The son treats her with compassion and understanding, conveying as well the news that her mother left her a plantation. Moll reacts to her kind fate with a combination of satisfaction and guilt: "Not on this Occasion only, but even on all other Occasions of Thankfulness, my past wicked and abominable Life never look'd so Monstrous to me, and I never so compleatly abhorr'd it, and reproach'd myself with it, as when I had a Sense upon me of Providence doing good to me, while I had been making those vile Returns on my part" (p. 337). Following the death of her former husband, she tells the complete story to her husband, whom she calls "as sincere a Penitent, and as thoroughly a reform'd Man, as ever God's goodness brought back from a Profligate, a Highway-Man, and a Robber" (p. 339). After eight years in America, they "resolve to spend the Remainder of our Years in sincere Penitence, for the wicked Lives we have lived" (p. 343).

With respect to what may be termed a discursive contract—the relation between textual presuppositions and narrative response to the presuppositions—*Moll Flanders* presents certain problems. The process of repentance, which carries great strength both in the preface and in the final part of the narrative, remains a verbal construct. There is minimal testing of Moll's professed conversion in the events following her release from Newgate. She is not alone, for her fourth husband accompanies her on a voyage to America and away from death. She is not poor, for she has no qualms about using stolen goods to ensure the most comfortable passage possible. She does not have to comply with her term as an indentured slave, for the fruit of her thefts allows her to buy her way out of the arrangement. In Virginia, fate is on her side. Her son is sympathetic to her plight, her mother rewards Moll in a generous will, her properties give her impressive profits, and her fourth husband repents and forgives. Moll Flanders, in short, has no trials to bear, no tests in which to exhibit her penitential nature, no mimetic equivalent to her diegetic reformation. The system of poetic justice established by the author of the preface depends on the authenticity of Moll's repentance and thus has little validation in the narrative. At the end of the preface, the author refers to the husband's account of the final years in England. He notes that Moll "liv'd it seems, to be very old; but was not so extraordinary a Penitent, as she was at first; it seems only that indeed she always spoke with abhorence of her former Life, and of every Part of it" (p. 5). The ambiguity of this passage, which intimates that Moll may be a nominal rather than an active penitent, moves away from the vision of a contrite and totally reformed sinner. The closing section of the preface marks a discursive rupture intensified by the closing section of the memoirs. The text substitutes providence for what the preface calls poetic justice.[4]

Moll Flanders inherits from her mother the infamy of Newgate Prison that will follow her through life. From the forced abandonment, Moll learns to fear solitude as the greatest enemy of her survival, and each episode features examples of her rhetoric of solitude, the expression of her need for companionship and material possessions. Her favored status in Colchester belies the stigma of her birth, and in this exceptional case, heredity does not rule out marriage with an aristocrat. Environment, however, does not rule out irrational behavior on Moll's part, as she favors the role of mistress to that of wife. Her self-imposed solitude following the death of her first husband represents not only a rhetorical shift but also a retrogression from her position as a gentlewoman. All of the marriages involve misrepresentation and fraud, often from both parties. The protagonist repeats her mother's action by deserting her children. The discursive analogue of the desertion is a text that disregards the children by failing to provide details about them and, at times, by failing to acknowledge their existence. When Moll returns to Colchester, for example, she does not inquire (or report having inquired) about the children of her first marriage. Similarly, when she makes the second trip to Virginia, she speaks of only one of the two children of her third marriage. The lamentation on seeing this son clashes with the earlier coldness as a mother, verifying the conversion or perhaps injecting a note of skepticism. Moll's rather late apprehension by the authorities is the most obvious source of poetic justice. The reprieve and the stolen money—and significantly a final and positive inheritance from her mother—guarantee security in the New World, and the forgiveness of her son and fourth husband mark the final stage of her salvation by forces from without. For those forces from within, the reader must analyze the intricate elements of her discourse.

The authorial presence, according to the discourse of the preface, rewrites Moll Flanders's memoirs to fit specific criteria of decorum and to conform to a unity established by the author, and not by the narrator. The encoded message is didactic in nature, illustrating to the reader the dangers of sin and the benefits of repentance. The implied redirection of the original structure is suspect in itself and made more problematic by the failure of the (rewritten) text to comply with the message announced in the preface. One obstacle to didacticism is the protagonist's independence of action and language. When she admits that she would prefer being her first lover's mistress to being his brother's wife, she reveals an antisocial inclination despite her social pretensions. When she sacrifices maternal love for economic considerations, she initiates a discourse that will characterize her narration: the discourse of economics, in which money speaks and by which Moll measures her success and happiness. Accordingly, this discourse of economics—and its corollary, the discourse of deception—silences the discourse of love and motherhood. Each of the five marriages re-creates those preceding it, showing Moll's inability to profit from experience. The repeated cries of despair against solitude become ironic, for the protagonist is rarely as alone as her discourse would indicate, and she comes across more as the forger of her destiny than the victim. In the description of her exploits as a thief, Moll deals openly with robbery as an addiction. Once she begins to acquire money and possessions, survival is no longer the question; she continues to ignore warnings of doom to fatten the coffer. In this section, the narrator supplies the moral instruction (in the form of consciousness of her vices) alluded to in the preface, but it is overshadowed by the excitement and variety of the crimes and the enduring luck of the criminal.[5]

Before repenting of her sins, Moll Flanders becomes an expert thief and, once imprisoned, a hardened criminal. The revised manuscript presents only diegetic evidence of the descent in Newgate. From her lowest state, she does penance to atone for her crimes and to avert the threat of death. In economic terms, she invests her time and efforts in salvation, primarily earthly and secondarily divine. Moll convinces the minister that her conversion is genuine, and the reward is a reprieve. Given the minimal proof of the enduring effects of the repentance, the author of the preface and the narrator herself require the reader's faith in their word, in their discourse. Since the text does not entirely live up to its premises, one may search for a rationale for the discrepancy between the proposal and its execution. A device associated with the Spanish picaresque, as well as with earlier narrative, is the creation of an instructive intention to legitimize an entertaining text. The author of the preface may be a construct to provide a moral frame for the adventures of Moll Flanders. A second possibility would be the use of discursive ambiguity to symbolize conceptual ambiguity; in this case, the contradictions on the formal level match mankind's contradictory nature and the difficulty of true repentance. From the perspective of a discursive contest of sorts between the author/editor and the narrator/protagonist, the text represents not so much the limitations of writing as the limitations of rewriting. The voice of Moll Flanders pervades the narrative, unable to be "silenced" by the imposing presence of the author. The revisions add a discernible moral base and a cleansed linguistic base, but Moll succeeds in conveying a personality of her own, reflected in both story and discourse. Her identity depends in part on the feminine qualities of her voice.

Moll Flanders's literary femininity raises doubts from the beginning of the text. The author claims to alter and to censor the language of the (nonexistent) original manuscript, an act (or device) that eliminates the purity of voice of the narrator. The prefatory remarks of the author provide clues to the uncensored voice. The words of Moll Flanders are less modest than those of the narrative before the reader, less humble and penitential in spirit. The wickedness of Moll's past survives in her discourse, if not in her life, according to the author. The early manuscript seems to have possessed an anti-Aristotelian biographical unity, a linear account of the evil deeds countered by repentance. The author takes the reformation as the point of unity, supplying doses of caution and poetic justice. The preface also lauds society and its institutions for the rehabilitation of the criminal, citing diligence and application as means to the end of earthly salvation. If the author redeems the narrator as society redeems the sinner, one may deduce that the original text had a less notable correspondence between diction and dénouement than the "corrected" version and that the narrator's avowed repentance does not produce a linguistic analogue in modified speech. The author intervenes to create the analogue, thus casting doubt on the validity of the penitence, which is necessarily more abstract than discourse. The reference to Moll's decreasing piety (at the end of the preface) makes conversion, untested in the final portion of her narrative, especially problematic. The imposition of the author works to silence Moll in much the same way that Castillo Solórzano silences his protagonists, yet Defoe's character comes closer to having a mind and a voice of her own.

Moll Flanders, "real" or created, never seems as helpless or as desolate as her words would indicate. She makes decisions for herself and abides by the consequences. When destiny or trickery works against her, she resists the agents that would undo her to face and invent new challenges. She speaks eloquently of the plight of the orphan, the education of women, and the glories of passion. She is less traditionally "feminine" when addressing the issues of wifely devotion and maternal responsibility. Of course, this tradition is man-made, and *Moll Flanders* covers new discursive ground, despite the authorial intrusion. Moll's self-analysis in the opening section of the narrative centers on the conquest of virtue by male desire and female vanity. Moll views her lost virginity through society's—that is, man's—eyes, but so might the majority of her sisters. Her attitude toward her two suitors in Colchester shows an anti-establishment favoring of passion over convention, and her schemes to win wealthy husbands equate her with men who dedicate themselves to advancing on the social ladder. Even when her family background catches up with her, Moll devises a means of escaping a deterministic legacy, a feat that Pablos in *El Buscón* cannot manage. In Newgate, she convinces a man of the cloth of her sincerity and returns in triumph to the scene of her humiliation. During her tenure as a thief, she disregards the signs of defeat, while as narrator (and penitent) she reprimands her former self for ignoring the inevitability of social and divine punishment. Within the context of redemption, the smooth course following the reprieve may attest to the genuineness of her conversion. The narrator speaks at the end of the narrative of her resolve to spend the remainder of her life in penitence, a promise that the author indirectly challenges in the closing of the preface. Moll Flanders has the final word here, as elsewhere in the text.

In a society dominated by men, a woman may express her independence or dissatisfaction through antisocial behavior and uncondoned speech. The male as figure of authority (in the text as well as in the world) censors, judges, and regulates both speech and behavior. In Moll Flanders, Defoe creates a character who rebels against a deterministic birthright and the limited possibilities for women without a dowry. Her actions are consistently defiant, if not consistently logical or ethical. It is possible to consider the resistance of Moll's narrative, even as revised by the authorial figure, to the premises of the preface as a discursive correlative of her (anti)social position. She refers at one point to things "which are not so proper for a Woman to write," a commentary that probably reflects the author/editor's presence rather than the narrator's modesty. The statement ironically foregrounds the separation of masculinity and femininity in terms of literary and social decorum. Moll Flanders flouts acceptable conduct, and society uses a punitive system to restore order. The ambiguity of the order in each case attests to Defoe's skill in the creation of character. While Castillo Solórzano distances himself from the narrator in the prologue to *Teresa de Manzanares*, his protagonist has no distinctive voice. The first-person narrator sounds like the omniscient narrator of *La garduña de Sevilla*. The similarity in tone and lexicon of the two works (and of prologue and text) shows a consciousness of generic conventions without a consciousness of or wish to re-create the discursive model of the picaresque archetypes. In *Moll Flanders*, Defoe follows the earlier pattern to distinguish the creator (and his alter ego) from the speaker. The result is a contest for control of text and subtext.

The events of the narrative demonstrate Moll Flanders's reaction against her "natural" place in society and against social conditioning. In a sense, she struggles against heredity and environment to forge a unique place for herself, and her adventures become a parody of women's search for a suitable match. A dominating factor is Moll's wish to prosper, a willingness to cast herself to fate to achieve the goal. The expression and reexpression of her fear of solitude carry less weight, diegetically and mimetically, than the fierce sense of independence that directs her life. Moll Flanders is a woman unafraid to speak of passion. She is not a victim in Colchester but a woman in love, translated into the terms of male society as a whore. Her favoring of the older brother and her subsequent flight from the comforts of Colchester suggest a subliminal escape from the traditional woman's role, an escape that forces her into the margins of respectable society. The new life is, by most standards, a descent into deception and crime, yet Moll is mistress of her actions, if not always of her destiny. Educated in the humanities and domesticity by her adoptive family, she embarks on a journey of self-education that emphasizes economics and interest. Her discourse reflects a monetary rather than a maternal perspective and a devotion to active (male) pursuits as opposed to passive (female) values. The time in Newgate is the nadir of her life, but the prison is also the setting for her redemption. Through her minister, she makes peace with God, and through the reprieve, with man. The return to Virginia, the scene of her fateful reunion with her mother, represents her own acceptance of maternal responsibility (and a rare display of maternal feelings) as a final stage of the redemptive process. The voyage to England at the end of the narrative completes a cycle of sin and penitence, in accord with the base of poetic justice elaborated in the preface. Nonetheless, Moll Flanders circumvents a predetermined existence and a predetermined narrative plan.[6]

What "escapes" the author/editor of *Moll Flanders* is the discourse of freedom on the part of the narrator. The feminine voice is not so much womanly as a contradiction of male-imposed categories and values. Moll enters the social domain to manage—sometimes badly—the course of her life. In doing so, she confronts established codes of conduct. As a writer, she enters a realm of prescriptions and restrictions, as well as censorship by an editor bent on conveying his message through her text. Because one can separate the authorial intention from the resulting story, the discourse of social conformity opposes the discourse of resistance. The text projects a dialectical relationship between a society capable of redeeming sinners and a society whose policies of exclusion lead its members to sin. The author fictionalizes himself to argue for the status quo while inventing a fictional character to argue (and act) for change. The end of the story signals a victory for order restored, but the discourse never fully complies with the edited story. The ambiguous treatment of Moll's conversion bespeaks an unresolved tension between the individual and society, between the upper and lower classes, and between man and woman. The unrelenting fate that consistently reminds Moll Flanders of her past becomes the protective fate that rewards her transformation. Moll herself changes very little in the rendering of her five marriages; events rather than psychology guide her through life, and she puts herself in a position to repeat mistakes. Need and the related vice of avarice push her into crime until the administration of justice fosters a movement toward introspection. From this moment, Moll conveys little of her innermost feelings, and circumstances do not require her to prove that her conversion is sincere. The ending of the narrative is happy yet somewhat forced and incomplete, in part because the female voice survives in the text.[7]

In *Roxana*, published two years after *Moll Flanders*, Defoe follows the general structure of the earlier work while underscoring excesses in story and discourse. The mediated narration presents a variation on the ironic discrepancy between the stated message and the elements of meaning in the text. The author/editor's emphasis on instruction clashes with the narrative events, the abrupt ending, and the characterization of the protagonist. While the motif of repentance may not be as strong in *Moll Flanders* as the reader of the preface would suppose, it almost disappears from Roxana's memoirs. The similarity of the two narratives sheds light on the discursive irony of *Moll Flanders*. The author of the preface to *Roxana* asks his readers to consider the private history a function of the didactic message, a condemnation of greed and immorality. Through her personal account, edited by

the authorial figure, Roxana reveals a class consciousness and a consciousness of her financial status more pronounced than that of Moll Flanders.
Like Moll, Roxana fights to stave off poverty, and when the threat no
longer exists, she refuses to cease her compromising activities. She conducts
her life and her discourse in terms of money and power. Independence
becomes a major priority, with fear of exposure as the greatest danger to her
happiness. Redemption takes an unusual form in *Roxana*, associating maternal guilt with a struggle to maintain a false identity. Roxana's discourse
centers on materialism, license, and illusion, so that motherhood and penitence seem as unconvincing in her narrative as they are unimportant in her
life. The negative aspects of Roxana's character stem more from the individual will than from determination, and the consequences of her choices—
notably, pursuit by a renounced daughter—clarify the roles of author and
narrator. The first pleads his case with a questionable rationale, while the
second evokes reader sympathy for a questionable cause.

The author of the preface reports (while undermining his statement)
that the history of Roxana "is to speak for itself," that it will be sweet and
useful, and, if not, "the *Relator says*, it must be from the Defect of his
Performance; dressing up the Story in worse Cloaths than the Lady, whose
Words he speaks, prepar'd it for the World."[8] Defoe repeats here much of
what he says in the preface to *Moll Flanders*, yet he distances himself from
the discourse by alluding to a process in which the text reaches him from
Roxana via an editor, or perhaps by referring to his editorial responsibilities
in the third person. He approaches the question of truth as Cervantes approaches it in *Don Quijote*, by equating historicity with details and witnesses
while subtly acknowledging the domain of fiction. Like Cervantes, Defoe is
a third hand in the act of composition, removed from the text and able to
judge its worth. The prefatory material stresses a unity based on the convention of negative exemplarity. The narrator does not "recommend her
Conduct, or indeed, any Part of it, except her Repentance to our Imitation:
On the contrary, she makes frequent Excursions, in a just censuring and
condemning her own Practice" (p. 2). Lest one admire Roxana's success in
the wicked course of life, the author of the preface notes, "Even in the
highest Elevations of her Prosperity, she makes frequent Acknowledg-
ments, That the Pleasure of her Wickedness was not worth the Repentance." As in *Moll Flanders*, the editor clears the text of indecent language
and thought. *Roxana* emulates its predecessor in the commitment to a didactic purpose (and in the narrative counterpoint to the commitment). The
author/editor/censor of *Moll Flanders* becomes the "writer" of *Roxana*, separated from the author of the preface and from the narrator by the third-
person masculine pronoun. The writer belongs to the realm of history and
projects truth from various perspectives, according to the presuppositions
of the preface.

In *Roxana*, Defoe adds reduplication to the prefatory base of *Moll
Flanders*, but otherwise the assertions are the same: the edited materials
reflect sinful events from the point of view of a reformed narrator/pro-
tagonist who rejects her past. Within the text, she will condemn her evil

deeds as she recounts them; beyond the text, the (virtuous) reader will savor message over mirth. The problematical areas of the narrative proper are those that concern self-recrimination and repentance, specifically the frequency and sincerity of one and the presence of the other. The significant but inconspicuous distinction between description and product in *Moll Flanders* illuminates the ambiguities of the word and the world. In this respect, the novel continues a discursive tradition foregrounded in the Spanish picaresque. *Roxana*, on the other hand, presents a glaring (and unambiguous) relation between the goals stated in the preface and the events of the memoirs. The preface to *Roxana* justifies a particular type of literary realism and a particular type of didacticism, but it only succeeds in the former. The latter, as often in the intertextual past, becomes a device employed for the sake of a scrupulous reading public or publisher, or as a self-conscious motif. The narrative analogue of the prefatory claim to morality is the ending of Roxana's history, as short on repentance as it is detailed on her immoral exploits. Between the preface and the concluding paragraph lies a unique version of the rogue's history, a social and economic elevation of the solitary orphan in search of prosperity. The voice of Roxana offers surprises in the juxtaposition of a damning self-interest and a praiseworthy spirit of independence. The character becomes an unlikely and ironic model of the liberated woman.

Following the author of the preface, the narrator vows to present her own character as impartially as possible, "as if I was speaking of anotherbody" (p. 6). Born in France and removed to England, Roxana enters an arranged marriage to a man she calls a fool. Left with five children after he abandons her eight years later, she delivers the children to relatives and faces destitution in the family home. Although "hitherto I had not only preserv'd the Virtue itself, but the virtuous Inclination and Resolution" (p. 29), Roxana allows herself to serve the passion of her landlord. Succumbing to poverty "at the dear Expence of Body and Soul, mortgaging Faith, Religion, Conscience, and Modesty, for . . . a Morsel of Bread" (p. 38), she establishes a pattern of existence that links the different stages of her progression in society. She enjoys her status as a kept woman, a situation marred by occasional pangs of conscience: "As much as I was harden'd, and that was as much, as I believe, ever any wicked Creature was, yet I could not help it; there was, and would be, Hours of Intervals, and of dark Reflections which came involuntarily in, and thrust in Sighs into the middle of all my Songs; and there would be, sometimes, a heaviness of Heart, which intermingl'd itself with all my Joy, and which would often fetch a Tear from my Eye" (p. 48). Roxana's contention that "there can be no substantial Satisfaction in a Life of Known Wickedness" (p. 49) appears to be an afterthought, for her vices increase along with her wealth. She bears her former landlord a son, accompanies him to France, and takes financial advantage of his death. She is once again alone but hardly impoverished. Early in life (and in the narrative), she is a pawn of avarice, as is Moll Flanders during her period as a thief. Roxana's solitude does not bear the burden of poverty, yet wealth breeds in her a hunger for luxury and rank.

Her discourse amplifies Moll's materialism to a maximum degree, relating her story almost exclusively in economic terms.

If she at first falls prey to poverty, Roxana now yields to vanity and greed. A powerful prince seeks her company and she becomes, as she calls herself, a queen of whores: "Never Woman, in such a Station, liv'd . . . in so compleat a fullness of Humane Delight; for to have the entire Possession of one of the most accomplish'd Princes in the World, and of the politest, best bred Man; to converse with him all Day, and, *as he profess'd*, charm him all Night; what could be more inexpressibly pleasing, and especially, to a Woman of a vast deal of Pride, as I was?" (p. 68). She spends eight years with the prince, bears him two sons, and travels with him to Italy. Passion for her lover and her way of life heighten her vanity. Although she laments the stained honor of her children, motherhood is above all an imposition, to the point at which Roxana feels no sorrow over the loss of a child. After the death of his wife, the prince repents of his indiscretions, leaving his mistress. Roxana's greatest concern is how to secure her wealth in order to maintain the style to which she has become accustomed. The Prince undergoes a reformation, both psychological and spiritual in nature, while Roxana changes settings and companions without a notable change of heart.

Resolved to return to England, Roxana consults a Dutch merchant living in Paris about the transferal of her money and jewels. After being caught in a lie about jewelry she had reported stolen from her former landlord, she escapes with the aid of the merchant. The journey on a tempestuous sea evokes a vow to turn away from evil: "Upon these serious Considerations, I was very Penitent . . . for my former Sins, and cry'd out, *tho' softly*, two or three times, *Lord have Mercy upon me*; to this, I added abundance of Resolutions, of what a Life I wou'd live, if it should please God but to spare my Life but this one time; how I would live a single and a virtuous Life, and spend a great deal of what I had thus wickedly got, in Acts of Charity, and doing Good" (p. 126). When the threat of death diminishes, so does the penitential zeal: "I had no thorow effectual Repentance; no Sight of my sins in their proper Shape; no View of a Redeemer, of Hope in him: I had only such a Repentance as a Criminal has at the Place of Execution, who is sorry, not that he has committed the Crime, as it is a Crime, but sorry *that he is to be Hang'd for it*" (p. 129). The lady of pleasure is now a woman of business, making her way to Rotterdam to settle accounts. Her merchant friend, a widower, pursues her and asks for her hand in marriage. Roxana's short-lived spirituality fades and is replaced by an obsessive practicality. She loves the merchant, but she loves freedom more. In this section of the narrative, she has a forum for her views on matrimony and on the rights of women. If her morality is questionable, her advocacy of a politics of economic equality is direct, theoretically sound, and pragmatically awkward.

Roxana opens her debate with a clever contrast of the position of wife to that of mistress, presenting both sides of the argument. In her personal history, however, she prefers the role of mistress: "I thought a Woman was a free Agent, as well as a Man, and was born free, and cou'd she manage herself suitably, might enjoy that Liberty to as much Purpose as the Men do; that the Laws of Matrimony were indeed, otherwise, and Mankind at this time, acted quite upon other Principles; and those such, that a Woman gave herself entirely away from herself, in Marriage, and capitulated only to be, at best, but *an Upper Servant*" (pp. 147–48). Roxana resents the passivity of married women, the forced indolence that deprives them of liberty, estate, and authority. She considers the merchant an exceptional and trust-worthy man, but she refuses to submit to the legal restraints of a marriage contract that would negate his promise of financial independence. Even when she becomes pregnant, Roxana adheres to her stance. Reflection in the narrative present casts her attitude in another light, as the preposterous act of a frivolous woman. Thought, discourse, and event answer to the dictates of an enigmatic freedom. Roxana holds up her story as a monument to pride, vanity, and ambition. The inversion of traditional roles—the man who insists on marriage and the woman who wishes to remain his mis-tress—accentuates the economic priorities of the protagonist and the com-promising security of marital ties. Roxana chooses solitude over servitude.

Roxana's wealth keeps her from being truly alone. She reestablishes herself in London and measures her social status in terms of acquisitions and appearance. The historical figure of Sir Robert Clayton, a noted economist, appears in the narrative, fittingly to aid Roxana in financial planning. Her independent spirit wins out over his advice to marry a merchant for se-curity; Sir Robert calls her speech on freedom for women "a kind of *Amazo-nian* language" (p. 171). Roxana moves from social queen to retreat as a mistress, always cognizant of her increasing wealth, which seems to grow in inverse proportion to her sense of guilt: "I may venture to say, that no Woman ever liv'd a Life like me, of six and twenty Years of Wickedness, without the least Signals of Remorse; without any Signs of Repentance; or without so much as a Wish to put an End to it; I had so long habituated myself to a Life of Vice, that really it appear'd to be no Vice to me; . . . I wallow'd in Wealth, and it flow'd in upon me at such a Rate . . . that I had at the End of the eight Years, two Thousand eight Hundred Pounds coming Yearly in, of which I did not spend one Penny, being maintain'd by my Allowance from my Lord _____" (p. 188). She does commend herself for a concern for the well-being of the five children she abandoned fifteen years earlier, and her attempt to find news of them effects a change of lifestyle and an emotional crisis, if not a genuine repentance.

Roxana discovers that her children suffered abuse at the hands of their aunt. The son who survives is an apprentice to a "mean trade" and the two daughters are maids. Through her companion Amy, Roxana arranges to train her son for a more distinguished position and to support her daugh-ters. It turns out that Susan, one of the daughters, is a maid in her mother's home. This stroke of irony determines the direction of Roxana's life and of her text. The curious and persistent Susan suspects that Roxana is her mother, and, to flee from exposure and from her wicked existence, Roxana takes up residence with a family of Quakers. She copies their habit and their speech, but her actions and her discourse continue to reflect self-interest.

The Dutch merchant appears in London and still wishes to marry her. Amy travels abroad to check on the whereabouts of the prince while Roxana stalls the merchant. Convinced that the Dutchman is her best bet, Roxana consents to marriage, and the two plan to settle in Holland. Meanwhile, Susan threatens to become her mother's nemesis, even endearing herself to the family of the ship's captain. Roxana must contend with her daughter's persistence, Amy's vow to kill Susan, the secrets she is hiding from her husband, and the imminent journey. Despite her triumphs, she does not find peace of mind, plagued as she is by the fear of ill fortune and the threat of exposure. Roxana overcomes all obstacles to arrive safely (and unexposed) in Holland.

The discourse of the final part of *Roxana* reflects the ambiguity and inconclusiveness of the ending. Directly following her marriage to the Dutch merchant, Roxana declares to have "put an End to all the intrieguing Part of my Life; a Life full of prosperous Wickedness; the Reflections upon which, were so much the more afflicting, as the time had been spent in the grossest Crimes, which the more I look'd-back upon, the more black and horrid they appear'd, effectually drinking up all the Comfort and Satisfaction which I might otherwise have taken in that Part of Life which was still before me" (p. 243). The statement implies a conscious will to reform, hindered only by memories of past evils, yet her commentary betrays her. Her professed concern for the children of her first marriage conflicts with her treatment of Susan, and she twice (both before and after the above quotation) admits her lack of love for her son by the merchant.[9] The closest thing to repentance in *Roxana* is a justifiably guilty conscience. Neither words nor deeds convince the reader of a transformation, for Roxana continues to plot, to conceal the truth, and to reject her daughter. From a rhetorical perspective, the most significant element of her discourse is the attempt to shift reader sympathy from Susan (the victim) to herself (the victimizer), as if she were an innocent pursued by an ingrate. The closing sections of the narrative detail a number of close calls that endanger her wedded bliss and bright prospects for the future. As narrator, Roxana offsets the self-criticism by calling on the reader to commiserate with her over the threat of exposure, again projecting Susan as the antagonist. In Holland, she worries that Amy may have killed Susan, a preoccupation that somewhat contradicts her actions. The past returns to haunt Roxana, but outside of the text.

Roxana devotes much literary space to the fears of her last days in London and to her fortunate escape. In contrast, she addresses one brief paragraph to the years in Holland: "Here, after some few Years of flourishing, and outwardly happy Circumstances, I fell into a dreadful Course of Calamities, and *Amy* also; the very Reverse of our former Good Days; the Blast of Heaven seem'd to follow the Injury done the poor Girl, by us both; and I was brought so low again, that my Repentance seem'd to be only the consequence of my Misery, as my Misery was of my Crime" (pp. 329–30). For a narrative that prides itself (in the preface) on its instructional value, the memoirs reveal in a most summary fashion the manifestations of poetic justice and of Roxana's penitence. The author of the preface summons the reader to note the narrator/protagonist's frequent self-reproach, but the text itself shows an unflinching character whose discourse remains as constant as her passion for wealth. The author says that "the Pleasure of her Wickedness was not worth the Repentance" while the narrator seems to be saying that sin is evil because it finally catches up with the sinner. She comprehends the reason for her punishment without indicating a knowledge of the nature of repentance. Although the preface maintains that conscience and repentance affect Roxana in the end, the penitential process that would counteract the moral and maternal crimes does not form part of the narrative. Roxana acknowledges childhood lessons in religion and honor, accuses the devil and avarice of corrupting her, yet she offers neither elaboration of her change nor narrative analogues of this change. The brevity and abruptness of the ending may testify to the presence of an author who wishes to control the textual message. His failure to do so, given the obviousness of this failure, attests to the priority of fiction by subordinating the preface to the level of pretext.[10]

The sense of history that pervades *Moll Flanders* is not as evident in *Roxana*. Moll Flanders is born at Newgate and returns to Newgate. Fate reunites her with her mother and with her fourth husband, and she makes significant return voyages to Virginia and to England. An ambiguous determinism accompanies her through life. Roxana, on the other hand, forges her own way, makes her own rules, and defines her own codes. The presence of her first husband in Paris—Amy, not Roxana, speaks with him—foreshadows the discovery of Susan's identity, but the past in *Roxana* is of the character's making. Roxana flees not so much from destiny as from her sins, a conflict incarnated in the flight from her daughter. Moll Flanders dedicates a good portion of her narrative to the motif of crime and punishment. The reader sees her edging closer and closer to apprehension by the authorities. Roxana describes a similar situation in the pursuit by Susan, but in this case the guilty party not only escapes but also elicits reader sympathy for her cause. The text concerns itself with crime; the punishment, as it were, occurs offstage. In *Moll Flanders*, the author battles with the narrator over the message of the private history. For the author, the story is a means to a didactic end, as confirmed by the instructive and penitential bent of the memoirs. The narrator seems to be telling a slightly different story, marked by the predominance of Moll's voice and the "original" manuscript. In *Roxana*, the tension between the competing voices diminishes because the gap between the mimetic and the diegetic widens. Social institutions and a representative of the spiritual order teach Moll Flanders the importance of penitence, and fate coddles the repentant sinner. Both the individual and society benefit from the reformation. Roxana is a character in stasis. The linear argument presents shifts in time and place but not in priorities. Repentance is a word, not an act. The payment for sins is a blast from heaven absent from the text.

The private histories, narrated in the first person and with a professed emphasis on impartiality, employ a discourse in which the lexicon of economic security replaces that of traditional domesticity. Moll Flanders and Roxana invent means to survive in society, and, when survival is no longer an issue, they seek greater wealth. Moll Flanders begins as a desolate orphan, and the relative prosperity she achieves as a thief reaches new heights in *Roxana*. Roxana moves from the burgeoning middle class to a déclassé ground of sexual and financial power. The two narratives show individuals dominated by materialism and forced by society and/or fate to suffer the consequences of their avarice. The eighteenth-century reader, if enlightened, may have focused on social redemption, while the more detached reader may see a dialectical connection between the social value of money and individual means of attaining wealth. The subtext seems to reflect this tension by presenting the problematic aspects of repentance. Moll has no action to prove her conversion, and Roxana's repentance has the force of one word in her memoirs. The discursive structure of the narratives captures—inaugurates—the complex system of message production shared by the two works.[11]

In *Guzmán de Alfarache*, the discourse functions as a validation or a refutation of the purported spiritual conversion of the narrator/protagonist. The linguistic contextualization—the means and variations of imparting messages—determines (as opposed to being determined by) the social content of the work. There is a relation not only between the mimetic and diegetic elements of the text but also between the multiple and complex diegetic elements, between the differentiated "voices" that tell the story or, more properly, stories. The discursive conflict between Guzmán as an ideal convert and Guzmán as an embittered sinner conveys messages that comprise the story. Analysis of the discourse creates a framework for the narrative events and for the discovery of the text. The irony of language and circumstance owes a debt to the implied authorial presence in *Lazarillo de Tormes*. Defoe revises the scheme by inserting a Cervantine editor, a fictionalized version of the author, into the work. The particular contribution of this figure is implied, but the presence is explicit. The interplay of preface and memoirs leads the way to a consideration of the "distorted" text and its literary and social significance. The author makes his presence and his motives known in the preface; the narrators, uncommitted to unified messages, write their private histories spontaneously and openly. The authorial censorship intrudes on but does not destroy the spontaneity and the openness of the edited narratives. The resistance of the memoirs to rewriting points to the art and the aims of narrative. Defoe's interest in the historical or realistic components of the story extends to his conception of the storytelling process. The female voices narrate events that explore the place of women in society and in texts.

Two message systems function in the private histories. The first, established in the preface, centers on the text in its exemplary role. The lives show a retreat from and then a return to moral values, according to the premises of the author, who acknowledges his modification of the original material while arguing that the narrators are mindful of the question of moral unity. The prefatory commentaries allow the reader to define the second system, based on the "independent" portions of the text, those narrative elements that do not support the reading and revision of the fictionalized author. The preface of *Moll Flanders* suggests a closer adherence to poetic justice, a more introspective narrator, and a more demonstrable repentance than the memoirs actually provide. *Roxana* extends the distance between the mimetic and the diegetic by exaggerating the narrative tension of *Moll Flanders*. Roxana's discourse is a gloss on the theme of interest, a linguistic displacement of economic categories for human feelings. Both Moll Flanders and Roxana deal with the particular problems of women in society. Moll enters the male domain to seek wealth and matrimony. She plays by the men's rules and suffers as they do. Roxana is more daring in her approach, and the stakes are higher. Ironically, her success as a mistress leads to the eloquent (and clearly pro-feminist) speech on legal inequities for women. She rejects the marriage proposal of the man she loves for the sake of her independence and for the love of her estate. Fate works for the repentant Moll while it conspires against Roxana to bring about her repentance. The society that rehabilitates Moll Flanders (with the aid of fate) is the object of Roxana's egalitarian plea. The two narratives illustrate the consequences of rebellion. *Moll Flanders* reforms the rebel, who in turn lauds the institutions that earlier caused her alienation; *Roxana* allows the rebel to prosper by flouting the conventions of morality and matrimony up to the final paragraph of the memoirs.

In *Moll Flanders* and *Roxana*, the male voices describe an order that the female voices do not fully respect. This discursive phenomenon relates to the multiple facets of the act of narration and to the social implications of sexual difference. The author within the text edits an unseen (imaginary) manuscript to agree with his real or ideal reading. If the narrator fails to recognize all that she reveals, the author similarly allows the narrator to go beyond and even to contradict the premises of the directed reading. The female voice becomes, in part, a voice of resistance, moving from the literary to the social perspective. *Moll Flanders* depicts a tension between the didactic intention alluded to in the preface and in the memoirs themselves, and *Roxana* expands the distance between professed message and "real" message(s). The conflicting semiotic systems constitute a valid and vital part of the texts, as in the case of *Lazarillo de Tormes*, *Guzmán de Alfarache*, and *El Buscón*. Apart from *La pícara Justina*, the early feminine picaresque novels stress incident over the question of narrative control. Defoe returns to and reexamines the poetics of discourse. While he does not give the female narrator an unmediated voice, he removes her from the silence of the Spanish models. Whether by design or not, he opens the way for the liberated (if not unmediated) voices of the future.

5 THE OBLIGING NARRATOR
Tristana and the Rhetoric of Irony

Oigo desde aquí las palomitas, y entiendo sus arrullos. Pregúntales por qué tengo yo esta ambición loca que no me deja vivir; por qué aspiro a lo imposible, y aspiraré siempre, hasta que el imposible mismo se me plante enfrente y me diga: "Pero ¿no me ve usted, so . . . ?" Pregúntales por qué sueño despierta con mi propio ser transportado a otro mundo, en el cual me veo libre y honrada.

From here I listen to the little doves, and I understand their cooing. Ask them why I have this crazy ambition that doesn't let me live; why I aspire to the impossible and will aspire always, until the impossible itself stands before me and says, "But don't you see me, you . . . ?" Ask them why I dream when I'm awake with my own being transported to another world, in which I see myself free and honorable.

When is a woman not a woman? Perhaps when a man creates her, puts words into her mouth, and allows a male-dominated society to defeat her. These are the obstacles that face the Spanish picaresque antiheroines, who somehow manage to register voices, identities, and subversive subtexts in narratives not entirely their own. From *La lozana andaluza* to *La garduña de Sevilla*, the authors become increasingly insensitive to the protagonists as victims and as women. The *pícaras* are wrongdoers to be punished by the community at large (if not by individual men) and by writers with social doctrine on their side and fate within their control. Even when an enlightened society redeems her, as in the case of Moll Flanders, the antiheroine employs a discourse that serves the saving powers while only summarily addressing the causes of delinquency and the uniqueness of womanhood. In an essay on women in eighteenth-century English literature, John J. Richetti uses the term "female impersonator" to describe Moll Flanders and Roxana: "For them, sexuality is simply an available and efficient means for self-advancement and survival. . . . They are essentially male creations, characters who use their dreadful female problems as opportunities for demonstrating their skill and cunning in survival. They remain to all intents and purposes untouched by the special quality of female experience."[1] The female experience becomes part of the antiheroine's text, but not without the mediation of society, male voices, and the intertextual past.

In nineteenth-century Europe, the industrial revolution brings an altered view of man. The work ethic and the economic changes it fashions overturn traditional hierarchies. Upward mobility is no longer an illusion. Even in Spain, where insistence on blood lines and resistance to manual labor are the markers of aristocracy, the middle class finds a new power and a new doctrine in financial security. Benito Pérez Galdós's *Tristana* reflects the transitional period by contrasting an elderly and impoverished gentleman with a young artist seeking to break the restraints of his heredity. Society accommodates both of these men but not the woman who stands between them. Tristana's intellectual promise and aspirations have no place in the so-called progressive order. She is a rebel not because she opposes progress but because she wants to be a part of it, because she does not know her place.[2] Galdós presents her predicament through a dialectic of language and event. Messages rest on judgment, and the narrator of *Tristana* judges the characters by way of a subtle and ironic discourse, a discourse that separates feminism from antifeminism.

The ironic reading of a literary text may produce a circle of ironies, levels of interpretation in which one irony leads to another, ad infinitum. An ultimate irony, in terms of literary criticism, may be the vastly different analyses of texts by those who read ironically and by those who do not. Acceptance of an ironic meaning forces rejection of a literal meaning, yet, as Wayne Booth has demonstrated in *A Rhetoric of Irony*, neither internal nor external clues are totally reliable for determining whether a given statement is accurate or misleading, to be taken literally or ironically.[3] The art of defining an author's perspective, both crucial and elusive, becomes one of learned intuition. At a certain point, the critic (and, less consciously, the reader) must make a decision that more often than not will be all right or all wrong, and the difficulties are heightened by the fact that there may be no consistent pattern of irony.

One does not have to be flightily romantic nor overly inclined toward symbolic interpretation to recognize, for example, that *Don Quijote* is a more complex, more sophisticated novel now than it was in 1615. Novelistic experimentation and the theory of the novel, on becoming more complex and more sophisticated, have illuminated aspects of the work that the seventeenth-century reader and critic could not have discerned. Similarly, *Tristana* is perhaps a more effective work now than in 1892 because the source of its irony has been more clearly elucidated and because its almost precognitive social stand has been verified. The novel focuses on a woman who must confront traditional and dogmatic social positions and who rejects accepted views regarding education, career potential, and feminine honor. The fact that Tristana is fighting a losing battle is not as significant as the battle itself, a battle that must be viewed in light of Galdós's system of absolute values. The self-conscious use of literature as a mediating factor (as in the depiction of Don Lope as a Don Quijote turned Don Juan, seducer of Tristana, whose name derives from the chivalric tradition) allows for the elaboration of a multifaceted analogic structure that illustrates Galdós's feminist position. The foundation of this structure is the ironic narrative voice.

Simply put, the storyteller, the manipulator of the literary events, loads the deck. The narrator is in full sympathy with Tristana. The novel is not parodic, but ironic. The impossibility of realization of Tristana's goals is not due to her mother's mental instability and the inheritance of insanity, nor to the defiance of natural law (in which the amputation of the leg may be seen as nature's revenge), nor because she has an incomplete and unrealistic vision of society, nor because she is too given to idealism. For Tristana, there is no hope from the beginning, no possible way to act, no way to plan for the future, no realistic course of action. Galdós has created a blind alley, and the subject, as in his early thesis novels, is intolerance and the cruelties of society, only here the treatment is more subtle, more ironic. The narrator is the mediator of Tristana and her circumstances, and he can manipulate character and situation. It is precisely the narrator's stance, the strength and nuances of his voice, that one must intuit to comprehend *Tristana*. Galdós's implied author is the creator of a double standard of discourse. The comic tone and the apparently happy ending belie the direction of the text. Discourse seems to be copying society and fate as it reacts against victimization. The narrator is Marc Antony to Don Lope's Brutus.

The tension between the narrative persona as observer and omniscient witness, his attitude toward the characters, the subtlety of his expression, the literary orientation of his rhetorical devices, and the development of an external viewpoint put Galdós in full control of his material. He creates an internal or covert irony to replace the obvious or overt irony of the thesis novels.[4] By establishing an open and unlimited perspective, Galdós can work (and play) on a number of levels. The final effect is tragicomic because the tragic potential of the major social theme is countered by a resolution that initially seems anticlimactic and, perhaps more significantly, by a reduction of the "real" attributes of the characters. Linked to literary prototypes and increasingly dependent on the narrator, the characters are so fictionalized as to become indistinguishable from the storyteller.

While recognizing Galdós as "the most complex presence in his novel," David I. Grossvogel believes that the characters of *Tristana* suffer at the hands of the powerful narrator, that "mocked and manipulated by the author, his people are prevented from achieving fully their fictional self-definition: a part of them exists as a function of his commentary."[5] For Grossvogel, the narrator's strength is the novel's weakness: "From a surrealist point of view, Galdós is twice a prisoner of his words. He uses them not for themselves (as pure sound, or *objects*) but as signs (symbols), and he does so not in order to create an object that will stand separate from him, but to inform mere phantasms with his commenting (mental) presence."[6] This reading denies an open structure, multiple sources of ambiguity, and all but the most inadvertent of ironies. Thus, "the author, having shaped his protagonists to his Procrustean bed, marries them off to each other without even the benefit of a bitter afterthought."[7] One could argue that the effect is precisely the opposite.

In *Tristana*, Galdós deals in literary terms with a social issue on which he takes a definite stand. The social issue forms part of a work of art that is determined but not restricted by thematic elements. The novelist must treat reality differently than the essayist by working indirectly to make a statement and by subjecting that statement to the rules of art. Thus, there can result a ricocheting effect between the social backdrop and the literary precedents, all within a newly created literary world. The narrator synthesizes the diverse elements and adds to them a commentary that, rather than closing the narrative by asphyxiating the characters, opens it by speaking ambiguously and by constantly changing the points of reference. In this system, the narrator (or the author controlling the narrator) makes no attempt to detach himself from the characters, as they unite to form a comprehensive perspective. The fact that the character cannot be separated from the storyteller, like the proverbial dancer and the dance, in no way undermines Galdós's vision and to a certain extent makes it more forceful. The narrator is the source of the discourse—the content and the mode of communication—and Galdós gives him the dual function of showing and telling. He is the intratextual ally of the implied author. Hardly a prisoner of his words, he is the master of both situation and diction, playing all sides, arguing all points, exploring the infinite uses of language, and dominating the universe he has created by providing a means of decoding the novel's ambiguities. The decoding of ambiguities in this case is synonymous with defining the ironic structure of *Tristana*. The wedding of Tristana and Don Lope is far more than a weak allusion to the marriage ending traceable to ancient comedy; it is the final irony of the novel and the culmination of an intricate series of ironies.

The narrative persona takes charge from the opening passages of the novel and maintains full authority throughout. He relies heavily on a synthesis of perspectives, on establishing a compatibility between seemingly incompatible conventions. *Tristana* begins with a description of Don Lope and his milieu, with clear allusions to *Don Quijote*: an *hidalgo* (lesser nobleman), a confusion of names (Don Juan López Garrido becomes Don Lope, "made up by the gentleman himself"), a quotidian schedule, and two female figures reminiscent of the housekeeper and niece of Cervantes's novel. Galdós has his narrator borrow a literary voice before his own voice can be heard; an anachronistic (derivative) discourse presents an anachronistic Don Quijote, a nineteenth-century *hidalgo* portrayed in incongruous terms. The gentleman, whose name and military bearing suggest the noble soldiers of old, inhabits cheap rented quarters with the sound of taverngoers and goats in the background.[8]

The chivalric overtones of the introductory chapter are purely ironic, for this gentleman is the antithesis of Don Quijote. Like the monkey dressed in silk who remains a monkey—Spain's version of the sow's ear—Don Lope is a despicable figure despite the knightly linguistic trimmings. The narrator seems fully conscious of the discrepancy, which becomes the basis of the novel's irony. The narrator's attitude toward Don Lope reflects the interplay between art and concept that characterizes Galdós's approach. The mock-serious, ultimately burlesque treatment of Don Lope makes a statement and makes it creatively. He is an egotist ("En afeitarse y acicalarse, pues cuidaba de su persona con esmero y lentitudes de hombre de mundo, se pasaban dos horitas," [p. 9; In shaving and sprucing himself up, since he cared for his person with the meticulousness and leisure of a man of the world, he spent a good two hours]), a man who takes himself too seriously ("O había que matarle o decirle don Lope," [p. 8; You either had to kill him or call him *Don* Lope]), and a womanizer ("Se preciaba de haber asaltado más torres de virtud y rendido más plazas de honestidad que pelos tenía en la cabeza," [p. 8; He prided himself on having assaulted more towers of virtue and having conquered more centers of purity than he had hairs on his head]).

Just as he initiates the novel with a voice not entirely his own, the narrator gives himself what may be termed a false presence, that of uninformed observer. He writes in a tentative style of his acquaintance with the characters and with studied uncertainty of the identity of Tristana and her relationship with Don Lope. During the course of the narration, the outsider looking in will become omniscient, and this discursive change will be matched by a change from the opening impression of the title figure. Tristana appears to be beautiful but lifeless, ironically detached from society. Her perfectly formed hands, like her body and her clothing, hold a mysterious virtue and seem to proclaim that the misery of the physical world cannot touch her ("Sus manos, de una forma perfecta . . . , tenían misteriosa virtud, como su cuerpo y ropa, para poder decir a las capas inferiores del mundo físico: *la vostra miseria non mi tange,*" p. 10). The first chapter ends with a partial clarification of Tristana's role in Don Lope's household: "No era hija, ni sobrina, ni esposa, ni nada del gran don Lope; no era nada y lo era todo, pues le pertenecía como una petaca, un mueble o una prenda de ropa, sin que nadie se la pudiera disputar; ¡y ella parecía tan resignada a ser petaca, y siempre petaca!" (p. 11; She was not the daughter, nor the niece, nor the wife, nor anything of the great Don Lope; she was not anything and yet she was everything, for she belonged to him like a tobacco pouch, a piece of furniture, or an article of clothing for which no one else could stake a claim. And she seemed so resigned to be a tobacco pouch, now and always!). The passages are, of course, ironic. Tristana will hardly be immune from the world's misery, and she will refuse to resign herself to a negligible social role until the moment of her final and ambiguous conversion. The narrator is asking the reader to analyze the written word, to question the apparent, and to search for meanings. From the beginning, he is asking the reader to read ironically.

The examination of Don Lope continues in the second chapter, in which the narrator purportedly attempts to be truthful, "so that one will not run the risk of considering him either better or worse than he really was." The narrator describes Don Lope as "muy amigo de sus amigos," "servicial hasta el heroísmo" (p. 15; a great friend to his friends, accommodating to the point of heroism). The praise seems straightforward until the reader becomes aware that the specific case used to demonstrate Don Lope's generosity is that of Don Antonio Reluz, Tristana's father. Don Lope saves his friend but destroys his friend's daughter; he frees Don Antonio from jail and later imprisons Tristana. Don Antonio was deceived by an unfaithful partner, and the man who brings about his salvation ultimately proves himself to be an unfaithful friend. The case of Don Antonio follows a series of general statements concerning the character of Don Lope, all of which emphasize his hypocrisy.

A motivating force in Don Lope's life is a resuscitated code of honor that is as shallow and dependent on appearances as its exponent. The industrial revolution is inimical to the views of the class-conscious Don Lope, in whose opinion society has created diverse mechanisms to persecute the well-born and to deprive them of their due. The narrative voice reaches its highest tenor in a supremely ironic passage that combines exposition and direct quotation to accentuate Don Lope's hypocritical nature while seeming to present him as an enemy of hypocrisy:

> Respecto a la Iglesia, teníala por una broma pesada, que los pasados siglos vienen dando a los presentes, y que éstos aguantan por timidez y cortedad de genio. Y no se crea que era irreligioso: al contrario, su fe superaba a la de muchos que hocican ante los altares y andan siempre entre curas. A éstos no los podía ver ni escritos el ingenioso don Lope, porque no encontraba sitio para ellos en el sistema seudo-caballeresco que su desocupado magín se había forjado, y solía decir: "Los verdaderos sacerdotes somos nosotros, los que regulamos el honor y la moral, los que combatimos en pro del inocente, los enemigos de la maldad, de la hipocresía, de la injusticia . . . y del vil metal." (pp. 14–15)

> As for the Church, he considered it a hoax, a practical joke that past centuries have bequeathed to the present and that people put up with out of fear and lack of character. But do not think that he was irreligious: on the contrary, his faith surpassed that of many who nose around the altars and keep company with priests. The ingenious Don Lope could not stand the sight of these people, since he could not find a place for them in the pseudo-chivalric system that his unoccupied imagination had forged, and he often said, "We who regulate honor and morality are the true priests, the ones who fight for the rights of the innocent, we who are the enemies of evil, of hypocrisy, of injustice, and of filthy lucre."

The narrator's message is playful but obvious. Subsequent affirmations of Don Lope's benevolence, even from the narrator himself, are not to be trusted.

In this chapter, Don Lope's view of the past is contrasted with Tristana's bleak vision of the future, a future that seems to hold nothing for her. Tristana's coming of age brings a wish for independence and a recognition of the absence of possibilities. The narrator employs verbal humor to capture the incongruity of the matter—"Ejercía sobre ella su dueño un despotismo que podremos llamar seductor" (p. 12; Her master exercised over her a despotism that one could call seductive)—so that once again the conceptual analogue finds a linguistic counterpart. The lack of decorum and the ironic courtly imagery relate deceptive diction to the deceptive behavior of Don Lope and to its effect on Tristana. Don Lope is an unceasing opponent of absolute justice. He abides by an anachronistic and retrogressive code, and his opposition to progress is mirrored on an individual level in the seduction of Tristana, a figurative destruction of her prospects for the future.

The Cervantine fictional world provides the backdrop for the third chapter, devoted primarily to Tristana's mother, Doña Josefina, a woman who finds release from the tribulations of the real world in the ideal world of chivalry. In her passion for the past, she gives her daughter a name that will be a constant reminder of an ideal society and that may help to block out crude and vulgar realities. After her husband's death, Doña Josefina enters a fantasy world in which she is dominated by two obsessions: moving from house to house and an inordinate concern for cleanliness. Before she dies, she realizes the error of her ways and rejects the fantasies, like the moribund Don Quijote. In this moment of apparent lucidity, Doña Josefina delivers her daughter to Don Lope.

The narrator imposes a pattern of idealism and a tendency to exalt the literary over the real not only on Doña Josefina but on Tristana as well. Within this system, one can rationalize Tristana's subsequent actions in terms of an inheritance of madness, absurd idealism, and a final awakening to reality. Like her mother, Tristana may escape the real by wishing for the impossible ideal, and she will be defeated in her irrational quest. Read ironically, on the other hand, the account of Doña Josefina can serve as an inverse analogue of Tristana's case. In the first instance a woman who cannot face reality hides behind a literary facade, while in the second instance a woman fights for absolute values in a society given to relative and arbitrary values. Don Lope, the so-called protector of Tristana, sacrifices his collection of arms to pay Doña Josefina's debts (without, however, giving up his collection of portraits of beautiful women), and as repayment he dishonors Tristana within two months. The stage is set for Tristana's confrontation with society.

In the third chapter, the narrator introduces what may be a false analogy between Tristana and her mother. In chapter 4, he introduces a startling simile, an omen of Tristana's fate. Speaking of Don Lope, he says, "Al sentido moral del buen caballero le faltaba una pieza importante, cual órgano que ha sufrido una mutilación y sólo funciona con limitaciones o paradas deplorables" (p. 23; The moral sense of the good gentleman was lacking an important part, like an organ that has suffered mutilation and only functions with limitations or deplorable halts). As with Doña Josefina, the comparison may underscore the differences. In the same chapter, the narrator presents Tristana in the context of Don Lope's perverse ethical code ("sus perversas doctrinas," p. 24), verified in his rationale for the seduction: "¿No me pidió Josefina que la amparase? Pues más amparo no cabe. Bien defendida la tengo de todo peligro; que ahora nadie se atreverá a tocarle el pelo de la ropa" (p. 25; Didn't Josefina ask me to protect her? Well, she couldn't ask for greater protection. I have her well defended against any danger, for now no one would even dare to lay a finger on her).

At first, Tristana accepts the ideas of her guardian without realizing the gravity of his actions. She is open to the imaginative notions, compatible with her readiness to idealize, to view things not as they are but as they should be. Soon, however, she recognizes the ludicrous position of Don Lope: "Bruscamente vio en Don Lope al viejo, y agrandaba con su fantasía la ridícula presunción del anciano que, contraviniendo la ley de la Naturaleza, hace papeles de galán" (pp. 26–27; All of a sudden she noticed that Don Lope was old, and in her imagination she magnified the ridiculous presumptions of the elderly gentleman who, violating the law of Nature, plays the role of ladies' man). At the same time, she recognizes something in herself, an intrinsic self-worth, a "consciousness of not being a vulgar person" ("consciencia de no ser una persona vulgar," p. 27). After eight months with Don Lope—and metaphorically linked to a premature infant— Tristana undergoes a spiritual awakening that will mark her future. Her new moral sense could hardly have been learned from Don Lope. His lessons have taught her to reject the future, and her aim now is to transcend the present. Certain of Tristana's ideas, such as a negative view of marriage, will conform to Don Lope's outlook, but the narrator makes it clear in this chapter that there is a distinction between the moral base of the two ideologies; the motives are different, even when the ideas are the same.

The friendship between Tristana and the servant Saturna produces a dialogue on the social restrictions of women. The conversation is not a debate. Both women feel that while those of their sex should be both free and honorable, society makes the two categories mutually exclusive. Nevertheless, Saturna adopts a realistic position ("pintándole el mundo y los hombres con sincero realismo," pp. 28–29), while Tristana in her idealism dreams of changes and castles in the air ("armando castilletes de la vida futura," p. 29). Saturna discusses the possibilities for women: "Sólo tres carreras pueden seguir las que visten faldas: a casarse, que carrera es, o el teatro . . . , vamos, ser cómica, que es buen modo de vivir, o . . . no quiero nombrar lo otro. Figúreselo" (p. 29; There are only three professions open to those who wear skirts: getting married, which is a profession, or the theater . . . , well, being an actress, which is a good way to live, or . . . , I refuse to name the other. You figure it out). Tristana is disturbed by the options because she has the inclination and the talent for none of them. What she would prefer is a so-called man's job: "Si nos hicieran médicas, abogadas, siquiera boticarias o escribanas, ya que no ministras y senadoras, podríamos . . ." (p. 30; If they would let us become doctors, lawyers, even druggists or clerks, if not ministers or senators, we could . . .). Tristana here is not groping at windmills. Conscious of the enemy and the difficulties implicit in the struggle, she feels a need for self-fulfillment and for exploration of her full potential: "Ideas, lo que llamamos ideas, creo que no me faltan" (p. 30; Ideas, what we could call solid ideas, I believe I have in me). In this chapter, the narrator lets the characters speak for themselves. There is no burlesque tone to weaken the argument, and the result is a clearly established bond between the women.

Chapter 6 marks the culmination of a literary transformation: Don Lope changes from an antithetical Quijote figure to a Don Juan grown old ("el Don Juan caído," p. 33). Faced with poverty and old age, he loses self-confidence but not pride. He is given to fits of jealousy, and when the narrator speaks of "the old man and the young girl," another literary tradition comes into play. Don Lope's jealousy prepares the way for the introduction of the third member of the amorous triangle in the following chapter. The scene is set, as well, for an ironic reversal. The narrator stresses the ridiculous egotism of Don Lope before introducing a young lover who, if the traditional literary analogue is completed, will make a fool of the old man and carry off the young lady. This would be the world of poetic justice, not the world of *Tristana*.

Before the meeting with Horacio, the narrator reaffirms the moral superiority of Tristana ("La tranquilidad de su conciencia dábale valor contra el tirano," [p. 37; The tranquillity of her conscience gave her strength against the tyrant]). Her profound sympathy for the blind children at the orphan asylum has self-referential and symbolic overtones. Tristana seems to see herself in the incomplete world of the handicapped as one whose mental processes surpass her options. Ironically, she notices Horacio as she is warning Saturna's son not to play with fire, and her love for the artist begins at that moment. From the beginning of their relationship, Tristana cannot bring herself to play conventional social roles, to subtly let herself be courted; her discourse is sincere and direct. In a manner of speaking, she enters blindly into the affair with Horacio. She is guided by the initial attraction—partly physical, partly idealized—and by her wish to abandon Don Lope. Because the narrator has consistently contrasted Tristana's honesty with Don Lope's hypocrisy, the reader may view the expression of Tristana's love as real and the progression of that love as credible.

Tristana's love for Horacio grows on two levels, based on her contact with him and her absence from him. In the first case, she becomes intrigued by the events of his life, which she sees as a type of martyrdom, and, in the second, she glorifies him in combined adulation and spiritualism ("un espiritualismo delirante," p. 45). Love is both immediate and atemporal—"Te estoy queriendo, te estoy buscando desde antes de nacer" (p. 44; I've been loving you, I've been searching for you since before I was born)—and the letters to Horacio offer Tristana a means of self-expression. Although, in her exaltation of Horacio, Tristana does not intuit the similarity of their backgrounds, the narrator focuses on the figurative slavery of each of them. The radical difference is that Horacio, once freed from the dominance of his tyrannical grandfather, is able to experience life, to make mistakes, and to continue to have society's approval of his actions, while Tristana will never be free of Don Lope. The narrator seems aware of the irony of Tristana's sympathy when he says that Horacio's story "almost seemed like a saint's life worthy of a small space in the martyrology" ("casi parecía vida de un santo digna de un huequecito en el martirologio," p. 51). In a society that is beginning to accept and to respect the concept of upward mobility, the new alternatives apply exclusively to men, and women are to remain the true martyrs of the will.

Tristana's idealism is matched by that of Horacio, who views his present idyllic state as the poetically just conclusion to a long period of misery and who is as prone as Tristana to verbalize his feelings of ecstasy. The narrator becomes part of this romanticized universe in his descriptions of the lovers' actions: "La separación, algunas noches tan dolorosa y patética como si Horacio se marchara para el fin del mundo y Tristana se despidiera para meterse monja" (p. 56; The separation, some nights so painful and pathetic, as if Horacio were marching off to the ends of the earth and Tristana were bidding farewell before entering a convent). This realm of mutual exaltation exists unencumbered by the presence of Don Lope, who does not appear in chapters 7, 8, and 9. When Don Lope returns in chapter 10, the narrator's recourse to courtly love imagery once again becomes ironic, with Tristana as a "captive" of the "tyrant." At this point, Tristana sees herself as a true romantic heroine, willing to suffer for her love, and in an ironic passage she says, "Créete que en vez de apurar la felicidad, nos vendría bien ahora algún contratiempo, una miajita de desgracia. El amor es sacrificio, y para la abnegación y el dolor debemos estar preparados siempre" (p. 61; You'd better believe that, instead of using up our happiness, a small setback, a little morsel of misfortune, would do us good. Love is sacrifice, and we always ought to be prepared for self-denial and pain). Tristana is a symbolic prisoner of love, a real prisoner of Don Lope and of social mores, and the victim of an ironist who makes her figurative speech literal.

After Tristana makes her confession to Horacio—quite possibly the sacrificial act she has imagined, but ironically only a minor indication of the suffering to come—she describes Don Lope in the same terms used by the narrator, as a Don Juan Tenorio with a wide range of victims. The characters draw from the narrator, who in turn draws from literature to create a contemporary social analogue. Don Lope, conscious of the role imposed on him by Doña Josefina, shows the outward signs of a gentleman whose only concerns are Tristana's well-being and the defense of her honor. Tristana calls him a hypocrite and a liar, and the narrator notes mockingly, "It's a shame he didn't speak in verse so he could be the perfect image of the *noble father* of the plays of old" ("¡Lástima que no hablara en verso para ser perfecta imagen del *padre noble* de antigua comedia!," p. 70). Don Lope's role-playing makes Tristana more determined than ever to escape the repressive environment. If he is to emulate the vengeful father of drama, she will justify the wrath by visiting Horacio in his study.

For the narrator, Tristana's decision marks a fusion of the real and the ideal: "Pasearon . . . en el breve campo del estudio, desde el polo de lo ideal al de las realidades; recorrieron toda la esfera, desde lo humano a lo divino, sin poder determinar fácilmente la divisoria entre uno y otro, pues lo humano les parecía del cielo y lo divino revestíase a sus ojos de carne mortal" (p. 75; They walked around in the small area of the study, from the pole of the ideal to that of reality; they covered the entire sphere, from the human to the divine, without being able to determine easily the dividing line between one and the other, for the human seemed like heaven to them and in their eyes the divine clothed herself in mortal flesh). The experience opens

Tristana's eyes, making her aware of the beauty of nature and art and aware of her own shortcomings. The contact with Horacio allows her to discover the inadequacy of her education and upbringing. The success of her early efforts at painting both emphasizes the wasted years and indicates that the opportunities available to Horacio, and to men in general, do not exist for women.[9]

The narrator takes care to provide a realistic rather than an idealistic backdrop for Tristana's paean to honorable freedom. The physical encounters with Horacio broaden her perspective and let her see that happiness is within her grasp. Present reality, to an extent, supports her idealism. As Tristana grows intellectually and as her goals increase, she affects both Horacio and Don Lope. With respect to Horacio, "empezó a notar que la enamorada joven se iba creciendo a los ojos de él y le empequeñecía. En verdad que esto le causaba sorpresa, y casi casi empezaba a contrariarle, porque había soñado en Tristana la mujer subordinada al hombre en inteligencia y en voluntad, la esposa que vive de la savia moral e intelectual del esposo y que con los ojos y con el corazón de él ve y siente" (p. 77; he began to note that the young woman in love was growing in his eyes and that he was getting smaller. In truth, this took him by surprise, and it almost— almost—began to bother him, because he had dreamed of Tristana as a woman subordinate to man in intelligence and in will, the wife who lives off the moral and intellectual energy of her husband and who sees and feels with his eyes and with his heart). The spiritual awakening is reciprocal, but although Horacio is profoundly moved by Tristana's ideas and recognizes the impact of these ideas on his life, he seems surprisingly conventional when his (apparently) progressive attitude is put to the test. He wants a woman who will be an extension of himself and whose inferior status will accentuate his own superiority. He accepts Tristana's idealism up to the point at which it could materialize. In his way, he is as hypocritical as Don Lope.

Blinded by love, Tristana mistakes Horacio's condescension for sincerity. Her faith in him, whether justified or not, gives her the courage necessary to defy Don Lope, and the old man dares not scold her, "supposing that, at the slightest provocation, the slave would show her intention of refusing to be one" ("adivinando que, al menor choque, la esclava sabría mostrar intenciones de no serlo," p. 79). Tristana seems to have won the love of a man willing to disregard the negative aspects of her past, and in doing so she has freed herself from dependence on Don Lope. The path has been cleared for her confrontation with society, for putting into practice her personal concept of freedom. Her trust in Horacio is unfounded, however. While outwardly supporting her, he thinks otherwise: "Esperaba que su constante cariño y la acción del tiempo rebajarían un poco la talla imaginativa y razonante de su ídolo, haciéndola más mujer, más doméstica, más corriente y útil" (p. 82; He hoped that his constant affection and the passage of time would reduce somewhat the fanciful and reasoning stature of his idol, making her more of a woman, more domestic, more typical and useful). If Tristana is overly optimistic in her hopes for social change,

Horacio seems to want to convert the "new woman" whom he loves into a domestic servant. Tristana's idealism becomes ironic when, on defending the position of a mother regarding her child, she tells Horacio that nature gives her more rights than it gives him. The reader will see that nature's rights mean very little when superseded by those of society. Tristana is bound by absolute principles in a world that exalts relative values.

In chapter 15, the narrator establishes a literary and at times symbolic base for the treatment of the social issue. The most obvious convention is the creation of a lovers' vocabulary, an intricate and intimate use of language by Tristana and Horacio.[10] The primary models for their expressions of love are Dante and Leopardi, and Horacio teaches Tristana Italian. The section is significant for a number of reasons. Tristana shows exceptional linguistic and histrionic skills, just as earlier she has shown a talent for art, and she is an expert at creating new language from old. The intellectual stimulus leads to introspection and to an awareness of her abilities. "Es que sirvo," she announces to Horacio, "que podré servir para las cosas grandes; pero que decididamente no sirvo para las pequeñas" (p. 94; I'm worth something, and I know I have the talent to do important things, but I definitely don't have a talent for small things). The passage may reflect a consciousness of her historic role, amplified by the narrator's commentary: "Sabía ser dulce y amarga, blanda y fresca como el agua, ardiente como el fuego, vaga y rumorosa como el aire" (p. 88; She could be sweet and bitter, soft and fresh like water, passionate like fire, vague and murmurous like air). She is water, fire, and air, everything but earth and a figurative Earth Mother. She and Horacio read selections from the *Inferno* and the *Purgatorio*, associating themselves with tragic lovers and perhaps intuiting that paradise will be denied them. Their lovers' vocabulary contains repetitions of the narrator's allusions to Don Juan and the *comedia*.

The glorification of language and the glorification of ideals through language, as well as Tristana's projection of a higher order, contrast with Horacio's views on love. While Tristana synthesizes her romantic idealism with reality, Horacio moves from one realm to the other with no intention of combining the two. Tristana tends to see the figurative as an expression of the real, but for Horacio the dichotomy will always remain. The distinction is important because Tristana takes her role seriously and Horacio considers it a lovers' game. On reentering reality, he is as conventional as before in expecting Tristana to conform to traditional domesticity: "Entrégate a mí sin reserva. ¡Ser mi compañera de toda la vida; ayudarme y sostenerme con tu cariño! . . . ¿Te parece que hay un oficio mejor ni arte más hermoso? Hacer feliz a un hombre que te hará feliz, ¿qué más?" (p. 93; Give yourself to me openly. Being my companion for life, helping me and sustaining me with your devotion. Do you think there's a better occupation or a more beautiful art? Making a man happy who will make you happy. What more could you want?). The ideological (and discursive) foundation of *Tristana* may hinge on this "¿qué más?"

The conceptual separation of Tristana and Horacio is mirrored in the following chapter by their physical separation, a separation that seems to affect Tristana more profoundly than it does Horacio. She suffers, while he "breathed a sigh of relief, like a worker on Saturday afternoon, after doing a full week's work" ("respiraba con desahogo, como jornalero en sábado por la tarde, después de una semana de destajo," p. 98). Anticipating her subsequent devotion to the Church, Tristana hears mass and prays during Horacio's absence. The two begin a correspondence that continues their recourse to a lovers' vocabulary. Even in his show of passion, Horacio sounds ironic in passages such as "la gloria de ser tu dueño" (p. 100; the glory of being your master), since the narrator has informed the reader of Horacio's attitude toward the separation. Tristana's letters reflect a growing illusion over what strikes her as ideal love—expressed ironically as "Soy tan feliz, que a veces paréceme que vivo suspendida en el aire, que mis pies no tocan la tierra" (p. 102; I'm so happy, that sometimes it seems that I'm living suspended in mid-air, with my feet not touching the earth)—in addition to a more contemplative tone in the references to her freedom. Her condemnation of marriage and a male-oriented society conflicts with Horacio's standpoint. Here, as in the passage on having children, Tristana apologizes for her audacity and for the absurdity of her position, but there are no disparities in her remarks. Her antimarital stance has nothing to do with the libertinism of Don Lope; it is, rather, a rejection of obligatory devotion in favor of love built on faith and a call to arms against a system that regards women as subservient to men. This is followed, again ironically, by Horacio's request that Tristana move to the country and marry him.

Tristana's self-conscious focus on her idealism seems to indicate that she can distinguish between her aspirations (the impossible) and her status in society (the real). Her introspection continues, and so do her efforts at self-improvement. Her study of English with Doña Malvina, a liberated woman who is free of the social strictures that inhibit Tristana,[11] gives her the opportunity to broaden her knowledge and to augment her linguistic and acting skills. The lovers' vocabulary now includes anglicisms and quotations from Shakespeare. While Tristana jests about Doña Malvina, writing Horacio, "You would think that she was of the masculine gender or of the neuter" ("La creerías del género masculino o del neutro," p. 108), she calls Lady Macbeth her friend and says, "*Unsex me here* makes me tremble and awakens I don't know what terrible emotions in the deepest part of my nature" ("Me hace estremecer y despierta no sé qué terribles emociones en lo más profundo de mi naturaleza," p. 112). Tristana uses the Shakespearean passage to express her dissatisfaction with the lot of women. She does not want to become manly or sexless, but she clings to the desire for a change in role models: "Eso de que dos que se aman han de volverse iguales y han de pensar lo mismo, no me cabe a mí en la cabeza. . . . Sea cada cual como Dios le ha hecho, y siendo distintos, se amarán más" (p. 111; The idea that two people who love each other have to become equal and have to think the same doesn't seem right to me. Let each one be as God made him, and being different, they will love each other more). At this point in the narrative, Tristana has become a standard for the women's cause, and the individual and the subjective are relegated to the universal. Even Horacio loses his distinctive features to become pure spirit ("se me ha borrado tu imagen," "te me vuelves espíritu puro," p. 114).

In chapter 19, Tristana makes her first allusion to the pain in her leg. In the preceding chapter, she speaks of Don Lope's temporary illness as a vengeance of sorts: "El reuma se está encargando de vengar el sinnúmero de maridillos que burló, y a las vírgenes honestas o esposas frágiles que inmoló en el ara nefanda de su liviandad" (p. 108; His rheumatism is taking charge of avenging the endless number of poor little cuckolded husbands and the chaste maidens or fragile wives he sacrificed on the vile altar of his licentiousness). The reversal of fortunes puts Tristana in the position to judge her own illness in terms of retribution. Chapter 19 contains three allusions to her illness as an act of God:

> ¿No te parece cruel lo que hace Dios conmigo? ¡Que a ese perdulario le cargue de achaques en su vejez como castigo de una juventud de crímenes contra la moral, muy santo y muy bueno; pero que a mí, jovenzuela que empiezo a pecar, que apenas . . . , y esto con circunstancias atenuantes; que a mí me aflija, a las primeras de cambio, con tan fiero castigo! (p. 116)

> Doesn't what God is doing to me seem cruel? To load ailments on that old wastrel in his final years as punishment for a youth of crimes against morality is well and good, but on me, a young girl who has just begun to sin, who hardly . . . and even that with extenuating circumstances. That He would inflict upon me, at the first signs of change, such a fierce punishment!

> ¿Qué crimen he cometido? ¿Quererte? ¡Vaya un crimen! Como tengo esta maldita costumbre de buscar siempre el *perché delle cose*, cavilo que Dios se ha equivocado con respecto a mí. (p. 119)

> What crime have I committed? Loving you? What kind of crime is that? Since I have this damned habit of always looking for the reason behind things, I have to conclude that God has made a mistake in my case.

> ¿Me querrás tú cojita? No, si me curaré . . . ¡Pues no faltaba más! Si no, sería una injusticia muy grande, una barbaridad de la Providencia, del Altísimo, del . . . no sé qué decir. (p. 120)

> Would you love me as a little cripple? No, I'll get well. That's all I need! If not, it would be a very great injustice, an outrage of Providence, of God, of . . . I don't know what to say.

The irony here is especially complex. Tristana at first is willing to rationalize the events in a framework of divine or poetic justice and then is forced to seek another explanation. The reader may note, however, that her logic is valid. Her illness can be explained as a divine order operating to punish her for her sins, but this system would call for a more severe punishment of Don Lope's moral offenses. Since this is not the case, Tristana resolves that either there is no absolute system of retribution or a mistake has been made. If one accepts this position, the inescapable conclusion will be that poetic justice is not being served, or that Tristana's sins are more serious because she is a woman. Tristana puts her faith in an egalitarian fate, in the love of Horacio, and in the dream of social change. The letters document the process of her destruction and the beginning of her reintegration.

After establishing a foundation of irony, the narrator to a degree stays in the background. While he is as manipulative as in the early part of the novel, the events themselves become increasingly ironic. Tristana's decision to become an actress, for example—to follow a path acceptable in society's eyes—comes at the moment of her debilitating illness, and there seems to be a type of unconscious insight in her wish to become a performer "in the tragic mold." Even more ironic is the narrator's treatment of Don Lope. Mimesis and diegesis point to Don Lope as the quintessential hypocrite, the true culprit of the text. In chapter 20, the narrator criticizes while pretending to praise: "Fuera de su absoluta ceguera moral en cosas de amor, el libertino inservible era hombre de buenos sentimientos y no podía ver padecer a las personas de su intimidad. Cierto que él había deshonrado a Tristana, matándola para la sociedad y el matrimonio, hollando su fresca juventud; pero lo cortés no quitaba lo valiente; la quería con entrañable afecto" (pp. 121–22; With the exception of his absolute blindness in the area of love, the useless libertine was a man of good sentiments, and he could not stand to see the people closest to him suffer. It is true that he had dishonored Tristana, ruining her for society and for marriage, trampling on her wholesome youth, but the courtly misdeeds did not take away from his praiseworthy qualities; he loved her with deep affection). If telling has been modified somewhat, showing remains the same. In this chapter, Don Lope deigns to pardon Tristana for her sins, offering her "total absolution," and advises her to avoid marriage, which "will plunge you into vulgarity." The irony and the veracity of the advice reach culmination in the final chapter, as does Don Lope's continued emphasis on "ridiculing the foolish life, the eternal union with a vulgar being, and the florid prose of marital intimacy" ("ridiculizar la vida boba, la unión eterna con un ser vulgar y las prosas de la intimidad matrimoñesca," pp. 128–29).

The tendency toward idealization, combined with suffering, leads Tristana to a dependence on abstraction. It is not the narrator but Tristana herself who first reveals the creation of a perfect lover modeled after, but distinct from, Horacio. Her letters convey a passion for the ineffable; no longer relying on the lovers' vocabulary of the past, they demonstrate Tristana's belief in a higher spiritual realm in which love is unaffected by physical matters: "Tan espiritualmente amaré con una pierna, como con dos" (p. 133; I will love you as spiritually with one leg as with two). The narrator may bring to light the danger of her retreat from reality, but he continues to make it clear that no alternative exists for her. She is the victim not only of an unkind fate but also of the failure of those around her to provide the love she merits. Tristana is not ranting thoughtlessly when she writes to Horacio, "Si tú no tuvieras brazos ni piernas, yo te querría lo mismo" (p. 143; If you didn't have any arms or legs, I would love you just the same). But he is a "beautiful phantom," a God of her own invention, and she is at the mercy of her oppressor, Don Lope, who delights in his triumph: "Triste es mi victoria, pero cierta. . . . Quiso alejarse de mí, quiso volar; pero no contaba con su destino, que no le permite revoloteos ni correrías; no contaba con Dios, que me tiene ley . . . , no sé por qué . . . , pues siempre se pone de mi parte en estas contiendas" (pp. 143–44; My victory is sad but certain. She tried to get away from me, she tried to fly, but she didn't count on her destiny, which doesn't permit excursions or flitting around; she didn't count on God, who must respect me—I'm not sure why—since He always takes my side in these conflicts). This is man's version of natural law.

Following the amputation of Tristana's leg, the enemies seem more and more like ideological brothers. Don Lope, conspicuous by his hypocritical presence, and Horacio, conspicuous by his absence and by the narrator's failure to include his letters after chapter 18, serve a mutual and paradoxical cause. Both suggest the purchase of an organ for Tristana, clearly intended as a replacement for the lost limb. At their initial meeting, each man feels respect for his opponent. Don Lope considers Horacio "a reasonable man who in the long run will view things as I view them" ("un hombre sesudo, que al fin y a la postre verá las cosas como las veo yo," p. 162). Declaring that Tristana is "now and forever a useless woman," Don Lope frees his rival of any obligation to her: "¿Como sostener su promesa ante una mujer que ha de andar con muletas? . . . La Naturaleza se impone" (p. 165; How can you be expected to keep your promise to a woman who has to walk on crutches? It's nature's will). He speaks of the inevitable separation as a figurative divorce, based on "incompatibility of character, absolute incompatibility, irreconcilable differences." In the conversation with Horacio, Don Lope's words betray him. With absolutely no conviction, he pretends to see Tristana's attitude as a vision of truth: "Quizá ve más que todos nosotros; quizá su mirada perspicua, o cierto instinto de adivinación concedido a las mujeres superiores, ve la sociedad futura que nosotros no vemos" (p. 168; Perhaps she sees more than all of us; perhaps her perspicuous view, or a certain instinct for divination granted to superior women, sees a future society that we don't see). Artfully manipulated by the narrator, the words of a hypocrite, intending to be deceptive, comply with a message system of another (social) order.

After Tristana's operation, the narrator writes of "the slow and sad awakening of Señorita Reluz, her new life, after that simulacrum of death, her resurrection, leaving behind a foot and two-thirds of a leg" ("el despertar lento y triste de la señorita de Reluz, su nueva vida, después de aquel simulacro de muerte, su resurrección, dejándose un pie y dos tercios de la pierna," p. 147). The arrival of the new organ, a gift from Horacio with music lessons courtesy of Don Lope, is also "like a sudden resurrection" for its owner. The organ is symbolic not only of the amputated leg but also of Tristana's conversion, of her withdrawal into full spirituality. Once again separated from Horacio, this time permanently, Tristana replaces the man she has made into a god with God and the idyllic visions of love and a new society with religious fervor. Tristana at the novel's end is an accomplished musician, an expert pastry cook, and the wife of Don Lope. She is no longer the Tristana of honorable freedom, of conceptual precocity, and of verbal wit.

The fact that Tristana says very little in the text after the operation makes examination of her conversion difficult (while making a statement about her predicament). During Horacio's first visit, the narrator expresses Tristana's disappointment that the man she has worshipped treats her with pity rather than with love. In their conversations, Tristana and Horacio stop speaking of the past, and her "spiritual stagnation" is broken only by the delivery of the organ. Even before the announcement of Horacio's marriage, Tristana has committed herself to self-imposed seclusion and concentration on music. Don Lope fares better. The final chapter begins, "In his old age, Don Lope did not have the sadness and solitude that he deserved as the conclusion to a dissolute and depraved life" ("No tuvo la vejez de Don Lope toda la tristeza y soledad que él se merecía, como término de una vida disipada y viciosa," p. 180). The narrator seems to be warning the reader that justice is not at work, that what will follow may be disguised as a logical consequence of the events but is really an elaborate system of contradictions.

The narrator has demonstrated that Tristana, on awakening into maturity, has been able to assimilate Don Lope's antisocial ideology to form her own view of society and specifically of women's role in it. Her standpoint, based on equality and absolute values, is radical only in the sense that it clashes with the relative and oppressive ethical codes of her society. This is a society that insists on a rigid distinction between what is manly and what is womanly, while Tristana's ideal refuses to admit dichotomies of this type. Her rejection of domestic duties, traditional marriage, and conventional careers is not a rejection of femininity but an assertion of the potential of women, who should be free to emerge from the kitchen to enter the realm of ideas. Her own prodigiousness, attested to by Doña Malvina and the music teacher, indicates the validity of her position. She is not fighting for a libertinism for women as a counterpart to that of Don Lope, but rather she submits that the new social freedom accorded to men should apply to women as well. Tristana's idealism is a necessary consequence of her undertaking, and the major element of her disillusionment is the realization that Horacio, the model of male superiority for her new society, is of the same cast as Don Lope, representative par excellence of the old society. The narrator formulates a pattern of Don Lope's hypocrisy and defamation of women, as well as a discrepancy between the progressive nature of what Horacio says and the reactionary nature of his thoughts concerning social roles. As a supporter of Tristana's cause, the narrator gives an ironic twist to Don Lope's words and silences Horacio.

The narrator goes to great lengths to promote reader sympathy for Tristana, a strategy that he seems to negate in the final conversion. Yet at that point the reader has been made privy to the ironic level of the narrative and may not be surprised by an ironic final reversal. The narrator says in the last sentence of the text that one cannot be sure if Tristana and Don Lope are happy as a married couple. Perhaps, he tells the reader, Tristana has found final consolation in religion, a spiritual support to match the crutches that have become a part of her. Perhaps Don Lope is content with his financial independence and his victory over a rebellious spirit. The relative happiness of the characters is less significant than the implications of the novel's open-endedness. Just as in the thesis novels, Galdós allows the triumph of intolerance to underline the need for tolerance, and in *Tristana* he creates a narrator to convey his message in the indirect terms (and discourse) of art. In chapter 23, Tristana writes to Horacio, "¿Te acuerdas de aquel grillo que tuvimos, y que cantaba más y mejor después de arrancarle una de las patitas?" (p. 143; Remember that cricket we had, that sang more and better after we pulled out one of his little legs?). Like this symbolic cricket, the resonance of Tristana's voice becomes stronger and more effective after the amputation, even though she seems to have been silenced.

A factor in the narrator's use of irony is the literariness of the work. In the early part of the text both the narrator and the characters depend on literary allusions, while in the second part the literary figures become products of the narrator's self-referential method and characters in their own right. Don Lope, for example, goes from an anachronistic Don Quijote, a sedentary knight, to an aged and ridiculous Don Juan, and he finally surpasses the derivative identities to become a unique image of hypocrisy incarnate. His idiosyncrasies are brought to light in comparative terms, and the narrator's intervention diminishes once the character has been defined. The narrator can play more subtly with his own creation because he has shown the reader what to expect from the character. This technique allows the narrator to strengthen the textual message(s) by exaggerating the moral distance between the characters while apparently increasing his own critical detachment.

Criticism of *Tristana* relies very little on Galdós's ironic strategies. For Emilia Pardo Bazán, Galdós's contemporary, the crux of the narrative events lies in Tristana's willingness to cast herself into an unequal battle to escape the indignities of her life with Don Lope. Pardo Bazán's essay stresses the feminist orientation of *Tristana*, and in recognizing the impossibility of victory it hints (probably unconsciously) at the novel's ironic potential.[12] Several more recent studies discount both Galdós's feminism and the irony of the text. A case in point is an article by Leon Livingstone.[13] The great equalizing agent for Livingstone is the incontrovertible harmony of nature. Man errs when he attempts to contradict nature, yet it is always nature that ultimately triumphs: "The denaturalization process consists of the imposing of artificial constraints or unattainable goals on the individual by himself or by others." The first example of one who carries an attitude to unreasonable extremes is Doña Josefina; the description of her two manias "establishes the author's basic position and sets the burlesque tone of the novel." The second is the case of Don Lope, "who, the author takes pains to let us know, outside of his one obsession is an essentially decent and even exemplary character." The idea of a burlesque tone is disregarded here, even

though Don Lope's single flaw involves destroying women's lives by dis-
honoring them and their families, and Livingstone's analysis depends on an
absence of ambiguity in the text. The critic says that Don Lope is finally
obliged to recognize the absurdity of his role as gallant—"contraviniendo la
ley de la Naturaleza," opposing the law of nature—but is this really true?
Moreover, he believes that Don Lope is "so contrite in the presence of
Tristana's misfortune that he is willing to make the greatest of all sacrifices
and surrender her to his rival," but Don Lope makes this gesture only when
he is positive that Tristana is tied to him forever.[14]

Basing his discussion of *Tristana* on the intricacies of the love triangle,
made more complex by literary self-reference, Germán Gullón rejects the
idea of an ironic ending, since the characters show through resignation an
acceptance of their destiny and an understanding (via Calderón's *La vida es
sueño*) that "even dreams are dreams."[15] Throughout the novel, however,
resignation is portrayed as something less than consistent, and the final
resignation is more the recognition of a lack of possibilities than an awakening. What Gullón calls Tristana's conformity to her destiny comes only
after man, society, and nature (illness) have destroyed her dreams, after all
hope has disappeared. The narrator calls the marriage plan an "absurd project" and underscores Tristana's indifference to the plan and to all earthly
things: "No sentía el acto, lo aceptaba como un hecho impuesto por el
mundo exterior, como el empadronamiento, como la contribución, como
las reglas de policía" (p. 182; She didn't feel the act but accepted it as an
event imposed by the exterior world, like the census, like taxes, like police
rules).

Tristana's spirit has been broken and Don Lope has fallen into the
vulgarity of the conventionalism he abhors. This is ironic because the force
of her struggle remains and because the man whom destiny has favored is
made to seem especially ridiculous and part of a dying breed. Tristana fades
into the background in the final chapters of the novel not because she ceases
to be important but because she ceases to be important as a person. She is
now a symbol of the need for equality and of the search for social and poetic
justice. *She* is now the literary allusion, and her name—echoed in the numerous uses of the word *triste*, sad, in the concluding chapters—evokes the
idea of a continuing struggle. The final image of a contented Don Lope with
his crippled and dominated pastry cook cries for revision in the same way
that the social analogue cries for revision. The story has ended for Tristana
the person but not for Tristana the symbol, and the open ending is fully
appropriate. Dreams are dreams not because they are distinct from reality—
as Gullón would have it—but because they are the mainstay of reality.

Michael Nimetz speaks of the ending as a sign of the "irony of incongruity," in which the incongruous relationship between Tristana and
Don Lope continues and is legalized. For Nimetz, the irony lies in the
unexpected events rather than in the symbolic implications of these events.
The two characters readjust, make compatible the incongruities, and so
compromise themselves that they are "seemingly unaware of their descent
into vulgarity. The wonderful old rake and the unique girl cease to be

interesting. When the reader perceives this, he confronts the culminating irony of the novel: Tristana and Don Lope are oblivious to their fate."[16] Nimetz, in his discussion of the irony of *Tristana*, fails to consider the ironic voice of the narrator, who provides the reasons for Tristana's uniqueness and treats Don Lope as more than a "wonderful old rake." The narrator's voice gives meaning to the characters and to the events, so that the novel's actions are more than conditioning agents. If Tristana and Don Lope are oblivious to their fate, it is not because they are vulgar but because they are symbolic. Only symbolically does the final compromise make sense. Tristana is predestined to fail because the society of her time will not permit "honorable freedom," but—and this is a crucial element of the textual irony—Galdós has created a woman who could succeed.[17] It takes a stroke of fate to definitively frustrate the goals of a woman who single-handedly defies society. Her failure is inevitable, but to an extent she is doomed not by the social system but by her creator, who shows that success is within her grasp. Within this perspective, it is thematically more than socially imperative that Tristana fail.

The irony of *Tristana* may be the irony of contradiction. Literature competes with life and with itself. The narrator defines the characters, and although they remain consistent with his definitions, he begins to shift his position, but only to foreground the validity of the initial stance. The impossibility for Tristana—the reason for her struggle and for her defeat—is the intrinsic contradiction between a socially realistic attitude (as expressed by Saturna) and true self-respect. Tristana's goal of honorable freedom is a chimera not because it contradicts absolute morality but because it contradicts the social conscience of her time; self-respect and social respectability operate on different and mutually exclusive planes. In *Tristana*, not only is reconciliation (Tristana's entry into the world of spiritual seclusion) apparent at best, but the dichotomy of reality (the real Horacio) and illusion (the ideal Horacio) is overshadowed by Tristana's false perception of reality. Her inaccurate "reading" of Horacio negates the dichotomy while it extends the social vision. In his manipulation of narrative recourses, Galdós accentuates the impossibility of synthesis by denying the dialectic, by fusing and confusing reality and illusion, and by silencing Tristana in the final chapters.

If in *Fortunata y Jacinta* Galdós chooses what John Sinnigen calls "redemption rather than revolution" for Fortunata,[18] the ambiguity of Tristana's retreat into a type of mysticism seems to strengthen the novel's subtle revolutionary spirit. The consciously absurd rendering of a union between Tristana and Don Lope, together with the unexplained illness, is—if anything—a parody of redemption, and Tristana's final convictions do not make their way into the text. The narrator creates a literary imbalance to equal a social imbalance, yet within this structure he becomes a proponent of Tristana's cause. Stephen Gilman says that the theme of all great novels since *Don Quijote* is "the creation of significance out of insignificance, or, as Lukacs tells us, a search for values which in apparent failure nevertheless succeeds."[19] This is what makes *Tristana* artistic and what makes it ironic.[20]

It is not the anachronistic gentleman described in Cervantine terms but a woman fighting social windmills who most resembles Don Quijote. It is not the victim of a tyrannical grandfather in his clean transition into bourgeois society but a woman denied the benefits of her intellectual and artistic potential who achieves the status of martyr. It is not nature but society's dogmatic and male-oriented codes that reduces women to subservience. It is not God but man acting as God who determines the limits and abuses of morality. And, finally, it is not Tristana's redemption but Galdós's refusal to redeem her that points toward a new society. The reader is left, then, to intuit the novel's irony, to understand when the narrator is mocking his subject and when he is respecting it, and when an apparent volte-face is consistent with a previously established perspective.

The third of Wayne Booth's four steps for reconstruction of stable irony is that "a decision must . . . be made about the author's knowledge or beliefs," an undertaking that Booth admits brings the critic dangerously close to committing the "intentional fallacy."[21] To attribute to Galdós an unrelenting faith in tolerance and in a system of absolute values seems reasonable, and for him to favor Tristana's views over those of an intolerant society and its relative values would follow. To read *Tristana* literally is to accept or to rationalize intolerance and an unjust and arbitrarily derived system of values. To read *Tristana* ironically is to decide both that Tristana must lose her struggle and that her defeat is a defeat for poetic justice. The defeat and the novel are ironic because they are stages of a victory and because Galdós is an eloquent spokesman for poetic justice.

Discourse in the picaresque models operates in the space between the narrative voice and textual messages. The opposition of narrator and implied author attests to the duplicity and the multiplicity of signification. The reading (and critical) process becomes a search for markers of internal structure and meaning production. The unity of *Lazarillo de Tormes*, *Guzmán de Alfarache*, and *El Buscón* may rest more on the implied author's "story"— exposure of the rhetorical strategies of the narrator and a directed rewriting of the text—than on prefaces and premises. In the conceptist metalanguage of the baroque period, meanings stand behind rhetorical strategies, in the extended sense of the term; wordplay and defensive maneuvers make semiotics a game and a frame for storytelling. Quevedo's stylistic display in the *Buscón* establishes a notable distance between the narrator and the implied author. The one who invents the linguistic flourishes is the same one who controls the fate and self-betrayal of Pablos, whose flawed narrative performance is a discursive variation of the determinism that hinders his chance for success in society. The figurative or literal silence of the Spanish anti-heroines is the principal marker of (implied) authorial intervention, again linking the narrator's marginal position in the text to its social analogue. In the picaresque, irony results from the flexibility of the word and the illusion of power, which place meaning in the realm of dialectics. In *Tristana*, a text that also makes a social statement through silence, the distance between narrator and implied author is an illusion.

Tristana builds on Galdós's thesis novels, with their structure of overdetermined injustice, and the later novels, in which the narrator walks a discursive tightrope between observation and omniscience, the comic and the tragic, artifice and message. The blend of storytelling, commentary, and linguistic play—Galdós's idiolect includes conventions and points of reference from the intertextual tradition—is a testament to the inseparability of story and discourse. Don Lope and Tristana are anachronisms, he the relic of a misnamed age of gallantry and she the harbinger of a new feminism. The narrator combines the neochivalric, grandiose, and declamatory rhetoric of the past with the rhetoric of honorable freedom and with a subtly judgmental tone to take sides in the social and sexual struggle. He damns Don Lope with faint praise and demonstrates a flagrant abuse of women. He makes Horacio the embodiment of a deceptively conservative and hypocritical present, then removes him from discourse and story. And most importantly, he converts Tristana from free spirit to victim to martyr. She disappears from the text but not from the larger picture or from the historical record.

The general movement in *Tristana* is from diegesis to mimesis. The narrator outlines a plot and the characters validate his position; they comply with his story as he intrudes on their discourse. The implied author relinquishes the explicit thematics of the thesis novels in favor of a more complex form of overdetermination. The patterns of irony in *Tristana* develop from a stability of stance, the speakers' relation to the messages they are uttering. What changes—to heighten the irony—is the narrator's contact with the reading public, a public that may be increasingly attuned to the rhetoric of liberation and to the ironies of history.

6 THE MARGINATED NARRATOR

Hasta no verte Jesús mío and the Eloquence of Repression

El Ser Supremo nos envía a la tierra a lavar nuestras almas porque nos hizo limpios la primera vez y para poder retornar a él tenemos que regresar como nos mandó. ¿Y cómo nos vamos a limpiar? A fuerza de dolor y de sufrimiento. Nosotros creemos que El se equivoca, y no; los que nos equivocamos somos nosotros porque no oímos, no entendemos, no queremos reconocer el verdadero camino, porque si la mayoría de la gente llegara a reconocer el camino limpio de Dios no habría hombres abusones ni mujeres que se dejaran.

The Supreme Being sends us to earth to cleanse our souls, because we were born pure and to be able to come back to Him we have to return the way He sent us out. And how are we going to purify ourselves? Through pain and suffering. We believe that He makes mistakes, but that's not so; we're the ones who make mistakes because we don't hear, we don't understand, we don't want to accept the true path, because if the majority of the people would recognize the pure path of God, there would be no men who abuse women and no women who allow it.

Lazarillo de Tormes initiates a discursive irony that makes the production of meanings in fiction a counterpoint to the narrator's text. The result is a complex linguistic and artistic product, as well as an analogue of the pro- tagonist's role in society and a reflection of the implied author's sympathy or antipathy toward the narrator/protagonist. Within the dialectic of narra- tive, the authorial presence provides a synthesis of sorts by siding with the prevailing social ideology or with the created figure who in some way opposes the established position. The textual conflict mirrors and becomes part of a construct of ideas. Lázaro attempts to change history by imposing semiotic barriers to interpretation (and to the ever-problematic issue of truth). The elimination of consciously deceptive language may lead to a modified relationship between author and narrator and to alternative means of dealing with history. Elena Poniatowska's *Hasta no verte Jesús mío* centers on the status of woman in her society, and the authorial level is ironic in an innovative and compassionate way. The writer uses a real informant and encodes the material of her interviews to produce a persona, Jesusa Palan- cares. The account vacillates between the unmediated narration of docu- mentary and the self-conscious reinvention of a nonfictional character through narrative and rhetorical strategies. Set against the Mexican Revolution, Poniatowska's text accentuates the lack of recourses for Jesusa in a male-dominated society, despite her strength and her commitment to independence. While the underlying premises of the novel differ greatly from those of *Lazarillo de Tormes*, the beauty and force of *Hasta no verte Jesús mío*—as in the earlier work—lie in ironic discourse.

Jesusa Palancares narrates a series of events, while Poniatowska adds to the linguistic eloquence—the eloquence of simplicity—an organization of the material that serves to illuminate circumstantial irony. Although conditioned to accept her destiny, Jesusa cannot obscure the need for social change, nor can the reader ignore the skill and ingenuity that allow her to survive in a world that constantly rejects her. Her isolation and lack of options confirm Jesusa's archetypal role, relating her to the picaresque tradition through plot, discourse, and, as in *Moll Flanders*, a potentially radical subtext.[1] In this particular transformation of the picaresque, the text articulates a social injustice by giving a voice to a woman silenced by her society. The implied author turns resignation into resistance and the sediment of revolution into the seeds of liberation. If Lázaro's text breaks a silence to incriminate him, Jesusa's text breaks a silence to incriminate a repressive society.

In *Hasta no verte Jesús mío*, history competes with fiction. The uncertainty and transformations wrought by the revolution form the backdrop of Jesusa's oral history, which the authorial figure—real and implied—transfers into the terms of narrative fiction. The raw materials of history include the autobiographical frame, the continuing political conflict, and the social struggle of the Mexican woman and the poor. The author, in turn, devises a structure in which to project the messages of the text, based in part on her own "reading" of Jesusa's story. Jesusa supplies what the Russian formalists call *fabula*, the sum total of narrative events, and the author organizes these events into a plot, *sjuzet*.[2] The ordering affects story and discourse, for the author may pattern words as well as events through a rhetorical strategy aimed at producing a particular reader response. Repetition, circularity, and a defined system of pathos broaden the impact of the individual episodes. More importantly perhaps, the unconscious power of Jesusa's words, consciously arranged by the author, reveals meaning on multiple levels. Far more than a transcription of interviews,[3] the text develops a narrative space in which to expand the content and the context of Jesusa's account.

Through narrated action, recorded (remembered) dialogue, and subjective commentary, Jesusa Palancares discusses her life and times. The recurring features of her discourse include a cynical attitude toward men based on their insensitivity to and abusive treatment of women; a condemnation of the well-to-do for their selfishness, of educators for their self-serving methods, and of the clergy for its hypocrisy; and a pessimistic view of the revolution and its promise of freedom. There exists, however, a tension between this type of negativism and an indisputable concern for people, as exemplified in the events and words of the text. Just as the narrative refutes the silenced position of the protagonist, the discourse exposes Jesusa's acceptance of the solitary existence as a response to experience rather than as a desired state. Unable to depend on others, she advocates solitude over the risk of betrayal, yet she continues to love and to serve her neighbors. Her faith requires suffering on the road to immortality, and a sense of spirituality determines both her resignation to fate and her reaction to the hardships of this life. Poniatowska appropriates the spiritual perspective to frame the narrative, which operates exclusively in the here and now of social consciousness. As she narrates her story, Jesusa seems unaware of her powers of endurance, her strong will, her magnanimity, and her intelligence. It is the implied author's task to foreground these qualities in directing an ironic reading of the text, a reading that elevates the antiheroine while decrying the conditions that inhibit her growth.

Jesusa's narrative defines a causal structure inspired by her faith. Atonement leads to salvation, and reincarnation offers an outlet for repentance. The sinner must return to earth a number of times to reach the proper degree of retribution. In another life, Jesusa was a queen. Now she is impoverished and alone, so, she reasons, her guilt must be great. To eradicate the guilt, her present suffering must be commensurate with her culpability. In this occult variation of Christianity, penitence demands earthly trials, and only divine justice matters. Jesusa's studied complacency acknowledges her submission to the precepts of a higher order that dictates suffering for the individual soul. Despite her adherence to spiritual causality, Jesusa binds herself to this world by seizing upon the mundane pleasures of dancing, drinking, and fighting, activities that contradict the goals of her faith. More emphatically, her ties to human need are unmistakable. Poniatowska makes the disparity a function of the theme of rebellion. The events that mark Jesusa's progression toward perfection illustrate society's discrimination against the lower classes and against women. Persecution is the narrator's cross to bear, while at the same time the implied author is standard bearer of social equality. Jesusa says that she feels no inclination to share life with others, but her protective nature belies this contention. Similarly, she points toward eternity yet builds a place for herself in this world. The authorial figure captures the internal conflict, incorporating it into the narrative scheme and the thematic movement of the text. Using the literary tension as a marker, the author transfers the problem to the social plane and to the historical rebellion. As in *Lazarillo de Tormes*, a narrator "unconsciously" depicts what an implied author chooses to present. *Hasta no verte Jesús mío* inverts the formula by adding an ironic dimension to a preexisting oral record.

In her role—figurative and literal—as editor of the narrative materials, Poniatowska transforms the spoken word into a structured whole. The symmetrical frame (a beginning and ending in the present, with allusions to the spiritual realm) surrounds the autobiographical account, which is divided into the conventional chapters of fiction as it re-creates dialogue from the past. Through memory, Jesusa Palancares reappropriates events and speech, and the author takes the process one step further by imposing a form borrowed from fiction. Selection, placement, and recurrence provide aesthetic means to social ends. Jesusa's shrewd perception of her environment and her grasp of human psychology, products of a keen but unanalytical mind, derive from experience. Intuition rather than introspection motivates her response to those who surround her, and faith rather than reason—or perhaps a rationale based on faith—justifies the social oppression. Underlying the passivity of her spiritual orientation, nevertheless, is an unformed social conscience that resists the dominance of one group over another. For Poniatowska, Jesusa's life seems to suggest an analogical design that portrays the mistreatment of an individual and extends to the community at large. Revolution here is not so much the great equalizer as the synthesis of society's ills. Until the revolution defines itself in terms of the broadest areas of the class struggle, it will be an exercise in futility, a series of changes without advancement. This message, implicit in Jesusa's story and in her discourse, becomes a unifying thread of Poniatowska's work. Repressed by society, Jesusa Palancares finds an identity in the spiritual congregation that gives purpose to her suffering. She distances the social significance by externalizing the problem that her alter ego internalizes. Focusing on the sources and manifestations of repression, Poniatowska employs the force of narrative disposition to make the "untold" story a part of the text.

At the beginning of *Hasta no verte Jesús mío*, Jesusa Palancares views her life as a stage in a divine plan of retribution. God has placed her in the world—poor, alone, and a woman—to work toward salvation. As her narrative ends, she awaits death and probably another reincarnation. Laconically self-critical, she realizes that she has not yet reached the degree of acceptability required by the spiritual order: "En esta última reencarnación he sido muy perra, pegalona y borracha. Muy de todo. No puedo decir que he sido buena" (In this last reincarnation I've been very mean, quick to fight and drink. All that sort of thing. I can't say that I've been good).[4] The self-deprecating tone suits the narrative beautifully. Jesusa attempts to serve truth rather than her own interests, a recourse that adds to the documentary flavor of the text. Equally significant is the relation between the narrator/protagonist's humility and the establishment of ironic levels of discourse. Few readers will share Jesusa's negative attitude toward her behavior because there is a discrepancy between what she tells and what she shows. Poverty and exclusion cannot conceal her strength of character, nor can a denial of her goodness destroy the benevolent portrait contained in the text. The narrative situation is similar to that of *La familia de Pascual Duarte*, in which Pascual inadvertently provides a psychological explanation of his actions while addressing other issues. The implied author allows the reader to see—ironically, through the words of a speaker unable to comprehend the significance of his own discourse—the interaction of environment and heredity in the formation of the protagonist. As narrator, Jesusa emphasizes her unworthiness while unknowingly demonstrating her heroic traits. As in Cela's novel, determinism has textual and extratextual bases.

Jesusa's childhood ends at an early age. She loses her mother and her innocence: "Mi mamá no me regañó ni me pegó nunca. Era morena igual a mí, chaparrita, gorda y cuando se murió nunca volví a jugar" (p. 20; My mother never fussed at me or beat me. She was dark like me, short and plump, and when she died I never played again). At the funeral, Jesusa jumps into her mother's grave, in a type of symbolic mourning or anticipation of her own death. The widowed father treats his daughter responsibly but without affection. He changes jobs with frequency and takes up with a succession of women, who abuse Jesusa or fail to give her any attention. "Ni mi nombre supo" (p. 23; She didn't even know my name), says Jesusa of one of her father's mistresses, as if to confirm the suppression of her youth and of her identity. The partial exception is her stepmother Evarista Valencia, whom Jesusa credits with teaching her not to be idle. The work day for the nine-year-old begins at four, and her rewards include beatings by her stepmother, which Jesusa accepts with precocious resignation: "Ella me golpeaba pero yo no decía nada porque como ya estaba más grande comprendía mejor. Pensaba yo: 'Bueno, pues ¿qué ando haciendo de casa en casa? Pues me aguanto en donde mi papá esté... ¿A dónde me puedo ir que más valga?' Y esta señora se dedicó a enseñarme a hacer quehacer; me pegó mucho con una vara de membrillo, sí, pero lo hacía por mi bien, para que yo me encarrerara" (p. 35; She used to beat me, but I didn't say anything because since I was older I understood better. I thought to myself: "Okay, so what good would it do to go from one house to another? I'll stick it out where my father is. Where could I go where things would be better?" And this lady did devote herself to teaching me how to do chores; she beat me a lot with a switch from the quince tree, but she did it for my own good, so that I would head in the right direction).

The rigors of her life impress Jesusa as natural, while the reader will probably note the irony of a discourse that proposes hard labor for a young child as an antidote for idleness. The work takes place at a prison, where Evarista's mother is warden, so that history provides a metaphor for the conditions that mark Jesusa's childhood. This section of the text introduces a major motif: the silence that Jesusa must endure. Evarista, like many of those with whom Jesusa comes into contact, rarely speaks to her. Consequently, Jesusa develops no voice, no means of representing herself before the world, no sense of self. The solitary existence becomes an extension of the silence of her formative years, and the individual spirit must mature in the other world of faith. In the narrative, Jesusa gives utterance to her thoughts and by so doing stabilizes her identity, made public for the first time and altered by enunciation; the teller of the tale transforms herself in the narrative process.

Another related motif is the contemptible conduct of men toward women, with a corollary in the limited recourses open to women. Jesusa's brother Efrén, a drunken loafer, brings home Ignacia, an orphan with no social possibilities, and continually beats her. Having no blood line, no education, and no money, Ignacia exists only as a receptacle for Efrén's violence. Correspondingly, she has no role in the dialogue or in the action of the text. Jesusa's sister Petra is kidnaped, beaten, and held prisoner by a corporal for three years only to be rescued by a man who subsequently tries to kill her. Petra's social rebellion is circumscribed by her sex and class. Her only outlet is the bad life, which leads to imprisonment and to a tragic relationship. These examples expand the perspective by characterizing the problem as general rather than as isolated. Society neglects the women of the lower classes by denying them means of upward mobility, schooling, and justice. In the following sections of *Hasta no verte Jesús mío*, Jesusa emerges as victim of the system, and her text illuminates the system of motifs.

Jesusa enjoys a short respite on the road with her father, as the only woman in his life. When she returns to Evarista, she once more suffers at the hands of her stepmother. Evarista's mother rebukes her daughter for the cruelty and sends Jesusa to work for a lady who continues the abusive treatment. The woman speaks to Jesusa only once a day to issue orders, gives her no salary and no free time to eat her meals. Jesusa sleeps in her employer's bedroom, but on the balcony, "like a dog." Her comment, "¡Si de chiquilla hicieron leña de mí" (p. 48), translates roughly as "Even as a child they treated me like dirt!" With little malice in her retrospective vision, Jesusa notes that the *madrina* (or protectress) was not a bad woman but, like all prosperous people, oblivious to the status of the poor and unwilling to share her wealth. The *madrina* dispatches Jesusa to the port of Salina Cruz as a type of mother's helper for her daughter, again without benefit of salary and without a recognized position in the family. Her work, which she describes as "not very difficult," consists of caring for five children, washing, ironing, and other household duties. Jesusa at this time is eleven or twelve years old, a child in charge of children. She says of the experience: "Fuera de los chiquillos no tenía con quién hablar, porque mi único amigo era el metate" (pp. 55–56; Except for the kids I had no one to talk with, because my only friend was the *metate* [stone surface used for grinding]). She leaves her job when she hears that her father has left Evarista and is now in Salina Cruz, but she is disowned by him for reasons that are unclear. She becomes an orphan in a place where everyone considers her a stranger. The renunciation by her father removes the final trace of a connection with home, family, and lineage. It is not, unfortunately, the nadir of Jesusa's life.

After the death of Jesusa's only surviving brother, her father reclaims her, and the two head for the capital with the troops of General Jesús Carranza. The women who accompany the infantry have a definite role in the military operations. They enter a new location ahead of the soldiers to mislead the enemy as to the size and strength of the force. On one occasion, General Emiliano Zapata himself returns Jesusa and four other women to their company unharmed and protected. As in the past, Jesusa competes for her father's attention with his mistresses. One of them, La Guayabita, mistreats and curses Jesusa in public. Forced to defend her honor, Jesusa badly wounds her enemy. Pride rather than jealousy motivates her. As she becomes increasingly disenchanted with her position and alienated from her father, she seeks a means to leave the company. Aided by General Genovevo Blanco, she makes an escape. The causes of her flight are multiple but relate to the themes of silence and abuse. Jesusa's father condemns her for speaking in the Zapotec language (a knowledge acquired during her period with Evarista) with soldiers from Tehuantepec. When he moves to strike her, she demands her freedom, a freedom that will continue to elude her.

While traveling to Acapulco with the company of General Blanco, Jesusa finds herself pursued by Captain Pedro Aguilar, whose fervor contrasts with her indifference. Through an unhappy turn of fate, the general gives Jesusa's hand in marriage to Aguilar, despite her disinterest. Jesusa is fifteen, her husband is seventeen. Aguilar's character and his zeal change immediately after the ceremony. Piqued by rejection, he weds Jesusa to retaliate, to cure her of her presumption, to put her in her place. If Jesusa had previously lost her childhood, she now loses her freedom. She has no role in determining her future, and, when given the opportunity, her father offers no assistance. It is crucial to note that Jesusa does everything possible to discourage Aguilar's pretensions, yet her resistance becomes the catalyst of his pursuit. The earlier examples of male-female relationships culminate in the ruthless conduct of Pedro Aguilar toward Jesusa, whose only fault is a wish for independence. A less than ideal reality turns into a nightmare.

In concise but graphic terms, Jesusa describes her married life:

> No podía voltear a ver a nadie ni me podía cambiar ni me podía peinar. . . . El me pegaba, me descalabraba y con las heridas y la misma sangre me enllagué y se me acabó el pelo que era largo y rizado. Allí en la cabeza estaba la plasta de mugre y allí seguía, porque yo no me podía bañar ni me podía cambiar, así es que sufrí como Santa María en los desiertos. ¿Iba yo a tener voluntad de quererlo? Le cogí tirria, le agarré inquina. Con un cuchillo me podía raspar la mugre del vestido de lo gruesa que estaba. Anduve con el mismo vestido todo el tiempo aunque él me llevaba mucha ropa, pero no me la podía poner. Me la compraba donde nos detuviéramos para presumir con los soldados y con las mujeres: —¡Miren cómo la tengo! . . . El se divertía bien y bonito pero allá lejos, conmigo no. Por eso yo le pedía a toda la corte celestial que lo mataran. . . . . Así que yo fui mártir. Ora no, ora ya no soy mártir. Sufro como todo el mundo pero no en comparación de lo que sufrí cuando tenía marido. (pp. 96-97)

> I couldn't get out to see anyone or change clothes or comb my hair. He beat me, he hit me in the head, and with the wounds and the blood and all it got worse and I lost my hair, which was long and curly. There on my head was the grimy paste and there it stayed, because I couldn't bathe or change clothes, so I suffered like Saint Mary in the wilderness. Was I going to feel like loving him? I despised him, I hated his guts. I needed a knife to get the grime off my dress, it was so thick. I had to wear the same dress all the time although he brought me a lot of clothes, because he wouldn't let me wear them. He bought them for me at the places where we stopped, so he could put on airs for the soldiers and the women. "Look what I've got to put up with!" He was all sugar and spice outside, but not with me. That's why I asked all the heavenly court to kill him. So I was a martyr. Not now, I'm not a martyr any more. I suffer like everyone else, but not compared with how I suffered when I was married.

The calculated guile of Pedro Aguilar further eradicates Jesusa's self-hood: "Jamás oí mi nombre con él" (p. 97; He never even spoke my name). Careful to maintain an air of respectability, he charms people in public and punishes his wife in private; society sees him as a man who must bear a woman unworthy of his benevolent nature. When Jesusa finally decides to defend herself or die trying, she wins an important victory. With Aguilar's vacillation comes a new-found vigor in Jesusa. Moved by a pride that had earlier eluded her, she fights her husband and his female admirers, yet she is only happy when he is away. Fearing her increasing self-sufficiency, Aguilar takes her into combat dressed in male clothing, an act that ironically foregrounds her role as a dependent woman. When they go north to Coahuila to visit his grandmother, they discover that the revolution has had a negligible effect on the way of life in the region. If anything, hunger and indigence are more pronounced. Frustration on the historical level underscores the utter disillusionment of Jesusa's marriage and foreshadows Aguilar's death on the battlefield shortly thereafter. Jesusa's commentary extends the battle imagery: "Cuando Pedro se quedó con el corazón atravesado yo no había cumplido dieciocho años. El decía que cuando la viera perdida, me mataría. Quería mandarme por delante, pero no se le hizo. Aquí estoy todavía dando guerra" (p. 133; When Pedro had his heart pierced through by a bullet, I wasn't even eighteen years old. He always told me that when he saw that it was a lost cause, he would kill me. He wanted to send me out ahead of him, but it didn't happen that way. Here I am, still waging war). Jesusa loses her husband and the protection that marriage has afforded her. The solitary orphan becomes a solitary widow. Liberated from the (literal) bonds of matrimony, she must now confront the specter of abject poverty.

Jesusa spends one month in Marfa, Texas, as a prisoner of war. On her arrival in Mexico, General Espinosa y Córdoba asks her to remain in command of her husband's troops. She refuses, still anxious to return to Tehuantepec. Awaiting a train in Mexico City, she is robbed of all her belongings and finds herself "sin centavos, sin ropa y sin nada, encuerada viva" (p. 134; without a penny, without clothing, and without anything, skinned alive). She seeks a widow's pension from President Venustiano Carranza ("an evil man masquerading as good"), who refuses her on the basis of youth. A kindly lady lets her sleep on the floor in her hallway, and Jesusa spends ten months without work and almost without food, wandering the streets in search of a job yet unaccustomed to verbalizing her needs. She has neither space nor voice; her solitude and her silence very nearly lead to starvation. In a moment of great despair, God sends Jesusa a guardian angel in the person of Isabel Chamorro, who arranges for her to work as a maid for a Spanish woman. For a year and a half, she washes, irons, and cleans the floor daily. Because she suffers from rheumatism caused by the dampness, her employer fires her for fear of having to suffer a sick person in her house. The guardian angel goes to the house to claim Jesusa's salary. Her next employer makes her sleep in the doorway with the dog, gives her little food, and forces her to spy on an errant husband. She subsequently gets her first of many factory jobs, earning enough to live frugally and establishing a pattern of existence that continues to the present.

A small but steady income and friendship with co-workers remove Jesusa from the destitution of her first months in the city. Her attitude changes, and her actions become more aggressive. She has leisure time to go to movies, to dance, and to drink. She works in a canteen and has a second job as a waitress on Sundays, enjoying her time off with several dancing partners in what she calls fraternal relationships. For a time, she manages the canteen while the owner is away, then she takes another factory job, learns the fundamentals of carpentry, and spends three days in jail for striking a drunkard who was pursuing her. Too proud to return to the factory after her stay in jail, Jesusa finds a new job. During this period, she cares for a neighbor's child, Angel, who dies during a stay in the country. A dog she takes in dies suddenly. Disillusionment seems to follow Jesusa, making her cynical and slow to offer affection, a stance that extends to the time of narration. When hunger and silence cease to be key issues in Jesusa's life and key motifs of her text, they are replaced by disillusionment—hope turned to rejection, voluntarily or involuntarily—and, as a consequence, by a shift from the concerns of this world to a heightening spirituality.

The homosexual dancer Manuel el Robachicos, her class-conscious friend Antonio Pérez, and the canteen owner Adelina de la Parra and her family take advantage of Jesusa's generosity. The corps of teachers who come to the hospital where Jesusa is working as a nurse insult her intelligence and her sensibility. When an act of friendship evolves into a run-in with a policeman, Jesusa leaves the city to work as a maid and cook for the Second Artillery Regiment in Oaxaca, thus resuming her ties with the military. She discovers that her father's brother lives there in relative luxury. At their meeting, her uncle greets her with the statement that she has come too late if she expects to receive her father's inheritance, since his share was confiscated by the government during the revolution. Jesusa reacts with dignity, noting that she was raised poor and will stay poor until she dies, that she has no beneficiaries and no need of an inheritance. She realizes that she does have a claim but neither the resources nor the desire to go to court. Her behavior is a model of restraint, yet her words indicate the disappointment of rejection and an increased skepticism. Poverty and hunger are gone, but solitude remains.

Another term in jail (for fighting) causes Jesusa to miss a train carrying the company of soldiers to a new destination. Back in the city, she cares for the grandmother Adelina's family has abandoned and then manages a barber shop owned by her carpenter friend. She finds the job confining, a threat to her freedom, and returns to the soldiers: "Como a nadie le tengo que rendir cuentas, nomás me salgo y adiós. Me voy por allí sin rumbo o por un camino que yo sola discurro. Así soy, hija de la mala vida, acostumbrada a ir de un lado a otro y a poner en cualquier parte los palos de mi sombrajo" (p. 238; Since I don't have to answer to anybody, I can pack up and go whenever I please. I can travel with no set direction or set my own direction. That's how I am, a daughter of the wild life, used to going from one place to the next and putting up stakes anywhere at all). Jesusa takes in an orphan, Rufino, who stays with her for two years, robs her, and flees, and she vows never to fall into the same trap. She travels on foot from San Luis Potosí to Mexico City, finding more charity among the poor of the country than within the urban middle class.

In the city, history seems to repeat itself. Jesusa works as a maid, and, while she is willing to do menial labor, she refuses to be treated as subhuman. When her mistress offers her scraps from the table, she quits. She tries her hand at selling but is too good-natured to make a profit. She changes jobs—working in a drugstore, washing mattresses, cleaning—yet her living conditions remain the same. She is always alone, able to depend on no one but herself. She works for the Torres family but sleeps outside the house, leaning against a wall. José Torres wants to marry Jesusa, and when she refuses he marries another woman, whom he abuses. Jesusa establishes contact with the Vidales family, which includes nine children. After the death of the mother, Jesusa breaks her resolve never to provide shelter for another child by caring for Perico, the youngest son. He leaves her lonely and remorseful, as in the earlier cases, only to return years later, near the time of narration. She receives him coolly, recognizing that his attentions stem from self-interest. Perico is the ultimate and archetypal male, the last in a line of men who expend a certain amount of energy but show no real concern for her: "Por eso digo que a los hombres de hoy no les llama la atención más que aprovecharse. Nadie estima a su mujer ni la cuida. Al contrario, entre más le sacan, mejor. Cualquier día no podré hacer ya nada y ni modo de decir: 'Mi muchacho va a ver por mí.' No, hombre, mejor me largo. Ya para qué le sirvo, estoy imposibilitada de lavarlo ni hervirle sus frijoles. Cuando ya no pueda más, agarro mi morral y como sé que en el camposanto no hay pozo para mí, me voy al cerro a que me coman los zopilotes" (p. 314; That's why I say that men today aren't interested in anything but taking advantage. Nobody respects his woman or cares for her. Just the opposite, the more they can get out of her, the better. Any day now I might not be able to do anything, and there's no way I can say, "My boy will see after me." No, sir, it would be better for me to leave. What good am I to him if I'm too weak to wash for him and cook his beans? When I can't go on any longer, I'll grab my bag, and since I know that there's no hole for me in the cemetery, I'll go over to the hill and let the buzzards eat me).

Because her social experience degrades her at every stage of her life, Jesusa finds comfort in the promise of eternal tranquillity. She borrows from Christianity the concept of earthly suffering as necessary preparation for the afterlife, mixing this belief with a belief in indigenous myths, reincarnation, and the contact with dead souls provided by the Obra Espiritual, the religious organization that influences her from her early days in Mexico City. Through a medium, Jesusa hears the voice of her father, who proffers more advice from the beyond than he had on earth, admonishing her to act moderately and to avoid confrontations. Given the opportunity, she refuses to conjure Pedro Aguilar, a presence she wishes to leave as part of the past. She credits her protector, Manuel Antonio Mesmer, with narrow escapes from death—from serious illness and accidents—and dedicates herself to spiritual study to repay the Supreme Being. At one point, she vows to stop drinking and fighting as a sign of respect for the Obra Espiritual. Her bond with spirituality gives meaning to her pain and to her alienation: "Entiendo que yo no iba solita sino que el mundo espiritual estaba conmigo" (p. 226; I realize that I wasn't alone but that the spiritual world was with me). Nonetheless, she understands that total detachment from the temptations of this world is impossible. She reacts strongly, for example, to those who envy her rapid progress through the spiritual exercises: "En una cátedra el Señor dijo que debía tener calma, porque con esa calma daría yo el paso de la oscuridad a la luz divina que ninguna de esas envidiosas había traspasado. Pero yo era de carne y hueso, sigo siendo de carne y hueso, y no me gusta que me digan nada. Todavía siento lo material y me defiendo" (p. 251; In a session the Lord said that I ought to be calm, because with that calm I could pass from darkness to the divine light that none of those jealous women had crossed. But I was made of flesh and blood—I'm still made of flesh and blood—and I don't like them telling me what to do. I still feel contact with material things and defend myself).

The realm of the senses imposes itself on the ethereal. If spirituality provides a remedy for despondency, the human spirit cannot eliminate spontaneous responses within the objective world, and Jesusa's struggle becomes the eternal conflict between morality and mortality. The disillusionment that pervades the earthly course of events makes its way into the divine scheme. As Jesusa grows older, she maintains her faith but isolates herself from the congregation, which to her mind has become a business rather than a holy community. Spiritual visions occur in a world of injustice and cruelty; people can pray and kill, learn the path of righteousness and waver from it, pretend to love their neighbor and do violence to their spouses. God's work is difficult, according to Jesusa, because mankind is inherently evil. Only man's desire for transcendence gives goodness a place on earth, and even the contests for freedom ignore basic rights. The text suggests that true revolution must have as its point of departure a search for equality and not a stratagem for power. If not, the struggle loses all meaning except the ironic.

The historical setting of *Hasta no verte Jesús mío* stands in contrast to the individual case of Jesusa Palancares. The equality that serves as the motivating factor of the revolution can only have relative significance. Ideological ambiguities may bring into question the ends of the combatants, but the social issues are ambiguous only when they pertain to men. The political revolution does not have a sexual counterpart. Women are categorically excluded from the aspirations of a society seeking freedom from oppression. They are at best sacrificial victims, allowed to precede the soldiers into combat, and are at worst ciphers in the social perspective. General Blanco forces Jesusa's marriage to Pedro Aguilar with no regard to her protests. Aguilar subjugates her in the cruelest possible manner, satisfying his carnal needs at the expense of her human status, while society considers him an exemplary husband. President Carranza's denial of a pension to Jesusa tacitly negates her identity and threatens her chances of survival; he consolidates the harm done by her husband. Historical change, in its multiple and fluctuating forms, does not alter the position of women. On the contrary, it accentuates the lack of change through a consistent pattern of discrimination that extends beyond the revolution. Although participants and historians may view the matter in political and economic terms, the text focuses on sexual inequity—ultimately both political and economic in nature—with implied male superiority as the principal referent.

The exempla of Jesusa's story add a universal quality to the experiences of her life. Her sister Petra is kept prisoner by a soldier, her sister-in-law Ignacia is beaten by her husband, other women are destitute when alone and repressed when married. Through the trope of synecdoche, in which the part stands for the whole, Jesusa represents women in general and specifically the poor woman in Mexico. In this society, the thesis that men are morally inferior carries little weight; survival is not an ethical matter. Jesusa herself recognizes the advantages of being a man: "Para todas las mujeres sería mejor ser hombre, seguro, porque es más divertido, es uno más libre y nadie se burla de uno. En cambio de mujer, a ninguna edad la pueden respetar, porque si es muchacha se la vacilan y si es vieja la chotean, sirve de risión porque ya no sopla. En cambio, el hombre vestido de hombre va y viene: se va y no viene y como es hombre ni quien le pare el alto. ¡Mil veces mejor ser hombre que mujer!" (p. 186; For all women it would be better to be a man, surely, because it's more fun. You're free and nobody hassles you. But a woman can't get respect at any age, because if she's young they fool around with her and if she's old they make fun of her, treating her with scorn because she's all out of wind. On the other hand, a real man can come and go as he pleases, or he can go out and not come back and no one will stand in his way. It's a thousand times better to be a man than a woman!). In short, men enjoy freedom and women do not. Women are subservient in their prime and the object of scorn in their maturity, and their identity depends on their relationship to a man and on laws written and enforced by men. President Alvaro Obregón, significantly, enacts a nine o'clock curfew for women, reserving the streets of Mexico City for the male population. Jesusa Palancares, equally significantly, ignores the curfew.

Men are to be admired, it seems, not for their character but for their privileged status. Jesusa does not like men and, in fact, does everything within her power to avoid them, yet she clearly envies them their position in the social hierarchy. The men who abuse her in one way or another—her father, her brothers, her husband, her uncle, President Carranza, Antonio Pérez, José Torres, Manuel el Robachicos, among others—include blood relatives incapable of love, a spurned suitor bent on revenge, a government official misusing his authority, a decent man unwilling to marry beneath himself, a man forcing his attentions on her, a homosexual attracted to her money. Despite obvious differences, the men share an egotistical vision of their masculinity, a vision that works to destroy feminine self-esteem. When the woman is alone and poor, she becomes distanced from her environment, from human warmth, and from herself. Speaking of her time in Oaxaca, Jesusa reflects on her place in society, and her words convey an acceptance of defeat: "Al fin de cuentas, yo no tengo patria. Soy como los húngaros: de ninguna parte. No me siento mexicana ni reconozco a los mexicanos. Aquí no existe más que pura conveniencia y puro interés. Si yo tuviera dinero y bienes, sería mexicana, pero como soy peor que la basura, pues no soy nada. Soy basura a la que el perro le echa una miada y sigue adelante. Viene el aire y se la lleva y se acabó todo... Soy basura porque no puedo ser otra cosa" (p. 218; All things considered, I don't really have a homeland. I'm like the gypsies: from nowhere. I don't feel Mexican or acknowledge the Mexicans as my own. Here nothing matters but pure profit and pure interest. If I had money and property, I'd be Mexican, but since I'm worse than garbage, I'm nothing. I'm the garbage the dog pisses on before he goes on his way. A breeze blows and carries it off and that's it. I'm trash because I don't know how to be anything else).

Reduced to nothingness, Jesusa believes only in her insignificance, trusting neither her fellow man nor the possibility of change. Her faith, with its emphasis on a miraculous world far removed from present reality, offers consolation and a logic of moderation in this life and a dream of peace for the future. The religious synthesis mediates good and evil, making suffering an agent of salvation, and only when Jesusa acknowledges a divine plan does she consider herself part of a collectivity. Her role in the social order remains the same, but she has compensatory and multiple identities in the spiritual order. She is not only a penitent in search of salvation but also a former queen, who even as a penniless vagrant has the protection of spiritual beings. In society, the higher one's rank, the better the chance of success; in the eternal domain, the lower one's status, the greater the means of attaining perfection. The Obra Espiritual actualizes the world-as-stage metaphor to deliver Jesusa from solitude, to provide new associates and new associations, and to reconcile social contradictions. It gives her more than a promise for the future. It gives her a self-image for the world to come.

Jesusa Palancares's narrative wavers, to a degree, between life as a series of tribulations and life as a preparation for and anticipation of eternal life. Jesusa favors the second, but her text—as a product of this world—operates in the field of the first. Her situation and her discourse, a mixture of faith and frustration, present a devotee striving for acceptability in the spiritual order and an old woman awaiting an end to her suffering as a social outcast. Jesusa's commentary reaches its final form through the intervention of the author, who provides a structure for the words. The narrative breaks with strict chronology by introducing a spiritual explanation in the first chapter. In life, experience precedes faith, while in the text faith precedes and influences the presentation of experience. Jesusa's resignation to poverty and mistreatment depends on her beliefs, and this resignation sustains her, even though story and discourse often forsake the higher sphere for a spontaneous reaction to the immediate circumstances. The author seizes upon the tension to lead the reader away from a passive response and toward an involvement with the social problems posed by the text. Jesusa's unconscious stand against oppression, in actions and narration that prioritize the present moment, validates a reading of *Hasta no verte Jesús mío* that would focus on a social subtext. Message production stems here from a narrator who does not comprehend the full implications of her discourse and from an implied author who structures the discourse to stress the protagonist's strength and society's weaknesses.

The linear progression of the text advances from incident to response (resistance) to commentary, all within the spiritual frame. The war imagery unifies the narrative both verbally and thematically, and the recurrent images effect an intensification of the struggle. Jesusa must deal with a difficult father and the women he pursues, with a far more difficult husband and the women who pursue him, and finally with a hostile society and the prospect of starvation. As her economic situation improves, her pride increases, and so does the scope of her resistance. As her world becomes less silent and less solitary, she defends herself with greater frequency, but only in her text does she generalize about social inequities. Among the turning points in Jesusa's life are decisions related to self-preservation: to fight her father's mistress, to arm a counterattack against Pedro Aguilar, to leave an employer who treats her unfairly, to turn down those who would abuse her, to dedicate herself to the Obra Espiritual. The individual cases, when viewed collectively and brought into the public domain (through commentaries and the presence of the book as object), acquire an expressive force. Jesusa finds a form of release through faith, but her text repeatedly invokes the signs of a battle against society. Her discourse provides a forum denied by her fellow man.

The narrative linearity of *Hasta no verte Jesús mío* contains a circular movement that helps to define Jesusa's character and her attitudes. The pattern begins with an event in which someone abuses Jesusa, followed by a feeling of mistrust on her part and a vow to detach herself from others, continued service to those in need, continued abuse, disillusionment, and so on. Her mother's death, competition with her father's companions, and rejection by him open a cycle that ends with Perico, the adoptive son who takes advantage of Jesusa's emotional and financial support. Although faith goes beyond history, the inescapable present breeds cynicism. The text manifests the contradiction through the juxtaposition of resigned acquiescence with heightened aggression and of skepticism with human kindness. The dichotomies of male versus female and rich versus poor complement the sense of opposition, while paradoxically both sides of the revolution seem to merge into a mass of undisciplined acts and unclear ambitions. The final test of sustained interaction comes not from the revolution but from the discursive model.

The discourse of *Hasta no verte Jesús mío* combines the directness of an elderly speaker totally lacking in social pretensions with an unpremeditated indictment of social institutions. Tempered by memory and by the transformations of time and state of mind, Jesusa Palancares's narrative recaptures experience and at the same time reflects the past from the vantage point of the present. Jesusa reduplicates herself in the process of narration; she has the authority of hindsight and, more importantly, of speech. Social repression finds a verbal correlative in the silence imposed by those who fail to communicate with her, most notably her husband. The oral history removes the barrier of silence, creating a voice and a new identity for Jesusa. While her acts of resistance take place almost exclusively on the individual level, the speech act allows her to confront society directly and in comprehensive terms. Her method is intuitive as opposed to introspective, but this distinction only strengthens the verisimilitude of the text and the validity of its argument. By telling the story in her "own words"—which are, in fact, not entirely her own—she gives the text a documentary air. Jesusa is a reliable narrator who becomes unreliable only when she fails to see her own courage or to respect her own intelligence, but again the discrepancy between self-image and the image projected within the text underscores narrative realism and the need for social reform. The narrator calls herself "very mannish" ("muy hombrada"), a pejorative term, yet her text, in its conscious and unconscious condemnation of the traditional role of women, converts the antifeminine into a profeminist position.[5]

It is crucial to note that Jesusa Palancares is illiterate. Her exposure to the world of books comes from Pedro Aguilar, who reads to her and tests her mnemonic and comprehensive skills. She will have acquired a basic sense of plot from these books, from film, and perhaps from radio serials, and the passages in which she traces her family history and the reminiscences in general attest to her sharp memory. Nonetheless, Jesusa's contribution to the narrative is an oral performance, transformed into a written text by a second author (to use Cervantes's term). While the words belong to Jesusa, the literary object indicates that the oral history has been subjected to the devices of narrative, that it has been edited to adhere to the laws of written (hi)story. The work respects such conventions as the division of the material into chapters, the re-creation of dialogue, and the development of structural unity. The dynamics of authorship begin with Jesusa Palancares and move to the narratee and the second author/editor, who produce a written version of the speech act.

Just as Jesusa functions as narrator and protagonist, the authorial figure has multiple roles in the creation of the text. The narrator directs the final words of her story to a narratee one could identify as "Poniatowska": "Ahora ya no chingue. Váyase. Déjeme dormir" (p. 316; Don't bother me anymore. Go away. Let me get some sleep). The literary conventions imply that the relationship between the two is more than that of informant and passive receiver. The publishing house responsible for the text's entry into the world calls it a novel, fostering a reading as such and distancing the object from the realm of nonfiction.[6] Despite this link with fiction, the narrative premise of an oral performance evolving into a written text inverts the traditional fictional circumstances. The author does not compose on a tabula rasa but builds on and revises an existing story. The result is an adaptation whose source is inaccessible to the reader. The narrator/informant provides the basis for the composition of the text, so that the rhetorical strategies of the implied author come into play after the fact. If the implied author of *Lazarillo de Tormes* puts words into his narrator's mouth, the corresponding presence in *Hasta no verte Jesús mío* controls preexisting words to help determine the production of meaning.

In *Moll Flanders*, Defoe "rewrites" Moll's memoirs but makes his work as editor and censor a part of the text. The final version is a combination of Moll Flanders's unmediated (and fictitious) original manuscript and the moral presence of the author (as fictionalized in the preface). The interplay has a precedent in the ambiguous prologue of *Lazarillo de Tormes*, but Defoe legitimizes—that is, makes explicit—the authorial imposition. The reader may seek to differentiate the two voices or to reconstruct elements of the original text based on the rewriting. The gaps between the premises of the author and the discourse of the narrator extend the scope of literary and social messages. Rather than resolve the intricacies of the text, the intervention of the author challenges the semantic and ethical bases of this particular narrative and broadens the range (and art) of discourse. Poniatowska, for her part, explains her editorial role in *Hasta no verte Jesús mío* outside of the text, and the difference is significant. Defoe "reads" Moll Flanders's manuscript, revises it according to his own notions of poetic justice, and directs a reading of the modified narrative. Poniatowska reenacts this fictional situation in real life, devising a plot and an idiolect for the recorded voice of Jesusa Palancares, but directing the reader only through the recourses of the narrative proper. She returns to the concept of an implied author whose contact with the narrator takes place within the text. The reader recognizes Jesusa as the speaker and tacitly acknowledges the presence of the second party who converts the raw material into an established literary form. The rewriting here is distinguishable from Defoe's authorial device by the absence of an overt thematic center such as that provided by the preface of *Moll Flanders*. Defoe's author competes with his narrator, while Poniatowska collaborates with hers.

In the discursive scheme of *Hasta no verte Jesús mío*, Jesusa Palancares addresses herself to "Elena Poniatowska," the narratee who has a fictional identity within the text and who in some way differs from the woman who is (re)writing the oral history. This second figure exists outside of the text as author and within not only as narratee but also as implied author. The fragmentation of the author follows the model of discourse initiated in the *Lazarillo*, with a variation in the point at which the implied author enters the process. The reader may accept the author's statement (made beyond the limits of the text) that much of the work owes its discourse to Jesusa herself or may prefer to consider everything within the text as fiction. In either case, it is clear first that the oral performance is a stable feature of the narrative premise and secondly that the narrator/protagonist could not have produced the manuscript on her own. The original receiver of the enunciation incorporates herself into the written text while she revises Jesusa's story to suit narrative conventions and to reach an implied reader. That is, she encodes the material according to the techniques of narrative fiction, and she encodes the altered discourse into systems of message production and irony. The markers of meaning and irony interact within the narrative format to fashion a subtext that complements and amplifies Jesusa's perspective.

The raw material of the account illustrates the plight of a (perhaps *the*) poor woman in Mexico during and after the revolution.[7] Jesusa Palancares is neither self-absorbed nor self-pitying, yet the text presents a sympathetic portrait of her, a portrait that foregrounds her forthrightness, her bravery, her perseverance, and her intelligence. The religious frame breaks the chronology to introduce the protagonist's means of rationalizing her suffering. The hope for a peaceful future serves as a constant counterpoint to the rigors of earthly existence. Divine justice is a last resort when social injustice prevails. In the text, social injustice does prevail, most strikingly in the presentation of the indigent and women, and the social vision overshadows the spiritual revision. The intensification of solitude, the use of parallel episodes and foreshadowing, and the placement of commentary at critical points offer further evidence of the presence of an implied author. The concept of irreconcilability may serve as a source of unity for both story and discourse, and the guiding trope of this unity, as would follow, is irony.

The Obra Espiritual endorses an alternative to abusive men and abused women, yet the reality of the present is far removed from this ideal. In accord with her faith, Jesusa views earthly suffering as a necessary prelude to eternal life, without sacrificing her social conscience and a sense of absolute values in this life. The implied author uses the resulting tension to pattern variations of inequality within Jesusa's narrative. The text presents a narrator/protagonist who, while criticizing her brusqueness and belligerent attitude, demonstrates kindness and a true spirit of love in her dealings with others. Only when provoked does she defend herself. As creator of the literary order, the author makes the contradictions between speech and action the determinant and the rationale of the ironic structure. For Jesusa, the events of her narrative are fact, and the commentaries would thus be spontaneous reactions to the narrative events. For the implied author, these events seem to belong to a panorama of irony. The fictionalized Poniatowska is the narratee, the object of an oral performance that, when made public, calls on an implied reader to decipher clues to the narrative and rhetorical structure of a text.

A primary stage in the development of irony in *Hasta no verte Jesús mío* relates to the dialectic of diegesis and mimesis, to the distance between the self-deprecating Jesusa and the heroic (and antiheroic) Jesusa. The key here is a discourse that goes beyond the speaker's comprehension to reveal a verbal and vital resistance to oppression. Jesusa cannot read or write, but her discourse is direct, unself-conscious, and articulate, and, like her story, the discourse finds unity in contradiction. The story centers on the spiritual and the social, on resignation and reaction. It takes place during a time of revolution, yet the revolution ignores—or worse, exploits—women. The conflict effects little change and reflects a general misdirection in society.

Civil rights must have a place in a struggle for freedom. As presented in the narrative, the Mexican Revolution omits women from its political and social goals. The predominant battle in *Hasta no verte Jesús mío* is not so much the revolution as the fight for survival of a representative and symbolic woman, whose major weapon is a text that delivers her from silence.

7 THE MYTHIC NARRATOR
Tereza Batista and the Utopian Alternative

Juntei quanto pude ouvir e entender, pedaços de histórias, sons de harmônica, passos de dança, gritos de desespero, ais de amor, tudo de mistura e atropelo, para os desejosos de informações sobre a moça de cobre, seus afazeres e correrias. Grande coisa não tenho para narrar, o povo de lá não é muita conversa, e quem mais sabe menos diz para não tirar diploma de mentiroso.

I gathered together all bits and pieces I heard and could make sense of—anecdotes, tunes on the harmonica, dance steps, cries of desperation and moans of love, all jumbled together—and brought them back to tell to people who wanted to know about that copper-colored girl's ups and downs, and all her wanderings. It still doesn't add up to an awful lot: folks in these parts aren't what you'd call real talkers, and the ones who know the most say the least. Nobody out there hankers to get a diploma for telling tales.

The rediscovered faith in the saving power of society, as evidenced in the plots (and especially in the dénouements) of the eighteenth-century novel, suffers at the hands of economic determinism in the nineteenth century and disintegrates in the twentieth century. A new age of skepticism brings with it new narrative relationships, including an increased distance between the narrator and tradition, both social and literary. The Brazilian novel *Tereza Batista cansada de guerra* would seem to verify this thesis. Jorge Amado's particular treatment of a geographical backdrop, often Bahia, gives his novels a sense of place that converts the representational into the mythic. Through what may be termed naturalistic impressionism, Amado re-creates the setting to conform to a plot and to a focal character. The vision is selectively panoramic, faithful in a synecdochic sense. Characters may simultaneously exist in time and space and transcend time and space, as quotidian reality interacts with a reality of a higher order. In *Tereza Batista*, interaction becomes intersection, symbolism. The individuation process moves forward and backward to provide a definitive perspective and to transform an antiheroine into a heroine. Somewhat paradoxically, the heroics of *Tereza Batista* relate the work to another backdrop, the intertextual realm of the picaresque tradition. The result is an idealization of the picaresque protagonist and a significantly new use of point of view.

Orphaned at an early age, Tereza Batista is sold by her aunt to Captain Justiniano Duarte da Rosa, whose interest in her is purely and cruelly sexual. Implicated in the Captain's death, she is rescued by the benevolent Don Emiliano Guedes, dances her way to samba stardom, combats a smallpox epidemic, leads a strike of prostitutes against police corruption, and is finally reunited with Captain Januário Gereba, the sailor whose passion and heroism match her own. The third-person narrator creates a tension of sorts by incorporating into the biographical structure a temporal frame based on the collection of data concerning Tereza Batista, now both a historical and legendary figure. The process involves the interplay between truth and fiction, and, perhaps more importantly, the invention of a narrative perspective that becomes a structuring agent of the novel. The separation of Tereza and her lover at the beginning of the novel and their reunion at the end gives the work the form of romance, but the superseding form has as its focal point the relationship between Tereza and her society. The narrator, as mediator, provides the judgmental base that reveals the validity and the paradoxical nature of Tereza's social role. Only by isolating his subject from the narrative discourse can he exalt her attitudes and accomplishments and expose the hypocrisy of a society that condemns her. If *Moll Flanders* in its own way substantiates the social order as had Quevedo in *El Buscón*, Amado's novel obliterates this perspective. *Tereza Batista* negates society— and society's derogatory view of Tereza—by converting the antiheroine into the symbol of an ideal society.

Marginated by a class-conscious society and by an unwritten doctrine of male supremacy, Tereza Batista undergoes stages of rejection, or variations of solitude. With little control over her destiny, she serves many masters and suffers numerous hardships, and the narration of her experiences accentuates her position on the lower rungs of the social ladder. Unlike other descendants of Lazarillo de Tormes, however, Tereza has no desire to rise in the social hierarchy. She chooses the freedom of prostitution over the servitude of the kept woman, follows a standard of absolute values in her treatment of others, and finds respectability, seemingly unconsciously, beyond her community, in the abstract realm of the spirit and in the narrative itself. An idealistic sensibility moves beyond the realistic direction of the text to create an ironically heroic offense against social ostracism. By exposing the derogatory aspects of social conditioning, the narrative recourses define an analogical structure: romance supersedes literary realism as a utopian vision supersedes social realism.

The storyteller is the fictionalized author seeking facts and legends concerning Tereza Batista from informants whose reports are quoted directly or are incorporated into the narrative events. The narrator emphasizes the quest for authenticity while recognizing that unconditional truth is impossible. Tereza is no longer merely real but mythic as well. The collected data allow the narrator to approximate omniscience, to give form to Tereza's life, to progress in his written account (as does Tereza as a character) from earthly to transcendent themes. He employs the protagonist's antisocial behavior as an ironic counterpoint to established codes. Through this inversion of traditional dichotomies, the activities that a relativistic society considers inferior, immoral, and unjust become—within the ethical and narrative consciousness of the text—superior, moral, and just. Discourse here is an end in itself, a means of validating a social position and the representative of that position. The narrative discourse and disposition project the reversal of priorities that ends in Tereza's transformation from social outcast to romantic heroine.

Amado's rhetorical strategy is a synthesis of the diegetic and the mimetic, of telling and showing. The narrator and his literary accomplices (the informants and those characters most worthy of praise, though not necessarily in the accepted and conformist sense) extol Tereza while making prejudicial statements against her enemies. Those who condemn her are presented negatively or are shown to be hypocrites. Diegetically speaking, Tereza is portrayed in heroic terms, and her actions mimetically confirm the description; her "reconstructed" words operate on both levels, to her advantage. Equally significantly, her strength and courage are to a great extent unrecognized and unrewarded by society, thus serving to increase reader sympathy. Her enemies are especially demonic, so that her oppression is especially fierce. The text offers a radical denial of the factors that alienate Tereza and at the same time counters that alienation by making itself the vehicle of her redemption and of her legend. The literary document becomes a defense against solitude, partial truths, and rejection, as the narrative voice joins the protagonist in her fight against social inequity. The war imagery of the title and within the text suggests a battle against the forces of evil masquerading as truth, a battle in which the narrator uses his discursive strength to uncover deception and to achieve a spiritual triumph for Tereza Batista. As in the case of the *Buscón*, the implied author manipulates story and discourse for social effect, but in *Tereza Batista* society rather than the protagonist suffers at the hands of narrative causality.

The introduction to *Tereza Batista* defines a context (and a pretext) for Amado's fiction through the narrative situation, whereby the "author"/narrator travels to various locales to interview people acquainted with Tereza. Because the subject has risen above conventional documentary, the legendary and mythic aspects of her story are inseparable from historical events and linked to the question of truth. No one, of course, knows the whole truth, and history alone is but another fiction; exploiting the fragile base of objectivity, the narrator and his informants magnify, embellish, intuit, and prioritize event and character to arrive at a poetic truth. The final version of this truth depends on the shaping of the text: the organization and ordering of episodes, commentaries, indeterminacies, and rhetorical framework. It is here that the reader may feel the presence of an implied author who controls the story by controlling the discourse. Poetic license serves poetic truth or, from a social standpoint, poetic justice. Narrative perspective unifies the text as both process and product. The "author" not only discovers facts and fictions but also arranges them in such a way as to orient, perhaps reorient, reader response. The poetic license allows myth and history to converge in a narrative structure that deviates from strict chronology and fills in gaps to devalue the social record. The design of *Tereza Batista* reveals a calculated irony whose matrix and principal marker is the narrative voice.

The first section of the novel, chronologically the third of five parts,[1] displays the key elements of Amado's narrative strategy. An informant praises Tereza in terms of her powers of endurance and her ability to compete with men while retaining her feminine qualities. Alone and the victim of bad luck, she is nonetheless prepared to defend the oppressed. A reference to her childhood leads to the statement that Tereza could never bear to see a man hit a woman. The informant presents the initial characterization of the protagonist in the context of a recognized legend and of a legend being created. Diegesis shifts to mimesis as the notorious Libório das Neves strikes his mistress on the dance floor of a cabaret in the port city of Aracaju on the night of Tereza Batista's scheduled debut as samba star extraordinaire. Tereza intervenes on behalf of the woman and, in the ensuing tumult, loses a tooth to Libório and her heart to Januário Gereba, the noble sailor who rescues her. The incident postpones the debut until a dentist can provide the gold tooth that will become her trademark and sets into motion the two interrelated plot lines of this section, which are based on the paradoxes of justice and love.

Tereza's friend, the lawyer Lulu Santos, is defending the impoverished Joana das Folhas against Libório, a usurer who has forged a document to seize control of the widow's property. Although his infamy is widely known, Libório has thus far been successful in court. In order to nullify the contract, Tereza devises a plan to teach the illiterate Joana to sign her name. She spends many hours tutoring Joana, and Lulu convinces a respected teacher to testify that she has instructed the pupil. Justice grows from injustice, from fighting fire with fire. The teacher is willing to commit perjury, and the judge willingly accepts the deception for the sake of absolute justice. Tereza Batista, the author of the scheme, forsakes conventional morality for a higher cause, and justice is served. The incident reflects Tereza's ingenuity and special code of ethics; it also reflects the inversion of traditional values that marks the novel as a whole. If the ultimate victory belongs to the forces of resistance, it is because the narrative establishes its own criteria for judgment from the very beginning of the text.

The interrupted debut brings Tereza into contact with Captain Januário Gereba, described in the idiom of Afro-Brazilian mythology as her protector. She falls madly in love with the noble sailor, whose sense of duty to his invalid wife creates an obstacle to their union. The joy of Libório's defeat mixes with the sorrow of Januário's departure. The samba queen takes to the stage, oblivious to the applause that greets her performance and conscious only of her lover's promise to return. The idyllic time with Januário remains a memory, but passion burns in Tereza's heart and she cannot be at peace until they meet again. As in romance, this meeting will take place at the novel's end, after both have endured a series of tribulations.

The opening section treats Tereza's debut in a double sense, as a dancer and as protagonist. The narrator alludes to her masters as a lead-in to the succeeding sections of the novel, which are unified by her courage, dedication, and stamina, and by her mistreatment by these men and the community at large. The one exception is Emiliano Guedes, who saves her from death only to die in her arms. As her mourning nears its close, Tereza finds a new cause for grief in her ill-fated love for the sailor. In Januário Gereba, Amado introduces an antiheroic hero to match Tereza Batista in lofty yet unorthodox idealism, offensive to polite society while exemplary in the realm of fiction and aesthetic response. The adversity that faces them in separation frames the text and influences the arrangement of events. Not only the heroine of romance, Tereza is also a woman with a history. The first part of the novel places her life story in medias res, implying a foreknowledge of her beauty, goodness, and willingness to sacrifice all for the man she loves.

The second section of *Tereza Batista* centers on the period of Tereza's servitude to Captain Justiniano Duarte da Rosa, a wealthy businessman with a penchant for young girls. When her parents are killed in a bus accident, Tereza is given shelter by her mother's sister Felipa. Suspicious of her husband's attentions to his niece and mindful of the captain's quest for virgins, Felipa sells Tereza to Justiniano Duarte da Rosa. Childhood innocence ends abruptly for Tereza, who is not yet thirteen years old. Her rites of passage take her from resistance to fear to submission. Only after a brutal branding by the captain does Tereza accept her sexual slavery. Defeated at last, she becomes another ring on his chain of conquered maidens, the receptacle into which he pours his semen as he would empty his urine in the chamber pot.[2] She is his servant and his favorite, keeping the books in his store by day and always on call in his bed, one commodity more under his violent, usurping spell. Into this world divested of pleasure and desire for Tereza comes Daniel Gomes Neto, a judge's son and gigolo from Bahia, handsome, gentle, resembling the image of the Angel of the Annunciation on the wall of the captain's farmhouse. During the captain's absence, Daniel finds a way to seduce Tereza, who responds to love for the first time. For eight days Tereza lives in rapture and feels herself to be born again; each moment with Daniel eradicates months of pain with the captain. Daniel is, however, a fallen angel, and his promise to carry Tereza off is merely a pretense. A spinster slighted by Daniel informs the captain of the affair, and he rushes in intent on humiliating Daniel and torturing Tereza. It is she who grabs a knife and kills the captain, saving Daniel and ending over two years of imprisonment, fear, and repression.

This part of the novel presents Tereza in her utmost solitude, forsaken by God and her fellow man, according to one informant. Orphaned by a tragic accident and betrayed by her closest relative, Tereza is weaned on pestilence, famine, and war. Justiniano Duarte da Rosa takes away her freedom and her youth. Excited by her ripening beauty and her spirit of resistance, he is proud of his possession, second only to his fighting cock. This demonic character finds a false nemesis in the angelic countenance of Daniel, who leads Tereza to love and then to despair. Ironically, the genuine angel of the second section is Tereza herself. Dona Brígida, Justiniano's mother-in-law, prays for an Angel of Vengeance to redeem her and her granddaughter from the hellish existence they have had to bear since the death of the captain's fifteen-year-old bride. The old woman, ragged, half-crazed, and contemptuous of Tereza, refuses to allow her to associate with the child, yet only when Tereza kills the captain does Dona Brígida recover her sanity and her former opulence. Emiliano Guedes, Tereza's eventual redeemer, appears in this section to buy cattle from Justiniano and offers to purchase the "little heifer" ("novilha") in the house at any price. The captain refuses, preferring to hold on to Tereza for his gratification, and she is forced to be her own avenging angel.

The text informs through a studied detachment, graphically detailed and oriented toward the process of victimization. To depict Tereza's spiritual nadir, the narrator relies primarily on incident rather than on commentary. He condemns Felipa's ignoble act through the unarticulated thoughts of her husband, but once the captain has taken possession of Tereza, the narrative presence recedes to emphasize her solitude and to focus on the events that produce this solitude. Chapters 15 through 18 of part 2, which refer to Tereza's sexual initiation and conditioning, portray an involuntary descent into depravity of the lowest order. All of the characters, and most especially the captain, dehumanize Tereza as she stands unprotected and helpless before them, unable to influence her destiny. Felipa trades her, Emiliano Guedes bids for her, Daniel views her as one in a series of amorous triumphs, and Justiniano Duarte da Rosa subjugates her through fear. She responds, mechanically and without feeling, to the captain's every whim. Daniel offers her a rose, tenderness, and the promise of liberation as symbols of his love, but they are more properly symbols of his hypocrisy; later, Emiliano Guedes will make them valid, if impermanent, symbols of true love. The narrator recounts the stages of Tereza's abuse without defending her, for she needs no defense. The protagonist and the reader face the unknown rites of forced sexuality from the temporal frame of experience. Although Tereza is silent throughout much of this section, the effect of the events on her future behavior and attitudes is evident.

The third section of the novel, centering on Tereza Batista's war against the black smallpox, takes place after her encounter with Januário Gereba. After Daniel produces a deposition charging that Tereza had lured him into the captain's bedroom, she spends time in jail and is rescued by Emiliano Guedes and his lawyer Lulu Santos. Don Emiliano gives her a new life and, for the first time, a justified trust in the human race. This interlude ends with the death of her mentor, and, following a period of mourning, her heart is at peace, until she meets the valiant sailor. Despondent over Januário's absence and pressured to accept propositions from certain wealthy gentlemen of Aracaju, Tereza agrees to accompany Dr. Oto Espinheira, director of a public health clinic, to Buquim. In this relationship totally devoid of sentimental commitment, Tereza may continue to be faithful to Januário. He alone can deliver her from the somnambulistic existence.

Fate has it that Tereza's arrival in Buquim coincides with the outbreak of a smallpox epidemic. The inexperienced Dr. Espinheira, biding time in Buquim while awaiting a more favorable appointment, reacts in panic to the crisis. When his nurse runs off and his elderly colleague dies, the unnerved doctor shelters himself in his room. Tereza volunteers her services in carrying out the plans developed by the old doctor; she learns quickly and acts spontaneously to aid the sick. Threatened by the loss of his smooth skin and perhaps his life, Dr. Espinheira flees, under the pretext of going to Aracaju for more serum, in a train bound for Bahia. Deserted once again, the temporary nurse becomes a temporary doctor. Enlisting the prostitutes of Muricapeba as her staff, Tereza vaccinates most of the townspeople and many of those in the countryside. The epidemic takes its toll, but a severe tragedy is averted.

The abecedarian format of the chapters of this section and the sustained use of war imagery indicate lessons in combat against disease, incompetence, hypocrisy, and grief. This part of *Tereza Batista* is a perfect example of the interplay between social discourse (convention) and textual discourse. The narrator's account of the incidents in Buquim displays an ironic disparity between society's interpretation of the events and the underlying paradox of selflessness. It is important to note that at the beginning of part 3 the narrator presents the consequences of Justiniano Duarte da Rosa's murder. Daniel swears before the court that he had merely succumbed to feminine wiles, that Tereza had insisted to him that she was the captain's servant and that she had not had intercourse with him for over a year. The subtlety of evil strikes Tereza more sharply than the captain's beatings, and she retires to her cell in an animal state. Daniel, society's darling, is a coward protected by rank and wit. Tereza, who has defended herself and Daniel against the captain's wrath, must endure the cruelest result of victimization, the loss of faith.

The smallpox epidemic is an analogue of the earlier situation. The official nurse, an untrained woman who has received the position through family influence, deserts the town, and the doctor entrusted with the lives of the inhabitants follows her. Tereza becomes nurse and doctor, with the prostitutes as able assistants. When an eight-member medical team finally arrives, there are no new cases and no recent deaths from smallpox. In recognition of meritorious service, society chooses to bestow honors and promotions on Dr. Espinheira and his nurse and to eulogize the medical team. The prostitutes who have volunteered their services maintain their health, but now as social pariahs they sacrifice their source of income. Tereza must sell a few of her trinkets to buy a train ticket. She leaves Buquim as the pious women congregated in church call it an injustice that so vulgar a person has escaped unscathed while many righteous souls have suffered.

Narrative discourse favors Tereza as society rejects her; the antisocial characters, led by Tereza, are unsung heroes who receive their due within the text. The narrator exposes the irony of the outcome as a type of axiom, implying that through its inverted value system society rewards the guilty and punishes the innocent. Literary discourse reveals the inconsistencies and falsehoods of society's story to set the record straight. Tereza and the least respected segment of the community wage war against disease while the narrator wages a verbal battle against prejudice. The narrative strategy includes a juxtaposition of the irresponsibility of so-called professionals and the dedication of marginated figures, as well as a set of circumstances in which Tereza and the prostitutes can be accused of no ulterior motives. Tereza escapes death and refuses the proffered liaisons. She cannot be truly free until she is reunited with Januário, but now she is free to continue her search.

If part 3 of *Tereza Batista* is a stylized lesson in social responsibility, the following section offers an unconventional perspective to correspond to the six years that Tereza spends with the influential Doctor Emiliano Guedes, owner of a sugar mill. The fourth part opens with the death of Don Emiliano in bed with Tereza. The individual chapters alternate flashbacks drawn from the time of Tereza's implication in Justiniano Duarte da Rosa's death and from her life as Don Emiliano's mistress. Dona Beatriz, Don Emiliano's cousin and Daniel's mother, requests her relative's intervention on behalf of the "innocent victim." When he senses the truth of the matter, Don Emiliano arranges for Tereza's release from prison and for her protection in a convent. Misunderstanding his motives, Tereza leaves the nuns to become a prostitute. The aged knight rescues her once again, carrying her off to his home in Estância. The two live in a state of perfection until death comes to make Tereza widow and orphan of her teacher of shared love. The reward for her dedicated service, as in the smallpox episode, is disdain and a voluntary departure.

Rather than producing an anticlimax, the death of Don Emiliano at the beginning of this section serves to underscore both the cyclical progression of Tereza Batista's experiences and the ahistorical use of time in the novel. In figurative terms, the period with the captain and the betrayal by Daniel bring death to Tereza, who is resurrected by Don Emiliano only to die a second time. The implicit second resurrection will be the reunion with Januário Gereba in the final part of the narrative. Time is not as crucial in this structure as the emotional impact of events and the cumulative effect of struggles past and present. The self-conscious temporal scheme calls attention to the imposition of form in the text, a form constructed around reader response and the representation of unwitnessed intimacy.

An informant in the early part of the fourth section notes that much of the story of Tereza's life with Don Emiliano is based on hearsay and advises the "author" to discuss the matter with informants who have had a first-hand knowledge of the affair. While the author/narrator may get closer physically, he can ultimately find only additional versions of the truth. The private story of the relationship between Tereza and Don Emiliano, as presented in the text, is a judgmental compendium of hearsay, legend, and partial truths; it is, in short, a fiction based on tenuous and varying facts, a metafiction. The shift from chapter 2, in which the informant stresses hearsay, to chapter 3, an intimate conversation between Tereza and Don Emiliano, illustrates the narrator's control and power of organization over the material. His authority derives from his role as reporter, as he turns field experience into literary omniscience. An informant quoted in part 3 remarks that Tereza could never learn to order servants around or to assume the position of mistress of the manor. In part 4, Don Emiliano admonishes Tereza for refusing to play a dominant role in the household. The informant's "fact" has thus made its way into the fiction, as do similar facts throughout the act of narration.

As in the preceding sections of the novel, the text projects a perspective that contrasts with public opinion regarding Tereza Batista. The principal spokesperson for society is Nina, Don Emiliano's servant, envious of Tereza's position and willing to condemn her on moral grounds as an opportunist whose sexual debauchery finally kills her master. After the death, the members of the family make a proper show of grief, but the narrator has previously presented Don Emiliano's lack of faith in his second wife and children and his expressions of love for Tereza, whom he considers his true wife. Their mourning ritual comes across as performance, while Tereza, as if oblivious to them, bids farewell to Don Emiliano. She leaves with a rose (a constant symbol of his love for her) in one hand and a suitcase in the other. Her departure is final; she will start anew with the memories of her years with the kindly Don Emiliano. He has taught her love and respect, and she has given him unrelenting devotion, asking nothing in return. When Tereza becomes pregnant, Don Emiliano forces her to choose between her life with him and motherhood. She makes the sacrifice for him, for he has brought her to life by showing her the joy of living. He intends to provide for her after his death but does not finalize his plans, and Tereza makes no demands. One more stage of life is over for her, and she is content with her memories of the perfect time with Don Emiliano. She is too marginal a social being to wish for more.

In the fifth and final section, also the last chronologically, Tereza Batista is very much a social (or antisocial) being. An informant, the spirit-guide Iyá Nassô, raises Tereza's story to the mythic level of voodoo religion, yet the issues of part 5 are indisputably of this world. As in part 1, which establishes the framework of romance, the central questions are social justice and love, and the dual plot is repeated and intensified. Tereza defends a group rather than an individual, and she must contend not only with Januário's absence but also with a report of his death. After Emiliano Guedes's death, Tereza once again becomes a prostitute to work her way to Bahia, in the hope of a reunion with Januário Gereba. Following the death of his wife, Januário had sought Tereza, had been misinformed that she had died in the smallpox epidemic, and, discovering the error, had set out to find her on the *Balboa*. To complete the symmetrical structure (and the penultimate stage of romance), Tereza receives a report of Januário's death at sea. While bearing the burden of death multiplied, Tereza loses herself in a struggle for civil rights and, consistent with former battles, finds herself on the wrong side of the law but not of justice.

To protect the society ladies who have complained of the plague of prostitution and to protect their own interests in ancillary economic enterprises, the police of Bahia resolve to move the red-light district to a more discreet location. The prostitutes, with Tereza as their spiritual leader, resist to the point of declaring the Closed Basket Strike ("A Greve do Balaio

Fechado"), a threat to police-controlled sale of drugs and sexual aids. The servants of law and order answer the strike by attempting to open the brothels by force, in time to serve troops of American soldiers scheduled to land in the port city. Tereza's mania for fighting injustice and her notoriety make her a prime target for police officials, who harass and jail the prostitutes. At one point the only prostitute still imprisoned and beaten by the officer she has mocked in public, Tereza spends her twenty-sixth birthday in jail, as she had spent her fifteenth following the death of Justiniano Duarte da Rosa. With Tereza and apparently their patron saint Onofre, the voodoo gods, and the deceased poet Castro Alves behind them, the prostitutes conquer the policemen, who must watch a good portion of their drugs burn in a fire in the new zone of prostitution. It is clear that the guardians of justice may be more appropriately termed the enforcers of corruption, for they abuse both society and the prostitutes. The fire may signal a ritual cleansing of wrongdoing and hypocrisy and the need for a new perspective on social justice. Used figuratively in the case of Joana das Folhas, the fire imagery has a literal effect in the episode of the strike.

As a samba dancer and prostitute, Tereza bides time until the return of her lover. Love burns, and along with it goes a last, faint hope for happiness. Released from jail to take refuge in a voodoo temple, she dreams of Januário's death, but the priests and priestesses assure her that she is well protected by the gods, that faith under all adversity will bring her success. When she receives the news of the wreck of the *Balboa*, she succumbs to despair. Three times she has carried death on her back and three times she has overcome it, but now the burden is too heavy. Tereza wishes to return to her native region; she is a widow home from the wars, too weak to fight any longer. She is awakened from the daydream of death by her friend and suitor Almério das Neves, whose son Zeques is suffering from meningitis. Convinced that Januário is dead and that Zeques needs a mother, Tereza agrees to marry the honorable Almério. On the day of the wedding, Januário reappears and carries Tereza—reborn once more and definitively—away from death, toward plenitude, self-realization, and possibly motherhood. The lovers have overcome the mightiest of obstacles and now may drift away into the wish-fulfilling realm of romance.

The ending of *Tereza Batista* reverses, even transcends, death. The good Emiliano Guedes pours death into Tereza and subtly persuades her to abort their child. With Januário Gereba, Tereza's future is reborn, and they will have a baby to celebrate life made more precious by its victory over death. The last of the informants views Tereza symbolically, as an icon for the Brazilian spirit and for the oppressed of the world: "Lhe digo, meu senhor, que Tereza Batista se parece com o povo e com mais ninguém. Com o povo brasileiro, tão sofrido, nunca derrotado. Quando o pensam morto, ele se levanta do caixão" (p. 455; "I tell you, sir, that Tereza Batista is just like the people, that's who. The Brazilian people, who've had to suffer so much and never know when they're beaten. When you think they're done for and dead, that's the time they hop right out of the coffin," [p. 547]). The message here seems to be that one must continue fighting injustice, that change is possible, and that death may be averted through a consistent faith in the superiority of life. Tereza, Januário, and their off-spring may forge a better world, a new society in which absolute truth and honor prevail. When Tereza leaves Almério das Neves for Januário, he falls in love with the prostitute Anália, who promises to be an ideal wife and mother. The narrator comments on the coincidence and symmetry of this match: "Ora, já se viu, até parece coisa de romance!" (p. 461; "Now isn't that like something right out of a novel?" [p. 554]). The self-consciousness of the statement draws the reader to the literary product as an analogue of social reality and at the same time as an imaginative creation, a utopian fantasy. Amado attempts to synthesize the socio-historic problem with fictional license; the first determines the events and the second their or-dering and outcome.

The imposition of form in *Tereza Batista* follows standard literary pat-terns (the beginning and ending of romance, the epic opening in medias res, the multiple marriage dénouement of classical comedy) and a literary pre-text in the collection of materials related to the protagonist. Self-referen-tiality is incorporated into the text as the author/narrator encodes his data into the life story of Tereza Batista. Because the sources are incomplete, the "author" uses his powers of deduction and narrative license to fill in gaps. By making the search for facts and (significantly) legends part of the final product, the "author" informs the reader of the inevitable ambiguities and indeterminacies of his work. The informants who make their way into the text verify the problem of objectivity. Yet it is clear that the creator of the narrative is seeking something beyond accuracy of detail, something higher than social truth. The literary conventions, and specifically the fantasy world of romance and the mythic regions of the gods, extend the scope of the text to idealistic levels. The structural scheme exposes social ills and proposes practical and utopian alternatives. Resistance from within and destiny from without defeat the agents of oppression. Employing the devices of fiction, the narrative design punctuates the motives, both person-al and universal, of Tereza Batista's struggle. It is not so much the biograph-ical and legendary considerations as the resistance that determines the or-ganization of the novel.

Tereza's life is a statement against a repressive society, and the arrange-ment of events relies on popular and literary tradition to eternize the life by eternizing the struggle. The narrator combines repetition with intensifica-tion. The injustice of part 1, involving Libório das Neves and Joana das Folhas, finds an analogue in the persecution of the prostitutes in part 5. In each case, Tereza helps to secure a victory for the underdog by fighting fire with fire, and each episode contains an interrelated plot concerning Tereza's love for Januário Gereba. This love for the sailor frames the progression of sexual brutality with Justiniano Duarte da Rosa, deception by Daniel Gomes Neto, and redemption by Emiliano Guedes. As Tereza gets closer to love, she must at the same time bear the burden of death. The joy mixed with sorrow of the first section is amplified in the concluding section with the triumph of the prostitutes and the news of Januário's death, but the mood is reversed in the symbolic climax. Tereza defends Libório's mistress, Joana, Daniel, the smallpox victims, and the prostitutes of Bahia. She receives temporary respite from her suffering from Daniel and Dr. Oto Espinheira, who prove to be false prophets of peace, and from Don Emiliano, himself a pawn of time. With Januário, suffering and love reach their highest points, as the rite of resignation (the imminent marriage to Almério das Neves) is transformed into a true wedding feast to celebrate the long-awaited union.

The unifying element in Tereza Batista's saga is paradox, the textual assertion that a prostitute turned samba queen may use injustice to serve justice (part 1), that the seemingly defenseless servant may kill her authoritarian master (part 2), that a kept woman and a group of prostitutes may successfully ward off a smallpox epidemic after medical personnel have deserted the cause (part 3), that a concubine may find greater love and moral dignity than her social superiors (part 4), and that a coalition of so-called undesirables, led by a fallen woman, may impede police corruption (part 5). The narrative creates a dichotomy between respectable society and a rejected demimonde, only to reverse the hierarchy by demonstrating the moral laxity of the upper classes. Prostitution becomes a symbol of the paradox. Within the confines of the text—and presumably beyond—one can be a prostitute and do good deeds, just as one committed to serve society may do evil. The modified system of values makes it possible for Tereza to sell herself yet remain faithful to Januário and to rise above those who hold her in contempt. The text shows that society misreads itself and others and implicitly proposes to correct the false judgment. This, in essence, is the task of the narrator.

The narrator of *Tereza Batista* conveys to the reader the information that society does not know about the protagonist; the social perspective makes its way into the text, but only to be negated by the narrative facts. The mythification of Tereza Batista, replete with voodoo ritual characters and incantations, coincides with a demythification of social virtues. The narrator joins the informants in praising Tereza's willingness to fight for her beliefs and then offers specific cases of her war against injustice. Tereza's enemies, often the most socially acceptable characters, thrive on the power of wealth to usurp the poor and unprotected, and their self-righteousness contrasts with her indefatigable magnanimity. Part 1 illustrates her skills at physical and mental retribution, part 2 her will to endure, part 3 her unselfish devotion and intelligence, part 4 her dedication and quiet dignity, and part 5 the culmination of her rebellion and of her devotion. Were it not for Tereza's intervention, Joana das Folhas would have lost her property, Justiniano Duarte da Rosa would have continued to victimize young girls, the population of Buquim would have greatly diminished, and the working ladies of Bahia would have been at the mercy of corrupt officials. In none of these cases does society give Tereza credit for her heroic actions, but instead it ignores or reproves them. The narrator seeks poetic justice for Tereza Batista and social change for those she symbolizes.

The temporal shifts within the individual sections and within the text as a whole correspond to the multiple levels on which the novel operates. The narrative development adheres to a strategy of plotting based on conceptual and emotional impact rather than on biographical chronology. The first section—the chronological center—initiates an analogical structure based on the righting of social wrongs and a linear structure based on romance. In the trial of Joana das Folhas, Tereza stays in the background socially but in the foreground textually. Her ingenuity brings about what the legal system had been unable to achieve: the defeat of Libório das Neves. The worthy end justifies the questionable means. Not just the story but also the discourse provides the judgmental direction that complements the narrative design. Tereza acts and the narrator speaks for her, informing the reader of her courage, her tribulations, and her agonizing solitude. The motif of men beating women attains its full force in the second part, which records Tereza's time with Justiniano Duarte da Rosa, and appears in the final section in a more comprehensive social context. With no advantages, the oppressed Tereza Batista fights and succeeds, and the narrative places this success in society and beyond. As Tereza sails away with her godlike protector, she seems destined to lose all identity but the mythic. Story and discourse point toward a new order in which present fantasy may become future reality.

To satisfy the mythic and socio-political facets of the text, as well as to heroize the protagonist in human terms, discourse must be mediated by someone other than Tereza Batista. The first-person narration of the archetypal picaresque leads to an ironic distinction between story and discourse. The telling of the story reveals character as well as plot, that is, the "true" plot. The early picaresque novels share the possibility of an ironic interpretation resulting from the disparity between the vision the narrator purports to project and the vision(s) encoded in the discourse. Irony shatters the illusion of oneness between the narrator and the protagonist and asserts the presence of an implied author. The narrator compromises himself, himself being, of course, the protagonist. In *Tereza Batista*, the narrator is an "author" of the mindset of the author. Having synthesized legend, history, and supposition, he is free to convert this material into literary time and space and to predetermine perspective.

In Amado's novel, there is no incompatibility between story and discourse. Tereza's actions show and the narrator tells of an enduring faith in justice, love, and life in a world beset with injustice, evil, and death. Tereza is, like society, oblivious to her strength. Her behavior is partly intuitive, partly the effect of accumulated experience. Her lack of introspection allows the narrator to foreground her spontaneous benevolence; analytical commentary reaches the reader without jeopardizing the purity of Tereza's characterization. The distanced (though hardly objective) narrator spares Tereza the incriminating self-evaluation of her predecessors. He "reads between the lines" before beginning to write, so that an intelligible point of view becomes part of the narrative line. Because narrator and author are not working at cross purposes, reader response is less subtly directed than in the picaresque models. Mediation of the discourse is, in *Tereza Batista*, a means of predisposing a response. The fictionalization of the author and the self-conscious references to the writing process make content a function of form by abstracting the spirit of experience (as opposed to the re-creation of experience) as the guiding principle of the text. The narrator becomes a new mythmaker, the text a new myth.

Tereza Batista's womanhood is a decisive and variable factor in the novel. From the first informant onward, the narrative perspective associates Tereza's fortitude and perseverance with masculinity: "Tereza carregou fardo penoso, poucos machos agüentariam com o peso" (p. 3; "Tereza had a hard row to hoe, no doubt about that. Not many men could have pulled such a load," [p. 3]). Lest one get the wrong idea, the informant adds, "Nem mulher-macho, nem paraíba, nem boca-suja—ai, boca mais limpa e perfumosa!—, nem jararaca, nem desordeira, nem puxa-briga; se alguém assim lhe informou, ou quis lhe enganar ou não conheceu Tereza Batista" (p. 5; "She wasn't mannish, or a dyke, or dirty-mouthed—Oh, how her mouth smelled of perfume—or shrewish, or a slut, or spoiling for a fight; and if anybody told you different, he was either kidding you or he didn't know Tereza Batista, one," [p. 5]). In a male-dominated society, the allusions to Tereza's manly qualities are a compliment, yet the protagonist manages to incarnate the best of both worlds. If Tereza must bear the burden of her identity as object and as outsider, she will not resign herself to suffer passively. The motif of prostitution fits the struggle, in that women take advantage of their status to turn servitude into profit and dependence into self-reliance. In this system, victory is incomplete, perhaps uncomfortable, but not pyrrhic. The text rejects society as inferior, just as society rejects women as inferior. Narrative discourse makes unacceptability desirable, or at least preferable to the status quo. The insiders lose their privileged status, and the outsiders point forward to a new and just society, in which marriage and motherhood will bring freedom rather than bondage.[3]

The narrator of *Tereza Batista*, the truth- and legend-gatherer, records the events of the protagonist's life in a manner that emphasizes (paradigmatically) her heroic actions and self-sacrifice and (syntagmatically) the symbolic force of her collective actions, arranged in a carefully controlled sequence. The question of authenticity, posed in the introduction and sustained throughout the text, refers to the literal as opposed to the symbolic. The separation of the lovers in the early part of the novel mythicizes a relationship that ends, significantly, as a type of figurative resurrection. The ironic mode of presentation subverts the present social order in favor of a future or utopian society embodied in Tereza.

With respect to the impact of discursive structure, which conveys conceptual structure, *Tereza Batista* is, to a degree, the antithetical counterpart of *El Buscón*. The conflict between society and the individual remains the same, but while Quevedo reinforces the social hierarchy by denying upward mobility, Amado invents an antisocial narrator to strengthen the ideological force of his antiheroine. The supposedly unmediated voice of Pablos is, in fact, mediated by the baroque idiom and by the ironic manipulation of the narrator by Quevedo. The mediated form of expression in

Tereza Batista, in contrast, serves to link the actions of the protagonist with the reactions of the narrator. Both cases are paradoxical: in one, union brings separation, and in the other, separation brings union. The discursive model for picaresque narrative produces not only a transformation but also an inversion of the structure of the *Buscón* in *Tereza Batista*.

Both authors are judgmental in an indirect way. Quevedo makes Pablos the agent of his own downfall while presenting the social code as indisputable. Amado manages to make even the most blatant acts of social defiance superior to the accepted modes of behavior. Fate and chance, as well as authorial determinism of another variety, function to elevate Tereza. Unlike Quevedo, Amado cannot sacrifice the individual for the so-called collective good. Unlike Defoe, he cannot force an integration of the individual into the system that fosters alienation. And unlike Galdós in *Tristana*, he does not rely on discursive subtleties to tip the balance in favor of the antiheroine. Amado operates instead in the dialectical space between rejection and conversion—in the margins of present society with an eye on radical change, for now the stuff of romance—presenting a heroic antiheroine in the margins of discourse who is imposing in her silence and aided by an eloquent and loving narrator.

8 THE PRECOCIOUS NARRATOR
Fanny and Discursive Counterpoint

> To dress as a Boy gave one Privileges no Woman could e'er possess: first,
> the Privilege of being left in Peace (except by Robbers, who prey'd almost
> equally upon both Sexes); second, the very substantial Privilege of Dining
> where'er one wisht without being presum'd a Trollop; third, the Privilege
> of moving freely thro' the World, without the Restraints of Stays,
> Petticoats, Hoops, and the like. For I had form'd the Theory that Women
> should ne'er be entirely free to possess their own Souls until they could
> ride about the World as unencumber'd as possible. The Hoop Skirt, I
> reason'd, was an Instrument of Imprisonment. I might shudder with
> Horror at the Idea of the legendary Amazons cutting off one Breast, but
> sure I could not but understand their Motives.

The notion that children should be seen and not heard applies, in some
circles, to women. What might be considered precocity in a man could be
antinatural in a woman. The feminine transformations of the picaresque
share a common problem in the creation of narrative voice. Gender invades
literature as it invades society, where it has traditionally been less onerous to
be a man than a woman. It is easier for a man to be published, to be a
protagonist, to be a narrator. Verbal wit may become intrusive, intimidat-
ing, or incongruous if the speaker is a woman. Recent novels, aided by
modified sensibilities, establish new directions in narrative discourse by
seeking ways to project the feminine voice. Methods vary, as do the results,
in this difficult synthesis of characterization, message, and narrative presence.

In *Hasta no verte Jesús mío*, Elena Poniatowska breaks a silence imposed
by society through the recorded words of the protagonist. Despite her
dignified resignation to her fate and her admirable will to endure, it is not
Jesusa Palancares's text but Poniatowska's subtext that contains a reaction
against sexual politics. The passive resistance of the central character—
adeptly arranged within the narrative format—may promote an active response from the reader. The discourse is ironic because the speaker is unaware of its social implications. The seemingly absent author supplies a
structure for the text and a vehicle for its social statement. Historically and
textually, rebellion is in the background of the novel. Just as she is detached
from society, the narrator/protagonist is detached from the impact of her
own discourse. Poniatowska's rhetorical strategy depends on the presentation of oppression by Jesusa and on the disposition or plotting of the data by
an authorial figure, one unconscious and the other conscious.

In *Tereza Batista*, Jorge Amado reverses the formula of Quevedo's *Buscón* by aligning the antiheroine and the implied author against the social hierarchy. While Jesusa Palancares's strength lies in her "own words," Tereza Batista's lies in the words of a third-person narrator who discredits her enemies. Informing the narrator's search for material and Tereza's search for her absent lover is a call for radical social reform, in a utopian world whose literary analogue is romance. The synthesis of novel and romance effects a mythification of Tereza Batista, placing her above the social order while idealizing her aggressive feminism. She is not the female warrior, the affirmative woman who disregards sexual difference in order to break the bondage of inferiority. Romance delivers her from this evil, allowing her to be both a love object and an emblem of absolute justice. To an extent, the strategy risks sacrificing the immediacy of present social reality for the utopian vision or wish-fulfillment of idealistic fiction. The text works, however, because Tereza is realistic, because her actions and her words are credible, because her courage is unending, because her antisocial stance is fully justifiable, and because she (and the reader) never forgets that she is a woman. She is a beautifully realized character, full of heart, but without a voice of her own, a liberated (anti)heroine without discursive power to match her sustained spirit.

The protagonist of Erica Jong's *Fanny, Being the True History of the Adventures of Fanny Hackabout-Jones* is spirited and loquacious, and her narrative follows the lines of picaresque story and discourse. A foundling, she suffers at the hands of many masters before becoming mistress of her destiny, triumphant in personal and antisocial terms. If Amado synthesizes novel and romance in *Tereza Batista*, Jong synthesizes linguistic and plot conventions of the eighteenth century with an indisputably contemporary sensibility. The result is a foregrounding of both intertextuality (the literal or figurative presence of novelistic precursors) and an anachronistic social context, a self-conscious manifestation of the narrative craft and a self-conscious feminist manifesto. Fanny Hackabout-Jones speaks for herself in the idiolect of her time, but while the discourse points backward, its message points forward. The stylized language and the progressive attitude that informs the text are antithetically anachronistic. The new content takes a borrowed form to create a distinctive and ironic narrative voice. Behind the discourse (and beyond the story) lies a feminist tract in literary guise. The text cleverly acknowledges its debt to earlier narrative conventions and Fanny freely comments on the act of writing, yet the complex intertextual mechanisms highlight an ongoing struggle for freedom. The device of an unrevealed identity parallels not only a process of individual growth but also a change in the status of women, a fighting spirit that unites Fanny with her sisters in succeeding generations and that represents, in the final analysis, the quest for an authentic identity.

The explicit feminism of *Fanny* suggests a relation between the emergence of the liberated woman in society and the emergence of the liberated woman in literature. Male domination promotes male-oriented social systems and codes of behavior, administered by men and often associated with divine law in order to limit objections. Women must adhere to these rules or suffer the consequences. When men control literary production, a similar imbalance occurs, in works that reflect the social status quo. Female characters—and even female protagonists and narrators—may conform to stereotypes propagated by male authors. When women write about women, new energies and a new independence may arise, only to lead to the nuptial couch and a return to normalcy. Jong's antiheroine asserts herself through her actions and her words. Fanny's social stance is a literary stance as well, a response to inequities against women in the world and in print, so that her acts of rebellion extend to the depiction of women in fiction. Her own text defines and exemplifies the alternate position. While *Tereza Batista* mythifies the antiheroine, *Fanny* demythifies male supremacy in the community and in the republic of letters.

The formal trappings of *Fanny* showcase narrative tradition. Language and artifice accentuate a debt to the picaresque novel, to *Don Quijote*, and to the eighteenth-century English novel, as well as to romance and pseudo-didactic literature. Fanny experiences the solitude of the orphan, disillusionment at the hands of man, and the lack of professional opportunities for women. Her options seem to include only poverty or perdition. Fate conspires against her to link the past irretrievably with the present and to predetermine the future. Separation from her beloved, a less than desirable vocation, motherhood, and a series of tribulations and betrayals bring her full circle to bestow a concealed and poetically just identity. In addition, Fanny achieves a special status as a writer and iconoclast, moving from victim to beneficiary of sexual politics. Exploiting her role as author, she offers advice to her daughter Belinda, corrects a misguided survey of her life (John Cleland's *Fanny Hill*), provides a theoretical and practical refutation of her literary predecessors, and prescribes a formula for independence and happiness outside of marriage. This is a success story with a number of twists, ranging from incest to witchcraft to ironic poetics. Before Fanny resolves that there is no place like home, she transforms herself and her home and memorializes her development in a text that is both a record and a manual.

The list of dramatis personae that precedes the novel describes Fanny as "the Beauteous Heroine of our Tragi-comical, Mock-heroical Memoirs,"[1] identifying not only the protagonist but also an author behind the author. Fanny is an eighteenth-century thinker with contemporary ideas. Erica Jong is a contemporary feminist with a background in narrative fiction. Their point of contact is an implied author who employs anachronism for ironic purposes. The plot of *Fanny* mixes social issues with literary debates, presented through the diction of a bygone era but encompassing current issues and debates. The reader, as witness to the feminist enterprise, may view the proceedings historically and ironically, relishing early triumphs and yet detached enough to notice the victories still unwon after two hundred years. The implied author supplies the bittersweet distance between fact and fiction by exaggerating the literary contrivances to strengthen the analogue and, paradoxically, the seriousness of the social questions. Literature is a means and an end in *Fanny* because the text, even in its utopian extremes, mirrors life. The discourse calls attention to itself in order to heighten the irony of the story, and the dual temporal frame (one explicit, one implicit) brings the text into the world. As a literary artifact, *Fanny* finds its significance in intertextuality, in a fictional past. As an ironic set piece, it expands this significance to contemporary society. The narrator rewrites literary history, and the implied author refocuses social history. As Fanny speaks for herself, the narrative liberates itself from the restrictions of time and creates its own discursive space.

Like *Lazarillo de Tormes*, *Fanny* has a narratee and a pretext: the work is a legacy to Fanny's daughter Belinda and "if these Pages oft' tell of Debauchery and Vice, 'tis not in any wise because their Author wishes to condone Wickedness, but rather because Truth, Stark-Naked Truth, demands that she write with all possible Candour, so that the Inheritor of this Testament shall learn how to avoid Wickedness or indeed transform it into Goodness" (p. 17). The use of negative examples to promote positive behavior is a literary commonplace that is overtly ambiguous as a doctrinaire method or ironic motif. In a text such as the fourteenth-century *Libro de Buen Amor*, reader response to this device will affect any interpretation of the narrative. In *Fanny*, the admonition has an intertextual identity and serves as the point of departure both for Fanny's autobiography and for her treatment of men of letters. Since Fanny serves truth rather than conventional morality, vice is not always punished nor virtue rewarded in the manuscript. Yet by respecting truth, she avoids the narrative extremes of her day, of authors such as Henry Fielding and Samuel Richardson, who either "prate of Female 'Vartue,' a Luxury which few Women can afford, and only the dullest and most witless can tolerate, or . . . condemn Female Vice in such Terms that upon reading these Male Authors, any spirited Young Woman should resolve to slit her own Throat forthwith" (p. 18). Fanny's life and her story belie the reductionist image of woman by establishing new (and variable) contexts for virtue and vice. It is difficult to be a man but more so to be a woman, in the world and in the text. Fanny's work offers a revisionist theory of female conduct and responsibilities, copied from nature yet undistorted by male prejudice.

Abandoned as an infant on the doorstep of Lord and Lady Bellars's home, Fanny has no identity. She receives kind treatment from her philandering master and long-suffering mistress and unkind treatment from their daughter Mary and son Daniel, unattractive types inside and out. A displaced bookworm subject to the pedagogical biases of the time, Fanny recognizes early on the advantages of learning. Marriage is but a form of indentured service, while the literary wit may enjoy fame, fortune, and freedom. Her admittedly quixotic goal is to thrive as a writer in London, unencumbered by husband, children, and domestic travails. From Lord Bellars, she learns to beware of men, a lesson verified in Alexander Pope's *The Rape of the Lock* and transmitted to Belinda (named for the poem's protagonist). Pope himself, a friend of Lord Bellars, visits Lymeworth and excites Fanny's professional yearnings. When she asks the illustrious writer,

"Is it vain for a Woman to wish to be a Poet, or e'en the first Female Laureate someday?," he breaks into a gale of derisive laughter and replies, "Fanny, my Dear, the Answer is implied in the Query itself. Men are Poets; Women are meant to be their Muses upon Earth. You are the Inspiration of the Poems, not the Creator of Poems, and why should you wish it otherwise?" (p. 41). To add insult to injury, Pope, "so lofty and so low" (p. 44), proposes that Fanny become his mistress at Twickenham. Fate has not been generous to Fanny, an orphan, a female, and an aspiring writer, yet these disadvantages make her even more committed to endure.

The first of a series of tests comes shortly thereafter. The seventeen-year-old Fanny, as innocent as she is beautiful, escapes the seduction attempts of Alexander Pope and Daniel Bellars but succumbs to the treachery of the experienced Lord Bellars, who swears to kill himself if she will not submit to his amorous pleas. When Fanny discovers a mocking description of the scene in a letter from Lord Bellars to his mistress in London, she loses her ingenuousness as quickly as she has lost her virginity. The moment of truth is a moment of disillusionment. Dressed in male clothing, she flees toward London on the faithful steed Lustre. A victim of fate, she is pushed forward by fate to pursue her dream.

The solace of the road provides an opportunity for reflection. Fanny realizes that only the male disguise allows her to travel in peace and wonders why those who speak of Christian charity and love address themselves exclusively to the behavior of men toward each other. Mankind seems to disregard womankind, and self-interest seems to win over innate virtue. The exemplary Mr. Pope proves that great poets do not great men make, so that the aspiring poet should imitate his words but not his deeds. If the female writer cannot seek inspiration from the Muses, she can seek it from wisdom. Experience leads to wisdom, and the rites of passage have begun. At the time of narration, Fanny has achieved success as a writer; she knows that she was right and that Pope was wrong, but society is slow to acknowledge the victory. In the retelling, the narrator blends the adventures and perceptions of the past with a commentary in the present. The lessons intended for Belinda illustrate the reciprocity of the discourse, which is aimed as well at Fanny's twentieth-century daughters. On one level, the narrator attempts to set the record straight. On another, the implied author binds the text to a social work in progress.

Fleeing from a wicked entrepreneur intent on stealing Lustre, Fanny finds herself among a coven of witches, benevolent creatures devoted to a Great Goddess. Isobel White and Joan Griffith initiate her to the intricacies of witchcraft and prophesy a successful but difficult path for Fanny, calling on her to create her own destiny. While attending a meeting of the coven, Fanny witnesses a brutal attack on the women by a group of blackguards, who invite her (in her male garb) to join in the assault. The defenseless Fanny departs, bearing a red garter from the witches, a prophecy for her future, and an unforgettable image of suffering womanhood. The episode presents a feminist worldview. Just as the Grandmaster of the witches' ritual is a woman, the deity is likewise a goddess. Men invent a supreme being in their image and enforce their laws as His. The female cult of the Great Goddess evolves, at the hands of man, into the antifeminist myth of witch-craft. Under the battle cry of blasphemy, men may torture women to preserve their own myths and to stabilize their own control. Linked to the witches by the prophecy and by a confidence in the will of the Great Goddess—and by a mysterious bond with her protectress Isobel White—Fanny continues her journey in the male world.

If man may walk the earth in haughty strides and woman must dally behind him, Fanny has a taste of male superiority in her disguise. Her feigned masculinity gives her authority and an enjoyable impudence, per-haps too enjoyable. Forced to share a room in an inn with a male guest, she flirts with a maid and forms part of a threesome in bed. This episode is ironically juxtaposed with Fanny's philosophical ruminations of the theme of "greater Justice betwixt Men and Women upon the Hearth and in the Bedchamber." Working from the thesis that "neither Sex must have Do-minion o'er the other" but instead "they should fit together, like Lock and Key, both indispensable, both precisely made and well-oil'd," Fanny envi-sions a literary undertaking of the highest order:

> 'Twas fit Matter for a Poem, I thought; my first great Philosophical Poem. I should call it *The Lockiad*, and in it I should expose the Folly of the Age, the Folly of Mankind, the Need for Great Change in Human Society, and I should call for Equality betwixt the Sexes. For, if I truly believ'd that Mankind was essentially good (tho' corrupted by Ignorance, Folly, and False Dominion o'er his Sisters), then surely my Affection for the whole Human Race must make me strive to help that Race perfect itself. And what was Poetry but a rhyming Means of leading the Human Race towards Perfection? And what was the Poet but a Human Creature inspir'd to raise his Fellow Creatures closer towards the Divine Spirit? (p. 102)

At this point in her life, Fanny's fantasies outweigh her maturity. Her theoretically sound proposal falters in a world of men abusing women. Her lofty aspirations dissolve at the first (incongruous) sexual encounter; she is, like Pope, willing to exchange the meditative for the carnal. She is headed in the right direction but needs to understand why clothes do not make the man. This experimental training will come from suffering, love, and fate. As if a punishment for her sin against the maid and against nature, Fanny is robbed of Lustre and must take the stage to London. A group of highway-men overtake the stage and strip the passengers of their clothes and valu-ables. The leader of the thieves is Lancelot Robinson, a neo–Robin Hood who prizes justice more than gold, humanity more than human law, and—to Fanny's dismay—men more than women. The unconventional protago-nist finds an equally unconventional love object, a soul brother who resists her touch and her belief in a Great Goddess, yet who touches her with his beauty and his words. Lancelot gives her the surname Hackabout-Jones to commemorate her trials as a victim of fate and to instill modesty in her. When he informs her that he once loved a woman, Fanny pursues him with renewed vigor. In a moment of tenderness, Lancelot is about to succumb to Fanny's admirable charms when Horatio, a black former slave who became part of the group at the same time as Fanny, interrupts to rescue the damsel and ends by stealing Lancelot from her. Forgotten by the two men, Fanny dreams of Lord Bellars, Isobel White, and Lancelot. With an uncertain identity, a dream of literary success, and an unsatisfying fraternal love, she enters London with Lancelot's Merry Men. The thieves immediately enter into combat, and Fanny is forced to flee, involuntarily abandoned by her new family.

Alone and innocent in the ways of the big city, Fanny falls prey to a pickpocket and is saved by Mrs. Coxtart, a lady of means with several "daughters" who turn out to be women of easy virtue. The ladies wish to partake of the young lad and are only momentarily daunted by the generic confusion. Regaled by Mrs. Coxtart and encouraged to sell and resell her maidenhood, Fanny becomes a prisoner of poverty and of the brothel, where her clients include Theophilus Cibber (son of Colley), Jonathan Swift, William Hogarth, and John Cleland. While Fanny suffers the humiliations of prostitution, Lancelot Robinson is languishing in Newgate Prison. In addition to her chores at the brothel and her commitment to raise funds for Lancelot's comfort in prison, Fanny discovers that she is pregnant from her moment of weakness with Lord Bellars. After a painful and unsuccessful attempt at abortion, she determines to have the baby and to join Lancelot in his escape plans. Under the strain of prostitution and impending motherhood, Fanny is ill-prepared for the reappearance of Lord Bellars in her life.

Fanny's colleague Melinda introduces her to the world of private clubs. Dressed in a nun's habit amid a select group of gentlemen in monks' robes, Fanny finds herself pursued by Lord Bellars and in the company of his mistress. She swears revenge, yet she enjoys a second seduction as she submits to passions that overcome her reason. She whets Lord Bellars's sexual appetite through the allure of her physical presence and the spell of her disguise, winning him with disdain. The more she puts him off, the more his love grows. He breaks relations with his mistress, granting Fanny a part of her vengeance, and pines for her company. A jealous co-worker foils Fanny's escape from the brothel following the prisoners' rebellion, and she remains a captive of Mrs. Coxtart's professional zeal and Lord Bellars's burning desire. Separated from Lancelot at least until the birth of her baby, Fanny survives through what she terms a pact with the devil: she demands a house with a servant, a single nocturnal visit by Lord Bellars per week, and the right to wear a mask throughout the relationship. The ironies of fate bring another separation and another union. Fanny, as destiny's plaything, relies on her body and her wit to endure.

Book 1 of *Fanny* traces the protagonist's journey to London, from the loss of innocence to the incipient wisdom of experience to an enigmatic love. In the hubbub of London represented in book 2, there is little room for innocence but great opportunity to acquire experience and to experience love in its multiple forms. Fanny must contend with the indiscretion at Lymeworth, the prophecy of the witches, and an unrequited passion for

Lancelot Robinson. The present is an intensification of the past, adding pregnancy, prostitution, Lancelot's incarceration, and the reunion with Lord Bellars to the agents affecting Fanny's will and her course of action. Mrs. Coxtart's brothel offers new rites of passage and contact with the city's literati, and it becomes an unlikely refuge from Lancelot's suffering and Lord Bellars's obsession. Virtue, in turn, becomes increasingly relative as Fanny struggles to cope with the mounting complications due to past errors and the whippings of fate. In an atmosphere of uncertainty, necessity dictates behavior and self-preservation motivates Fanny's response to the forces that conspire against her. Lancelot, Lord, Bellars, and the unborn baby move her to emotional extremes. Passion of one type or another dominates her private and professional identities. She is alternately independent and vulnerable, reflective and impulsive. This is the part of Fanny's biography most subject to critical scrutiny, given the temptations of London (and the flesh) and her association with artists who would incorporate life into their work.

If prostitution is the middle ground for the events of book 2—the consequence of the incident at Lymeworth and the means to rescue Lancelot—the artistic use of prostitution forms the basis of the novel's intertextuality. Fanny recognizes that a prostitute must entertain the mind as well as the body, and, as in the case of Pope, her customers are often superior in mental rather than bodily functions. The brilliant but tactless Jonathan Swift, who visits Fanny prior to the publication of *Gulliver's Travels*, sets out to prove with her aid that a horse is more rational than a man, winning his point when said horse refuses to copulate with the somewhat bewildered human offering. William Hogarth visits the brothel to satisfy his lust and to sketch the girls. He sees in Fanny a synthesis of country maid and queen, and she becomes his principal model and sexual partner. Some eight years later, "The Harlot's Progress" comes out, featuring Fanny as the subject of this representation of the wages of sin. John Cleland, a fifteen-year-old virgin despite his braggadocio, proposes a role reversal in which he and Fanny exchange clothes before engaging in sex. Other reversals occur when he re-creates her character in the *Memoirs of Fanny Hill*, published in 1749.

Two surveys of Fanny's life precede her text. Hogarth portrays the fate of the rustic lass corrupted by the inescapable debauchery of London. The prostitute is society's (or man's) scapegoat, more the victim than the cause of wickedness: "Canny Hogarth knew that 'tis the Woman who always suffers for the Sins of all Mankind" (p. 226). Fanny shudders at the thought of the artist seeing her doomed to die for the crimes of her fellow man, but she respects the moral intention and concern for women implicit in the sketches. John Cleland, on the other hand, depicts prostitution as merrymaking and the prostitute as a contented ravager of men. Fanny objects that "the Portrait he paints of *his* simp'ring Strumpet leaves the World to think that the Whore's Life is nought but a Bed of Roses. Of Clap, Consumption, the Evils of Drink, Death in Childbed . . . , he hath nought to say" (p. 227). The works of art are lessons in perspectivism. Hogarth casts Fanny's life in the mold of tragedy, while Cleland views it as comedy. The only opinion that matters, Fanny instructs Belinda, is one's own. The world cannot set absolute standards of judgment, and there is no biography as valuable as an autobiography and no writer as suitable to narrate a woman's story as a female author. Cleland's *Fanny Hill* is not only a falsification of history but also an example of man's incapacity to capture a woman's character. Until men understand that "a Woman is made of Sweets and Bitters, that she is both Reason and Rump, both Wit and Wantonness" (p. 176), they will be unable to deal with her in society and in literature.

Fanny strives—in contemporary theoretical parlance—to deconstruct *Fanny Hill*. A first step is the autobiographical framework of her manuscript, and a second step is the laudatory reaction to the validity (if not truthfulness) of "The Harlot's Progress." Hogarth employs poetic license to a moderate and logical degree. Cleland, in contrast, abuses this privilege. The third and decisive step in the process of deconstruction is a discrediting of Cleland as a human being and as an author. A pimply virgin claiming to be a man of the world, Cleland chooses to play the bride in his games with Fanny, and she classifies him as someone between male and female. Tracing his subsequent history, she notes a scandal in the East (perhaps of a sexual nature) and debtors' prison in England. The want of money, as opposed to the Muses, inspires *Fanny Hill*, a prevarication posing as truth and a source of embarrassment to Fanny Hackabout-Jones. Fanny considers it poetically just that Cleland remained poor while his bookseller prospered from the memoirs, and she relishes the thought that her "true history" will eradicate the veneer of honesty from the maligning fiction. She deserves better, and so do her sisters in print.

Consider Pamela Andrews, for example. The virtuous heroines invented by male authors in their one-dimensional frame of mind and their inflexible double standard give legitimate virtue a bad name, according to Fanny. The difference lies in susceptibility to human feelings and errors versus a calculating chastity, "as witness Mr. Richardson's cloying Pamela Andrews, who ensnares her Squire, Lord B., by holding fast to her Maidenhead until the very Moment after Marriage and thereby receiving the very best Goods in Exchange for it" (p. 209). Fanny the false virgin is an honest whore who sells her body (but not her mind) to save Lancelot and her child. Pamela's virtue is a vice and Fanny's vice is a virtue. Richardson and his colleagues defame women by presenting them as spiritless icons, while Fanny reveals her own complexity and the contradictions of her personality, warts and all.

As the narrator of her story, Fanny has the option of selecting only those incidents that would reflect her positive qualities, but she prefers to deal honestly with her actions and with her emotions. In a text directed to Belinda, she painfully describes the abortion attempt and offers no justification other than her youth and desperation. She deals with the question of Lord Bellars in a similar manner, refusing to place all the blame on him. She admits to a love-hate relationship, yet she finds Lord Bellars at the source of her rage against men. In her contemplation, she becomes the archetypal woman, a pawn of male whims. Men abuse and betray women, and the result is the procreation of the race. Were the situation to be reversed, life would perish because man cannot bear unselfish suffering. Men, who demand constant homage to themselves, give little of themselves. In spite of the hardships of her existence, for which she accepts partial responsibility, Fanny dotes on the moral superiority of women. She marches forward on a road covered with man-made obstacles, to serve her fellow man and woman and to comply with her destiny. That she errs proves that she is human; her successes are personal and feminist triumphs.

Fanny degrades herself to aid Lancelot only to suffer his scorn toward her means of livelihood. The antisocial bisexual rebel is a male chauvinist at heart, intent on changing the world and disposed to accept Fanny's money but obsessed with the norms of society. It will take Fanny (in book 3) to bring out his masculinity, to add substance to his utopian ideas, and to establish a site for the modified version of his "deocracy." This happens because Fanny insists on defending her position on decency and on women's rights, topics that her enemies consider mutually exclusive. A case in point is her stand for greater compensation for the employees of Mrs. Coxtart, who makes the concessions when the ladies support Fanny and threaten to leave the brothel. Fanny is calling on Belinda not only to be true to herself but also to fight for her own advancement and that of her sisters. At this point, Fanny's fight has just begun. Separated once again from Lancelot, she must come face to face with the demonic Lord Bellars.

Book 3 opens in the final months of Fanny's pregnancy and continues to the publication of *Fanny Hill* and the composition of the true history. Fanny entertains Lord Bellars once a week without further revealing her identity. During her "six-day Chastity" (p. 294), she reads and begins work on a romance after dabbling in other genres. Lord Bellars rightly but ironically believes that the child is his, and Fanny notes in him a new tenderness and concern for her and the baby. The major point of debate is the choice of a midwife, as recommended by Fanny's faithful mulatto servant Susannah, versus the accoucheur favored by Lord Bellars. Fanny accepts Bellars's candidate, Dr. Smellie, who proves to be as insensitive as he is incompetent. Susannah's quick thinking produces a midwife who saves mother and child and who turns out to be Isobel White. Claiming that "the Goddess spar'd me for a Purpose" (p. 316), Isobel bears the sign of the cross on her forehead from the scene of torture witnessed by Fanny. She confers with Lord Bellars as he is about to reveal the secret of Fanny's identity, and he goes off to atone for his sins.

Fanny vows, above all, that Belinda's fate will be better than her mother's. Unable to nurse the baby, she hires a wet nurse named Prudence Feral, a proponent of the swaddling clothes theory. Fanny's disagreement with the child-rearing policies forces a dismissal, but Prudence escapes by boat with Belinda. The leisurely days of enjoying her baby and completing her romance are abruptly ended, as Fanny and Susannah embark on a perilous journey to redeem the kidnaped child. Disguised as men, they board a ship with the aid of the first mate, are discovered by a captain with sadomasochistic tendencies, and are forced to submit to his perversions. When the overwrought Susannah commits suicide, Fanny becomes more determined than ever to survive. The ship's surgeon, Bartholomew Dennison, befriends Fanny and informs her that he has been working for fourteen years on a book condemning the excesses of the slave trade. He sees himself as God's amanuensis and his exposé as the definitive revelation of man's cruelty to man. Fanny, in turn, becomes the amanuensis of Captain Whitehead, whose musings provide an antithetical variation of Dennison's manuscript, full of hypocrisy and racial prejudice. Much to Fanny's dismay, the captain plans a secret slaving expedition, thwarted by the providential arrival of a pirate ship headed by Lancelot Robinson and Horatio. In the ensuing melee and its aftermath, both Whitehead and Dennison die, the latter after expressing his love for Fanny and bequeathing his book to her.

The idealistic Lancelot reads a list of "Sacred Articles" to the new recruits, articles that feature equality among men of all races but with an antifeminist bias perceived at once by Fanny. Her objections effect a capitulation of sorts, and the pirates set off in pursuit of Belinda. As the flotilla grows to four ships, so grows the "unrequited Lust" of Fanny, Lancelot, and Horatio, who adopt a "dog in the manger" approach to lovemaking. A catalyst enters the picture in the form of the notorious pirate queen, Annie Bonny, whose storytelling and sexuality enchant the two men and, to her chagrin, Fanny. With Annie at the helm, the four engage in extended amorous activity, paradoxically binding two men who love each other with two women who resent each other. Fanny ultimately admires her competitor for encouraging the "Daring Pyrate" to win out over the "Vapourish Lady" in a battle for supremacy within her soul and, most significantly, for offering a clue to the whereabouts of Belinda. While Annie is Lancelot's nemesis—her men rob the ship during the sexual encounter, proving, Fanny says, that a woman can rape a man—Fanny thinks of her as a messenger sent by the Great Goddess to lead her to her true fate. With the information provided by Annie Bonny, the pirates track down Prudence Feral, who jumps into the sea with Belinda. Fanny and Horatio save the baby, but the gallant servant loses his life to sharks. Reunited with her daughter and with Lancelot and his men by her side, Fanny longs to return to her childhood home.

The impoverished but hopeful group, animated by the discovery of Lustre, reaches Lymeworth on Christmas Eve. Lord Bellars, who had fled to Switzerland to become a monk, and his son Daniel are now dead. Lady Bellars, weak and infirm, asks Fanny to read a letter from her husband. The ever-disagreeable Mary protests, while a "healer" called in to look after Lady Bellars—Isobel White—insists that the letter be read. The contents are startling. Fanny is Lord Bellars's daughter by Isobel, a fact he did not know at the time of the seduction. Mary Bellars, sent from Lymeworth to a wet nurse, died at three months, and the nurse (Isobel's colleague Joan Griffith) substituted the daughter of a chambermaid transported to the plantations for theft. The second Mary goes from mistress of the manor to changeling, and Fanny from orphan to heiress. Isobel calls Fanny the instrument of the Goddess's vengeance and Lord Bellars's retribution. Fanny wins not only an abundant inheritance but also the love of Lancelot, finally come to terms with his sexuality and settled in Lymeworth (renamed Merriman Park) as his promised land.

In an epilogue, Fanny speaks of the events following her homecoming. Mary, progressing from bitter to obsequious, marries one of Lancelot's men, and the two torment each other for the duration of their lives. Having lost her original romance in the days on the sea, Fanny creates an epic adventure of piracy based on her own experiences and publishes *The Pyratiad* under the name of Captain F. Jones. The work is a huge popular and critical success until, at the invitation of the King, Fanny journeys to London and lays her womanhood bare to the literary world. The scandal promotes sales but alienates the critics, whose perspective and objectivity change radically. Fanny also publishes the memoirs of Bartholomew Dennison, but a materialistic society is indifferent to the evils of the slave trade, just as a sexist society is indifferent (or worse) to the merits of the female writer. In terms of her lifestyle, Fanny responds to this sexist society by establishing her own rules for peaceful coexistence with Lancelot Robinson:

> O we lov'd each other truly now—join'd as we were by Love, by Lust, by shar'd Adversity, and by Belinda, our lovely Daughter (whom Lancelot lov'd as if he'd sir'd her himself, nay better). Still we ne'er married, for I'd be damned if I'd give a Man—e'en a Man as loving as my Lancelot—Pow'r o'er my Lands and Houses, Stocks and Bonds! Lancelot might share all that I had, but under the Law, if I married him, he would have Title to all, not I; for thus were Wives treated under Britannia's Statutes. I was resolv'd, therefore, ne'er to marry (which Lancelot, who was no Friend to the Law himself, fully applauded and understood). (p. 492)

This is precisely the situation facing Defoe's Roxana, who leaves the Dutch merchant rather than forfeit her independent wealth through marriage. Roxana represents a precarious synthesis of demeaning sexuality (as a kept woman) and egalitarian spirit (as a proponent of women's rights); her self-interested feminism demands economic equality. Defoe reverses traditional roles, having the merchant insist on marrying his pregnant lover and Roxana refuse the offer. Reunion comes years later when she agrees to marriage. Jong's (fore)knowledgeable couple settles on living together, thus preserving the economic legality while challenging the social and moral codes in a manner fully acceptable to modern liberal sensibility. Fanny echoes Roxana's speech and updates her solution, with the aid of a man as antisocial as she.

When Cleland's book comes out, Fanny suffers a certain humiliation, as well as mixed emotions regarding the possibility of a rejoinder. Her desire for truth vies with fear of a charge of witchcraft, the unfashionable status of autobiographical literature, the shortage of feminine protagonists, and a reluctance to incite literary revenge. The reservations notwithstanding, she writes her history for her daughter, as Belinda begins her own journey around the globe and toward independence. *Fanny Hill* becomes a blessing in disguise for Fanny, who may assert herself as a writer and as a woman, and for Belinda, who may begin to know herself by knowing her mother.

Fanny Hackabout-Jones, writer and protagonist, makes herself a rarity in literature, a woman who falls between virtue and vice. Whoredom, motherhood, and the distractions of love block a woman in her quest for nobility of destiny, and Fanny's confrontation with each of these elements marks the course of her story. She sacrifices her dignity to protect the imprisoned Lancelot Robinson, who berates her for her lowly behavior until she brilliantly defends prostitution as a means to sell the body to save the soul. The bittersweet joys of motherhood imply a sacrifice of another kind, a different giving of the self for the other. Fanny responds rather analytically to motherhood, elaborating the phases of pregnancy, studying John Locke and Mrs. Aphra Behn on the education of children, and scrutinizing potential wet nurses according to philosophical modes. The rift with Prudence Feral and the frenzied search for Belinda stem, in fact, from questions of child psychology. Ultimately, however, Fanny views the birth of her daughter as a matter of the heart: "Only when a Woman bears a Daughter doth she journey through the Pier-Glass of her Destiny and see the World thro' her own Mother's Eyes. To *be* a Daughter is but half our Fate; to *bear* one is the other. And suddenly that Bearing changes all our Views: our Fury at the Fates, or grim Denunciations of our Destinies, our very Rage at Womanhood itself—such Things are soften'd by the Bearing of a Daughter" (p. 414). Fatherhood in this case is even more problematic, and Fanny admits to feelings of intense passion for the satanic Lord Bellars, the cause of profound distractions of love and mental confusion. Fanny's identity as a woman depends on her ability to convert the obstacles into the pillars of feminine strength.

Man is capable of redemption, but redemption denotes sin, and woman is the sinned against, the scapegoat in man's redemptive process. Lord Bellars's atonement comes after the incestuous relationship that controls Fanny's future. Lancelot Robinson founds his deocracy from Fanny's labors and on her property. *The Rape of the Lock* warns women to beware of men, and Fanny must apply the admonition to Pope himself. Both social intercourse and intellectual pursuits teach Fanny that philosophy ignores one-half of the human race and that the sexes bear out the myths created about them. Pope the man is an eloquent propagator of these myths, noting, for example, that "a Woman Poet is an Absurdity of Nature, a vile, despis'd Creature whose Fate must e'er be Loneliness, Melancholy, Despair, and eventually Self-Slaughter. Howe'er, if she chooses the sensible Path, and devotes her whole Life to serving a Poet of the Masculine Gender, the Gods shall bless her, and all the Universe resound with her Praise." The fact is indisputable because "whate'er exists in Nature is but an Expression of God's Will, and if He hath placed Women below Men, you can be sure 'tis for a Noble Purpose. In short, whate'er is, IS RIGHT" (p. 42). The early lesson is important in Fanny's development as a destroyer of social and literary myths. The disillusionment with Pope provokes her to seek a synthesis of nature and poetry and a negation of the false synthesis (or false theology) accepted by man and by society at large. The dream to be a writer becomes an extension of the social struggle. The righting of wrongs against the prostitutes, the feminist modifications of Lancelot's articles and Lord Bellars's will, and the final independence out of wedlock challenge the social system and at the same time offer an alternative to literary convention. Fanny's revisionist history even provides for the transcendent—for a final judgment, so to speak—in the presentation of the myth of the Great Goddess, a redemption for women from male bias.

Fanny's role as nun to Lord Bellars's monk conceals the further irony of their familial ties and of his atonement among the Swiss monks. The prostitute's pact with the devil leads to the revelation of Fanny's genuine identity as a counterpoint to her coming to terms with her womanhood, socially and professionally. As in the reunion with Lancelot, which follows the formula of romance, the fateful meetings with Isobel White and Lord Bellars suggest causality of a literary variety, a narrative determinism ruled by poetic justice and thematic symmetry. The composition of the book as part of the book relates to the self-referentiality of art and to the textual and extratextual implications of identity. Fanny comes full circle as an artist and as the model for her work, surrounded by her old and new families (and enlightened by the epistolary message from her father) at Lymeworth. Her story rewrites history while proposing an emended approach to future history.[2]

Fanny has a rich intertextual identity. The perennial orphan of the picaresque tradition, she lives marginated from social acceptability and separated from her adopted families. Like Pablos in *El Buscón*, she cannot escape the specters of the past, but Jong (an ally of her narrator/protagonist, as opposed to Quevedo) transforms Lord Bellars from nemesis to benefactor, from agent of disgrace to agent of respectability. The desired end is not a return to normalcy but a new social plan transposed on the old. The literary analogue of the projected social change is the female writer, whose aspirations echo the description of Don Quijote's madness: "For I had conceiv'd the most foolish Passion a Country Lass may entertain: that of going to London as a Lit'ry Wit. O I dreamt of London Coffee-Houses, Playhouses, Masquerades, and Balls. But chief amongst my Dreams was that of becoming a Famous Scribbler! If 'twas a risible Ambition for a Lad, then how much more ridiculous for a Lass" (p. 30). Fanny's is not the first feminine history but rather the first history that reflects a feminine sensibility; it is not the male authors but the pervasively male worldview of these histories that Fanny wishes to combat. Just as a male-dominated society constructs a hierarchical natural order to substantiate its claims to superiority (and then insists that the natural order preceded and determined the social), so the male author uses female characters and allegedly feminine discourse to solidify the opposing viewpoint. The resulting works feature women's problems and men's solutions. Nowhere are the absence of empathy and the presence of male priorities more evident than in John Cleland's *Memoirs of Fanny Hill*, the primary intertextual source of *Fanny*.

As the model for both narratives, Fanny enjoys the strategical advantage of authoring the true history in contrast to Cleland's fictionalized account. Experience and sensitivity call attention to the contradictions of her competitor, who "understanding almost nothing of the Thoughts and Sensations of the Fair Sex, fashion'd from my Life a nauseously sugar'd Tale (as studded with Inflaming Scenes as a Plum Pudding with brandied Fruits) about a poor Country Girl who comes to the City, quite inadvertently becomes a Whore, but nonetheless is faithful at Heart (if not at some lower Organ) to her belovèd Charles, and becomes an Honest Woman at the Last, concluding her Days in 'the Bosom of Virtue' (as Mr. Cleland quaintly styles it)" (p. 175). The definitive sign of a male presence, according to Fanny, is the overbearing emphasis on naming and describing the male organ. Fanny's reaction, perhaps subconscious, is a similar emphasis on the female organ, with the most complete listing supplied by Lancelot Robinson. Fanny Hackabout-Jones concerns herself with the position of women in society, while Cleland presents variations on male erotic themes. Fanny Hill's separation from her true love Charles fulfills the archetypal pattern of romance, but the overriding structure places the protagonist in scene after scene of public and private love with clients of diverse social and sexual categories. Fanny Hill and her cohorts cover the spectrum of lovemaking from the deflowered virgin to the seasoned veteran, from participant to voyeur. The survey predominates over the story, and the discourse of *Fanny Hill* corroborates the male orientation of the text.

The plot elements of *Fanny Hill* bear a strong resemblance to those of *Fanny*. The protagonist addresses herself to a narratee ("Madam"), presumably to answer an inquiry concerning her past. As in the case of the later work, the pretext opens the way for a success story in which the narrator refuses to delete scandalous material at the expense of truth. The orphaned, abandoned, and innocent Fanny Hill faces the unknown dangers of London. A Mrs. Brown gives her a home, sisters in leisure, and her first exposure to the "male machine." She loses her virginity to the handsome and noble Charles, and the two live in harmony for eleven months, until he is forced to leave the city. The pregnant Fanny suffers a miscarriage and initiates a life of prostitution to "repay" her landlady. She spends about two years with Mrs. Cole, a madam posing as a milliner, and her three employees. A good portion of the narrative centers on the varied sexual adventures of the prostitutes, which are presented in catalog fashion. Fanny's associates introduce themselves by recounting the circumstances of their first sexual encounters. The tone of their stories and the commentary of the narrator inspire titillation rather than compassion. Fanny's work is not pure sacrifice; she often enjoys her profession and at times gives more than the job requires. When fate brings her together with Charles, she resumes her single-minded devotion to him, grateful that she has the means to support him if necessary. The couple lives happily, honorably, and blessed with offspring.

The magnanimous, and certainly atypical, Charles disregards the infidelities of Fanny Hill and honors her in marriage. Her move from vice to virtue occurs without psychological development or moral justification.

Prostitution is an interlude to occupy the time of separation. When Charles returns, so does the lost virtue. While Fanny laments the conditions that cause the ruin of innocent girls, only at the end of the narrative—in what she calls a "tail-piece of morality"—does she inject commentary on proper conduct:

> Thus, at length, I got snug into port, where in the bosom of virtue, I gathered the only uncorrupt sweets: where, looking back on the course of vice I had run, and comparing its infamous blandishments with the infinitely superior joys of innocence, I could not help pitying, even in the point of taste, those who, immersed in gross sensuality, are insensible to the so delicate charms of VIR-TUE, than which even PLEASURE has not a greater friend, nor VICE a greater enemy. This temperance makes men lords over those pleasures that intemperance enslaves them to: the one, parent of health, vigour, fertility, cheerfulness, and every other desirable good of life; the other, of diseases, debility, barrenness, self-loathing, with only every evil incident to human nature.[3]

The self-consciousness of the narrator toward her closing statements accentuates the incongruity of the moral turn, a weak and tardy attempt at didacticism. The happy ending, like the erotic fantasies and realities of the text, belongs to a literary universe devoid of poetic justice, a universe in which virtue and vice are as fickle as fate. Fanny's companion on the trip to London warns her that if she serves a man virtuously, she may win him in the end. Fanny submits to vice, yet the prize is still hers.[4]

Cleland's eighteenth-century fiction imitates the social reality of the period, in that men and destiny determine the course of women's history. Fanny Hackabout-Jones works to alter history by shattering the myths that history sustains. Her text and her life refocus such social phenomena as marriage, motherhood, prostitution, and witchcraft. Fanny succeeds through unconventional and largely unacceptable behavior. Her career choices, writing and prostitution, defy the rules of decorum and the so-called natural order. She wants not to be manly but to possess civil liberties denied to women. This she achieves by avoiding legal marriage. Fate amplifies the paradox by making her father the father of her child and the male love object a bisexual. Fanny presides over Merriman Park with its version of the nuclear and extended families, enjoying love, wealth, notoriety, and positive prospects for the future. This future makes its way into the text through the double field of Fanny's discourse, which extends the social reality to the present struggle for liberation.

Fanny imagines *The Lockiad* as a poetic means to expose the folly of inequality between the sexes. The road to human perfection cannot deny entry to women, and society must change to meet this need. The text in which Fanny inscribes the message is not *The Lockiad* but her "true history," motivated not only by the wish to instruct and to protect her daughter but also by an extension of the narrative pretext that suggests another "true history." In the second part of *Don Quijote*, the fictionalized Cervantes repudiates the pseudonymous Alonso Fernández de Avellaneda, author of a spurious sequel to the 1605 *Quijote*. Cervantes takes the lead from Mateo Alemán's revelation and exorcism of Juan Martí, alias Mateo Luján de Sayavedra, in part 2 of *Guzmán de Alfarache*. Similarly, Fanny brings John Cleland into the text and lambastes him for transforming—none too accurately—her life into the *Memoirs of Fanny Hill*. Her own account will be refutation, as well as a lesson and an artistic product. And the true heroine or antiheroine receives fame and fortune (if not a lofty literary reputation from her fictions), satisfaction from her nonconformist lifestyle, and support for her loved ones. One could say, via *Lazarillo de Tormes*, that she is living in prosperity and at the height of all good fortune.

Jong's novel presents an impressive balance of picaresque consciousness with social consciousness. Her text occupies the middle ground between its literary precedents and contemporary feminist questions. Looking backward and pointing forward, its discourse is consummately ironic. If Quevedo in *El Buscón* is the puppeteer who puts baroque diction in the mouth of his narrator while serving as a social and textual nemesis, Jong devises a neo-Augustan style in which to make her presence known. Through the masterful union of archaic discourse with a precognitive social—more properly, antisocial—posture, language addressed to the narratee (Belinda) contains a message for the implied reader. Much of the text's significance lies in its potentiality for double meaning. A primer for the freedom of body and soul, Fanny's story attests to an individual triumph in a collective struggle. Her discourse simultaneously links her to and isolates her from the present. The magnificent literary synthesis fails to produce a social solution. The male authors exclude Fanny from their ranks, and she in turn detaches herself from traditional society and its institutions. The final stage of Fanny's odyssey depicts a utopian community but hardly a utopian society. The microcosm projects no macrocosm, except perhaps of conscience, of sensibility. Peaceful coexistence between the sexes remains a dream of the future, which, the implied author reminds the reader, is the here and now.

Fanny Hackabout-Jones's legend is conveyed through her own discourse, a highly stylized and sophisticated idiolect. Both the studiedly anachronistic diction and the studiedly precocious content (spiritual links to the third-person narration of Galdós's *Tristana*) imply a guiding presence armed with contemporary ironic detachment. Intertextually, Fanny evokes her fellow (or sister) outsiders and narrators from the picaresque tradition, performing at the same time a deconstruction of *Fanny Hill* and the stereotypical females of fiction. Contextually, she raises her voice for a battle in which her successors will engage. One of these successors is her daughter Belinda, about to embark, as the novel ends, on a voyage that will include a stay in America, a land of free men and unliberated women.[5]

9 READING AS A PERSON
A Voice of One's Own

That which you are, that only can you read.
  Harold Bloom, *Kabbalah and Criticism*

The roles men and women play not only are complementary or capable of
inversion but are doubled by individuals playing both at once. Women
and men function as mutual signifiers and signifieds.
  Margaret R. Higonnet, *The Representation of Women in Fiction*

If there is a distinctly "female" voice—if there is a distinctly "male"
voice"—surely this is symptomatic of inferior art? . . . Of course the
serious artistic voice is one of individual *style*, and it is sexless; but perhaps
to have a sex-determined voice, or to be believed to have one, is, after all,
better than to have no voice at all.
  Joyce Carol Oates, "Is There a Female Voice?"

The world of St. Augustine's *Confessions* displays an author in control of the
text yet under the control of the Holy Scriptures and a theological "reading"
of the universe. Verbal signs serve predetermined meanings; that is, they
serve God. When literal interpretation fails to produce a desired (or desirable) result, the exegete must move to the figurative realm.[1] The literary
object is a microcosm within the macrocosm of the world as God's book, so
that the word functions more as an agent of conformity than as an agent of
invention. In this system, polysemy and the optional recourse to figurative
meaning protect rather than subvert dogma, and semiotics is a religion
rather than a science. The overdetermined moral base of Don Juan Manuel's
fourteenth-century collection of stories, *El conde Lucanor*, shows the continuation of the word at the service of faith and social codes. In contrast,
Juan Ruiz's *Libro de Buen Amor* reflects a world in crisis through problematic
signifiers that belie their traditional and sacrosanct values. Despite repeated
commentary on intention, words simply do not perform in accordance with
the narrative premise or with established modes of signification. The episode of the courtship of the nun Doña Garoza, for example, challenges good
love and bad love by seeking to invert the categories and to confuse the
terms. Good love fails to keep its distance from bad love, and the attempt to
maintain the dichotomy by redefinition and verbal masks is as unsuccessful
as the archpriest's pursuit of women. Morality's loss is art's gain. Rhetorical strategies posit new meanings for old and in the process transform

220

narrative hierarchies. The fictional act mediates the word and the world, with point of view as a principal marker of the change from a closed to an open structure. The narrator and the reader assume increased responsibility in the new order, exemplified in the picaresque and its variations of theme and voice.

Reflecting a modified view of the individual, secular autobiography and pseudoautobiography acknowledge subjective visions of the world. Narrative perspective places the reader above social reality (in idealistic and didactic forms) and in the midst of social intercourse (in the picaresque and other realistic forms). *Lazarillo de Tormes* and succeeding novels build on discrete perceptions of events, literary precedents, and writing as a self-conscious art. The picaresque uses the lowly status of the narrator/protagonist to deconstruct the myth of the epic and chivalric hero and the saint, and the corresponding motifs of the quest and the journey toward perfection. Aided by the voice-over of an implied author, the reader stands at a distance to note textual ironies and to pass judgment. The principal markers of the implied author are discrepancies between the narrator's revelations and the protagonist's best interests. The competing voices add an ambivalent, often self-defeating, quality to Lázaro de Tormes's defense of his actions and choices in the past, to Guzmán de Alfarache's exposition of his conversion, and to Pablos de Segovia's story of disillusionment and his subtle cries for sympathy. In each case, individual efforts yield to collective principles, the antisocial yields to the status quo. The protagonists rebel against a society that would deny them upward mobility, but the restrictive social doctrine ultimately wins out. The archetypal picaresque texts, like the community they portray, contain the mechanisms necessary for the preservation of the accepted hierarchy. The literary text conforms to the social subtext as the narrator/protagonist becomes an outsider in the discourse as well as in the story.

In the Spanish picaresque, narrative autonomy is an illusion. The defensive maneuvering of Lázaro, Guzmán, and Pablos signals an exercise in self-betrayal, casting doubt on the sincerity, innocence, and authority of the speaker. The authorial figure makes his way into the prologue of *Lazarillo de Tormes*, and the unity of the narrative depends not so much on Lázaro's explanation of the case as on the implied author's subversion of his discourse and rhetorical stance. *Guzmán de Alfarache*, in the prefatory materials and in the text proper, postulates a postconversional metamorphosis that the tone, diction, and preachments of the narrator do not bear out. The result is a parody of spiritual evolution. The baroque language of *El Buscón* suggests the presence, or intrusion, of a stylist who turns defense into indictment. Conceptism is the weapon and the verbal analogue of Quevedo's battle against deviation from the norm. Dominated by an almost visible puppeteer, Pablos becomes the object of mockery and scorn within the text that purports to be his own. Like Lázaro and Guzmán, he falls victim to the inventor of the deceptively individuated self, circumstance, and discourse. If deconstruction is the point of origin of the picaresque mode—a deconstruction of the intertext—it also provides an approach to the strategies of the narrator and, significantly, of the implied author. Discourse is not a means to an end but a key to message production. Narrative voice, in turn, is a complex of voices linked by irony and ambiguity. Literature emulates itself and the society in which it exists, placing the antihero in a textual environment as hostile and as inhibiting as its counterpart in the real world.

While the individual life and the record of that life achieve greater respect and attention from the Renaissance onward, the picaresque novel fashions a dialectical interplay between the created voice (and persona) and the creator who undermines the search for freedom of expression and upward mobility. The Spanish feminine picaresque expands the distance between the protagonist and the implied author, as female identity takes a turn toward the burlesque, with hints of interiority and the special problems of women. Francisco Delicado's *La lozana andaluza*, which predates the *Lazarillo*, fictionalizes the author and gives the antiheroine a role in the dialogue. The delineation of Lozana and the elaboration of her voice comprise part of a portrait of Rome in decline and, notably, a portrait of the artist. Although Lozana serves as the symbol of an imminent fall, she befits her milieu in speech and actions, and she is perhaps the most fully individuated and motivated of the *pícaras*. Francisco López de Ubeda allows his protagonist Justina to address the reader directly, but her voice satirizes the plot and the moral digressions of *Guzmán de Alfarache* at the expense of her selfhood and her femininity. The author enters the text as poet, moralizer, and ironist who appropriates the discursive power of the narrative. Justina manages, however, to outsmart the men who threaten her safety and her virginity and to register a protest against the double standard. Her ingenuity assures her survival in a male-dominated society and in a self-consciously parodic text. Together with the antiheroines of Alonso Jerónimo de Salas Barbadillo and Alonso de Castillo Solórzano, Justina belongs to the world of carnival, of wish-fulfillment, of momentary liberation from the confines of reality.[2] Poetic justice takes the form of male justice, but not before the women demonstrate their ability to succeed on their own.

Whatever their concessions to masculine codes, *La lozana andaluza* and *La pícara Justina* focus on women trapped by their rank and their sex yet endowed with intelligence, wit, and discernible voices. In his "reading" of the picaresque models, Salas Barbadillo favors incident over morality and story over discourse. Narrated in the third person, *La hija de Celestina* relates a life of crime punished by death, with emphasis on situational and linguistic humor as opposed to the motives and the social disadvantages of the protagonist Elena. At this decisive juncture in the history of the feminine picaresque, the death of the antiheroine coincides with the silencing of the female voice, redeemed briefly and half-heartedly by Castillo Solórzano in *Teresa de Manzanares* and abandoned once more in *La garduña de Sevilla*. As a type of reversal of the cult of the Virgin, the picaresque gives female characters the opportunity to act out their fantasies and male authors the opportunity to criticize and satirize from a detached position. While social justice (and man) emerges triumphant, the texts—at times in spite of themselves—

capture the plight of women, outsiders in a society in which the relative poses as the absolute and in which equality and expressive freedom are lacking.

Daniel Defoe's *Moll Flanders* presents delinquency in an age of redemption. With Enlightenment England as backdrop, the antiheroine transgresses, claims to see the light, and repents. The fictionalized author edits the "original" manuscript to honor literary decorum and social practice. The altered version bears the editor's mark on discourse, arrangement of events, and theme. Just as Pablos in the *Buscón* is forced to speak against challenging the social hierarchy, Moll is forced to speak on behalf of the saving powers of society, the same society that promotes her marginated status. The subtext of *Moll Flanders* is essentially a reconstruction of the original version, which would seem to stress isolation rather than reintegration, the individual rather than the collectivity, and survival rather than repentance. Fate conspires to aid Moll as it conspires to harm Pablos, yet (as in *Guzmán de Alfarache* and earlier in *La lozana andaluza*) the text makes conversion part of the story without making it part of the discourse. Morality, as society views it, may be imposed on Moll and on her narrative, redefining from within what social institutions determine from without.

Moll Flanders represents a break in ideology, for society continues to reign supreme but now takes responsibility for alienated souls. Literary causality—at the discretion or the whim of the author—elevates society by leading the antiheroine to penitence and conversion. Baroque society takes pride in quelling rebellion, Enlightenment society in transforming rebels into model citizens. The antithetical social policies lead to similar narrative strategies, with the narrator/protagonist under the direction of an (implied) author who devises a plot and an idiolect to suit his purposes. Benito Pérez Galdós's *Tristana* responds to the industrial revolution, an economic and ideological phenomenon that affects class consciousness as it pertains to men and offers women a new mode of suppression. In his early novels, Galdós is explicit in his condemnation of hypocrisy and intolerance, while in *Tristana* he makes a subtle shift from generational discord and a comic tone to sexual prejudice and a calculatedly serious discourse. The differentiation between Don Lope and Horacio is a mask for their complicity in denying Tristana her full potential. The Galdosian narrator damns both men with faint praise as he demonstrates Tristana's moral and intellectual superiority. As in the thesis novels, the protagonist must suffer for the good of the group she represents. Man, nature, and narrative determinism conquer the woman who aspires to be free. She loses a limb and her privileged position in the text, but the effect is ironic. Tristana's "honorable freedom" stands against inequality, human law treated as divine, and exclusive progressivism. If one accepts the markers of irony, the passivity and the silence of the antiheroine articulate her defeat and the injustice of that defeat. Unlike his predecessors, the implied author of *Tristana* puts his rhetorical skills at the service of the individual and the feminist perspective.

Elena Poniatowska's *Hasta no verte Jesús mío* combines the editing of Defoe with the antisocial tenor of twentieth-century narrative. The oral transmission of Jesusa Palancares's story leads to a "rewriting" that accentuates the protagonist's strength, gives her a voice, and denounces the society in which she occupies a marginal role. The complex irony of *Tristana* lies in the distance between showing and telling and in the paradoxical victory in defeat. The silencing of Tristana aids her cause. In *Hasta no verte Jesús mío*, Jesusa's voice attests to her wisdom, common sense, and courage. The implied author (or editor) foregrounds a heroism of which the narrator/protagonist seems unaware. The text deals with two revolutions, one political and centered on men, the other social and centered on women. As her symbolic name would suggest, Jesusa is a martyr of sorts, a poor orphan, abused wife, uneducated woman, and a silent member of society who comes into her own within the narrative and in the act of narrating. Following the discursive method of the Spanish picaresque, Poniatowska derives the textual message and irony from the interplay of voice and voice-over. Here, however, the two agents of discourse align themselves against the oppressive environment and open the way for new voices of change.

In *Tereza Batista*, Jorge Amado creates a woman of action, unaware of the extent of her fortitude, who defies a corrupt social establishment in the name of absolute justice. The narrator is an author in the process of synthesizing fact and fiction concerning Tereza Batista, and the movement involves a devaluation of the conventional and an exaltation of the unconventional. Officers of the law are the antagonists and Tereza and her band of prostitutes are the heroines of this literary universe, which uses a romance framework to project an alternate reality. Events, chronology, legend, fate, and narrative commentary provide a structure for the elevation of the antiheroine. The manipulation is as clear as in the early models, while the beneficiary is now the underdog, silenced not to thwart her development but to preserve her mythical dimension.

Erica Jong finds in the picaresque archetypes and their progeny a vehicle for contemporary feminism. The protagonist of *Fanny*, like Tereza Batista, is larger than life and unrestricted by time and space. Unlike Amado's heroic antiheroine, Fanny narrates her own story. She combines words and deeds, distance and immediacy, to forge and to discover her identity in a story that may be termed antiromance. The implied author shows her influence in the mixture of anachronisms. The "true history" of Fanny Hackabout-Jones addresses the feminist question in a stylized version of eighteenth-century English and a precociously revisionist intertext. Male literati and men of all ages bear the brunt of Fanny's—and Jong's—humor, wrath, and agile pen. The happy ending puts men in their place without transcending the problems of women's place. Full of talent, ideas, and eloquence, Fanny retreats with her daughter and bisexual lover into a predominantly female society, a type of liberation in isolation and justifiable reverse discrimination, yet hardly a long-range solution. The combination of voices manages to rewrite the past, but only to mock the present. *Tristana*, *Hasta no verte Jesús mío*, *Tereza Batista*, and *Fanny* set forth a message of tolerance, absolute justice, and the need for reform. The subversive concepts of the past are the lemmas of these works, and each of the narratives depends on an ironic relation between story and discourse.

Picaresque narrative begins, to a degree at least, as a comic response to spiritual autobiography and Renaissance humanism. Unreliability is fundamental to the structure of the picaresque, which capitalizes on the humble status and defensive stance of the narrator. An implied author, advocate of the conservative social order, disrupts the antisocial efforts of the narrator/protagonist while producing evidence of rhetorical strategies on both sides. There is a definite place—and space—for subversion in the text. The space widens in the case of the Spanish feminine picaresque, in which the *pícara* must contend with male consciousness in the literary as well as the real world. Discourse and dénouement illustrate her precarious position in society, thus defining an analogue and ironically converting impotence into (subtextual) strength. The progressive silencing of the antiheroine underscores her lack of authority in a text that professes to represent her viewpoint. She is an object of beauty in a male morality tale and an object of repression in a tale of sexual politics. Worshiping her from afar or limiting her options, the male establishment holds woman, saint or sinner, in check and deprives her of the voice that would proclaim her identity.

In the transformations of the picaresque, the antiheroine encounters attitudes and feminism in transition. Defoe proves in *Moll Flanders* that an enlightened society can rehabilitate errant women as well as men. The deterministic plotting and forced diction of the Spanish models serve the community and the individual, although the account of Moll's success requires the intervention of an editor who censors her manuscript. Her feelings, her story, and her voice must meet the standards of society—or be altered—before they make their way into print. The crucial voice in *Tristana* is that of the narrator, whose commentary and contact with the reader unite story and discourse. A rhetoric of irony breaks the neutrality of narration, as does the logic of a woman who wishes to enjoy the freedoms granted to men. The incongruity of defeat and the role of "natural law" in the defeat make the irony and the message more emphatic. Accordingly, Tristana's silence at the end of the narrative heightens the sense of loss. For Galdós, the thesis lies in the disintegration of hope and in the absence of poetic justice.

The twentieth-century transformations share a common enemy in male-oriented society and a common ally in the implied author. In *Hasta no verte Jesús mío*, Poniatowska "edits" interviews with her informant in much the same way that the fictionalized Defoe edits Moll's writings, in order to contrast social evils with the virtues of Jesusa Palancares. Like the narrator of *Tristana*, the authorial figure in *Tereza Batista* devises a mode of presentation that works with the raw material to determine reader response. Amado's method, though more direct than that of Galdós, similarly relies on the power of silence and on the superiority of the protagonist to her society. *Fanny* synthesizes the antiheroine's voice, temerity, and literary acumen with the implied author's propensity for irony to propose a feminist (and anachronistic) alternative to male dominance.

Narrative discourse, at least from the time of Lázaro's response to Vuestra Merced, conveys a dual message system, a juxtaposition of the outsider's viewpoint and the implied author's reaction to that viewpoint. The authorial presence in the text mediates language and meaning, social doctrine and rebellion. Lázaro, Guzmán, and Pablos deny their ignoble blood in an attempt to invade mainstream society only to be thwarted by a rigid hierarchy and the implied author's support of the inflexible code. As a travesty of the ideal citizen and the idealistic hero, the *pícaro* has little credibility and less respect. His creator subdues him within the text while society punishes his presumption; the consequence is an ironic and incriminating discourse and failure to achieve his goals. The feminine picaresque novels repeat these patterns, magnifying the parodic nature of the protagonist and her distance from social acceptability. No sooner does woman appear in the novel than she suffers an identity crisis that plagues her to the present. Male authors inhibit (and often inhabit) her discourse, mock her, judge her, and ultimately ensure her survival by formulating a narrative structure that is both self-revealing and reversible, ironically deconstructive.

The texts of the picaresque antiheroines provide a respite from reality and at the same time an accurate vision of the status of women. They allow for harmless insurgence without threatening social stability, and they rarely, if ever, take their subjects seriously. Authors portray the *pícaras* as licentious, unscrupulous, money-hungry, and as perfectly willing to use their physical charms to defraud men. Social and poetic justice, as defined by the male establishment, guarantee that their freedom is as short-lived as their success, their beauty, and their health. The requisite moral note redeems the authors as it castigates the protagonists. Women enjoy only negligible middle ground between chastity and promiscuity, allegiance and betrayal, good and evil. Men regulate their behavior and their speech, and in that sense literature mirrors life. By bringing antiheroines into the scheme, the writers refashion the picaresque to draw dichotomies along sexual lines, with women as delinquents and men as standard bearers. Subsequent novelists, usually with kindness in their hearts, strive to redeem the wayward women by converting them into heroines, but identity remains a problem.

The novel's preoccupation with identity objectifies women and their social roles, but heroism has its price. From one polarity (the picaresque), the novel shifts to the idealized and equally closed realm of the fictional heroine. In *Becoming a Heroine*, Rachel M. Brownstein notes, "The woman-centered novel in the Richardsonian tradition claims to be realistic, but in effect it contradicts itself when it makes a woman and her inner life central as they are not, in fact, in the bourgeois real world—but as they are in aristocratic romance. This paradox reflects and generates others involved in becoming a heroine. The novel heroine is both a representation (a girl trembling on the brink of a sexual and moral decision) and a metaphor (for an erotic-moral-aesthetic-psychological ideal). She is not only a believable image of a person but also the image of an ideal."[3] Whether narrative views her as inferior or superior to male society—whether she is an antiheroine or a heroine—the female protagonist tends to lose her battles. The picaresque offers her temporary wish-fulfillment, the opposing tradition a pyrrhic spiritual victory, and the enlightened synthesis of *Moll Flanders* a victory for society. The means are different, but the end is the same: to keep women in their place.[4]

That place is in the home, according to social morality and feminine variations of the bildungsroman, which prescribe for women a separate range of experience associated with domesticity: "Instead of testing their self-image through adventures in the outside world, they are initiated at home through learning the rituals of human relationships, so that they may replicate the lives of their mothers. . . . Women who rebel against the female role are perceived as unnatural and pay the price of unhappiness, if not madness or death."[5] Tristana's truncated story and its parody of the happy ending illustrate, if ironically, society's and nature's revenge on the woman who would stray from the hearth, who would envy man his freedom. Matrimony is the goal and the undoing of ingenious and aggressive women of fiction. Like the women of Spanish Golden Age comedy, they exert their energy and unquestionable talent on winning the prize that ensures their relegation. Diana Trilling points out, "Among heroines undoubtedly the most influential in the evolution of our present-day liberated woman has been the heroine of spirit. She is also the most treacherous of projections of a desirable female image for it is the heroine of spirit who has for so long led women to be deceived that their possibilities in life are bigger than they usually turn out to be and confirmed men in the not wholly mistaken belief that high spirit exists in woman only to seduce them and then expire."[6] Proving herself, the female protagonist establishes an identity. When she succeeds, that identity becomes part of her dowry.

Some heroines of literature sacrifice their lives to protect their virginity. Others sacrifice personal development, individuality, and pride to please men or to marry the man of their choice. The picaresque antiheroines make a mockery of purity, matrimony, and conventionality. They serve their instincts, physical and pecuniary, and go to great lengths to ridicule a society that is not only hierarchical but also decidedly misogynous. The men win out, but the *pícaras* leave their imprint on the (sub)text and to an extent foreshadow modern feminism. The crucial distinction between the Spanish feminine picaresque and the contemporary transformations is the implied authorial attitude toward society. The male-oriented social structure ceases to be the symbol of justice, so that the female rebel—underprivileged and victimized—comes to stand for individual, minority, and women's rights. Rhetorical manipulation works to win reader sympathy for the antiheroine in her struggle against the acknowledged order. *Tereza Batista* shows the moral superiority of a prostitute over enforcers of the law and endows Tereza not only with a heart of gold but also with the happy ending of romance. Society writes one version of the story, the fictional author another. *Hasta no verte Jesús mío* and *Fanny* also provide the "untold story" of those denied a voice in the real world. *Fanny* postulates new directions for social and literary history, imposing feminism on the past and urging it on the present. The past in *Hasta no verte Jesús mío* is a revolution that excludes the woman whom the implied author engages to address a present, and feminist, revolution. Poniatowska writes Jesusa Palancares into the history and future of Mexico, and the document records—constitutes— her triumph.

The self-consciousness of the picaresque—its emphasis on the soul and on forms of expression—approaches the inner self through an exploration of language. Perspectivism applies to personality and to the elaboration of thought. The feminine picaresque, with well-defined levels of social commentary and discourse, brings sexual difference to bear on the structures, goals, and limits of the verbal sign. Social protocol, controlled by men, includes speech and writing. Gender affects women's discourse and, more importantly perhaps, response to women's discourse. There is an increased self-consciousness, as well as increased potential for dialectic, when a woman speaks in a text, when a woman writes a work of fiction, and when an author creates a woman's voice.[7] The feminine picaresque accentuates the ironic voice-over. The intrusion of the author in the narrative (*La pícara Justina*), the man's voice claiming to be a woman's (*Teresa de Manzanares*), and the silencing of the antiheroine (*La hija de Celestina*, *La garduña de Sevilla*) parallel the relegation of women in society. Similarly, the editing and censorship of Moll Flanders's manuscript correspond to eighteenth-century social conditioning, and the feminist revisionism of *Fanny* corresponds to contemporary sensibility and fashionably antisocial behavior. In *Fanny*, the play of voices comes full circle to all but eliminate the male perspective.

The discursive model established in the early picaresque novels subjects its literary and social foundations to an internal critical mechanism, or metacommentary. Every text puts forth a "reading" of preceding texts and of society; a given text works metonymically with narrative tradition and metaphorically with social reality. The relationship between story and discourse, based on the shifting alliances of the implied author, operates in the mode of irony. If the voice-over rejects the words of the narrator, message systems oppose each other. If it confirms or amplifies them, the antihero(ine) becomes a hero(ine). The self-critical discourse lends itself to analysis of the stratified "I" and, in the case of the variations and transformations, to projections of feminist theory. The motif of "women's place" characterizes this theory, which seeks to define the structures of female consciousness, its reflections in literature and in life, and the ramifications of the sexual dialectic on woman as reader, writer, character, symbol, and metaphor.[8] Feminist theory is a history of repression and an ongoing story that may rethink social and poetic justice to the benefit of men and women. The works considered in this study capture the history and the story through meaningful silences and through the articulation of the antiheroine's voice, a changing voice and perhaps ultimately the voice of change.

Notes

NOTES TO INTRODUCTION

1. Victor Erlich notes that the phrase for the "laying bare of the device" (*obnazenie priëma*) was introduced by Roman Jakobson. See *Russian Formalism*, 3d ed. (New Haven and London: Yale University Press, 1981), esp. pp. 77 and 190–91; and Victor Shklovsky, "Art as Technique" and "Sterne's *Tristram Shandy*: Stylistic Commentary," trans. Lee T. Lemon and Marion J. Reis, in *Russian Formalist Criticism: Four Essays*, ed. Lemon and Reis (Lincoln and London: University of Nebraska Press, 1965), pp. 3–57.

2. In "Conditions and Limits of Autobiography," Georges Gusdorff writes, "Any autobiography is a moment of the life that it recounts; it struggles to draw the meaning from that life, but it is itself a meaning in the life" (p. 43). The essay, translated by James Olney, is in *Autobiography: Essays Theoretical and Critical*, ed. James Olney (Princeton: Princeton University Press, 1980), pp. 28–48. See also William L. Howarth, "Some Principles of Autobiography," *New Literary History* 5 (1974): 363–81; Paul Zumthor, "Autobiography in the Middle Ages?," trans. Sherry Simon, *Genre* 6 (1973): 29–48; and Jean Starobinski, "The Style of Autobiography," in *Literary Style: A Symposium*, ed. and trans. Seymour Chatman (New York: Oxford University Press, 1971), pp. 285–96. Howarth addresses issues of narrative technique in autobiography: "Autobiography is . . . hardly 'factual,' 'unimaginative,' or even 'nonfictional,' for it welcomes all the devices of skilled narration and observes few of the restrictions—accuracy, impartiality, inclusiveness—imposed upon other forms of historical literature" (p. 365).

3. Eugene Vance, "The Functions and Limits of Autobiography in Augustine's *Confessions*," *Poetics Today* 5, 2 (1984): 399 (399–409). See also Ralph Flores, "Double-Making St. Augustine's *Confessions*," in *The Rhetoric of Doubtful Authority* (Ithaca and London: Cornell University Press, 1984), pp. 44–65, esp. 46–50.

4. In *Of Grammatology*, trans. Gayatri Chakravorty Spivak (Baltimore and London: The Johns Hopkins University Press, 1976), and in other writings, Derrida speaks of logocentrism, the (unfounded) faith in a direct route from signifier to signified. This word-centered universe, the foundation of Western thought, creates a false sense of completeness, a "metaphysics of presence" more accurately seen in terms of absences, of deferred or deflected meanings (*différance*).

5. See, for example, Wolfgang Iser, *The Act of Reading: A Theory of Aesthetic Response* (Baltimore and London: The Johns Hopkins University Press, 1978), esp. pp. 225–31.

NOTES TO CHAPTER I: THE WOR(L)D IN CRISIS

1. At one extreme, the picaresque would include *Guzmán de Alfarache* and *El Buscón*, with *Lazarillo de Tormes* reduced to precursor. At the other end of the spectrum, the definition—open or closed, according to the critic or the model—could lend itself to a large number of works. For approaches to the Spanish picaresque, see Francisco Rico, *La novela picaresca y el punto de vista* (Barcelona: Seix Barral, 1970) (*The Spanish Picaresque Novel and the Point of View*, trans. Charles Davis with Harry Sieber [Cambridge: Cambridge University Press, 1984]); Maurice Molho, *Introducción al pensamiento picaresco*, trans. Augusto Gálvez-Cañero y Redal (Salamanca: Anaya, 1972); Jenaro Talens, *Novela picaresca y práctica de la transgresión* (Madrid: Ediciones Júcar, 1975); Gustavo A. Alfaro, *La estructura de la novela picaresca* (Bogotá: Instituto Caro y Cuervo, 1977); Alán Francis, *Picaresca, decadencia, historia* (Madrid: Editorial Gredos, 1978); Peter N. Dunn, *The Spanish Picaresque Novel* (Boston: Twayne Publishers, 1979); and Francisco Carrillo, *Semiolingüística de la novela picaresca* (Madrid: Ediciones Cátedra, 1982). Among the studies that deal with the continuity of the picaresque are Frank Wadleigh Chandler, *The Literature of Roguery*, 2 vols. (Boston: Houghton Mifflin, 1907; rpt. New York: Burt Franklin, 1958); Robert Alter, *Rogue's Progress: Studies in the Picaresque Novel* (Cambridge: Harvard University Press, 1964); Al-

exander A. Parker, *Literature and the Delinquent: The Picaresque Novel in Spain and Europe, 1599–1753* (Edinburgh: The University Press, 1967); Stuart Miller, *The Picaresque Novel* (Cleveland: The Press of Case Western Reserve University, 1967); Christine J. Whitbourn, ed., *Knaves and Swindlers: Essays on the Picaresque Novel in Europe* (London: Oxford University Press, 1974); Harry Sieber, *The Picaresque* (London: Methuen, 1977); Richard Bjornson, *The Picaresque Hero in European Fiction* (Madison: The University of Wisconsin Press, 1977); Alexander Blackburn, *The Myth of the Picaro: Continuity and Transformation of the Picaresque Novel, 1554–1954* (Chapel Hill: The University of North Carolina Press, 1979); Walter L. Reed, *An Exemplary History of the Novel: The Quixotic versus the Picaresque* (Chicago and London: The University of Chicago Press, 1981); Arnold Weinstein, *Fictions of the Self: 1550–1800* (Princeton: Princeton University Press, 1981); William Riggan, *Pícaros, Madmen, Naifs, and Clowns: The Unreliable First-Person Narrator* (Norman: University of Oklahoma Press, 1981); and Helen H. Reed, *The Reader in the Picaresque Novel* (London: Tamesis, 1984). See also J. V. Ricapito, *Bibliografía razonada y anotada de obras maestras de la picaresca española* (Madrid: Castalia, 1980); and Joseph L. Laurenti, *Bibliografía de la literatura picaresca: Desde sus orígenes hasta el presente / A Bibliography of Picaresque Literature: From Its Origins to the Present* (Metuchen, New Jersey: Scarecrow Press, 1973), and *A Bibliography of Picaresque Literature, 1973–1978* (New York: AMS Press, 1984).

2. Daniel Eisenberg, "Does the Picaresque Novel Exist?," *Kentucky Romance Quarterly* 26 (1979): 203–19. For commentary and metacommentary on the picaresque, see D. J. Dooley, "Some Uses and Mutations of the Picaresque," *The Dalhousie Review* 37 (1957–1958): 363–77; W. M. Frohock, "The Idea of the Picaresque," *Yearbook of Comparative and General Literature* 16 (1967): 43–52, and "The Falling Center: Recent Fiction and the Picaresque Tradition," *Novel: A Forum on Fiction* 3 (1969): 62–69; Harry Sieber, "Some Recent Books on the Picaresque," *MLN* 84 (1969): 318–30; Claudio Guillén, "Toward a Definition of the Picaresque," "On the Uses of Literary Genre," "Genre and Countergenre: The Discovery of the Picaresque," in *Literature as System* (Princeton: Princeton University Press, 1971), pp. 71–158; Fernando Lázaro Carreter, "Para una revisión del concepto 'novela picaresca,'" in *"Lazarillo de Tormes" en la picaresca* (Barcelona: Ariel, 1972), pp. 195–229, and "Glosas críticas a *Los pícaros en la literatura* de Alexander A. Parker," *Hispanic Review* 41 (1973): 469–97 (as well as Parker, "Sobre las *glosas críticas* de Fernando Lázaro Carreter," *Hispanic Review* 42 [1974]: 235–39, and Lázaro Carreter, "Contrarréplica," *Hispanic Review* 42 [1974]: 239–41); Frank J. Kearful, "Spanish Rogues and English Foundlings: On the Disintegration of Picaresque," *Genre* 4 (1971): 376–91; Ulrich Wicks, "Pícaro, Picaresque: The Picaresque in Literary Scholarship," *Genre* 5 (1972): 153–192, "The Nature of Picaresque Narrative: A Modal Approach," *PMLA* 89 (1974): 240–49, "Onlyman," *Mosaic* 8, 3 (1975): 21–47, "The Romance of the Picaresque," *Genre* 11 (1978): 29–44, and "Narrative Distance in Picaresque Fiction," *College Literature* 6 (1979): 165–81; Maximillian E. Novak, "Freedom, Libertinism, and the Picaresque," in *Racism in the Eighteenth Century*, ed. Harold E. Pagliaro (Cleveland: The Press of Case Western Reserve University, 1973), pp. 35–48; Barbara A. Babcock, "'Liberty's a Whore': Inversions, Marginalia, and Picaresque Narrative," in *The Reversible World: Symbolic Inversion in Art and Society*, ed. Barbara A. Babcock (Ithaca and London: Cornell University Press, 1978), pp. 95–116; Alison Weber, "Cuatro clases de narrativa picaresca," pp. 13–18, Edmond Cros, "Aproximación a la picaresca," pp. 31–38, José L. Alonso Hernández, "Signos de estructura profunda de la narración picaresca," pp. 39–52, and Jaime Ferrán, "Algunas constantes en la picaresca," pp. 53–62, in *La picaresca: Orígenes, textos y estructuras*, ed. Manuel Criado de Val (Madrid: Fundación Universitaria Española, 1979); Howard Mancing, "The Picaresque Novel: A Protean Form," *College Literature* 6 (1979): 182–204; John P. Kent and J. L. Gaunt, "Picaresque Fiction: A Bibliographic Essay," *College Literature* 6 (1979): 245–70; Peter N. Dunn, "Problems of a Model for the Picaresque and the Case of Quevedo's *Buscón*," *Bulletin of Hispanic Studies* 59 (1982): 95–105; and Edward H. Friedman, "Novel Groupings: The Order of Things," *Rocky Mountain Review* 37 (1983): 237–61.

3. The distinction between the story and the process of narration develops from the linguistic dichotomy *histoire/discours* of Emile Benveniste in *Problems in General Linguistics*, trans. Mary Elizabeth Meek (Coral Gables: University of Miami Press, 1971), esp. pp. 205–15. See Jonathan Culler, *Structuralist Po-*

etics (Ithaca: Cornell University Press, 1975), pp. 192–202; and Seymour Chatman, *Story and Discourse* (Ithaca and London: Cornell University Press, 1978).

4. For commentary on intertextuality, see Julia Kristeva, *Desire in Language: A Semiotic Approach to Literature and Art*, ed. Leon S. Roudiez, trans. Thomas Gora, Alice Jardine, and Leon S. Roudiez (New York: Columbia University Press, 1980), and for metacommentary, see Jonathan Culler, *The Pursuit of Signs: Semiotics, Literature, Deconstruction* (Ithaca: Cornell University Press, 1981), esp. pp. 100–18.

5. See, among the numerous studies devoted to the text, Otis H. Green, "Medieval Laughter: The *Book of Good Love*," *Spain and the Western Tradition*, vol. 1 (Madison: The University of Wisconsin Press, 1963), pp. 27–71; A. D. Deyermond, "The Greeks, the Romans, the Astrologers, and the Meaning of the *Libro de Buen Amor*," *Romance Notes* 5 (1963): 88–91; Anthony N. Zahareas, *The Art of Juan Ruiz* (Madrid: Estudios de Literatura Española, 1965), and "Structure and Ideology in the *Libro de buen amor*," *Corónica* 7 (1979): 92–104; Roger M. Walker, "'Con miedo de la muerte la miel non es sabrosa': Love, Sin and Death in the *Libro de buen amor*," in *Libro de buen amor Studies*, ed. G. B. Gybbon-Monypenny (London: Tamesis Books Limited, 1970), pp. 231–52; A. A. Parker, "The Parable of the Greeks and the Romans in the *Libro de Buen Amor*," in *Medieval Hispanic Studies Presented to Rita Hamilton*, ed. A. D. Deyermond (London: Tamesis, 1976), pp. 139–47; Cesáreo Bandera, "De la apertura del *Libro* de Juan Ruiz a Derrida y viceversa," *Dispositio* 2 (1977): 54–66; Alfonso Rey, "Juan Ruiz, don Melón de la Huerta y el yo poético medieval," *Bulletin of Hispanic Studies* 56 (1979): 103–16; M. K. Read, "Man against Language: A Linguistic Perspective on the Theme of Alienation in the 'Libro de buen amor,'" *MLN* 96 (1981): 237–60; Dayle Seidenspinner-Núñez, *The Allegory of Good Love: Parodic Perspectivism in the Libro de Buen Amor* (Berkeley: University of California Press, 1981); Rosalie Gimeno, "Women in the *Book of Good Love*," in *Women in Hispanic Literature: Icons and Fallen Idols*, ed. Beth Miller (Berkeley and Los Angeles: University of California Press, 1983), pp. 84–96; and Marina Scordilis Brownlee, *The Status of the Reading Subject in the "Libro de Buen Amor,"* North Carolina Studies in the Romance Languages and Literatures, no. 224 (Chapel Hill: University of North Carolina Press, 1985). Brownlee's point of departure is the Augustinian paradigm as key to reception.

6. Julio Cejador y Frauca, in his edition of the text (Madrid: Espasa-Calpe, 1967), vol. 2, p. 176, notes: "*Don Polo* llama la vieja al clérigo enamoradizo, en torno del cual ella anda sirviendo, y al cual mira como los navegantes a la estrella polar." See also *Libro de Buen Amor*, ed. Joan Corominas (Madrid: Editorial Gredos, 1967), p. 498; *Libro de Buen Amor*, ed. Raymond S. Willis (Princeton: Princeton University Press, 1972), p. 360; and Dorothy Clotelle Clarke, "Juan Ruiz as Don Polo," *Hispanic Review* 40 (1972): 245–59. The stanzas (*coplas*) contain four Alexandrine (fourteen-syllable) verses with monorhyme, called *cuaderna vía*. All quotations from the *Libro de Buen Amor* will refer to the Willis edition and English paraphrase, and verse and page numbers will be indicated in parentheses.

7. For connotative aspects of the fables, see Seidenspinner-Núñez, *The Allegory of Good Love*, esp. pp. 80–85.

8. See Cejador, ed., *Libro de Buen Amor*, vol. 2, p. 183; Corominas, ed., *Libro de Buen Amor*, p. 522; and James Burke, "Love's Double Cross: Language Play as Structure in the *Libro de buen amor*," *University of Toronto Quarterly* 43 (1974): 257 (231–62).

9. Robert Edwards, "Narrative Technique in Juan Ruiz' History of Doña Garoza," *MLN* 89 (1974): 266 (265–73).

10. Edwards, "Narrative Technique," pp. 266–67.

11. See Chatman, *Story and Discourse*, esp. chapters 4 and 5, and Gérard Genette, *Narrative Discourse: An Essay in Method*, trans. Jane F. Lewin (Ithaca: Cornell University Press, 1980), esp. chapter 5, for distinctions between and forms of mimesis and diegesis.

12. See Hayden White, *Metahistory* (Baltimore: The Johns Hopkins University Press, 1973), esp. pp. 31–38, and *Tropics of Discourse* (Baltimore: The Johns Hopkins University Press, 1978), esp. pp. 1–25 and 81–100, for the relationship between the tropes of traditional poetics (and of modern language theory) and modes of presentation.

13. Zahareas, *The Art of Juan Ruiz*, p. 34.

14. See esp. stanzas 64–79, which deal with the act of interpretation.

15. Stanzas 1520–1575 present the archpriest's reaction to Trotaconventos's death. See Frank P. Casa, "Toward an Understand-

ing of the Archpriest's Lament," *Romanische Forschungen* 79 (1967): 463–75.

16. Read, "Man against Language," p. 260.

17. Ibid., pp. 251–260. The essay appears in Read's *The Birth and Death of Language: Spanish Literature and Linguistics, 1300–1700* (Madrid: José Porrúa Turanzas, 1983), pp. 22–48.

18. Marta Ana Diz, "Relato, fabulación, semiosis: la producción del significado en el *Conde Lucanor*," *MLN* 90 (1981): 403–13. Diz expands her analysis of *El conde Lucanor* in *Patronio y Lucanor: La lectura inteligente "en el tiempo que es turbio"* (Potomac, Maryland: Scripta Humanistica, 1984). For a historical consideration of signs, their interpretation, and their changing status, see Stanley E. Fish, "The Aesthetic of the Good Physician," in *Self-Consuming Artifacts: The Experience of Seventeenth-Century Literature* (Berkeley and Los Angeles: University of California Press, 1972), pp. 1–77. See also Marina Scordilis Brownlee, "Autobiography as Self-(Re)presentation: The Augustinian Paradigm and Juan Ruiz's Theory of Reading," in *Mimesis: From Mirror to Method, Augustine to Descartes*, ed. John D. Lyons and Stephen G. Nichols (Hanover, New Hampshire: University Press of New England for Dartmouth College, 1982), pp. 71–82; Michael E. Gerli, "*Recta voluntas est bonus amor*: St. Augustine and the Didactic Structure of the *Libro de buen amor*," *Romance Philology* 35 (1982): 500–508; and Cyrus Hamlin, "The Conscience of Narrative: Toward a Hermeneutics of Transcendence," *New Literary History* 13 (1982): 205–30. Hamlin shows how a principle of transcendence, exemplified in the *Confessions* of St. Augustine, "may apply also to secular narrative, including *Tristram Shandy*, if only by negation with regard to the limits of language and verbal signification" (p. 218).

NOTES TO CHAPTER 2: NARRATIVE ACTS, NARRATIVE ACTORS

1. Seymour Chatman, *Story and Discourse* (Ithaca and London: Cornell University Press, 1978), p. 148. See Wayne C. Booth, *The Rhetoric of Fiction* (Chicago and London: The University of Chicago Press, 1961), esp. pp. 67–86 and 211–40; and Félix Martínez Bonati, *Fictive Discourse and the Structures of Literature*, trans. Philip W. Silver (Ithaca and London: Cornell University Press, 1981), esp. pp. 102–19.

2. See Chatman, *Story and Discourse*, pp. 149–50. In *The Implied Reader: Patterns of Communication in Prose Fiction from Bunyan to Beckett* (Baltimore and London: The Johns Hopkins University Press, 1974), Wolfgang Iser states, "This term incorporates both the prestructuring of the potential meaning by the text, and the reader's actualization of this potential through the reading process. It refers to the active nature of this process—which will vary historically from one age to another—and not to a typology of possible readers" (p. xii). See Iser, *The Act of Reading: A Theory of Aesthetic Response* (Baltimore and London: The Johns Hopkins University Press, 1978); and Jane E. Tompkins, ed., *Reader-Response Criticism from Formalism to Post-Structuralism* (Baltimore and London: The Johns Hopkins University Press, 1980).

3. Susan Sniader Lanser, *The Narrative Act: Point of View in Prose Fiction* (Princeton: Princeton University Press, 1981), p. 112.

4. Ibid., p. 93. Lanser discusses the concept of the implied author, which she finds problematic (pp. 49ff.) and for which she substitutes the term *extrafictional voice*: "The voice of a text, then, is endowed with the authority of its creator and of the community in which it is published and produced. But can we properly speak of an authorial voice in relation to a book that is fictional? Is not one of the hallmarks of fiction the absence of the author (as opposed to a narrator) from the text? As far as the fiction itself extends, the narrating voice may indeed have little in common with the authorial personage. In every text, however, even a fictional text, an authorial voice is an *extrafictional* entity whose presence accounts, for example, for organizing, titling, and introducing the fictional work. This extrafictional voice, the most direct textual counterpart for the historical author, carries all the *diegetic authority* of its (publicly authorized) creator and has the ontological status of historical truth. This is the voice of scientific and 'utilitarian' discourse as well as cultural communication. It is a voice that, but for the degree to which literary criticism has removed the author's historical presence from the text, could simply be called the authorial voice rather than the qualifying *extra*fictional" (p. 122).

5. See Gerald Prince, "On Readers and Listeners in Narrative," *Neophilologus* 55 (1971): 117–22, "Notes Toward a Categorization of Fictional 'Narratees,'" *Genre* 4 (1971): 100–105, "Introduction à l'étude du nar-

rataire," *Poétique* 14 (1973): 178–96 (reprinted in English as "Introduction to the Study of the Narratee" in *Reader-Response Criticism,* ed. Jane P. Tomkins, pp. 7–25), and "Narrative Analysis and Narratology," *New Literary History* 13 (1982): 179–87; Mary Ann Piwowarczyk, "The Narratee and the Situation of Enunciation: A Reconsideration of Prince's Theory," *Genre* 9 (1976): 161–77; Chatman, *Story and Discourse,* pp. 253–62; and Lanser, *The Narrative Act,* pp. 174–84. See also chapter 5 ("Voice") of Gérard Genette, *Narrative Discourse: An Essay in Method,* trans. Jane E. Lewin (Ithaca: Cornell University Press, 1980), pp. 212–62.

6. The seminal article is F. Courtney Tarr, "Literary and Artistic Unity in the *Lazarillo de Tormes,*" *PMLA* 42 (1927): 404–21. Other studies that examine the question of unity include Claudio Guillén, "La disposición temporal del *Lazarillo de Tormes,*" *Hispanic Review* 25 (1957): 264–79; Raymond S. Willis, "Lazarillo and the Pardoner: The Artistic Necessity of the Fifth *Tractado,*" *Hispanic Review* 27 (1959): 267–79 (complemented by Gethin Hughes, "*Lazarillo de Tormes:* The Fifth 'Tratado,'" *Hispanófila* 61 [1977]: 1–9); Norma Louise Hutman, "Universality and Unity in the *Lazarillo de Tormes,*" *PMLA* 76 (1961): 469–73; Stephen Gilman, "The Death of Lazarillo de Tormes," *PMLA* 81 (1966): 149–66; Andrée Collard, "The Unity of *Lazarillo de Tormes,*" *MLN* 83 (1968): 262–67; Fernando Lázaro Carreter, "Construcción y sentido del *Lazarillo de Tormes,*" *Abaco: Estudios sobre literatura española* 1 (1969): 45–134; Francisco Rico, "*Lazarillo de Tormes,* o la polisemia," *La novela picaresca y el punto de vista* (Barcelona: Seix Barral, 1970), pp. 13–55; Bruce W. Wardropper, "The Strange Case of Lázaro Gonzales Pérez," *MLN* 92 (1977): 202–12; Javier Herrero, "The Great Icons of the *Lazarillo*: The Bull, the Wine, the Sausage and the Turnip," *Ideologies and Literature* 1, 5 (1978): 3–18, and "The Ending of *Lazarillo*: The Wine against the Water," *MLN* 93 (1978): 313–19; Eugenio Suárez-Galbán, "El proceso caracterizador del *Lazarillo*: Una revaloración," *Sin Nombre* 9, 2 (1978): 49–66; Douglas M. Carey, "*Lazarillo de Tormes* and the Quest for Authority," *PMLA* 94 (1979): 36–46; Robert L. Fiore, "*Lazarillo de Tormes*: Estructura narrativa de una novela picaresca," pp. 359–66, S. B. Vranich, "El caso del *Lazarillo*: Un estudio romántico en apoyo de la unidad estructural de la novela," pp. 367–

73, James A. Parr, "La estructura satírica del *Lazarillo,*" pp. 375–81, and José A. Madrigal, "El simbolismo como vehículo temático en el *Lazarillo de Tormes,*" pp. 405–12, in *La picaresca: Orígenes, textos y estructuras,* ed. Manuel Criado de Val (Madrid: Fundación Universitaria Española, 1979).

For general studies of *Lazarillo de Tormes,* see R. O. Jones, Introduction, *La vida de Lazarillo de Tormes* (Manchester: Manchester University Press, 1963); Marcel Bataillon, *Novedad y fecundidad del "Lazarillo de Tormes,"* trans. Luis Cortés Vázquez (Salamanca: Ediciones Anaya, 1968); Fernando Lázaro Carreter, *"Lazarillo de Tormes" en la picaresca* (Barcelona: Ediciones Ariel, 1972); A. D. Deyermond, *Lazarillo de Tormes. A Critical Guide* (London: Grant and Cutler, 1975); Harry Sieber, *Language and Society in La vida de Lazarillo de Tormes* (Baltimore and London: The Johns Hopkins University Press, 1978); Víctor García de la Concha, *Nueva lectura del Lazarillo: El deleite de la perspectiva* (Madrid: Editorial Castalia, 1981); and Robert L. Fiore, *Lazarillo de Tormes* (Boston: Twayne Publishers, 1984). See also Robert Alter, *Rogue's Progress: Studies in the Picaresque Novel* (Cambridge: Harvard University Press, 1964), pp. 1–10; Alexander A. Parker, *Literature and the Delinquent: The Picaresque Novel in Spain and Europe, 1599–1753* (Edinburgh: The University Press, 1967), esp. pp. 1–17; Alberto del Monte, *Itinerario de la novela picaresca española,* trans. Enrique Sordo (Barcelona: Editorial Lumen, 1971), pp. 17–61; Richard Bjornson, *The Picaresque Hero in European Fiction* (Madison: The University of Wisconsin Press, 1977), pp. 21–42; Peter N. Dunn, *The Spanish Picaresque Novel* (Boston: Twayne Publishers, 1979), pp. 17–35; Alexander Blackburn, *The Myth of the Picaro: Continuity and Transformation of the Picaresque Novel, 1554–1954* (Chapel Hill: The University of North Carolina Press, 1979), pp. 26–59; Arnold Weinstein, *Fictions of the Self: 1550–1800* (Princeton: Princeton University Press, 1981), pp. 19–31, and Walter Reed, *An Exemplary History of the Novel: The Quixotic versus the Picaresque* (Chicago and London: The University of Chicago Press, 1981), pp. 43–58.

7. For questions of language and narrative discourse, see L. J. Woodward, "Author-Reader Relationship in the *Lazarillo de Tormes,*" *Forum for Modern Language Studies* 1 (1965): 43–53; A. D. Deyermond, "The Corrupted Vision: Further Thoughts on *Lazarillo de*

Tormes," *Forum for Modern Language Studies* I (1965): 246–49; Frank Durand, "The Author and Lázaro: Levels of Comic Meaning," *Bulletin of Hispanic Studies* 45 (1968): 89–101; R. W. Truman, "Parody and Irony in the Self-Portrayal of Lázaro de Tormes," *Modern Language Review* 63 (1968): 600–605; Douglas M. Carey, "Asides and Interiority in *Lazarillo de Tormes*: A Study in Psychological Realism," *Studies in Philology* 66 (1969): 119–34; Victoria Windler, "Alienación en el *Lazarillo de Tormes*: La fragmentación del 'yo' narrativo," *Estudios Filológicos* 8 (1972): 225–53; A. Bell, "The Rhetoric of Self-Defence of 'Lázaro de Tormes,'" *Modern Language Review* 68 (1973): 84–93; Howard Mancing, "The Deceptiveness of *Lazarillo de Tormes*," *PMLA* 90 (1975): 426–32; José Varela Muñoz, "El *Lazarillo de Tormes* como una paradoja racional," *Revista Canadiense de Estudios Hispánicos* I (1977): 153–84; Harry Sieber, *Language and Society in La vida de Lazarillo de Tormes*; Alfonso de Toro, "Arte como procedimiento: El *Lazarillo de Tormes*," in *La picaresca*, ed. Manuel Criado de Val, pp. 385–404; Antonio Gómez-Moriana, "La subversión del discurso ritual: Una lectura intertextual del *Lazarillo de Tormes*," *Revista Canadiense de Estudios Hispánicos* 4 (1980): 133–54 ("The Subversion of the Ritual Discourse: An Intertextual Reading of the *Lazarillo de Tormes*," *Sociocriticism* I [July 1985]: 111–35), "Autobiografía y discurso ritual: Problemática de la confesión autobiográfica destinada al tribunal inquisitorial," in *L'Autobiographie en Espagne* (Aix-en-Provence: Université de Provence, 1982), pp. 69–94, and "Intertextualidad, interdiscursividad y parodia: Sobre los orígenes de la forma narrativa en la novela picaresca," *Dispositio* 8, 22–23 (1983): 123–44; George A. Shipley, "The Critic as Witness for the Prosecution: Making the Case against Lázaro de Tormes," *PMLA* 97 (1982): 179–94; and Malcolm K. Read, *The Birth and Death of Language: Spanish Literature and Linguistics, 1300–1700* (Madrid: José Porrúa Turanzas, 1983), esp. pp. 108–19. See also Alfonso Rey, "La novela picaresca y el narrador fidedigno," *Hispanic Review* 47 (1979): 55–75.

8. At the end of chapter 7, Lázaro alludes to warning those who would speak ill of his wife to beware ("Mirá, si sois amigo, no me digáis cosa con que me pese, que no tengo por mi amigo al que me hace pesar"). See Francisco Rico, ed., *La novela picaresca española*, vol. I (Barcelona: Editorial Planeta, 1967), p. 80. Subsequent quotations from *Lazarillo de Tormes* will refer to this edition, and page numbers will be indicated in parentheses. For an English version, see *Two Spanish Picaresque Novels*, trans. Michael Alpert (Middlesex, England: Penguin Books, 1969).

9. In the final sentence of the prologue, Lázaro is clearly attempting to cast himself as one of the humble people who have made good by dint of their own efforts ("los que . . . con fuerza y maña remando, salieron a buen puerto," p. 7). The novel proper concludes with the narrator's statement of success: "en este tiempo estaba en mi prosperidad y en la cumbre de toda buena fortuna" (p. 80).

is subjected form the basis of Sieber's *Language and Society*: "The relationships between Lázaro and his masters . . . will be slightly redefined in order that I may discuss their 'linguistic' rather than their social implications. Lázaro learns something from each of them about the nature of language" (p. xi).

11. In the brief fourth chapter, Lázaro says of the friar, "Este me dio los primeros zapatos que rompí en mi vida, mas no me duraron ocho días, ni yo pude con su trote durar más. Y por eso y por otras cosillas que no digo, salí dél" (pp. 66–67; He gave me the first pair of shoes that I wore out in my life, but they didn't even last a week, and I couldn't keep up with his hustling around any more. So on account of that and other little things that I won't go into, I left him). Marcel Bataillon contends that the omission of additional facts could allow the reader to suppose the worst about the relations between this master and his young servant (*Novedad y fecundidad del "Lazarillo de Tormes,"* p. 72). See Sieber, *Language and Society*, pp. 45–58. Note also the episode of the painter in chapter 6: "Después desto, asenté con un maestro de pintar panderos, para molelle los colores, y también sufrí mil males" (p. 75; After this, I set myself up with a tambourine painter to grind his colors, and once again I suffered a thousand ills). See George A. Shipley, "A Case of Functional Obscurity: The Master Tambourine Painter of *Lazarillo*, Tratado VI," *MLN* 97 (1982): 225–53, and "Lazarillo and the Cathedral Chaplain: A Conspiratorial Reading of *Lazarillo de Tormes*, Tratado VI," *Symposium* 37, 3 (1983): 216–41.

12. Note, for example, Lázaro's revelation of Zaide's crimes and his forced (gastronomical) confession in the episode of the

NOTES— ·—235

sausage in chapter 1, the involuntary confession made in his sleep in chapter 2, the squire's story (confession) and Lázaro's thoughts (articulated silence) in chapter 3, the incomplete narration in chapters 4 and 6, the false confession of the constable in chapter 5, and the conflict between speech (the instrument of the town crier) and silence (the mainstay of the cuckolded husband) in chapter 7.

13. Note Lázaro's "yo determiné de arrimarme a los buenos" (p. 79). See Richard Bjornson, "Lazarillo 'arrimándose a los buenos,'" *Romance Notes* 19 (1978): 67–71.

14. See Anson C. Piper, "The 'Breadly Paradise' of Lazarillo de Tormes," *Hispania* 44 (1961): 267–71; and Walter Holzinger, "The Breadly Paradise Revisited: *Lazarillo de Tormes*, Segundo Tratado," *Revista Hispánica Moderna* 37 (1972–1973): 229–36.

15. Rico, *La novela picaresca y el punto de vista*, pp. 24–25.

16. Despite the frequent association of the end of chapter 7 with the time of writing, there is an obvious passage of time. Critics have offered several temporal theories based on historical allusions in the text. For a presentation of major opinions, see Bataillon, *Novedad y fecundidad*, esp. pp. 11–25, and Rico, in the introduction to *La novela picaresca española*, vol. 1, ix-xxvi. In "The Fictional Context of *Lazarillo de Tormes*," *Modern Language Review* 80, 2 (1985): 340–50, Robert Archer offers the thesis that the addressee is the archpriest himself and that Lázaro's text is "an insidious blackmail letter masquerading as ingenious autobiography" (p. 350).

17. Lázaro speaks of a soldier who risks his life to gain praise, a theologian interested in audience reaction to his oratorical style, and a jester willing to offer praise even when none is due (p. 6).

18. The concept of reading as misreading is associated with Harold Bloom. See *The Anxiety of Influence* (Oxford and New York: Oxford University Press, 1973), *Kabbalah and Criticism* (New York: Seabury, 1975), *A Map of Misreading* (Oxford and New York: Oxford University Press, 1975), and *Poetry and Repression* (New Haven: Yale University Press, 1976).

19. Jonathan Culler, *The Pursuit of Signs: Semiotics, Literature, Deconstruction* (Ithaca: Cornell University Press, 1981), p. 15.

20. In "Critical Factions/Critical Fictions," the introductory essay of *Textual Strategies: Perspectives in Post-Structuralist Criticism*, ed. Josué Harari (Ithaca: Cornell University Press, 1979), Harari writes, "Deconstruction, as Derrida practices it, is as much a matter of substance as it is a matter of form. Tradition is neither discarded, nor attacked from the outside. Derrida's strategy consists of working within metaphysics, of finding its weak point and of trying to widen the breach thus uncovered. His aim is to show that metaphysics has never had the plenitude it claims to have, and, also, that its entire history involves a dissimulation of this lack of fullness. Time and time again, Derrida denounces the illusion of a full presence or plenitude in Western metaphysics. . . . The Derridean demonstration consists of showing that the whole edifice of Western metaphysics rests on the possibility of compensating for a primordial nonpresence by way of the supplement. Once it is proven that the supplement is an integral part of the metaphysical machinery, it becomes easy to show how in every instance the notion of supplement serves to demystify full presence" (pp. 33–35). Derrida's "The Supplement of Copula: Philosophy *before* Linguistics" appears in the collection (pp. 82–120). See also Christopher Norris, *Deconstruction: Theory and Practice* (London and New York: Methuen, 1982).

21. Vincent B. Leitch, *Deconstructive Criticism: An Advanced Introduction* (New York: Columbia University Press, 1983), pp. 175–76.

22. Jonathan Culler, *On Deconstruction: Theory and Criticism after Structuralism* (Ithaca: Cornell University Press, 1982), p. 155.

23. Leitch, *Deconstructive Criticism*, p. 178.

24. See M. J. Woods, "Pitfalls for the Moralizer in 'Lazarillo de Tormes,'" *Modern Language Review* 74 (1979): 580–98, for a review of the critical conflict. The problem of morality is also treated in Bruce W. Wardropper, "El trastorno de la moral en el *Lazarillo*," *Nueva Revista de Filología Hispánica* 15 (1961): 441–47, and "The Implications of Hypocrisy in the *Lazarillo de Tormes*," in *Studies in Honor of Everett W. Hesse*, ed. William C. McCrary, José A. Madrigal, and John E. Keller (Lincoln: Society of Spanish and Spanish-American Studies, 1981), pp. 179–86; Didier T. Jaén, "La ambigüedad moral del *Lazarillo de Tormes*," *PMLA* 83 (1968): 130–34; and Georgina Sabat de Rivers, "La moral que Lázaro nos propone," *MLN* 95 (1980): 233–51. See also Roger Wright, "Lázaro's Success," *Neophilologus* 68 (1985):

529–33. Wright's minimalist view operates at a literal level, stressing the (double) allusion to entertainment in the prologue. He concludes, "The subtlety that has been expended on showing that the book means the opposite of what it says is unnecessary and probably anachronistic. *Lazarillo de Tormes* makes sense if we take it at face value" (p. 533).

25. Culler, *On Deconstruction*, pp. 123–24.

26. Enrique Moreno Báez stresses the didactic intention of the work in *Lección y sentido del "Guzmán de Alfarache," Revista de Filología Española*, Anejo 40 (Madrid, 1948). While recognizing the importance of Alemán's *converso* ancestry, Alexander A. Parker maintains, "He clearly *intended* to write an orthodox work, to contribute (as we now see it) to Counter-Reformation literature, and his book was passed by ecclesiastical censors in an age when the Inquisition was vigilant to protect both the purity and the dignity of the faith" (*Literature and the Delinquent*, pp. 32–33 [pp. 28–45]). Francisco Rico, in "Consejos y consejas de *Guzmán de Alfarache*" (*La novela picaresca y el punto de vista*, pp. 57–91), considers Guzmán's spiritual evolution—shown in his move from actor to author—as the basic theme of the novel. The history of a conversion and the analysis of a conscience employ antisocial misadventures because Alemán knew only too well that sinners do not read boring books (p. 70). Michel Cavillac makes a case for "la spiritualité alémanienne" in "La Conversion de Guzmán de Alfarache: De la justification marchande à la stratégie de la raison d'état," *Bulletin Hispanique* 85, 1–2 (1983): 21–44.

Recent critics generally have tended to be more skeptical concerning the validity of the conversion. Studies of the relation between status, conversion, and discourse include J. A. van Praag, "Sobre el sentido del *Guzmán de Alfarache*," *Estudios dedicados a Menéndez Pidal* 5 (Madrid: Consejo Superior de Investigaciones Científicas, 1954): 283–306; Edward Nagy, "El anhelo de Guzmán de 'conocer su sangre': Una posibilidad interpretativa," *Kentucky Romance Quarterly* 16 (1970): 75–95; Carroll B. Johnson, "Dios y buenas gentes en *Guzmán de Alfarache*," *Romanische Forschungen* 84 (1972): 553–63, and *Inside Guzmán de Alfarache* (Berkeley: University of California Press, 1978); J. A. Jones, "The Duality and Complexity of *Guzmán de Alfarache*: Some Thoughts on the Structure and Interpretation of Alemán's Novel," in

Knaves and Swindlers: Essays on the Picaresque Novel in Europe, ed. Christine J. Whitbourn (London: Oxford University Press, 1974), pp. 25–47; M. N. Norval, "Original Sin and the 'Conversion' in the *Guzmán de Alfarache*," *Bulletin of Hispanic Studies* 51 (1974): 346–64; Joan Arias, *Guzmán de Alfarache: The Unrepentant Narrator* (London: Tamesis, 1977); Hilary S. D. Smith, "The *Pícaro* Turns Preacher: Guzmán de Alfarache's Missed Vocation," *Forum for Modern Language Studies* 14 (1978): 387–97; Anthony J. Cascardi, "The Rhetoric of Defense in the *Guzmán de Alfarache*," *Neophilologus* 63 (1979): 380–88; Benito Brancaforte, *Guzmán de Alfarache: ¿Conversión o proceso de degradación?* (Madison, Wisconsin: The Hispanic Seminary of Medieval Studies, 1980); Genevieve M. Ramírez, "*Guzmán de Alfarache* and the Concept of Honor," *Revista de Estudios Hispánicos* 14, 3 (1980): 61–77; M. J. Woods, "The Teasing Opening of *Guzmán de Alfarache*," *Bulletin of Hispanic Studies* 57 (1980): 213–18; Carlos Antonio Rodríguez Matos, *El narrador pícaro: Guzmán de Alfarache* (Madison, Wisconsin: Hispanic Seminary of Medieval Studies, 1985); and Judith A. Whitenack, *The Impenitent Confession of Guzmán de Alfarache* (Madison, Wisconsin: Hispanic Seminary of Medieval Studies, 1985).

Edmond Cros, in *Protée et le gueux: Recherches sur les origines et la nature du récit picaresque dans "Guzmán de Alfarache"* (Paris: Didier, 1967), finds rhetorical and ethical unity in the narrative progression. For other studies of language in the *Guzmán*, see Barbara Davis, "The Style of Mateo Alemán's *Guzmán de Alfarache*," *Romanic Review* 66 (1975): 199–213; Vivian Folkenflik, "Vision and Truth: Baroque Art Metaphors in *Guzmán de Alfarache*," *MLN* 88 (1973): 347–55; and C. George Peale, "*Guzmán de Alfarache* como discurso oral," *Journal of Hispanic Philology* 4 (1979): 25–57. For general studies, see Gonzalo Sobejano, "De la intención y valor del *Guzmán de Alfarache*," *Romanische Forschungen* 71 (1959): 267–311; Donald McGrady, *Mateo Alemán* (New York: Twayne Publishers, 1968); Edmond Cros, *Mateo Alemán: Introducción a su vida y a su obra* (Salamanca: Anaya, 1971); and Angel San Miguel, *Sentido y estructura de Guzmán de Alfarache de Mateo Alemán* (Madrid: Gredos, 1971). See also Alberto del Monte, *Itinerario de la novela picaresca*, pp. 67–101; Harry Sieber, *The Picaresque*, pp. 17–23; Richard Bjornson, *The Picaresque Hero*, pp. 43–65; Peter N. Dunn, *The Spanish Picaresque*

Novel, pp. 41–63; Alexander Blackburn, *The Myth of the Picaro*, pp. 59–80; and Walter L. Reed, *An Exemplary History of the Novel*, pp. 58–64.

27. "De las cosas que suelen causar más temor a los hombres, no sé cuál sea mayor o pueda compararse con una mala intención; y con mayores veras cuanto más estuviere arraigada en los de oscura sangre, nacimiento humilde y bajos pensamientos, porque suele ser en los tales más eficaz y menos corregida." See Francisco Rico, ed., *La novela picaresca española*, vol. 1, p. 89. All subsequent quotations from *Guzmán de Alfarache* will refer to this edition. James Mabbe translated *Guzmán de Alfarache* into English in 1623 as *The Rogue, or the Life of Guzmán de Alfarache* (4 vols., intro. James Fitzmaurice-Kelly [London: Constable and Co., 1924]).

28. "Lo que hallares no grave ni compuesto, eso es el ser de un pícaro sujeto deste libro. Las tales cosas, aunque serán muy pocas, picardea con ellas" (p. 94).

29. See Donald McGrady, "Part II of *Guzmán*: Response to the Apocryphal Continuation," chapter 5 of *Mateo Alemán* (pp. 113–29), for a discussion and hypotheses concerning Alemán's strategies of exposure.

30. McGrady relates the content of the false continuation to parts 1 and 2 of Alemán's work in *Mateo Alemán*, pp. 123–27. See also Alán Francis, "Juan Martí y el *Guzmán* apócrifo," in *Picaresca, decadencia, historia* (Madrid: Editorial Gredos, 1978), pp. 152–61.

31. J. A. Jones, in "The Duality and Complexity of *Guzmán de Alfarache*," finds the argument convincing: "The nature of the conversion must be understood. It does not mean that Guzmán will in future lead a saintly life. His conversion consists of a realization and awareness of past failure and a determination to offer a fight in the future. In other words, it is only at that point that he decides to come to terms with concupiscence instead of being the willing victim of its motions. . . . The conversion then is not so much a glorious affirmation of spiritual victory as a pointer to that which is required in order to set out on the road to eternal life that, as Guzmán states in the closing lines of the novel, we all hope to attain. The work can thus be seen to end on a less triumphant but more realistic note" (pp. 40–41).

Benito Brancaforte (together with his disciples Carlos Rodríguez Matos and Judith Whitenack), Carroll B. Johnson, and Joan Arias represent the opposing viewpoint. Brancaforte signals an inverse progression in the narrative, a taking of sides with the Devil despite the moral and metaphysical trappings and the attempt of the implied author to conceal this state of affairs, perhaps to avoid his own psychic disintegration (*Guzmán de Alfarache: ¿Conversión o proceso de degradación?*, p. 198). Johnson sees Guzmán in dialogue with the Other, actually a part of himself. He concludes, "It is Guzmán's hatred and resentment of his father, joined paradoxically and conflictively to his desperate need to identify with him, which is displaced onto the ambiguous relationship between himself and God he develops in his text. God becomes the most important in a series of displaced representations of the father, . . . the maximum father-surrogate" (*Inside Guzmán de Alfarache*, p. 221). Arias observes, "If his life is a model for us, as he says it should be, his sermons would warn us against vengeance and trickery. But they excuse rather than reproach him for his evil thoughts" (*Guzmán de Alfarache: The Unrepentant Narrator*, p. 73).

32. On the question of conceptist language, see, for example, William H. Clamurro, "The Destabilized Sign: Word and Form in Quevedo's *Buscón*," *MLN* 95 (1980): 295–311, and "Interpolated Discourse in the *Buscón*," *Revista de Estudios Hispánicos* 15 (1981): 443–58, and Richard K. Curry, "La crítica del valor estético del *Buscón*," *Revista de Estudios Hispánicos* 18, 2 (1984): 259–76.

33. In "The Conflict between Author and Protagonist in Quevedo's *Buscón*," *Journal of Hispanic Philology* 2 (1977): 45–60, Edwin Williamson sees Pablos as Quevedo's puppet, "condemned for a crime he could not avoid—the accident of his dishonorable origins—and . . . made to stand in the dock before us uttering his abject piece of self-criticism under the direction of Quevedo." But "Pablos occasionally wriggles out of Quevedo's coercive grasp and seizes a fragile fictional life which follows the logical direction of his own ambition rather than the vicious circularity of his creator's manipulations" (p. 59). In *Estructura de la novela: Anatomía de El Buscón* (Madrid: Editorial Fundamentos, 1978), Gonzalo Díaz-Migoyo sees the novel as interplay between three "texts" in chronic tension: a "sub-text" consisting of the action narrated by the young Pablos, another "sub-text" narrated by the mature Pablos, and a "para-text" of the implied creative activity of Quevedo (pp. 167–68). James Iffland argues

against the separation of narrative voices in "Pablos's Voice: His Master's? A Freudian Approach to Wit in El Buscón," *Romanische Forschungen* 91 (1979): 215–43. Julia L. Epstein, in "Fiction-Making in Quevedo's *Buscón*," *Kentucky Romance Quarterly* 30, 3 (1983): 277–92, states, "Linguistic virtuosity is more than Quevedo's ingenious literary gamesmanship; its acquisition represents the *pícaro*'s true rite of passage" (p. 277). She concludes, "The *pícaro* goes through a process of learning which enables him to write his autobiography in the first place. He learns to recognize and use appropriately linguistic conventions which simultaneously create and disguise him" (p. 288).

For studies of narrative technique and discourse, see also C. B. Morris, *The Unity and Structure of Quevedo's Buscón: "Desgracias encadenadas,"* University of Hull Occasional Papers in Modern Languages, no. 1, 1965; Harry Sieber, "Apostrophes in the *Buscón*: An Approach to Quevedo's Narrative Technique," *MLN* 83 (1968): 178–211; Jenaro Talens, *Novela picaresca y práctica de la transgresión* (Madrid: Ediciones Júcar, 1975), pp. 11–106; Edmond Cros, *L'Aristocrate et le carnaval des gueux: Etude sur le Buscón de Quevedo* (Montpellier: Centre d'Etudes Sociocritiques, 1975), "Fundamentos de una sociocrítica: Presupuestos metodológicos y aplicaciones," *Ideologies and Literature* 1, 3 (1977): 60–68, "Foundations of a Sociocriticism: Methodological Proposals and an Application to the Case of the *Buscón* (Part II)," *Ideologies and Literature* 1, 4 (1977): 63–80, and "Ideología y genética textual en el *Buscón*," *Mester* 9, 2 (1980): 25–38; Anthony N. Zahareas, "Quevedo's *Buscón*: Structure and Ideology," in *Homenaje a Julio Caro Baroja*, ed. Antonio Carreira, et al. (Madrid: Centro de Investigaciones Sociológicas, 1978), pp. 1055–89, and "The Historical Function of Art and Morality in Quevedo's *Buscón*," *Bulletin of Hispanic Studies* 6, 3 (1984): 432–43; and James Iffland, *Quevedo and the Grotesque*, vol. 2 (London: Tamesis, 1982), pp. 76–140. See also Alberto del Monte, *Itinerario de la novela picaresca*, pp. 118–32; Richard Bjornson, *The Picaresque Hero*, pp. 106–26; Peter N. Dunn, *The Spanish Picaresque Novel*, pp. 64–75; Alexander Blackburn, *The Myth of the Pícaro*, pp. 80–92; Arnold Weinstein, *Fictions of the Self*, pp. 31–50; Donald Bleznick, *Francisco de Quevedo* (New York: Twayne Publishers, 1972), esp. pp. 70–92; and Manuel Durán, *Francisco de*

Quevedo (Madrid: EDAF, 1978), esp. pp. 120–34.

34. Francisco de Quevedo, *La vida del Buscón llamado Don Pablos*, ed. Fernando Lázaro Carreter, annot. Juan Alcina Franch (Barcelona: Editorial Juventud, 1968), p. 43. All subsequent quotations from *El Buscón* will refer to this edition. Michael Alpert translates the *Buscón* as *The Swindler* in *Two Spanish Picaresque Novels*.

35. "Vimos los muros de Segovia, y a mí se me alegraron los ojos, a pesar de la memoria, que, con los sucesos de Cabra, me contradecía el contento. Llegué al pueblo y, a la entrada, vi a mi padre en el camino, aguardando ir en bolsas, hecho cuartos, a Josafad [Jehosaphat, the valley in Jerusalem where the Final Judgment will take place]" (p. 136).

36. Critics debate the *Buscón* along two major lines, or schools of thought, associated with Alexander A. Parker and Fernando Lázaro Carreter. Parker believes, "It is impossible to read it correctly without reading it as a profoundly moral story" (*Literature and the Delinquent*, p. 62). Lázaro Carreter, in "Originalidad del *Buscón*," in *Studia Philologica: Homenaje ofrecido a Dámaso Alonso*, vol. 2 (Madrid: Gredos, 1961), pp. 319–38 (reprinted in *Estilo barroco y personalidad creadora*, pp. 109–41), argues that the novel is first and foremost a display of wit, an "obra de ingenio," without a moral purpose. See Parker, "The Psychology of the *Pícaro* in *El Buscón*," *Modern Language Review* 42 (1947): 58–69, and *Literature and the Delinquent*, pp. 56–73; T. E. May, "Good and Evil in the *Buscón*: A Survey," *Modern Language Review* 45 (1950): 319–35; Peter N. Dunn, "El individuo y la sociedad en *La vida del buscón*," *Bulletin Hispanique* 52 (1950): 375–96; Richard Bjornson, "Moral Blindness in Quevedo's *El Buscón*," *Romanic Review* 67 (1976): 50–59; and Elizabeth S. Boyce, "Evidence of Moral Values Implicit in Quevedo's *Buscón*," *Forum for Modern Language Studies* 12 (1976): 336–53, for one side of the polemic. For the other, see Lázaro Carreter, "Glosas críticas a *Los pícaros en la literatura* de Alexander A. Parker," *Hispanic Review* 41 (1973): 469–97 (and Parker's response and Lázaro Carreter's counterresponse in *Hispanic Review* 42 (1974): 235–41); Francisco Rico, *La novela picaresca y el punto de vista*, pp. 120–29; W. M. Frohock, "The *Buscón* and Current Criticism," in *Homenaje a William L. Fichter: Estudios sobre el teatro antiguo hispánico y otros ensayos*, ed. A.

David Kossoff and José Amor y Vásquez (Madrid: Castalia, 1971), pp. 223–27; and for a demystification of Don Diego Coronel as a moral exemplar, Carroll B. Johnson, "El Buscón: Don Pablos, Don Diego y Don Francisco," Hispanófila 51 (1974): 1–26, and Augustín Redondo, "Del personaje de don Diego Coronel a una nueva interpretación de El Buscón," in Actas del Quinto Congreso Internacional de Hispanistas, ed. Maxime Chevalier, et al. (Bordeaux: Presses Universitaires de Bordeaux, 1977), pp. 699–711.

Edwin Williamson maintains that the divergence in critical opinions regarding the Buscón "arises initially, not so much from opposed interpretative standpoints as from certain inconsistencies and problems inherent in the work itself" ("The Conflict between Author and Protagonist," p. 45). Peter N. Dunn reviews the controversy ("not a debate but a mêlée") in "Problems of a Model for the Picaresque and the Case of Quevedo's Buscón," Bulletin of Hispanic Studies 59 (1982): 95–105. In the closing paragraph, he writes, "The prerequisite for interpreting picaresque novels is to forget that they are picaresque, and to suspend judgement on whether or not they are novels; to read them as fictional discourses" (p. 104).

37. For studies that deal with Cela's novel and the picaresque tradition, see Sherman Eoff, "Tragedy of the Unwanted Person in Three Versions: Pablos de Segovia, Pito Pérez, Pascual Duarte," Hispania 39 (1956): 190–96; Gonzalo Sobejano, "Reflexiones sobre 'La familia de Pascual Duarte,'" Papeles de Son Armadans 117 (1968): 19–58; Juan María Marín Martínez, "Sentido último de 'La familia de Pascual Duarte,'" Cuadernos Hispanoamericanos 337 38 (1978): 90–98; Ulrich Wicks, "Onlyman," Mosaic 8 (1975): 21–47; Ignacio Soldevila-Durante, "Utilización de la tradición picaresca por Camilo José Cela," pp. 921–28, and Hortensia Viñes, "Notas para una interpretación de Pascual Duarte: La novela virtual," pp. 929–34, in La picaresca, ed. Manuel Criado de Val. See also Paul Ilie, La novelística de Camilo José Cela (Madrid: Editorial Gredos, 1963), pp. 36–76; Mary Ann Beck, "Nuevo encuentro con 'La familia de Pascual Duarte,'" Revista Hispánica Moderna 30 (1964): 279–98; Robert C. Spires, "Systematic Doubt: The Moral Art of La familia de Pascual Duarte," Hispanic Review 40 (1972): 283–302; Michael D. Thomas, "Narrative Tension and Structural Unity in Cela's La

familia de Pascual Duarte," Symposium 31 (Summer 1977): 165–78; Leon Livingstone, "Ambivalence and Ambiguity in La familia de Pascual Duarte," in Studies in Honor of José Rubia Barcia, ed. Roberta Johnson and Paul C. Smith (Lincoln: Society of Spanish and Spanish-American Studies, 1982), pp. 95–107; Matías Montes-Huidobro, "Dinámica de la correlación existencial en La familia de Pascual Duarte," Revista de Estudios Hispánicos 16 (1982): 213–22; Arnold M. Peñuel, "The Psychology of Cultural Disintegration in Cela's La familia de Pascual Duarte," Revista de Estudios Hispánicos 16 (1982): 361–78; and John W. Kronik, "Pascual's Parole," Review of Contemporary Fiction 4, 3 (1984): 111–19.

38. Camilo José Cela, La familia de Pascual Duarte, ed. Harold L. Boudreau and John W. Kronik (New York: Appleton-Century-Crofts, 1961), p. 4. Subsequent quotations from La familia de Pascual Duarte will refer to this edition. For an English version, see The Family of Pascual Duarte, trans. Anthony Kerrigan (New York: Avon, 1972).

39. "Otra parte hubo que al intentar contarla sentía tan grandes arcadas en el alma que preferí callármela y ahora olvidarla" (p. 6).

40. "En una de las habitaciones dormíamos yo y mi mujer, y en la otra mis padres hasta que Dios, o quién sabe si el diablo, quiso llevárselos; después quedó vacía casi siempre, al principio porque no había quien la ocupase, y más tarde, cuando podía haber habido alguien, porque este alguien prefirió siempre la cocina. . . . Mi hermana, cuando venía, dormía siempre en ella, y los chiquillos, cuando los tuve, también tiraban para allí en cuanto se despegaban de la madre" (p. 14).

41. Cela presents another "reading" of the picaresque in Nuevas andanzas y desventuras de Lazarillo de Tormes (New Wanderings and Misfortunes of Lazarillo de Tormes, 1944). The new Lázaro assays circumstances in Spain prior to the Civil War through his contact with a series of masters and social types. Critics have related the text to its picaresque predecessor and to Cela's later interest in the travelogue. In Forms of the Novel in the Work of Camilo José Cela (Columbia: University of Missouri Press, 1967), David W. Foster notes, "Lázaro is the homo viator who goes out to meet life on its own highways in the tradition of the travelers in the works of Dante, Bunyan, Gracián, and Cervantes" (p. 56). Christopher Eustis sees the temporal

scheme of the narrative as a "concession to the social and political realities of Francoist Spain"; picaresque re-creation takes the form of a shift in emphasis "from a concern with physical survival to a preoccupation with personal identity, individual isolation and the lack of human communication in a chaotic and inhospitable world." See "Politics and the Picaresque in the 20th-Century Spanish Novel," *Revista de Estudios Hispánicos* 18, 2 (1984): 171 (163–82). The nature of his life—and of his discourse—makes Pascual Duarte a more introspective narrator than the reborn Lázaro, participant and spectator in the great theater of the world. The implied author of the *Nuevas andanzas* addresses the world in which he lives through the distancing effects of literature. The conflict between individual and society, so much a part of picaresque narrative, finds a form of expression in Cela's updating of *Lazarillo de Tormes*.

NOTES TO CHAPTER 3:
THE VOICELESS NARRATOR

1. See Barbara F. Weissberger, "'Habla el auctor': *L'Elegia di Madonna Fiammetta* as a Source for the *Siervo libre de amor*," *Journal of Hispanic Philology* 4 (1980): 203–36. The intertext for the feminine variations of the picaresque would include the autobiography of Leonor López de Córdoba, written early in the fifteenth century. See Reinaldo Ayerbe-Chaux, "Las memorias de doña Leonor López de Córdoba," *Journal of Hispanic Philology* 2 (1977): 11–33; Randolph D. Pope, *La autobiografía española hasta Torres Villarroel* (Frankfurt: Peter Lang, 1974), pp. 14–24; and Alan Deyermond, "Spain's First Women Writers," in *Women in Hispanic Literature: Icons and Fallen Idols*, ed. Beth Miller (Berkeley and Los Angeles: University of California Press, 1983), pp. 27–52.

2. Francisco Delicado, *La lozana andaluza*, ed. Bruno Damiani (Madrid: Editorial Castalia, 1969), p. 33. All subsequent quotations from *La lozana andaluza* will refer to this edition, and page numbers will be indicated in parentheses. See Francisco Delicado, *Retrato de la loçana andaluza*, ed. Bruno M. Damiani and Giovanni Allegra (Madrid: Ediciones José Porrúa Turanzas, 1975). M. Louise Salstad treats the narratives discussed in this chapter in *The Presentation of Women in Spanish Golden Age Literature: An Annotated Bibliography* (Boston: G. K. Hall, 1980). For background material in the European con-

text, see Ian MacLean, *The Renaissance Notion of Woman* (Cambridge: Cambridge University Press, 1980).

3. José María Díez Borque, in "Francisco Delicado, autor y personaje de *La lozana andaluza*," *Prohemio* 3 (1972): 455–66; Bruno M. Damiani, in *Francisco Delicado* (New York: Twayne Publishers, 1974); and José A. Hernández Ortiz, in *La génesis artística de La lozana andaluza* (Madrid: Editorial Aguilera, 1974) argue for a moral intention in *La lozana andaluza*. See also Juan Goytisolo, "Notas sobre *La lozana andaluza*," *Triunfo*, no. 689 (10 April 1976): 50–55; and Augusta E. Foley, *Delicado: La Lozana andaluza* (London: Grant and Cutler, 1977).

4. See Bruce W. Wardropper, "La novela como retrato: El arte de Francisco Delicado," *Nueva Revista de Filología Hispánica* 7 (1953): 475–88; and Valeria Scorpioni, "Un ritratto a due facce: *La loçana andaluza* di F. Delicado," *Annali Istituto Universitario Orientale, Napoli: Sezione Romanza* 22 (1980): 441–76. For studies of the portrait with Rome as backdrop, see Segundo Serrano Poncela, "Aldonza la andaluza lozana en Roma," *Cuadernos Americanos* 122 (1962): 117–32, and Lilia Ferrara de Orduna, "Algunas observaciones sobre *La Lozana andaluza*," *Archivum* 23 (1973): 105–15; and for a relation of the portrait to literary theory, see José M. Domínguez, "La teoría literaria en la época de Francisco Delgado [Delicado], c. 1474–c. 1536," *Explicación de Textos Literarios* 6, 1 (1977): 93–96.

5. On the use of the dialogue form, see Claude Allaigre, "A propos des dialogues de la *Lozana andaluza*: La Pelegrina du mamotreto LXIII," in *Essais sur le dialogue*, intro. Jean Lavédrine (Grenoble: Publications de l'Université des Langues et Lettres, 1980), pp. 103–14; and Augusta Espantoso Foley, "Técnica audio-visual del diálogo y retrato de *La lozana andaluza*," in *Actas del Sexto Congreso Internacional de Hispanistas*, ed. Alan M. Gordon and Evelyn Rugg (Toronto: University of Toronto, 1980), pp. 258–60.

6. For views on the role of the author, see Díez Borque, in "Francisco Delicado"; Hernández Ortiz, in *La génesis artística*, esp. pp. 119–27; and Peter N. Dunn, "A Postscript to *La lozana andaluza*: Life and Poetry," *Romanische Forschungen* 88 (1976): 355–60. Addressing himself to a great extent to Delicado himself, as opposed to his textual alter ego, Dunn writes, "The sack of Rome is read in light of a code which is also a the-

odicy: wicked peoples and nations are punished by God in exemplary fashion. Lozana, learning to read the signs of Providence, rewrites her life on the pattern of St. Mary of Egypt: she retires to an island and becomes a pious recluse. For his part, the author protests his serious purpose; afflicted now with disease and the onset of age, he reads his own life and its involvement with Lozana as a sign. All that careless fornication and insouciant indulgence, and the seemingly gratuitous note-taking for the unmotivated 'portrait' of Lozana, appear as if directed by the same finger of Providence which points to the catastrophic punishment that is to come. He writes his book at the convergence of life (his own and Lozana's) and myth" (p. 356).

7. For linguistic considerations of *La lozana andaluza*, see Manuel Criado de Val, "Antífrasis y contaminaciones de sentido erótico en *La lozana andaluza*," in *Studia Philologica: Homenaje ofrecido a Dámaso Alonso*, vol. 1 (Madrid: Editorial Gredos, 1960), pp. 431–57, and Damiani, in the introduction to *Retrato de la loçana andaluza*, esp. pp. 33–51.

8. The title of *mamotreto* 41 begins, "Aquí comienza la tercera parte del retrato, y serán más graciosas cosas que lo pasado" (p. 171).

9. In chapter 31 of Unamuno's novel *Niebla* (*Mist*, 1914), the fictionalized author debates the question of authenticity with the protagonist, Augusto Pérez. In the climactic confrontation, Augusto uses Unamuno's own words against him.

10. Bruno Damiani speaks of a "spirit of the Renaissance" in *La lozana andaluza*. The protagonist "takes pride in asserting her dignity and merit and her right to use the physical and intellectual attributes in full to enjoy what the world has to offer. The concomitant effect of this attribute is the formation of a strong individualism and a notable social amorality. Although this amorality existed without any sense of guilt, in the ethical sense of the word, it created, nevertheless, a milieu for the inevitable disenchantment man felt with worldly things" (*Francisco Delicado*, pp. 90–91).

11. For general studies of *La pícara Justina*, see Marcel Bataillon, *Pícaros y picaresca* (Madrid: Taurus Ediciones, 1969); Bruno M. Damiani, *Francisco López de Ubeda* (New York: Twayne Publishers, 1977); "Aspectos barrocos de *La pícara Justina*," in *Actas del Sexto Congreso Internacional de Hispanistas*, ed. Alan M. Gordon and Evelyn Rugg, pp. 198–

202, and "Notas sobre lo grotesco en *La pícara Justina*," *Romance Notes* 22 (1982): 341–47; Luz Rodríguez, "Aspectos de la primera variante femenina de la picaresca española," *Explicación de Textos Literarios* 8 (1979–1980): 175–81; Antonio Rey Hazas, "La compleja faz de una pícara: Hacia una interpretación de *La pícara Justina*," *Revista de Literatura* 45 (1983): 87–109. Peter N. Dunn treats "The Pícara: The Rogue Female" from *La pícara Justina* to the narratives of Castillo Solórzano in *The Spanish Picaresque Novel* (Boston: Twayne Publishers, 1979), pp. 113–33. See also Thomas Hanrahan, S. J., *La mujer en la novela picaresca española*, vol. 2 (Madrid: José Porrúa Turanzas, 1967), pp. 195–261; Richard Bjornson, *The Picaresque Hero in European Fiction* (Madison: The University of Wisconsin Press, 1977), pp. 87–96; Pablo J. Ronquillo, *Retrato de la pícara: La protagonista de la picaresca española del XVII* (Madrid: Playor, 1980); and José María Alegre, "Las mujeres en el *Lazarillo de Tormes*," *Arbor* 117, 460 (1984): 23–35.

12. [Francisco López de Ubeda,] *La pícara Justina*, ed. Bruno Mario Damiani (Madrid: José Porrúa Turanzas, 1982), pp. 44–45. All subsequent quotations from *La pícara Justina* will refer to this edition.

13. Joseph Jones studies "'Hieroglyphics' in *La pícara Justina*," in *Estudios literarios de hispanistas norteamericanos dedicados a Helmut Hatzfeld con motivo de su ·80 aniversario*, ed. Josep Sola-Solé, Alessandro S. Crisafulli, and Bruno M. Damiani (Barcelona: Hispam, 1974), pp. 415–29. For a study of semantic layering, see Claude Allaigre and René Cotrait, "'La escribana fisgada': Estratos de significación en un pasaje de *La pícara Justina*," in *Hommage des hispanistes français a Noël Salomon*, intro. Henry Bonneville (Barcelona: LAIA, 1979), pp. 27–47.

14. See, respectively, book 2 (first part), chapter 1, number 1, pp. 154–55; book 2 (second part), chapter 1, number 2, pp. 225–26; and book 2 (second part), chapter 4, number 3, pp. 294–96.

15. Bataillon (*Pícaros y picaresca*, esp. pp. 175–99) and Damiani (*Francisco López de Ubeda*, esp. pp. 49–60) discuss the influence of *Guzmán de Alfarache* on *La pícara Justina*. Alexander A. Parker, in *Literature and the Delinquent: The Picaresque Novel in Spain and Europe, 1599–1753* (Edinburgh: The University Press, 1967), states, "It seems to me that Ubeda . . . honestly thought that *Guzmán* was not the way to write a work of entertain-

ment combining pleasure and profit, that a low-life theme should not be treated seriously, and that the tone of realistic fiction should therefore be lowered. Ubeda's extraordinary language can be considered an intentional travesty of the 'low style' in order to counter the solemnity of Alemán. His aim was to make the new *genre* laughable, which is why the title page does not offer the 'Life' of the heroine, but a 'Book of Entertainment' concerning her" (p. 50).

16. Alonso J. de Salas Barbadillo, *La hija de Celestina* [ed. Angel Valbuena Prat], annot. C. Pastor Sanz, published with *Lazarillo de Tormes*, ed. F. Aguilar Piñal (Madrid: Editorial Magisterio Español, S. A., 1967), p. 132. All quotations from *La hija de Celestina* will refer to this edition. For general considerations of the text, see Alessandra Melloni, "Rilievi strutturali sulla *Hija de Celestina* di Salas Barbadillo," *Lingua e Stile* 7 (1972): 261–87; Myron A. Peyton, *Alonso Jerónimo de Salas Barbadillo* (New York: Twayne Publishers, 1973), esp. pp. 55–60; Leonard Brownstein, *Salas Barbadillo and the New Novel of Rogues and Courtiers* (Madrid: Playor, 1974), esp. pp. 79–94; Antonio Rey Hazas, "Novela picaresca y novela cortesana: *La hija de Celestina* de Salas Barbadillo," *Edad de Oro*, vol. 2 (Madrid: Departamento de Literatura, Universidad Autónoma de Madrid, 1983), pp. 137–56. Source and influence studies include Gregory G. LaGrone, "Salas Barbadillo and the *Celestina*," *Hispanic Review* 9 (1941): 440–58, and "Quevedo and Salas Barbadillo," *Hispanic Review* 10 (1942): 223–43; Francisco A. Cauz, *La narrativa de Salas Barbadillo* (Santa Fe, Argentina: Ediciones Colmegna, 1977); and Randall W. Listerman, "*La hija de Celestina*: Tradition and Morality," *Language Quarterly* 22, 1–2 (1983): 52–53, 56.

17. Brownstein notes, "*La hija de Celestina*, although it belongs to the tradition of novels of roguery, reveals Salas' desire . . . to fuse certain principles of poetic literary theory with his prose fiction. His use of the *in medias res* technique, the workings of fate to create *admiratio*, and of situations that lend themselves to moral teaching as well as to pleasure and delight are all apparent" (p. 93).

18. Peter N. Dunn, in *Castillo Solórzano and the Decline of the Spanish Novel* (Oxford: Basil Blackwell, 1952), traces the writer's use of the Italianate convention of the group of travelers or reunion of friends as a motive for storytelling, and notes a shift toward multiple

plots. *Las Harpías en Madrid* (*The Harpies in Madrid*, 1631) exemplifies the tendency toward greater formal complexity, and at the same time it represents the transition between the early collections of stories and the so-called picaresque narratives of Castillo Solórzano. In *Las Harpías*, two mothers and their four daughters undergoing financial difficulties fall under the patronage of an aristocrat, whose coach provides them with a means of carrying out a series of swindles. The four *estafas*, corresponding to each of the four girls and unified by the coach as actant, point to the swindles of the later narratives. See also Alan Soons, *Alonso de Castillo Solórzano* (New York: Twayne Publishers, 1978), and Mireya Pérez-Erdelyi, *La pícara y la dama: la imagen de las mujeres en las novelas picaresco-cortesanas de María de Zayas y Sotomayor y Alonso de Castillo Solórzano* (Miami: Ediciones Universal, 1979). In *The Spanish Picaresque Novel*, Dunn comments, "The novel, in the hands of Castillo Solórzano, becomes material for authorial ingenuity. The autobiographical mode has been abandoned. The plot moves, but in obedience to an urge to keep moving, rather than a sense of design or of truth in representation. There is also a sense of geographical movement, of traveling continually here and there in between adventures" (p. 103).

19. Alonso de Castillo Solórzano, *La niña de los embustes, Teresa de Manzanares, natural de Madrid*, in *Novela picaresca española*, vol. 3, ed. Alonso Zamora Vicente (Barcelona: Editorial Noguer, 1976), p. 138. All subsequent quotations from *Teresa de Manzanares* will refer to this edition.

20. Peter N. Dunn notes the influence of the *novela cortesana* on Salas Barbadillo and Castillo Solórzano in *The Spanish Picaresque Novel*, pp. 120–21 and 127–28.

21. For the text of the *Aventuras del bachiller Trapaza, quintaesencia de embusteros y maestro de embelecadores* (*Adventures of the Bachelor Trapaza, Quintessence of Swindlers and Master of Impostors*), see *Novela picaresca española*, vol. 3, ed. Alonso Zamora Vicente, pp. 311–518.

22. Alonso de Castillo Solórzano, *La garduña de Sevilla y anzuelo de las bolsas*, in *Novela picaresca española*, vol. 3, ed. Alonso Zamora Vicente, p. 706. All subsequent quotations from *La garduña de Sevilla* will refer to this edition.

23. Comparative views of the feminine picaresque include Ann Daghistany, "The

Picara Nature," *Women's Studies* 4 (1977): 51–60; and Julio Rodríguez-Luis, "*Pícaras*: The Modal Approach to the Picaresque," *Comparative Literature* 31 (1979): 32–46. Daghistany observes, "While the picara faces as much adversity as her male counterpart, she encounters it so often in the form of physical menace that the metaphysical meaning is clouded by the stress placed on her immediate surroundings" (p. 59). Following Claudio Guillén (and, to a lesser extent, Ulrich Wicks), Rodríguez-Luis stresses "the socioeconomic ambition of the *pícaro* and the verisimilitude of the genre" (p. 33) as the major criteria for judgment of female figures in European narrative.

NOTES TO CHAPTER 4:
THE ENLIGHTENED NARRATOR

1. This is the thesis of chapter 3 ("The Conversion of the Natural Man") of Alexander Blackburn, *The Myth of the Picaro: Continuity and Transformation of the Picaresque Novel, 1554–1954* (Chapel Hill: The University of North Carolina Press, 1979), pp. 93–144. See also Robert Alter, *Rogue's Progress: Studies in the Picaresque Novel* (Cambridge: Harvard University Press, 1964), pp. 35–57; Alexander A. Parker, *Literature and the Delinquent: The Picaresque Novel in Spain and Europe, 1599–1753* (Edinburgh: The University Press, 1967), pp. 99–110; and Richard Bjornson, *The Picaresque Hero in European Fiction* (Madison: The University of Wisconsin Press, 1977), pp. 188–206.

2. Nicholas Spadaccini addresses the question of *Moll Flanders*'s relation to picaresque narrative in "Daniel Defoe and the Spanish Picaresque Tradition: The Case of *Moll Flanders*," *Ideologies and Literature* 2, 6 (1978): 10–26.

3. Daniel Defoe, *The Fortunes and Misfortunes of the Famous Moll Flanders*, ed. G. A. Starr (Oxford: Oxford University Press, 1981), p. 1. All subsequent quotations from *Moll Flanders* will refer to this edition, and page numbers will be indicated in parentheses.

4. For a less skeptical view of repentance in the novel, see Brean S. Hammond, "Repentance: Solution to the Clash of Moralities in *Moll Flanders*," *English Studies* 61 (1980): 329–37.

5. For perspectives on value systems (including economics) in *Moll Flanders*, see Denis Donoghue, "The Values of *Moll Flan-*

ders," *Sewanee Review* 71 (1963): 287–303; Juliet McMaster, "The Equation of Love and Money in *Moll Flanders*," *Studies in the Novel* 2 (1970): 131–44; John Preston, *The Created Self: The Reader's Role in Eighteenth-Century Fiction* (London: Heinemann, 1970), pp. 8–37; Walter L. Reed, "*Moll Flanders* and the Picaresque: The Transvaluation of Virtue," in *An Exemplary History of the Novel: The Quixotic versus the Picaresque* (Chicago and London: The University of Chicago Press, 1981), pp. 93–116; and Lois A. Chaber, "Matriarchal Mirror: Women and Capital in *Moll Flanders*," *PMLA* 97 (1982): 212–26.

6. The following studies deal with the role of the individual (or individuated) self in *Moll Flanders*: Miriam Lerenbaum, "Moll Flanders: 'A Woman on her own Account,'" in *The Authority of Experience: Essays in Feminist Criticism*, ed. Arlyn Diamond and Lee R. Edwards (Amherst: The University of Massachusetts Press, 1977), pp. 101–17; Jim Springer Borck, "One Woman's Prospects: Defoe's *Moll Flanders* and the Ironies in Restoration Self-Image," *Forum* (Houston) 17, 1 (1979): 10–16; Nancy K. Miller, *The Heroine's Text: Readings in the French and English Novel, 1722–1782* (New York: Columbia University Press, 1980), pp. 3–20; and Arnold Weinstein, *Fictions of the Self: 1550–1800* (Princeton: Princeton University Press, 1981), pp. 84–100. Homer O. Brown uses *Robinson Crusoe* as a basis for comparison of Defoe's narrators in "The Displaced Self in the Novels of Daniel Defoe," *Journal of English Literary History* 38 (1971): 562–90; and Shirlene Mason establishes a typology of women in *Daniel Defoe and the Status of Women* (Montreal: Eden Press Women's Publications, 1978).

7. In "The Two Faces of Moll," *Journal of Narrative Technique* 9 (1979): 117–25, Henry N. Rogers, III, argues that Defoe and Moll Flanders share the same perspective and that the repentance is sincere. For other views on narrative structure in *Moll Flanders*, see Terence Martin, "The Unity of *Moll Flanders*," *Modern Language Quarterly* 22 (1961): 115–24; Robert R. Columbus, "Conscious Artistry in *Moll Flanders*," *Studies in English Literature* 3 (1963): 415–32; Douglas Brooks, "*Moll Flanders*: An Interpretation," *Essays in Criticism* 19 (1969): 46–59; William J. Krier, "'A Courtesy Which Grants Integrity': A Literal Reading of *Moll Flanders*," *Journal of English Literary History* 38 (1971): 397–410; J. A. Michie, "The Unity of *Moll Flanders*," in

Knaves and Swindlers: Essays on the Picaresque Novel in Europe, ed. Christine J. Whitbourn (London: Oxford University Press, 1974), pp. 75–92; and the book-length studies cited below in note 11.

8. Daniel Defoe, *Roxana, the Fortunate Mistress*, ed. Jane Jack (London: Oxford University Press, 1964), p. 1. All subsequent quotations from *Roxana* will refer to this edition.

9. Roxana remarks, "I cou'd not hear this without being sensibly touch'd with it; I was asham'd that he shou'd show that he had more real Affection for the Child, tho' he had never seen it in his Life, than I that bore it; for indeed, I did not love the Child, nor love to see it; and tho' I had provided for it, yet I did it by *Amy*'s Hand, and had not seen it above twice in four Years; being privately resolv'd that when it grew up, it shou'd not be able to call me Mother" (p. 228); and "It is with a just Reproach to myself, that I must repeat it again, that I had not the same Concern for it, tho' it was the Child of my own Body; nor had I ever the hearty affectionate Love to the Child, that he had; what the reason of it was, I cannot tell; and indeed, I had shown a general Neglect of the Child, thro' all the gay Years of my *London* Revels; except that I sent *Amy* to look upon it now and then, and to pay for its Nursing; as for me, I scarce saw it four times in the first four Years of its Life, and often wish'd it wou'd go quietly out of the World" (p. 263).

10. Ralph E. Jenkins offers a different reading of the ending of *Roxana* in "The Structure of *Roxana*," *Studies in the Novel* 2 (1970): 145–58, in which he justifies the brevity of the final paragraph. For additional perspectives on the novel, see Robert D. Hume, "The Conclusion of Defoe's *Roxana*: Fiasco or Tour de Force?," *Eighteenth-Century Studies* 3 (1970): 475–90; C. R. Kropf, "Theme and Structure in Defoe's *Roxana*," *Studies in English Literature* 12 (1972): 467–80; Wallace Jackson, "*Roxana* and the Development of Defoe's Fiction," *Studies in the Novel* 7 (1975): 181–94; Steven Cohan, "Other Bodies: Roxana's Confession of Guilt," *Studies in the Novel* 8 (1976): 406–18; and David Durant, "Roxana's Fictions," *Studies in the Novel* 13 (1981): 225–36.

11. Anne Robinson Taylor, in "This Beautiful Lady Whose Words He Speaks: Defoe and His Female Masquerades," in *Male Novelists and Their Female Voices: Literary Masquerades* (Troy, New York: The Whitson

Publishing Company, 1981), pp. 29–55, studies the differences in narrative voice in *Moll Flanders* and *Roxana* as compared with Defoe's male protagonists: "The female voice is the most congenial disguise through which Defoe can take extremely personal risks, risks not congruent with his ideal of masculinity. As Crusoe and Colonel Jack he felt a social pressure to present to the world a thoroughly idealized male. At the rhetorical level the male voice is primarily a means of asserting the necessity of moral, practical, and spiritual choices. The will is everything. Defoe's women are much more clearly vehicles for self-exploration, exploration of both wishes and fears. Less constrained by their sexual identity, he has created more interesting, more complex human beings when he writes as a woman. . . . Writing as a woman he can take these risks and as a man deny that he has taken them" (p. 50).

Possible points of departure for the critical polemics concerning Defoe are Dorothy Van Ghent, *The English Novel: Form and Function* (New York: Rinehart, 1953), and Ian Watt, *The Rise of the Novel* (Berkeley and Los Angeles: University of California Press, 1957). Numerous essays dedicate themselves to questions of irony posed in the two studies; see, for example, Howard L. Koonce, "Moll's Muddle: Defoe's Use of Irony in *Moll Flanders*," *Journal of English Literary History* 30 (1963): 377–94, which seeks to disprove Watt's notion that there is no ironic structure of any kind in *Moll Flanders*. For extended treatment of Defoe's narratives, including *Moll Flanders* and *Roxana*, see G. A. Starr, *Defoe and Spiritual Autobiography* (Princeton: Princeton University Press, 1965), esp. pp. 126–83, and *Defoe and Casuistry* (Princeton: Princeton University Press, 1971), esp. pp. 111–89; E. Anthony James, *Daniel Defoe's Many Voices: A Rhetorical Study of Prose Style and Literary Method* (Amsterdam: Rodopi, 1972), esp. pp. 201–53; Everett Zimmerman, *Defoe and the Novel* (Berkeley and Los Angeles: University of California Press, 1975), esp. pp. 75–106 and 155–87; John J. Richetti, *Defoe's Narratives: Situations and Structures* (Oxford: Clarendon Press, 1975), esp. pp. 94–144 and 192–232; David Blewett, *Defoe's Art of Fiction* (Toronto: University of Toronto Press, 1979), esp. pp. 55–92 and 116–45; Maximillian E. Novak, *Realism, Myth, and History in Defoe's Fiction* (Lincoln and London: University of Nebraska Press, 1983), esp. pp. 71–120; and Michael M.

Boardman, *Defoe and the Uses of Narrative* (New Brunswick: Rutgers University Press, 1983), esp. pp. 97–155.

NOTES TO CHAPTER 5:
THE OBLIGING NARRATOR

1. John J. Richetti, "The Portrayal of Women in Restoration and Eighteenth-century English Literature," in *What Manner of Woman: Essays on English and American Life and Literature*, ed. Marlene Springer (New York: New York University Press, 1977), p. 88.

2. In *Women and Fiction: Feminism and the Novel, 1880–1920* (New York: Barnes and Noble, 1979), Patricia Stubbs notes, "From Samuel Richardson in the eighteenth century up to the present day, beneath the shifts and changes in attitude which have undoubtedly taken place towards women, there is a fundamental continuity which firmly places them in a private domestic world where emotions and personal relationships are at once the focus of moral value and the core of women's experience. In the novel women are 'prisoners' of feeling and of private life. . . . Increasingly confined to the home, it was they who became the focus of the new value which was placed on private experience once the public 'outer' world of production was stripped of its satisfactions by industrialization and the division of labor" (pp. 228–29). See also Bridget Aldaraca, "*El angel del hogar*: The Cult of Domesticity in Nineteenth-century Spain," in *Theory and Practice of Feminist Literary Criticism*, ed. Gabriela Mora and Karen S. Van Hooft (Ypsilanti, Michigan: Bilingual Press/Editorial Bilingüe, 1982), pp. 62–87.

3. Wayne C. Booth, *A Rhetoric of Irony* (Chicago: The University of Chicago Press, 1974), pp. 10–11.

4. Booth's classification of ironies in *A Rhetoric of Irony*, esp. pp. 233–37, uses as a point of departure the categories of D. C. Muecke in *The Compass of Irony* (London: Methuen, 1969). Muecke speaks of three grades of irony: overt, covert, and private. Galdós's thesis novels, often called the novels of the first period, include *Doña Perfecta* (1876), *Gloria* (1877), and *La familia de León Roch* (*The Family of León Roch*, 1878).

5. David I. Grossvogel, "Buñuel's Obsessed Camera: Tristana Dismembered," *Diacritics* 2 (Spring 1972): 53 (51–56). The article compares Galdós's narrative technique with Luis Buñuel's style in his film version of *Tristana* (1970). See Theodore A. Sackett, "Creation and Destruction of Personality in *Tristana*: Galdós and Buñuel," ' *Anales Galdosianos*, supp. (1978): 71–90; and Beth Miller, "From Mistress to Murderess: The Metamorphosis of Buñuel's *Tristana*," in *Women in Hispanic Literature: Icons and Fallen Idols*, ed. Beth Miller (Berkeley and Los Angeles: University of California Press, 1983), pp. 340–59. Vernon Chamberlin uses a musical paradigm in "*Tristana*: Sonata Form and Narrative Transformation," *Kentucky Romance Quarterly* 31, 2 (1984): 197–205.

6. Grossvogel, "Buñuel's Obsessed Camera," p. 57.

8. See Benito Pérez Galdós, *Tristana* (Madrid: Alianza Editorial, 1969), p. 7: "En el populoso barrio de Chamberí, más cerca del Depósito de aguas que de Cuatro Caminos, vivía no ha muchos años un hidalgo de buena estampa y nombre peregrino, no aposentado en casa solariega, pues por allí no las hubo nunca, sino en plebeyo cuarto de alquiler de los baratitos, con ruidoso vecindario de taberna, merendero, cabrería y estrecho patio interior de habitaciones numeradas. La primera vez que tuve conocimiento de tal personaje y pude observar su catadura militar de antiguo cuño, algo así como una reminiscencia pictórica de los tercios de Flandes, dijéronme que se llamaba *don Lope de Sosa*, nombre que trasciende al polvo de los teatros o a romance de los que traen los librillos de retórica; y, en efecto, nombrábanle así algunos amigos maleantes; pero él respondía por don Lope Garrido." All subsequent quotations from *Tristana* will refer to this edition, and page numbers will be indicated in parentheses.

9. Tristana says, "Ahora me parece a mí que si de niña me hubiesen enseñado el dibujo, hoy sabría yo pintar y podría ganarme la vida y ser independiente con mi honrado trabajo. Pero mi pobre mamá no pensó más que en darme la educación insustancial de las niñas que aprenden para llevar un buen yerno a casa, a saber: un poco de piano, el indispensable barniz de francés y qué sé yo..., tonterías" (p. 76; Now it seems to me that if I had been taught drawing when I was a child, today I would know how to paint, and I could earn a living and could be independent with my honorable work. But my poor mother didn't know any better than to give me the unsubstantial education that taught girls what was necessary to bring home a good son-in-law: namely, a little bit of piano,

the indispensable smattering of French, and whatever, just nonsense). See Ruth A. Schmidt, "Tristana and the Importance of Opportunity," Anales Galdosianos 9 (1974): 137 (135–44); and Frank Durand, "Two Problems in Galdós' Tormento," MLN 79 (1964): 514–15 (513–25), for considerations of Galdós's representation of the education of women.

10. See Gonzalo Sobejano, "Galdós y el vocabulario de los amantes," Anales Galdosianos 1 (1966): 85–100. According to Sobejano, chapters 14 through 21 of Tristana constitute an exercise in the exploration of amorous language which reaches a level that no nineteenth-century writer—not even Galdós in his other works—can match (p. 86).

11. See Schmidt, "Tristana and the Importance of Opportunity," p. 138: "The one career woman whom Tristana meets does not fit into the three careers outlined by Saturna. Doña Malvina, an English woman who becomes Tristana's tutor in the English language, is described as a former sacerdota protestanta of the capilla evangélica who was forced to take up a second career when 'le cortaron los víveres.' It should be noted in passing that this one example in the book of a woman earning her own living is of a non-Spanish person whose two careers would generally be unavailable to a Spanish woman like Tristana—that of a Protestant minister and a teacher of English."

12. Emilia Pardo Bazán, "Tristana," in Nuevo Teatro Crítico, vol. 2, no. 17 (May 1892), pp. 77–90. Rather than pursue the idea of the awakening of consciousness in a woman roused to rebellion via Galdós's trajectory, Pardo Bazán allows her preoccupation with what Galdós might have done to overshadow what he has done.

13. Leon Livingstone, "The Law of Nature and Women's Liberation in Tristana," Anales Galdosianos 7 (1972): 93–100.

14. Ibid., pp. 93–97. Livingstone sees the ending in marriage as a restoration of natural harmony: "If their union was initially a violation of nature because of the disparity between them in age and experience, the maturing of Tristana and her physical suffering—which have aged her to the point that although only twenty-five she now looks forty—conveniently annul this imbalance" (p. 98). For this reading, the disparities as well as the irony of the marriage need to be ignored, and the partners must be seen as "comparable and compatible (but different) equals" in a union that "constitutes a positive

force in the onward movement of society" (p. 99). Livingstone calls on the reader to accept the supposition that one must adhere to society's criteria, here intimately connected with the law of nature, as being higher than the individuals who create (and precede) them. The reader must accept, as well, the possibility that a woman may be subservient yet maintain her dignity in this paradoxical separate-but-equal system. And, finally, the reader must accept—in an analysis based on the condemnation of excesses—that the most exemplary character is Don Lope.

For Sherman Eoff, in The Novels of Pérez Galdós: The Concept of Life as Dynamic Process (St. Louis: Washington University Studies, 1954), Tristana "exemplifies Galdós' interest in the 'inexorable law of adaptation'" (p. 50). In an earlier article, "The Treatment of Individual Personality in Fortunata y Jacinta," Hispanic Review 17 (1949): 269–89, Eoff emphasizes, "In the author's opinion the basic requisite for morality is first of all to be true to oneself" (p. 283), a concept which he disregards in the discussion of Tristana. According to Joaquín Casalduero in Vida y obra de Galdós, 3d ed. rev. (Madrid: Editorial Gredos, 1970), pp. 104–08, Tristana demonstrates Galdós's belief in the submission of woman to man by nature, a belief based on reading of antifeminist material. Tristana's failure is nothing more than a discovery of this natural law (which strongly resembles social law, despite Casalduero's distinction). Carmen Bravo-Villasante, in Galdós visto por sí mismo (Madrid: Colección Novelas y Cuentos, 1970), pp. 118–23, sees 1895 and the premiere of Voluntad as the beginning of Galdós's sympathy for women. But can Galdós's worldview and his system of values really be judged in terms of a pre–1895 set of beliefs versus a post–1895 set? And can an antifeminist bias be seen in the works prior to 1895? In "Tristana o la imposibilidad del ser," Cuadernos Hispanoamericanos 250–52 (1970–1971): 505–22, Emilio Miró attempts to show that woman must be submissive, faithful, and humble because if she were emancipated, independent, and free, the familial structure—and ultimately that of the state and society at large—would be destroyed. Carlos Feal Deibe, in "Tristana de Galdós: capítulo en la historia de la liberación femenina," Sin Nombre 7, 3 (1976): 116–29, attributes Tristana's idealistic propensities to José Ortega y Gasset's belief that the impossibility of fulfilling a desire leads to dependence on the ideal—that the glorious ideal supplants the adverse real. Though the direction is somewhat different, the conclusion—that the individual must always submit to higher forces—resembles those of Casalduero, Livingstone, and Miró.

In "Resistance and Rebellion in *Tristana*," *MLN* 91 (1976): 277–91, John H. Sinnigen compares *Tristana* to other novels in which Galdós presents an "outsider-society duality" and concludes that Tristana's failure stems from an inadequate vision of the society against whose conventions she is rebelling. And yet one wonders what success Tristana could have achieved if she had had a more accurate vision of society and of her role as dissenter. Sinnigen considers Don Lope, Horacio, and Tristana to be social rebels. Perhaps Don Lope, on the one hand, in his desire for a return to a former hierarchy, is, rather, the antithesis of a rebel, a retrogressive force in society. His marriage to Tristana has nothing to do with social consciousness; he has merely found one more sacred institution to mock. Horacio, on the other hand, never justifies Tristana's faith in him. Intrigued by Tristana's ideology and her physical presence, he condescends to her principles while consistently betraying his conventionality. His reaction to a repressive adolescence differs from Tristana's because his possibilities have not been destroyed as have hers. Don Lope, a symbol of the past, and Horacio, a symbol of the status quo, make Tristana a solitary rebel.

15. Germán Gullón, "*Tristana*: Literaturización y estructura novelesca," *Hispanic Review* 45 (1977): 27 (13–27).

16. Michael Nimetz, *Humor in Galdós* (New Haven: Yale University Press, 1968), p. 91. See Maryellen Bieder, "Capitulation: Marriage, not Freedom, A Study of Emilia Pardo Bazán's *Memorias de un solterón* and Galdós' *Tristana*," *Symposium* 30 (1976): 93–109, which views each of the works as a parody of conventional marriage; the humor in *Memorias de un solterón* is satiric, in *Tristana* ironic. Bieder's model for irony is Nimetz.

17. Marina Mayoral, in "Tristana: ¿una feminista galdosiana?," *Insula* 320–21 (July-August 1973): 28, notes that if Tristana had not become ill, if her leg had not been amputated, she would have achieved her goals ("Tristana se hubiera salido con la suya"). Depending in part on an unpublished dissertation by Elizabeth T. Stout ("Women in the Novels of Benito Pérez Galdós," University of New Mexico, 1953, esp. pp. 7–8), Ruth Schmidt draws the same conclusion ("Tris-

tana and the Importance of Opportunity," p. 137).

18. John H. Sinnigen, "Individual, Class, and Society in *Fortunata y Jacinta*," in *Galdós Studies II*, ed. Robert J. Weber (London: Tamesis, 1974), p. 66 (49–68).

19. Stephen Gilman, "The Consciousness of Fortunata," *Anales Galdosianos* 5 (1970): 59 (55–66).

20. See Roberto G. Sánchez, "Galdós' *Tristana*, Anatomy of a 'Disappointment,'" *Anales Galdosianos* 12 (1977): 121 (110–27): "To be sure, Galdós was sympathetic to the plight of Spanish women. He seems to acknowledge the injustice in the circumstances that barred Tristana from being a lawyer, doctor or minister, but he is more concerned with her personal quandary (her yearnings and her doubts) and with the way men would take to her and she to them. The world of feminine emotions had always fascinated Galdós and in Tristana's rebellion he heard discordant voices that held his attention. He was no longer the liberal reformer who would protest against injustice explicitly; his message could only come through in an implicit manner; any thesis must now succumb to the drama of his fictional characters."

21. Booth, *A Rhetoric of Irony*, p. 11. In "Art, Memory, and the Human in Galdós' *Tristana*," *Kentucky Romance Quarterly* 31, 2 (1984): 207–20, Noël Valis—who calls the narrative voice "a subject for another study" —notes "the frequent air of complicity between the narrator and Don Lope (paralleling somewhat the later collusion between Don Lope and Horacio) as both take on the same knowing and paternalistic attitude toward Tristana—and this despite the fact that the narrator just as often twits the decaying Lothario in other passages, thus demonstrating once more the ambiguous tonalities of distance and engagement within this sadly ironic novel" (p. 217). Irony, and ironic readings, may have many faces. See also Diane F. Urey, *Galdós and the Irony of Language* (Cambridge: Cambridge University Press, 1982); the analysis covers a number of Galdós's "contemporary novels" but does not include *Tristana*.

NOTES TO CHAPTER 6: THE MARGINATED NARRATOR

1. Charles M. Tatum notes a connection between Poniatowska's narrative and what may be termed the picaresque situation, operating at the levels of plot and social context,

in "Elena Poniatowska's *Hasta no verte, Jesús Mío [Until I See You, Dear Jesus]*," in *Latin American Women Writers: Yesterday and Today*, ed. Charles M. Tatum and Yvette E. Miller (Pittsburgh: Latin American Literary Review, 1977), pp. 49–58.

2. See Victor Erlich, *Russian Formalism*, 3d ed. (New Haven and London: Yale University Press, 1981), pp. 240–42.

3. Joel Hancock treats the compositional process in "Elena Poniatowska's *Hasta no verte Jesús mío*: The Remaking of the Image of Woman," *Hispania* 66 (1983): 353–59. See also Beth Miller, "Interview with Elena Poniatowska," *Latin American Literary Review* 7 (1975): 73–78, published in an expanded form and in Spanish in *26 autoras del México actual*, ed. Beth Miller and Alfonso González (Mexico City: Costa-Amic, 1978), pp. 301–21; Beth Miller, "Personajes y personas: Castellanos, Fuentes, Poniatowska y Sainz," in *Mujeres en la literatura* (Mexico City: Fleischer, 1978), pp. 65–75; Lucía Fox-Lockert, "Elena Poniatowska," *Women Novelists of Spain and Spanish America* (Metuchen, New Jersey: Scarecrow Press, 1979), pp. 260–77; and Ronald Christ, "The Author as Editor," *Review* (New York) 15 (1975): 78–79. Christ discusses the author/narrator relationship in the English translation of *La noche de Tlatelolco*.

4. Elena Poniatowska, *Hasta no verte Jesús mío* (Mexico City: Ediciones Era, 1969), p. 13. All subsequent quotations from *Hasta no verte Jesús mío* will refer to this edition, and page numbers will be indicated in parentheses.

5. See Hancock, "Remaking of the Image of Woman," p. 357: "The extensive range of Jesusa's verbal communication—expressing protest, anger, tenderness, approval, and humor—is reinforced by her use of language. She is capable of uttering the most abusive insults as well as revealing, with moving sensitivity, innermost feelings. Her vocabulary exhibits a lexical diversity incorporating regionalisms and colloquialisms, as well as words that are of Indian origin, archaic, or simply invented. It is a language which, like her personality, contradicts notions of what is 'feminine' expression."

6. The list of books published by Ediciones Era and listed at the end of the text includes essays, novels and short stories, poetry, and accounts (*testimonios*). *Hasta no verte Jesús mío* is classified as a novel, while Poniatowska's *La noche de Tlatelolco* and *Palabras cruzadas* are listed under *testimonios*.

7. In "Jesusa Palancares y la dialéctica de la emancipación femenina," *Hispamérica* 10, 30 (1981): 131–35, Monique LeMaître sees Jesusa's struggle as a resistance that marks the first stage of revolution.

NOTES TO CHAPTER 7: THE MYTHIC NARRATOR

1. The epigraph—"Peste, fome e guerra, morte e amor, / a vida de Tereza Batista é uma história de cordel" ("Plague, famine, war; love and death, / Tereza Batista's life is a ballad to sing in the streets")—leads Mark J. Curran to view the novel as a stylized form of Brazilian popular literature, the *literatura de cordel*. The five sections correspond to five pamphlets or *folhetos*. See *Jorge Amado e a Literatura de Cordel* (Salvador: Fundação Cultural do Estado da Bahia; Fundação Casa de Rui Barbosa, 1981), esp. pp. 51–87. Amado's interest in popular literature is evident in his commentaries on writing. See, for example, "Discurso de Posse na Academia Brasileira" and "Carta a uma Leitora sôbre Romance e Personagens," in Amado, et al., *Jorge Amado, Povo e Terra: 40 anos de literatura* (São Paulo: Martins, 1972), pp. 3–22 and 23–36; and "*PW* Interviews: Jorge Amado," *Publisher's Weekly* (23 June 1975): 20–21.

2. See Jorge Amado, *Tereza Batista cansada de guerra* (São Paulo: Martins, 1972), pp. 126–27: "Nem sequer imaginava pudessem tais coisas conter alegria, reciprocidade no prazer ou simplesmente prazer—sendo Tereza apenas vaso onde descarregar-se o capitão, nela vertendo seu desejo como vertia urina no penico." All subsequent quotations from *Tereza Batista* will refer to this edition; the English translations are by Barbara Shelby, in *Tereza Batista, Home from the Wars* (New York: Avon Books, 1977). Page numbers will be indicated in parentheses.

3. Using a concept discussed by Fredric Jameson, Daphne Patai focuses on *Tereza Batista* in "Jorge Amado's Heroines and the Ideological Double Standard," in *Women in Latin American Literature: A Symposium*, ed. Martha Paley Francescato, Daphne Patai, and Ellen McCracken (University of Massachusetts at Amherst Program in Latin American Studies Occasional Papers, Series No. 10, 1979), pp. 15–36. The double standard refers to literary works that pretend to abhor violence while exploiting the reader's vicarious pleasure in violence. For Patai, Amado's "offense" is, first, the inference that male dominance is acceptable as long as women's sexual

desires are satisfied and, secondly, the excessive (and exploitative) use of scenes of brutality against women. Patai expands the analysis in "Jorge Amado: Morals and Marvels," in *Myth and Ideology in Contemporary Brazilian Fiction* (Cranbury, New Jersey: Associated University Presses, 1983), pp. 111–40.

NOTES TO CHAPTER 8: THE PRECOCIOUS NARRATOR

1. Erica Jong, *Fanny, Being the True History of the Adventures of Fanny Hackabout-Jones* (New York: New American Library, 1980), p. 3. All subsequent quotations from *Fanny* will refer to this edition, and page numbers will be indicated in parentheses.

2. Anthony Burgess writes of Jong's enterprise in a critique in *Saturday Review* (August 1980): "A few critics will condemn what she has done because the writing of 18th-century literature is the task of 18th-century men and possibly women, and there is nothing to add to that. The romantic movement began with a pastiche of the past—the Rowley and Macpherson fabrications—but also with *The Ancient Mariner*, which used the vocabulary and metric of the old ballads. Most of our best-selling novelists write, because they know no better, in a calcified Victorian style. But Bernard Malamud, with *The Fixer*, wrote a 19th-century Russian novel that literature needed, and Ms. Jong may be said to have filled a gap in the great tradition of the picaresque novel. *Fanny* . . . had to be written, and Erica Jong was the right hermaphrodite to write or endite it. I am delighted to belong to her sex" (p. 55). One of the condemnatory critics is Susan Dworkin, whose review appears in *Ms.* (November 1980): "I suspect that the reason I preferred Fanny on her arse to Fanny Ascendant was that in these instances, the wise self-mockery of the true author shone through. The 18th century may be fun to Jong, but to this reader, it was just a dummy sitting on her knee and I only really relished those parts of the book when I could see her lips move" (p. 45). Julia M. Klein, in *The New Republic* (20 September 1980), notes a similarity between life and art: "Fanny's gift for love, hitherto wasted on men, is ignited by her child. When a puritanical wet-nurse steals the baby away, Fanny . . . is willing to brave pirates and perverts to find her. During her quest, after discarding her disguise as a man, she finally sheds the incapacities of her sex, by cropping her hair short, mastering the pi-

rate arts, and making love to another woman. Liberation at last. In the end, as form dictates, home and hearth beckon. But the new identity Fanny will assume includes a fusion which the immature Isadora of Jong's previous fiction could never accomplish. For Isadora, personal happiness and art were incompatible. Fanny, too, wonders whether art and motherhood, procreation and artistic creation, are mutually exclusive. But in *Fanny*, and through *Fanny*, Jong—who gave birth to a baby while she was writing this book—hints at a reconciliation of the two" (pp. 39–40).

3. John Cleland, *Memoirs of Fanny Hill*, intro. J. H. Plumb (New York: New American Library, 1965), p. 219.

4. William H. Epstein, in *John Cleland: Images of a Life* (New York and London: Columbia University Press, 1974), notes a shared interest in the "woman question" between *Fanny Hill*, *Pamela*, and the anti-*Pamela* novels. He considers Fanny's tone burlesque and ironic, and that her adventures—both experimental and narrative—capture this spirit: "Underlying Fanny's use of any formal system of philosophy is her quite pedestrian preoccupation with the superficiality of the world of quality. Behind all her attempts to develop a philosophy and a life style based on natural beauty is her recognition that a life of aristocratic luxury, the ultimate wishfulfillment of most men and women, is finally corrupt and debilitating" (p. 103). In *The Heroine's Text: Readings in the French and English Novel, 1722–1782* (New York: Columbia University Press, 1980), pp. 51–66, Nancy K. Miller sees a significant development from *Pamela* to *Fanny Hill*: "The disastrous downward curve of the harlot's progress is, in the final analysis, averted, indeed reversed, in favor of the 'happy end' of virtue rewarded. As she had wished in the beginning, Fanny reaps Pamela's recompense: she moves from rags to riches, the bottom of the social ladder to the top. Such is the telic power of the structure of ascent in the English novel" (p. 65).

5. In Margaret Atwood's *The Handmaid's Tale* (Boston: Houghton Mifflin, 1986), an inversion of Jong's formula, the future is a nightmarish realm in which women have been forced into servitude. The female inhabitants of the Republic of Gilead answer to a super-reactionary hierarchy and to the biological needs of male society. Those who disobey become "Unwomen" and are exiled "to the Colonies." Offred (of Fred), the narra-

tor/protagonist, describes her current life and ponders the unknown while reflecting on her earlier existence and lost freedom. The author makes Offred's text part of a scholarly inquiry into monotheocracies, recorded at a symposium in the year 2195. The implied author, who "reads as a woman," offers an ironic warning to readers about to live this narrative past.

NOTES TO CHAPTER 9:
READING AS A PERSON

1. See "Augustine: Words as Signs," in Stanley E. Fish, *Self-Consuming Artifacts: The Experience of Seventeenth-Century Literature* (Berkeley: University of California Press, 1972), pp. 21–43.

2. Bruce W. Wardropper treats the contrast in women's roles in the comic and serious dramas of Golden Age Spain in *La comedia española del Siglo de Oro*, published with Elder Olson, *Teoría de la comedia*, trans. Salvador Oliva and Manuel Espín (Barcelona: Editorial Ariel, 1978), esp. pp. 225ff. In comedy, male authors use female characters to mock social institutions and social myths. The women gain in fiction what eludes them in reality. Once married, they enter the domain of men (and of tragic drama).

3. Rachel M. Brownstein, *Becoming a Heroine: Reading About Women in Novels* (New York: The Viking Press, 1982), p. xxii.

4. After examining novels from Richardson to Virginia Woolf, Brownstein concludes, "The beautiful personal integrity the novel heroine imagines and stands for and seeks for herself is a version of the romantic view of woman as a desired object; as the image of the integral self, she is the inverted image of half of a couple. The literary associations that halo the heroine keep her in a traditional woman's place. The self-awareness which distinguishes her from the simple heroine of romance ends by implicating her further in fictions of the feminine" (p. 295). In the epilogue to *The Heroine's Text: Readings in the French and English Novel, 1722–1782* (New York: Columbia University Press, 1980), Nancy K. Miller argues, "The plots of these feminocentric fictions are of course neither female in impulse or origin, nor feminist in spirit. In the final analysis, moreover, despite their titles and their feminine 'I,' it is not altogether clear to me that these novels are about or for women at all" (p. 149).

5. Mary Anne Ferguson, "The Female Novel of Development and the Myth of Psyche," in *The Voyage In: Fictions of Female Development*, ed. Elizabeth Abel, Marianne Hirsch, and Elizabeth Langland (Hanover, New Hampshire, and London: University Press of New England, 1983), pp. 228–29 (228–43). Ferguson continues, "Perceived as part of nature, women in most novels are presented as incapable of autonomy and integrity. They simply *are*, their existence a part of the world that men test in their own search. The view of women as passive has been integral to the male novel of development. Most women authors have shared this view of women and have represented female characters either as finding satisfaction within their limited development in the domestic sphere or as expressing their dissatisfaction through various self-destructive means" (p. 229).

6. Diana Trilling, "The Liberated Heroine," *Partisan Review* 45 (1978): 506 (501–22).

7. Among the studies that examine men's versus women's language and questions of expression for women are Robin Lakoff, *Language and Woman's Place* (New York: Harper and Row, 1975); Casey Miller and Kate Swift, *Words and Women* (New York: Anchor Press/Doubleday, 1976); Cheris Kramarae, *Women and Men Speaking* (Rowley, Massachusetts: Newbury House Publishers, 1981); Lynn Sukenick, "On Women and Fiction," in *The Authority of Experience: Essays in Feminist Criticism*, ed. Arlyn Diamond and Lee R. Edwards (Amherst: The University of Massachusetts Press, 1977), pp. 28–44; Elaine Showalter, "Feminist Criticism in the Wilderness," in *Writing and Sexual Difference*, ed. Elizabeth Abel (Chicago: The University of Chicago Press, 1982), pp. 9–35; Jean Bethke Elshtain, "Feminist Discourse and Its Discontents: Language, Power, and Meaning," in *Feminist Theory: A Critique of Ideology*, ed. Nannerl O. Keohane, Michelle Z. Rosaldo, and Barbara C. Gelpi (Chicago: The University of Chicago Press, 1982), pp. 127–45; Joanna Russ, *How to Suppress Women's Writing* (Austin: University of Texas Press, 1983); and Nelly Furman, "The Politics of Language: Beyond the Gender Principle," in *Making a Difference: Feminist Literary Criticism*, ed. Gayle Greene and Coppélia Kahn (London and New York: Methuen, 1985), pp. 59–79.

8. Representative studies of female consciousness and feminist criticism include Judith Kegan Gardiner, "On Female Identity

and Writing by Women," in *Writing and Sexual Difference*, ed. Elizabeth Abel, pp. 177–91; Myra Jehlen, "Archimedes and the Paradox of Feminist Criticism," in *Feminist Theory: A Critique of Ideology*, ed. Nannerl O. Keohane, et al., pp. 189–215; Annette Barnes, "Female Criticism: A Prologue," in *The Authority of Experience*, ed. Arlyn C. Diamond and Lee R. Edwards, pp. 1–15; Mary Jacobus, "The Difference of View," in *Women Writing and Writing About Women*, ed. Mary Jacobus (New York: Harper and Row, 1979), pp. 10–21, and "The Question of Language: Men of Maxims and *The Mill on the Floss*," in *Writing and Sexual Difference*, pp. 37–52; Margaret R. Higonnet, introduction to *The Representation of Women in Fiction*, ed. Carolyn G. Heilbrun and Margaret R. Higonnet (Baltimore and London: The Johns Hopkins University Press, 1983), pp. xiii–xxii; Annette Kolodny, "Some Notes on Defining a 'Feminist Literary Criticism,'" *Critical Inquiry* 2 (1975): 75–92, and "A Map for Rereading: Or, Gender and the Interpretation of Literary Texts," *New Literary History* 11 (1980): 451–67; Elaine Showalter, "Toward a Feminist Poetics," in *Women Writing and Writing About Women*, pp. 22–41; Stuart Cunningham, "Some Problems of Feminist Literary Criticism," *Journal of Women's Studies in Literature* 1 (1979): 159–78; Sandra Gilbert, "What Do Feminist Critics Want?, or A Postcard from the Volcano," *ADE Bulletin* 66 (1980): 16–24; Jonathan Culler, "Reading as a Woman," in *On Deconstruction: Theory and Criticism after Structuralism* (Ithaca: Cornell University Press, 1982), pp. 43–64; Terry Eagleton, *Literary Theory: An Introduction* (Minneapolis: University of Minnesota Press, 1983), esp. pp. 142–50, 187–91, and 194–217; and Shoshana Felman, "Rereading Femininity," pp. 19–44, Gayatri Chakravorty Spivak, "French Feminism in an International Frame," pp. 154–84, Elissa Gelfand, "Imprisoned Women: Toward a Socio-Literary Feminist Analysis," pp. 185–203, Naomi Schor, "Female Paranoia: The Case for Psychoanalytic Feminist Criticism," pp. 204–19, Alice Jardine, "Pre-Texts for the Transatlantic Feminist," pp. 220–36, *Yale French Studies* 62 (1981); and Sneja Gunew, "Feminist Criticism: Positions and Questions," *Southern Review* 16, 1 (1983): 151–60.

Selected Bibliography

PRIMARY TEXTS

Alpert, Michael, trans. *Two Spanish Picaresque Novels*. [*Lazarillo de Tormes, El Buscón*.] Middlesex, England: Penguin Books, 1969.

Amado, Jorge. *Tereza Batista cansada de guerra*. São Paulo: Martins, 1972.

──────. *Tereza Batista, Home from the Wars*. Translated by Barbara Shelby. New York: Avon Books, 1977.

Castillo Solórzano, Alonso de. *Teresa de Manzanares, natural de Madrid. Aventuras del bachiller Trapaza, quintaesencia de embusteros y maestro de embelecadores. La garduña de Sevilla y anzuelo de bolsas*. In *Novela picaresca española*, vol. 3, edited by Alonso Zamora Vicente. Barcelona: Editorial Noguer, 1976.

Cela, Camilo José. *La familia de Pascual Duarte*. Edited by Harold L. Boudreau and John W. Kronik. New York: Appleton-Century-Crofts, 1961.

──────. *The Family of Pascual Duarte*. Translated by Anthony Kerrigan. New York: Avon, 1972.

Cleland, John. *Memoirs of Fanny Hill*. Introduction by J. H. Plumb. New York: New American Library, 1965.

Defoe, Daniel. *The Fortunes and Misfortunes of the Famous Moll Flanders*. Edited by G. A. Starr. Oxford: Oxford University Press, 1981.

──────. *Roxana, the Fortunate Mistress*. Edited by Jane Jack. London: Oxford University Press, 1964.

Delicado, Francisco. *La lozana andaluza*. Edited by Bruno Damiani. Madrid: Editorial Castalia, 1969.

──────. *Retrato de la loçana andaluza*. Edited by Bruno M. Damiani and Giovanni Allegra. Madrid: Ediciones José Porrúa Turanzas, 1975.

Jong, Erica. *Fanny, Being the True History of the Adventures of Fanny Hackabout-Jones*. New York: New American Library, 1980.

[López de Ubeda, Francisco.] *La pícara Justina*. Edited by Bruno Mario Damiani. Madrid: José Porrúa Turanzas, 1982.

Mabbe, James, trans. *The Rogue, or the Life of Guzmán de Alfarache*. Introduction by James Fitzmaurice-Kelly. 4 vols. London: Constable and Co., 1924.

Pérez Galdós, Benito. *Tristana*. Madrid: Alianza Editorial, 1969.

Poniatowska, Elena. *Hasta no verte Jesús mío*. Mexico City: Ediciones Era, 1969.

Quevedo, Francisco de. *La vida del Buscón llamado Don Pablos*. Edited by Fernando Lázaro Carreter, annotated by Juan Alcina Franch. Barcelona: Editorial Juventud, 1968.

Rico, Francisco, ed. *La novela picaresca española*. Vol. 1. [*Lazarillo de Tormes, Guzmán de Alfarache*.] Barcelona: Editorial Planeta, 1967.

[Ruiz, Juan, Arcipreste de Hita.] *Libro de Buen Amor*. Translated and edited by Raymond S. Willis. Princeton: Princeton University Press, 1972.

Salas Barbadillo, Alonso J. de. *La hija de Celestina*. [Edited by Angel Valbuena Prat], annotated by C. Pastor Sanz, and published with *Lazarillo de Tormes*, edited by F. Aguilar Piñal. Madrid: Editorial Magisterio Español, 1967.

CRITICAL STUDIES

Abel, Elizabeth, ed. *Writing and Sexual Difference*. Chicago: The University of Chicago Press, 1982.

—————; Hirsch, Marianne; and Langland, Elizabeth, eds. *The Voyage In: Fictions of Female Development*. Hanover, New Hampshire, and London: University Press of New England, 1983.

Alter, Robert. *Rogue's Progress: Studies in the Picaresque Novel*. Cambridge: Harvard University Press, 1964.

Arias, Joan. *Guzmán de Alfarache: The Unrepentant Narrator*. London: Tamesis, 1977.

Babcock, Barbara A. "'Liberty's a Whore': Inversions, Marginalia, and Picaresque Narrative." In *The Reversible World: Symbolic Inversion in Art and Society*, edited by Barbara A. Babcock, pp. 95–116. Ithaca and London: Cornell University Press, 1978.

Bataillon, Marcel. *Pícaros y picaresca*. Madrid: Taurus Ediciones, 1969.

Bell, A. "The Rhetoric of Self-Defence of 'Lázaro de Tormes.'" *Modern Language Review* 68 (1973): 84–93.

Bjornson, Richard. *The Picaresque Hero in European Fiction*. Madison: The University of Wisconsin Press, 1977.

Blackburn, Alexander. *The Myth of the Picaro: Continuity and Transformation of the Picaresque Novel, 1554–1954*. Chapel Hill: The University of North Carolina Press, 1979.

Blewett, David. *Defoe's Art of Fiction*. Toronto: University of Toronto Press, 1979.

Boardman, Michael M. *Defoe and the Uses of Narrative*. New Brunswick: Rutgers University Press, 1983.

Booth, Wayne C. *The Rhetoric of Fiction*. Chicago and London: The University of Chicago Press, 1961.

—————. *A Rhetoric of Irony*. Chicago: The University of Chicago Press, 1974.

Brancaforte, Benito. *Guzmán de Alfarache: ¿Conversión o proceso de degradación?* Madison, Wisconsin: The Hispanic Seminary of Medieval Studies, 1980.

Brownlee, Marina Scordilis. "Autobiography as Self-(Re)presentation: The Augustinian Paradigm and Juan Ruiz's Theory of Reading." In *Mimesis: From Mirror to Method, Augustine to Descartes*, edited by John D. Lyons and Stephen G. Nichols, pp. 71–82. Hanover, New Hampshire: University Press of New England for Dartmouth College, 1982.

—————. *The Status of the Reading Subject in the "Libro de Buen Amor."* North Carolina Studies in the Romance Languages and Literatures, no. 224. Chapel Hill: University of North Carolina Press, 1985.

Brownstein, Leonard. *Salas Barbadillo and the New Novel of Rogues and Courtiers*. Madrid: Playor, 1974.

Brownstein, Rachel. *Becoming a Heroine: Reading About Women in Novels*. New York: The Viking Press, 1982.

Cauz, Francisco A. *La narrativa de Salas Barbadillo*. Santa Fe, Argentina: Ediciones Colmegna, 1977.

Chatman, Seymour. *Story and Discourse*. Ithaca and London: Cornell University Press, 1978.

Criado de Val, Manuel, ed. *La picaresca: Orígenes, textos y estructuras*. Madrid: Fundación Universitaria Española, 1979.

Culler, Jonathan. *On Deconstruction: Theory and Criticism after Structuralism*. Ithaca: Cornell University Press, 1982.

Daghistany, Ann. "The Picara Nature." *Women's Studies* 4 (1977): 51–60.

Damiani, Bruno M. *Francisco Delicado*. New York: Twayne Publishers, 1974.

_____. *Francisco López de Ubeda*. New York: Twayne Publishers, 1977.

Derrida, Jacques. *Of Grammatology*. Translated by Gayatri Chakravorty Spivak. Baltimore and London: The Johns Hopkins University Press, 1976.

Deyermond, A. D. *Lazarillo de Tormes. A Critical Guide*. London: Grant and Cutler, 1975.

Diamond, Arlyn, and Edwards, Lee R., eds. *The Authority of Experience: Essays in Feminist Criticism*. Amherst: The University of Massachusetts Press, 1977.

Díaz-Migoyo, Gonzalo. *Estructura de la novela: Anatomía de El Buscón*. Madrid: Editorial Fundamentos, 1978.

Diz, Marta Ana. *Patronio y Lucanor: La lectura inteligente "en el tiempo que es turbio."* Potomac, Maryland: Scripta Humanistica, 1984.

Dunn, Peter N. *Castillo Solórzano and the Decline of the Spanish Novel*. Oxford: Basil Blackwell, 1952.

_____. "A Postscript to *La lozana andaluza*: Life and Poetry." *Romanische Forschungen* 88 (1976): 355–60.

_____. "Problems of a Model for the Picaresque and the Case of Quevedo's *Buscón*." *Bulletin of Hispanic Studies* 59 (1982): 95–105.

_____. *The Spanish Picaresque Novel*. Boston: Twayne Publishers, 1979.

Edwards, Robert. "Narrative Technique in Juan Ruiz' History of Doña Garoza." *MLN* 89 (1974): 265–73.

Epstein, William H. *John Cleland: Images of a Life*. New York and London: Columbia University Press, 1974.

Fiore, Robert L. *Lazarillo de Tormes*. Boston: Twayne Publishers, 1984.

Fish, Stanley E. *Self-Consuming Artifacts: The Experience of Seventeenth-Century Literature*. Berkeley: University of California Press, 1972.

Foley, Augusta E. *Delicado: La Lozana andaluza*. London: Grant and Cutler, 1977.

Friedman, Edward H. "Chaos Restored: Authorial Control and Ambiguity in *Lazarillo de Tormes*." *Crítica Hispánica* 3 (1981): 59–73.

_____. "Novel Groupings: The Order of Things." *Rocky Mountain Review* 37 (1983): 237–61.

García de la Concha, Víctor. *Nueva lectura del Lazarillo: El deleite de la perspectiva*. Madrid: Editorial Castalia, 1981.

Genette, Gérard. *Narrative Discourse: An Essay in Method*. Translated by Jane E. Lewin. Ithaca: Cornell University Press, 1980.

Gómez-Moriana, Antonio. "Intertextualidad, interdiscursividad y parodia: Sobre los orígenes de la forma narrativa en la novela picaresca." *Dispositio* 8, 22–23 (1983): 123–44.

Greene, Gayle, and Kahn, Coppélia, eds. *Making a Difference: Feminist Literary Criticism*. London and New York: Methuen, 1985.

Guillén, Claudio. *Literature as System*. Princeton: Princeton University Press, 1971.

Hancock, Joel. "Elena Poniatowska's *Hasta no verte Jesús mío*: The Remaking of the Image of Woman." *Hispania* 66 (1983): 353–59.

Hanrahan, Thomas, S. J. *La mujer en la novela picaresca española*. 2 vols. Madrid: José Porrúa Turanzas, 1967.

Heilbrun, Carolyn G., and Higonnet, Margaret R., eds. *The Representation of Women in Fiction*. Baltimore and London: The Johns Hopkins University Press, 1983.

Hernández Ortiz, José A. *La génesis artística de La lozana andaluza*. Madrid: Editorial Aguilera, 1974.

Howarth, William L. "Some Principles of Autobiography." *New Literary History* 5 (1974): 363–81.

Iser, Wolfgang. *The Act of Reading: A Theory of Aesthetic Response*. Baltimore and London: The Johns Hopkins University Press, 1978.

_____. *The Implied Reader: Patterns of Communication in Prose Fiction from Bunyan to Beckett*. Baltimore and London: The Johns Hopkins University Press, 1974.

Johnson, Carroll B. *Inside Guzmán de Alfarache*. Berkeley: University of California Press, 1978.

Kent, John P., and Gaunt, J. L. "Picaresque Fiction: A Bibliographical Essay." *College Literature* 6 (1979): 245–70.

Keohane, Nannerl O.; Rosaldo, Michelle Z.; and Gelpi, Barbara C., eds. *Feminist Theory: A Critique of Ideology*. Chicago: The University of Chicago Press, 1982.

Kramarae, Cheris. *Women and Men Speaking*. Rowley, Massachusetts: Newbury House Publishers, 1981.

Lakoff, Robin. *Language and Woman's Place*. New York: Harper and Row, 1975.

Lanser, Susan Sniader. *The Narrative Act: Point of View in Prose Fiction*. Princeton: Princeton University Press, 1981.

Lázaro Carreter, Fernando. *"Lazarillo de Tormes" en la picaresca*. Barcelona: Ediciones Ariel, 1972.

Leitch, Vincent B. *Deconstructive Criticism: An Advanced Introduction*. New York: Columbia University Press, 1983.

McGrady, Donald. *Mateo Alemán*. New York: Twayne Publishers, 1968.

Maclean, Ian. *The Renaissance Notion of Woman*. Cambridge: Cambridge University Press, 1980.

Mancing, Howard. "The Picaresque Novel: A Protean Form." *College Literature* 6 (1979): 182–204.

Miller, Beth, ed. *Women in Hispanic Literature: Icons and Fallen Idols*. Berkeley and Los Angeles: University of California Press, 1983.

Miller, Casey, and Swift, Kate. *Words and Women*. New York: Anchor Press/Doubleday, 1976.

Miller, Nancy K. *The Heroine's Text: Readings in the French and English Novel, 1722–1782*. New York: Columbia University Press, 1980.

Mora, Gabriela, and Van Hooft, Karen S., eds. *Theory and Practice of Feminist Literary Criticism*. Ypsilanti, Michigan: Bilingual Press/Editorial Bilingüe, 1982.

Morris, C. B. *The Unity and Structure of Quevedo's Buscón: "Desgracias encadenadas."* University of Hull Occasional Papers in Modern Languages, no. 1, 1965.

Novak, Maximilian E. *Realism, Myth, and History in Defoe's Fiction*. Lincoln and London: University of Nebraska Press, 1983.

Olney, James, ed. *Autobiography: Essays Theoretical and Critical*. Princeton: Princeton University Press, 1980.

Parker, Alexander A. *Literature and the Delinquent: The Picaresque Novel in Spain and Europe, 1599–1753*. Edinburgh: The University Press, 1967.

Patai, Daphne. *Myth and Ideology in Contemporary Brazilian Fiction*. Cranbury, New Jersey: Associated University Presses, 1983.

Peale, C. George. "*Guzmán de Alfarache* como discurso oral." *Journal of Hispanic Philology* 4 (1979): 25–57.

Pérez-Erdelyi, Mireya. *La pícara y la dama: la imagen de las mujeres en las novelas picaresco-cortesanas de María de Zayas y Sotomayor y Alonso de Castillo Solórzano*. Miami: Ediciones Universal, 1979.

Peyton, Myron. *Alonso Jerónimo de Salas Barbadillo*. New York: Twayne Publishers, 1973.

Pope, Randolph. *La autobiografía española hasta Torres Villarroel*. Frankfurt: Peter Lang, 1974.

Read, Malcolm K. *The Birth and Death of Language: Spanish Literature and Linguistics, 1300–1700*. Madrid: José Porrúa Turanzas, 1983.

Reed, Helen H. *The Reader in the Picaresque Novel.* London: Tamesis, 1984.

Reed, Walter L. *An Exemplary History of the Novel: The Quixotic versus the Picaresque.* Chicago and London: The University of Chicago Press, 1981.

Richetti, John J. *Defoe's Narratives: Situations and Structures.* Oxford: Clarendon Press, 1975.

Rico, Francisco. *La novela picaresca y el punto de vista.* Barcelona: Seix Barral, 1970. [*The Spanish Picaresque Novel and the Point of View.* Translated by Charles Davis with Harry Sieber. Cambridge: Cambridge University Press, 1984.]

Rodríguez-Luis, Julio. "*Pícaras*: The Modal Approach to the Picaresque." *Comparative Literature* 31 (1979): 32–46.

Rodríguez Matos, Carlos Antonio. *El narrador pícaro: Guzmán de Alfarache.* Madison, Wisconsin: Hispanic Seminary of Medieval Studies, 1985.

Ronquillo, Pablo J. *Retrato de la pícara: La protagonista de la picaresca española del XVII.* Madrid: Playor, 1980.

Salstad, M. Louise. *The Presentation of Women in Spanish Golden Age Literature: An Annotated Bibliography.* Boston: G. K. Hall, 1980.

Schmidt, Ruth A. "*Tristana* and the Importance of Opportunity." *Anales Galdosianos* 9 (1974): 135–44.

Shipley, George A. "The Critic as Witness for the Prosecution: Making the Case against Lázaro de Tormes." *PMLA* 97 (1982): 179–94.

Sieber, Harry. *Language and Society in La vida de Lazarillo de Tormes.* Baltimore and London: The Johns Hopkins University Press, 1978.

―――――――. *The Picaresque.* London: Methuen, 1977.

Soons, Alan. *Alonso de Castillo Solórzano.* New York: Twayne Publishers, 1978.

Spadaccini, Nicholas. "Daniel Defoe and the Spanish Picaresque Tradition: The Case of *Moll Flanders*." *Ideologies and Literature* 2, 6 (1978): 10–26.

Springer, Marlene, ed. *What Manner of Woman: Essays on English and American Life and Literature.* New York: New York University Press, 1977.

Starobinski, Jean. "The Style of Autobiography." In *Literary Style: A Symposium,* edited and translated by Seymour Chatman, pp. 285–96. New York: Oxford University Press, 1971.

Starr, G. A. *Defoe and Casuistry.* Princeton: Princeton University Press, 1971.

―――――――. *Defoe and Spiritual Autobiography.* Princeton: Princeton University Press, 1965.

Stubbs, Patricia. *Women and Fiction: Feminism and the Novel, 1880–1920.* New York: Barnes and Noble, 1979.

Tatum, Charles M., and Miller, Yvette E., eds. *Latin American Women Writers: Yesterday and Today.* Pittsburgh: Latin American Literary Review, 1977.

Taylor, Anne Robinson. *Male Novelists and Their Female Voices: Literary Masquerades.* Troy, New York: The Whitson Publishing Company, 1981.

Vance, Eugene. "The Functions and Limits of Autobiography in Augustine's *Confessions*." *Poetics Today* 5, 2 (1984): 399–409.

Wardropper, Bruce W. "La novela como retrato: El arte de Francisco Delicado." *Nueva Revista de Filología Hispánica* 7 (1953): 475–88.

Weinstein, Arnold. *Fictions of the Self: 1550–1800.* Princeton: Princeton University Press, 1981.

Whitbourn, Christine J., ed. *Knaves and Swindlers: Essays on the Picaresque Novel in Europe.* London: Oxford University Press, 1974.

White, Hayden. *Tropics of Discourse.* Baltimore: The Johns Hopkins University Press, 1978.

Whitenack, Judith A. *The Impenitent Confession of Guzmán de Alfarache.* Madison, Wisconsin: Hispanic Seminary of Medieval Studies, 1985.

—————. "Narrative Distance in Picaresque Fiction." *College Literature* 6 (1979): 165–81.

Wicks, Ulrich. "The Nature of Picaresque Narrative: A Modal Approach." *PMLA* 89 (1974): 240–49.

Williamson, Edwin. "The Conflict between Author and Protagonist in Quevedo's *Buscón*." *Journal of Hispanic Philology* 2 (1977): 45–60.

Woodward, L. J. "Author-Reader Relationship in the *Lazarillo de Tormes*." *Forum for Modern Language Studies* 1 (1965): 43–53.

Zahareas, Anthony N. *The Art of Juan Ruiz*. Madrid: Estudios de Literatura Española, 1965.

Zumthor, Paul. "Autobiography in the Middle Ages?" Translated by Sherry Simon. *Genre* 6 (1973): 29–48.

Index